AIDA Europe Research Series on Insurance Law and Regulation

Volume 10

The AIDA Europe Research Series on Insurance Law and Regulation is the first book series of its kind and area of specialization. It comprises volumes on topics researched and written with an international, comparative or European perspective.

The regulatory response to the financial crisis in 2008 has pushed towards the adoption of transnational principles and rules also in the field of insurance by encouraging the convergence of national regulations to common regulatory framework. The need for a common legal language emerges to fully understand the process of transnational convergence in place and its impact on national legislation. On the other hand, persisting national peculiarities must be examined in the light of the transnational convergence of rules and concepts. Moreover, new risks, business practices and customers' issues are emerging worldwide, so requiring increasingly global responses.

The scope of the series is to bring together academics, practitioners and policy makers in order to exchange views and approaches to the topics concerned, which are based on the new transnational dimension of insurance law, business and regulation. All contributions are peer reviewed.

Juan Bataller-Grau • Marcin Kawiński •
Pierpaolo Marano
Editors

Sustainability and the Insurance Market

Trends and Challenges

Springer

Editors
Juan Bataller-Grau
Mercantile Law 'Manuel Broseta Pont'
Universitat de Valencia
Valencia, Spain

Marcin Kawiński
Department of Social Insurance
Warsaw School of Economics
Warsaw, Poland

Pierpaolo Marano
Department of Legal Sciences
Catholic University of the Sacred Heart
Milan, Italy

ISSN 2662-1770 ISSN 2662-1789 (electronic)
AIDA Europe Research Series on Insurance Law and Regulation
ISBN 978-3-031-72185-4 ISBN 978-3-031-72186-1 (eBook)
https://doi.org/10.1007/978-3-031-72186-1

This work was supported by Universitat de Valéncia.

This Springer imprint is published by the registered company Springer Nature Switzerland AG
The registered company address is: Gewerbestrasse 11, 6330 Cham, Switzerland

Contents

Part I
The General Framework on the Sustainability for the Insurance Market

Principles for Sustainable Insurance: The European Perspective

Javier Vercher-Moll

1 Introduction

From the beginning of the twentieth century to the present day, corporate social responsibility (CSR) has been the subject of study by authors (Fleisher 2015), companies, organisations, numerous groups and legislators. There have been different evolutionary phases, but at present it is said that we are in the era of corporate social responsibility regulation (Caputo et al. 2020). This statement may have its details, but we could consider that the incipient regulation allows us to affirm the existence of a normative body (Bataller-Grau 2018). This is also helped by the fact that many companies have instituted CSR values and principles as a methodology of behaviour in the business world (Bice 2017).

When approaching the study of CSR, one must start from a basic premise which revolves around the idea that there is no single code or standard. Every company is different, with different needs and a different business culture, all of which affect the third parties around that company in a particular way (Freeman 1984). Thus, corporate social responsibility has become one of the areas where the difficulty lies in the fact that there is no single guide, but hundreds of them that try to respond to the needs and priorities of each business sector (Green 2021). Furthermore, because even companies in the same sector, but located in different parts of the world, may have different needs, their guidelines for action within the framework of corporate social responsibility may be different (Leipziger 2010).

J. Vercher-Moll (✉)
University of Valencia, Valencia, Spain
e-mail: javier.vercher@uv.es

J. Bataller-Grau et al. (eds.), *Sustainability and the Insurance Market*, AIDA Europe Research Series on Insurance Law and Regulation 10,
https://doi.org/10.1007/978-3-031-72186-1_1

This is why there are a number of organisations whose mission is to provide codes, principles and standards to create a socially responsible business culture.[1] The subject matter of such documents varies according to their scope of application, stakeholder focus, business sector and even the region where they are to be applied. In terms of scope, most documents are intended to shed light on corporate governance, anti-corruption, environment, labour issues, human rights and health. In terms of stakeholders, codes, standards, etc., are aimed at employees, suppliers, customers, trade unions, governments, civil society and shareholders. Depending on the business sector, the catalogue is broad, ranging from large manufacturers, the mining industry, the pharmaceutical industry, the oil industry, the textile industry, finance companies, etc. Finally, from a regional point of view, there are geographical areas where there is a greater culture of implementing socially responsible business principles. However, given the universality of corporate social responsibility, the tools used in one sector in a specific region can be extrapolated to another region where the same business sector is involved, as long as the needs are the same.

These questions lead us to consider whether corporate social responsibility channelled through principles, guidelines, codes, etc., in any way has a positive impact, not only on the company that implements them, but also on the stakeholders who experience the application of such principles, i.e. how they can help companies to achieve their objectives across a broad spectrum (Smith 2002). What is certain is that an effective code of conduct or standard can help to: raise companies' own awareness of the importance of corporate social responsibility, assist the company in setting strategies and objectives, assist in implementation and monitoring, assist in avoiding or limiting scandals for the company, encourage dialogue and collaboration with key stakeholders, enhance unity and identity among divergent companies (Leipziger 2010). In the short term, the code can help in an internal company crisis about its management, in the medium term the code can prevent a crisis and in the long term it allows the implementation of principles aimed at improving the condition of stakeholders, including shareholders (Aglietta & Rebérioux 2005), promoting confidence in the company's own business sector, improving its performance, etc... (Hertel 2003).

---

[1] See: *The Accountability Principles Standard 2008, AA1000 Assurance Standard, Business Principles for Countering Bribery, Ceres Principles, EMAS (Eco-Management and Audit Scheme), The Equator Principles, Ethical Trading Initiative: Base Code, Extractive Industry Transparency Initiative, Fair Labor Association: Workplace Code of Conduct, Global Compact, Global Reporting Initiative, ICC Business Charter for Sustainable Development, International Labour Organisation: Code of Practice on HIV/AIDS and Tripartite Declaration of Principles concerning Multinational Enterprises and Social Policy, ISO 14001, ISO 26000, Johnson & Johnson Credo, The Natural Steps Principles, Norms on the Responsibilities of Transnational Corporations and Other Enterprises with Regard to Human Rights, Global Agreement between the ICEM and Statoil, OECD Convention for Combating Bribery of Foreign Officials in International Business Transactions, OECD Guidelines for Multinational Enterprises, OECD Principles of Corporate Governance, Principles for Responsible Investment, Responsible Care, Rio Declaration on Environment and Development, Shell Business Principles, Social Accountability 8000, Universal Declaration of Human Rights, Voluntary Principles on Security and Human Rights*, etc.

To have a positive impact, codes or standards must have certain connatural characteristics to be effective, making their application not merely a formal exercise, but also produces practical effects on both the company and the stakeholders. Thus, it has been considered (Leipziger 2010) that codes or standards should be clear and concise, so that the management body of the company obligated to apply them does not necessarily have to be highly educated, and a concept of an administrator with average knowledge is advocated in this sense; codes or standards should also be flexible and dynamic because such documents are not revised very often, so they should be able to adapt to new needs and/or changes in the workplace according to new approaches that may arise; they should also take into account their practical application, so the code or standard should define a clear process for achieving compliance and how it can be achieved. In addition, it should emphasise which key norms of the standard or code have inspired these same documents, so it is not uncommon for reference to be made to the Universal Declaration of Human Rights or the International Labour Organisation; it is also considered that stakeholders should be involved in the development of the code or standard not only to give it legitimacy, but also to improve and facilitate its implementation (Helmold et al. 2020). Furthermore, through the implementation of the code or standard, there must be a company's desire for change, even if this is a matter of company culture that is beyond the code or standard itself. Finally, such documents should contain a system for complaints and conflict resolution that may arise as a result of the application of the code or standard, giving the application of such standards a mechanism for solutions to continue their application and protection.

This overview allows us to recognise the importance of principles, codes, standards, etc. in each business sector. The insurance market is no exception. The United Nations Conference on Sustainable Development (Rio+20) has established principles within the United Nations Environment Programme Finance Initiative aimed at addressing environmental, social and governance risks and opportunities.

As the Secretary General of the United Nations points out, "The Principles for Sustainable Insurance provide a global roadmap to develop and expand the innovative risk management and insurance solutions that we need to promote renewable energy, clean water, food security, sustainable cities and disaster-resilient communities. With world premium volume of more than $4 trillion and global assets under management of more than $24 trillion, insurers that embed sustainability in their business operations can catalyze the kinds of financial and investment flows and long-term perspectives needed for sustainable development."[2]

The *Principles for Sustainable Insurance* (PSI) aim to establish a cross-cutting framework that covers all aspects of the insurance company, both in its internal and external relations. A new long-term insurance business culture is thus advocated, not only from a financial point of view, but also from a non-financial point of view, i.e. according to the impact of its activity on the environment in which it operates

[2]Ban Ki-moon, Secretary-General of the United Nations. https://www.unepfi.org/fileadmin/documents/PSI_document-en.pdf.

(Bansal & Des Jardine 2014). The principles therefore affect the company's relations with all stakeholders such as shareholders, customers, and governments, but also its internal development, whether through the integration of environmental, social and governance issues (ESG issues) in its management or the development of new types of risk management products and services (Scordis et al. 2014).

As the United Nations stresses that the PSI are not legally binding, the lack of implementation by the insurance company cannot generate a sanction or procedure that imposes the obligation to implement them, or even a complaint to the United Nations due to their voluntary nature. However, the PSI rightly show that the actions for the implementation of the principles are subject to the legal provisions governing the insurance company, i.e. the insurer's behaviour in implementing the PSI can have an impact on stakeholders. Therefore, for practical purposes, the rules on consumers, distributors, partners of the company, etc. must be observed.

In this regard, the regulations governing the organisation and supervision of insurance companies, insurance contracts and distribution in each country will be key to being able to adapt the PSI to the insurer. Given the drafting style and breadth of the PSI, it is up to the insurance company to implement the principles according to the reality of its business, its scope of action and the legislative situation. Even so, the regulations on the supervision of insurance companies establish certain rules of conduct that insurance companies must observe in the conduct of their business, particularly on policies and tariffs, the duty of disclosure, dispute resolution mechanisms, etc.[3]

In any case, the PSI stipulate that it will be up to the insurance company to establish the timeframes for adapting the principles. This does not mean that they can be delayed in time, as this would imply a formal but material assumption of the lack of implementation of the principles in the insurance company, which could result in reputational damage for the company. This situation would allow the United Nations Environment Programme Finance Initiative Board the possibility of de-registering signatory insurers as long as they do not disclose progress in implementing the PSI.

On the other hand, the PSI are stand-alone principles that can be adopted by any insurance company, but they are directly linked to the Principles for Responsible Investment (PRI), which focus on the risks and opportunities associated with ESG issues. As an institutional investor, insurance companies should compose a portfolio of investments that are ESG in nature, but without forgetting the levels of solvency required of them. Here, the importance of combining PRI and PSI should be emphasised, but without ignoring their own autonomy. Insurance entities can adopt one or other of the principles, but in the interests of managing the entity in a manner consistent with the UN Global Compact Principles, both the PSI and the PRI can be adopted jointly, given their impact in the areas of human rights, labour, the environment and anti-corruption (Brogi et al. 2022).

[3]Directive 2009/138/EC of the European Parliament and of the Council of 25 November 2009 on the taking-up and pursuit of the business of Insurance and Reinsurance (Solvency II).

The PSI consist of four principles that are made up of actions to implement them. It should be noted that the drafting style is broad, as it attempts to cover all facets of the insurance company and all types of insurers, i.e. both those of a capitalist nature and those of a social economy nature. The latter in particular, because of their specific solvency regimes, system of governance, type of products, non-profit nature, etc., must adapt the actions to their size and complexity in line with the regulations in force, i.e. if positive legislation sometimes exempts social economy insurers from obligations to respect the principle of proportionality so as not to impose the same requirements as those of a capitalist nature, we consider that the same predicament applies to the actions that the company must take to implement the PSI.

The first principle seeks to integrate ESG issues into the insurance company's decision-making. To this end, it exemplifies a number of actions that the company can take. It may establish a business strategy to integrate ESG issues, develop processes to identify and assess ESG risks in its day-to-day business, develop products and services with an ESG focus, manage claims promptly and transparently, conduct sales and marketing in a customer-focused manner, manage investments from an ESG perspective.

The second principle addresses the insurer's external relationships. The insurer will work with its customers and business partners to raise awareness of environmental, social and governance issues, manage risk and develop solutions. Thus, the second principle offers possible actions to collaborate with customers and suppliers to implement ESG principles and with insurers, reinsurers and intermediaries.

The third principle addresses the insurer's relationships with governments, regulators and other key stakeholders to promote broad society-wide action on environmental, social and governance issues. As possible actions, the insurer may support policies and regulations aimed at mitigating risks and promoting ESG issues, as well as dialogue with NGOs, business associations, dialogue with academia and scientists, dialogue with the media to raise public awareness of ESG issues.

Finally, the fourth principle deals with the disclosure of the implementation of the PSI in the insurance company. The adoption of the PSI implies the need for structural changes within the insurer, so, given that it is not a positive standard, this adoption can only be known if the company discloses its developments and its report is subsequently validated by an independent expert.

2 Principles for Sustainable Insurance

2.1 Principle I

Principle 1 provides for the integration of environmental, social and governance issues (ESG issues) into the company's decision-making. The point to note is that there is already regulation on both social and governance issues affecting insurance companies. What the PSI do is turn existing regulations into a mandatory minimum standard, making them guidelines that improve on aspects not covered by existing regulations. Moreover, in line with the principle of territoriality, the regulation does not regulate cross-border issues, so it does not affect the value chain of which the insurance company can make use.[4]

These three issues are the ones that condition the actions that are exemplified in this principle. The authors have shown that the PSI do not facilitate the calculation of the impact that the adoption of ESG criteria will have on the insurer, which makes their implementation difficult.

On the environmental side, the insurer will address climate change, such as air pollution and greenhouse gases; environmental degradation such as water and soil pollution, unconventional mining practices and deforestation; protected sites and protected species; unsustainable practices such as inappropriate energy use, illegal fishing vessels and environmentally aggressive fishing techniques, animal welfare and animal testing. On the social side, the insurer will look at human rights. This includes child labour, human trafficking, forced labour, forced resettlement, the poor safety record of workers, violation of workers' rights, and misconduct of security personnel. The insurance company will also watch out for controversial weapons, especially when they violate any of the UN conventions. Finally, from a governance perspective, the insurance company will ensure that there is no bribery or corruption, particularly illegal and unethical payments; poor corporate governance such as anti-competitive practices, antitrust violations, and unethical conduct; poor product safety and quality, particularly those that may have a negative impact on the health of clients.

Possible Actions

1. Company strategy: The PSI mention the need to establish a strategy for identifying, assessing, managing and monitoring ESG issues in the company's operations. This function is entrusted to the management body, which will be responsible for establishing a specific ESG policy and aligning other policies with it. Furthermore, although the drafting of the ESG policy is a matter for the management body, the PSI invite the management body to engage in dialogue with the owners of the company, i.e. the shareholders, to make them aware of the importance of ESG issues in business strategy, so that the agreements they adopt in the areas within their competence include respect for ESG issues as a variable in all cases. Finally, the PSI highlight the integration of ESG issues into employee selection, training and recruitment programmes as a company strategy.
2. Risk management and underwriting: Risk management is one of the key elements of any insurance company. PSI stress the importance of establishing processes to identify and assess ESG issues inherent in the portfolio and to be aware of the potential ESG implications of the company's operations. This strategy can be laudable and has its raison *d'être* in the essential elements of CSR. However, designing the insurance company's investment portfolio with ESG criteria in mind is not straightforward.

[4]Proposal for a Directive of the European Parliament and of the Council on Corporate Sustainability Due Diligence and amending Directive (EU) 2019/1937.

The supervisory and solvency regulations[5] for insurance companies require that the composition of the investment portfolio, to compose the company's own funds, be based on assets and instruments whose risks can be properly identified, measured, monitored, managed and controlled. These risks shall be taken into account in the assessment of the overall solvency needs as part of the internal risk and solvency assessment. This implies that the composition of the investment portfolio is of adequate quality to ensure the dynamic solvency of the insurer (Gatzert et al. 2020). In this respect, the application of ESG criteria to the investment portfolio entails a restriction of the portfolio, since there may be securities with a very high rating which, under ESG criteria, cannot be used for the composition of the insurer's own funds. This circumstance leads to increased difficulty in the composition of the investment portfolio. In addition, it affects the company's risk tolerance and, consequently, a relaxation of the management's risk appetite.

This line of action may lead to certain problems in the composition of the company's technical provisions, making it difficult to comply with the principle of premium adequacy when designing an insurance product. This is because guaranteeing a portfolio of ESG investments does not necessarily entail a high degree of solvency of such securities (Barber et al. 2022). From the organisational point of view of the company, it means an increase in the demands for control over the investments made and an analysis of the reports that rating agencies provide to institutional investors.

On insurance underwriting, the insurance company must design its models, calculations, analyses and tools in accordance with ESG criteria. Thus, when accepting the risks proposed by customers, i.e. their coverage needs, the insurance company must ensure that the environmental, social and governance impact is minimised in the management of these risks. In this line, perhaps the problem for the company is how to determine the ESG impact in the management of insured risks.

3. Product and service development: Insurance companies should develop products and services that reduce risk, have a positive effect on ESG issues and promote better risk management. Thus, the insurer must respect ESG issues from the offer, contracting, management and compensation following a claim or the provision of the service in the case of assistance insurance (Stricker et al. 2022). In this sense, the main problem is the application of these principles in the value chain (Cappiello 2020). Outsourcing of services may mean that they are respected internally by the company, but not in the services that support the assistance or the insurer's obligation to provide services. The company's vigilance will be key to ensuring that the implementation of PSI is real and effective. In addition, the insurer must develop or support training programmes on risk, insurance and ESG

[5]Directive 2009/138/EC of the European Parliament and of the Council of 25 November 2009 on the taking-up and pursuit of the business of Insurance and Reinsurance (Solvency II).

issues. In this way, it may require outsourced services to provide evidence of ESG training to comply with the PSI.

4. Claims management: Insurers should respond to customers promptly, honestly, sensitively and transparently at all times and ensure that claims handling is clear and understandable. This entails strengthening the claims area of the company to have a sufficient organisation chart and deployment of resources, with procedure manuals that not only respect current regulations but also place the customer at the centre of management. Thus, they should inform loss adjusters, insurance agents, brokers, etc. using precise instructions to speed up the management of the claim.

   In addition, it will integrate ESG issues into repair, replacement and other claims-related services. This action is laudable, given the importance of the value chain, but it is difficult to implement given the large number of ancillary companies that provide services to the insurance company for it to carry out the insured service. Therefore, the company will have to set criteria for the selection of suppliers to respect ESG issues. The issue is whether the suppliers respect ESG criteria. In this regard, the insurer must provide them with a questionnaire to assess whether the candidate can collaborate with the company.
5. Sales and marketing: Insurance companies should train sales and marketing staff on ESG issues related to products and services, integrating key messages in a responsible manner into strategies and campaigns. Thus, when offering and marketing insurance, companies may use the integration of ESG issues into their products as an advertising message. This can lead to a problem of colour-washing, so the image of the insurance company is washed out; particularly on green-washing, the products offered are ESG-friendly without actually being so. Along these lines, the assurance company's sustainability report verification by an expert will determine whether and to what extent green-washing exists (Pugnetti et al. 2022).

   In addition, the insurer must ensure that product and service coverage, benefits and costs are adequate, clearly explained and fully understood. This goes beyond the information standards provided for in insurance distribution regulations,[6] Thus, it is up to the insurance company to tailor insurance policies to the needs of its customers and to provide them with information not only on a standard basis but also according to customer characteristics such as age, qualifications or training, etc.,
6. Investment management: The insurance company should integrate ESG issues into investment decisions and liability practices (e.g. by applying the Principles for Responsible Investment). Insurance companies can apply the PSI and PRI together, although the autonomy of the two standards should be emphasized (Sievänen et al. 2013).

[6]Directive (EU) 2016/97 of the European Parliament and of the Council of 20 January 2016 on insurance distribution.

Under the PRI, insurance companies will incorporate ESG issues into investment analysis and decision-making processes; they will be active owners so as to incorporate ESG issues into ownership practices and policies; and they will seek appropriate disclosure of ESG issues by the companies in which they invest; also, they will promote acceptance and implementation of the principles in the investment industry; including by working collaboratively to increase their effectiveness in implementing the principles; and finally, each insurance entity will report on its activities and progress with respect to implementation of the principles.

The authors (Majoch et al. 2017) have questioned the reasons why the insurance company may adopt the PRI. Although there may be many explanations, there are two powerful reasons why insurers implement the PRI. First, for reputational reasons because the image of the insurer is crucial in today's market, and second, because stakeholders demand it that they force the insurance company to make responsible investments, which results in giving stakeholders a greater role in the composition of the insurance company's investment portfolio.

2.2 *Principle II*

Principle 2 states that the insurer shall work with its customers and business partners to raise awareness of environmental, social and governance issues, manage risk and develop solutions. Before addressing the details of this principle and its actions, we need to carry out a mapping exercise on who the customers and business partners are, as this will enable the insurer to target its actions.

As far as clients are concerned, the legal provisions on insurance contracts shed light on this group (Bataller-Grau 2009). Clients are considered to be policyholders, insured persons, and beneficiaries, but also any potential client who, not having signed any contract with the company, maintains a relationship with the company, whether it be about pre-contractual information or of any nature that has legal transcendence.

On the other hand, the delimitation of the insurance company's business partners is more complex, given that their heterogeneity makes it impossible to be exhaustive so that we can focus the imposition of ESG obligations on business partners. We can consider as business partners insurance companies with which risks are shared within the same insurance policy, either through co-insurance or through the underwriting of particular risks within a multi-risk policy, relationships with reinsurers, relationships of the insurance company within a group of insurers, relationships with insurance agents and brokers, relations with insurance experts, relations between the company and service companies that assist the insurer to fulfil the insured service, relations between the insurance company and suppliers due to the outsourcing of services, relations that may occur due to legal requirements, such as auditing services or actuarial studies, etc.

Possible Actions

1. Clients and suppliers: The PSI set out as possible actions on customers and suppliers awareness-raising campaigns on the benefits of managing ESG issues and on the company's expectations and requirements on ESG issues. To this end, they will provide customers and suppliers with information and tools that can help them manage ESG issues, as well as encourage them to disclose ESG issues and to use appropriate structures for such disclosure or reporting.

   This awareness-raising process should be used by the insurer as a way to improve the adoption of PSI. In this sense, insurance distribution partners will inform the insurer about the opinions of their customers or potential customers. This is why providing customers with the necessary tools to manage and disclose ESG issues will, in turn, inform their opinion of the insurer.

   The action that PSI impose on insurance companies to integrate ESG issues into the supplier tendering and selection processes is of particular relevance. This action implies the establishment of a procedural manual to determine the characteristics to be met by the supplier that integrates ESG issues. The solution is to require suppliers that intend to provide services to the company to submit an assurance report accrediting the implementation of ESG issues (Vercher-Moll 2021). In this sense, the assurance report may be the only document that proves a diligent bidding process on the part of the insurance company that assumes the PSI.

   In addition, the request for the assurance report may result in some providers not having it, so either they offer an alternative system of accreditation of ESG issues or the number of possible candidates in the tender is reduced. This situation may be detrimental to the insurer as it may result in increased costs due to the low supply of certain services that have to be outsourced.
2. Insurers, reinsurers and intermediaries: The PSI also set out a series of actions for the insurance company to conduct an awareness-raising campaign in the insurance sector. They will promote the adoption of the PSI and support the inclusion of ESG issues in professional education and professional ethics in the insurance sector. Although the PSI refer to insurers, in reality, the obligation to promote the adoption of the PSI is also addressed to associations of insurers and reinsurers (Miazad 2023).

   There are associations of insurers that have created a roadmap that is more ambitious than the PSI principles. For example, the Association of British Insurers, also known as ABI, has established four thematic pillars on which to develop the insurance business: zero emissions, improving investment capacity through regulatory change, sustainable operations across the value chain, and improving conditions in society. These four pillars are aimed not only at its member insurers, but also at all its partners and even governments.[7]

[7] https://www.abi.org.uk/globalassets/files/publications/public/climate-change/abi-climate-roadmap%2D%2D-080622.pdf.

2.3 Principle III

Principle 3 establishes an obligation for insurance companies to work with governments, regulators and other key stakeholders to promote broad society-wide action on environmental, social and governance issues. This obligation may be too broad, so broad as to lead to the conclusion that in reality insurance companies can do little or nothing because the obligations are more that of a legislator or a nation's government than of a private entity. Even so, this principle tries to establish actions in which two distinct groups are distinguished. On the one hand, actions to be taken with governments, regulators and other policymakers and, on the other hand, actions on other key stakeholders.

Possible Actions

1. Governments, regulators and other policymakers: Insurance companies' relations with governments, regulators and policymakers must go beyond the legal framework in force in each country, i.e. the actions of the PSI do not seek to impose a culture of regulatory compliance, since the rules must be complied with by law, and in this respect, the regulations governing the supervision and solvency of insurance companies, insurance contracts and their distribution are clear. Even the PSI do not attempt to highlight the importance of compliance with the soft law of supervisory bodies, because a diligent insurance company will comply to keep its management up to date (Sonnenberger & Weiss 2021).

   The mandate that the PSI impose on insurers is aimed at supporting prudent policies and regulatory and legal frameworks that enable risk reduction, innovation and better management of ESG issues to facilitate the supervisor's subsequent work on compliance with this new ESG-focused framework. This proactive stance will result in insurers seeking clarification from supervisory bodies on gaps or obscurities in the rules; thus, they do not seek to benefit from these shortcomings in legislative technique but act in a way that is consistent with the promotion of ESG issues.

   In addition, the PSI also require companies to engage in dialogue with governments and regulators to develop integrated risk management approaches and risk transfer solutions. Thus, it is intended that insurers should inform the consultation phase of legislative texts in a clear manner about the possible solutions that a legal text can adopt on risk management and risk transfer, which may result in insurers only protecting their interests (Hansen et al. 2019).
2. Other key stakeholders: PSI require insurance companies to engage in collaboration and outreach with different stakeholders. The materialisation of this collaboration depends to a large extent not only on the insurer, but also on the stakeholder group that has a relationship with the company. In this sense, it is necessary to be aware of the possible existence of CSR codes, principles and protocols that also affect the development of the activities of non-governmental and intergovernmental organisations, business and industry associations, academia, the scientific community and the media.

In any case, as far as each stakeholder group is concerned, insurers will engage in dialogue with intergovernmental and non-governmental organisations to support sustainable development by providing expertise in risk management and risk transfer (Linnerooth-Bayer & Mechler 2007). Insurers should contribute to the aims of these organisations in a way that aligns with the interests of sustainable development, particularly in developing countries (Johnson et al. 2019).

Also, insurers will engage in dialogue with business and industry associations to better understand and manage ESG issues across sectors and geographic regions. The aim is to strategically reach out on ESG issues to all members who are part of the business association. One of the questions that the PSI do not resolve is whether these business associations have to be insurance companies or whether they can affect any sector of the economy. Indeed, it would be laudable if the dialogue of insurance companies were to be conducted with any business association with which they have contact, but this aspiration may be too broad. We therefore believe that its impact will be more likely to be felt by those business associations of insurance companies.

In addition, insurers will engage in dialogue with academia and the scientific community to promote research and educational programmes on ESG issues in the context of insurance business. As is well known, universities are places of teaching but also of science. This is evidenced by the enormous amount of research that seeks to clarify, systematise and investigate corporate social responsibility and ESG issues. For insurance companies, the academic world is an inexhaustible source of information and new results.

Finally, insurers will engage in dialogue with the media to raise awareness of ESG issues and appropriate risk management. Important in this regard are the insurer's relationships with media and advertising media associations, which establish policies on the truthfulness, honesty and legality of the information disseminated.

2.4 Principle IV

Principle 4 requires insurance companies to be accountable and transparent by publicly and regularly disclosing progress in implementing the principles. This principle intends to address the problem of greenwashing in CSR (Vives 2019; Caterino 2020; Tapia Sánchez 2020).

As the authors point out, the phenomenon of greenwashing can be defined as "the intersection of two company behaviours: environmental performance and positive communication about environmental performance" (Delmas & Burbano 2011). However, this phenomenon has different perspectives through which it can take different forms. Greenwashing can be observed from the environmental labelling of products to the sustainability reports of companies (Baldi & Pandimiglio 2022).

On the other hand, this principle also aims to ensure that PSI are adapted to social and economic realities through dialogue with stakeholders. Thus, the information provided to consumer associations, the content of contractual clauses, and the information provided to the stock market and to governments can facilitate the implementation of PSI. These principles set out a number of actions to provide information on a regular and objective basis. First, insurance companies must assess, measure and monitor the company's progress in managing ESG issues and disclose this information publicly on a proactive and regular basis. Second, they must participate in relevant surveys and sustainability disclosure or reporting programmes. Third and finally, insurance companies will engage in dialogue with customers, regulators, rating agencies and other stakeholders to achieve a mutual understanding of the value of disclosure through the principles.

The information disclosed by insurance companies should be subject to assurance to give credibility to the system of principles and actions created by the PSI. Thus, the preparation of documentation by the company, which accounts for the integration of socially responsible standards or codes in its organisation, leads to the preparation of a report whose immaterial value is of vital importance, since it affects its reputation (Vermiglio 2005). However, it is a sui generis document, given its multidisciplinary nature and the wide range of information it contains. The drafting of this type of documentation is typical of socially responsible companies, the evolution of which is gradually becoming more technical to provide stakeholders with clear information.

Italian authors (Rusconi 2006) have categorised it as a kind of social accounting, making it a key element in the concept of corporate social responsibility. Such a document should be inspired by uniform postulates, models, characteristics and style of writing to ensure continuity in the way information is transmitted. However, given its multidisciplinary nature, it is recommended that a thesaurus be drawn up that includes the lexicon of all branches of law, its definition and the relational structure that links the different terms (Curtit 2016). In this sense, as in the case of auditing, clear and uniform documentation should be created to guide the assurance auditor to establish a systematic approach to both procedure and content.

Social accounting is not an occasional document, but is intended for perpetuity, as it is thus instituted permanently within the company (López Cumbre 2012; Esteban Velasco 2014). This is precisely the document through which a close relationship is maintained between the company and its stakeholders. This goes beyond the economic vision of company reporting, as the primary social purpose, the objective of which is economic profit, must not be forgotten in a socially responsible vision. The question arises as to whether this document can have an economic value in such a way that it represents a real asset for the company that can be included in its balance sheet (Viviani 1999).

In this sense, the preparation and reporting of non-financial information can be considered as a parallel system to the reporting of financial information. Although they differ in terms of content and basis, it is possible to replicate the financial reporting scheme to create a non-financial reporting structure that complies with CSR codes or standards. The authors have expressed concern about the quality of the information contained in such social accounting, given that practice shows the vagueness of the reports and the biased nature of their information (Rühmkorf 2015). It is said that it is relatively easy to reach agreements to establish standards of conduct, but once this phase of the agreement is over, the reality shows the use of corporate social responsibility as a publicity tool for companies (Leipziger 2010).

For this reason, there is a need for the intervention of an independent third party who can guarantee to the stakeholder that the balance sheet drawn up by the company is in line with the reality of its management (Malecki 2018). The assurance must be based on certain basic principles: first, the review must be carried out in accordance with the codes or standards to verify that these rules have been correctly applied; second, the assurer must be a person qualified to assess assurance; finally, an independent authority must recognise this professional qualification and authorise the assurer to carry out this task (Hinna 2005). In recent years, an assurance market has emerged, focused on offering its services to companies that assume socially responsible standards. This assurance has the effect of legitimising the company in society at large (Malecki 2009; Devalle et al. 2017).

Some studies demonstrate the proactive behaviour of companies with regard to assurance (Vaz Ogando et al. 2018). They start from the premise that the stakeholder is the addressee, so all instruments must be made available to the assurance provider to certify the veracity of the information provided in the sustainability report. However, two fundamental elements must be distinguished here: one thing is the willingness to carry out the assurance and another is the reliability of the outcome of the assurance.

The authors have studied the importance of non-financial disclosure from three different perspectives: that which places the stakeholder as the central element, to reduce the asymmetry of information between the company and the third party that demands information (Hill & Jones 1992); disclosure can serve to legitimise the company in the social environment in which it carries out its activity (Barkemeyer 2007); finally, the signal theory describes how the company's management body organises the disclosure of non-financial information and its assurance as a business strategy (Spence 2002). The common element in all of them is the need for assurance of the information that is disclosed, all of this to give meaning to the theories referred to in compliance with the criterion of sustainability as a principle of the company's future development (Bagnoli & Watts 2017).

3 Conclusions

The implementation of CSR principles in insurance companies is bringing about a far-reaching change in the traditional idea of the insurance business. The PSI consist of a transversal framework that alters all the elements that make up an insurance company, both internally and externally. In this sense, a long-term culture is imposed that seeks to protect numerous actors such as stakeholders, suppliers, governments and even the insurance company itself so that ESG criteria do not damage its reputation.

These laudable principles do not violate any legal provisions but seek to improve the insurer's behaviour in the market. In this way, the current regulations provide a minimum standard of conduct that can be improved through the implementation of the PSI. In addition, the PSI can be combined with the PRI to respect ESG issues on investments made by the insurance company to match its risks in insurance premiums.

However, it should not be forgotten that insurance companies must guarantee solvency ratios that cannot be undermined by non-economic principles. Thus, the investments that support insurance premiums, and through which claims can be paid, must be sufficient to guarantee a solvent, safe insurance system without systemic risks.

In addition, the PSI should be applied proportionately. Since not all insurance companies are the same in terms of type of clients, external relations, volume of business, geographical area, legal form, etc., the principles should be applied by adjusting them to the reality of the insurance company. This is often the case in mutual-based insurers, where the members are the policyholders whose business volume is usually only for the needs of their members.

Finally, assurance will be a key element in determining whether the PSI have been implemented correctly by an insurance company. Thus, it will be necessary for an expert to determine whether the insurance company has implemented the PSI, whether it has done so correctly, or what modifications it needs to make to its business to correctly comply with the PSI. However, it should be noted that it is the insurance company that appoints the assurance provider, so there may be suspicions of collaboration leading to the greenwashing of the company.

References

Aglietta M, Rebérioux A (2005) Corporate governance adrift. A critique of shareholder value. Edward Elgar, Cheltenham, pp 146–159

Bagnoli M, Watts S (2017) Voluntary assurance of voluntary CSR disclosure. J Econ Manag Strateg 26(1):205–230. https://doi.org/10.1111/jems.12171

Baldi F, Pandimiglio A (2022) The role of ESG scoring and greenwashing risk in explaining the yields of green bonds: a conceptual framework and an econometric analysis. Glob Financ J 52. https://doi.org/10.1016/j.gfj.2022.100711

Bansal P, Des Jardine M (2014) Business sustainability: it is about time. Strateg Organ 12(1):70–78. https://doi.org/10.1177/1476127013520265

Barber D, Kopp A, Cottet R, Susinno G (2022) How to improve the ESG profile of portfolios while keeping a similar risk-adjusted return. J Risk Manag Financ Inst 15(1) https://ssrn.com/abstract=4076841

Barkemeyer R (2007) Legitimacy as a key driver and determinant of CSR in developing countries. In: The 2007 Amsterdam conference on the human dimensions of global environmental change 44, pp. 1–23

Bataller-Grau J (2009) Principles of European insurance contract Law (PEICL). Wissenschaftliche Verlagsgesellschaft, Stuttgart, pp 36–75
Bataller-Grau J (2018) Un concepto de Responsabilidad Social de la Empresa desde el Derecho Mercantil. Revista de Derecho Mercantil 310:73
Bice S (2017) Corporate social responsibility as institution: a social mechanisms framework. J Bus Ethics 143:27. https://doi.org/10.1007/s10551-015-2791-1
Brogi M, Cappiello A, Lagasio V, Santoboni F (2022) Determinants of insurance companies' environmental, social, and governance awareness. Corp Soc Respon Environ Manag 29(5): 1357–1369. https://doi.org/10.1002/csr.2274
Cappiello A (2020) The digital (r)evolution of insurance business models. Am J Econ Bus Adm 1(1):13. https://doi.org/10.3844/ajebasp.2020.1.13
Caputo F, Scuotto V, Papa A, Del Giudice M (2020) From sustainability coercion to social engagement: the turning role of corporate social responsibility. Corp Gov Res Dev Stud 2:20. https://doi.org/10.3280/cgrds2-2020oa10558
Caterino D (2020) Nome e labeling della società benefit: nuove frontiere del contrasto al greenwashing, L' impresa sostenibile. Alla prova del dialogo dei saperi, EuriConv, Lecce, pp. 227–249
Curtit F (2016) Un thésaurus pour cartographier les outils juridiques mobilisés par la RSE. In: La RSE saisie par le droit. Perspective interne et internationale. A. Pedone, Paris, pp. 15–23
Delmas M, Burbano V (2011) The drivers of greenwashing. Calif Manag Rev 54(1):64–87. https://doi.org/10.1525/cmr.2011.54.1.64
Devalle A, Fiandrino S, Cantino V (2017) The linkage between ESG performance and credit ratings: a firm-level perspective analysis. Int J Bus Manag 12(9):12. https://doi.org/10.5539/ijbm.v12n9p53
Esteban Velasco G (2014) Responsabilidad Social Corporativa: delimitación, relevancia jurídica e incidencia en el Derecho de sociedades y en el Gobierno Corporativo, Libro Homenaje al Prof. Juan Luis Iglesias Prada, Civitas-Thomson Reuters, Madrid, p. 271
Fleisher H (2015) Corporate social responsibility, Vermessung eines Forschungsfeldes aus rechtlicher Sicht. Die Aktiengesellschaft 15:509
Freeman RE (1984) Strategic management: a stakeholder approach. Pitman Publishing, Boston, p 25
Gatzert N, Reichel P, Zitzmann A (2020) A. Sustainability risks & opportunities in the insurance industry. ZVersWiss 109:311–331. https://doi.org/10.1007/s12297-020-00482-w
Green M (2021) Theoretical developments in corporate social responsibility. In: Crowther D, Seifi S (eds) The Palgrave handbook of corporate social responsibility. Palgrave Macmillan, Cham, p 48. https://doi.org/10.1007/978-3-030-22438-7_78-1
Hansen E, Carnes N, Gray V (2019) What happens when insurers make insurance laws? State legislative agendas and the occupational makeup of government. State Polit Policy Q 19(2): 155–179. https://doi.org/10.1177/1532440018813013
Helmold M, Dathe R, Dathe T, Groß DP, Hummel F (2020) Corporate social responsibility im internationalen kontext. Springer Gabler, Wiesbaden, pp 31–93. https://doi.org/10.1007/978-3-658-30899-5
Hertel S (2003) The private side of global governance. J Int Aff 57(1):41–50
Hill C, Jones T (1992) Stakeholder-agency theory. J Manag Stud 29(2):131–154
Hinna L (2005) Principi di revisione dei bilanci social. In: Sacconi L (ed) Guida critica alla Responsabilità sociale e al governo d'impresa. Bancaria Editrice, Roma, p 690
Johnson L, Wandera B, Jensen N, Banerjee R (2019) Competing expectations in an index-based livestock insurance project. J Dev Stud 55(6):1221–1239. https://doi.org/10.1080/00220388.2018.1453603
Leipziger D (2010) The corporate responsibility code book, 2nd edn. Greenleaf Publishing Limited, Sheffield, p 19

Linnerooth-Bayer J, Mechler R (2007) Disaster safety nets for developing countries: extending public—private partnerships. Environ Hazards 7(1):54–61. https://doi.org/10.1016/j.envhaz.2007.04.004
López Cumbre L (2012) La dimensión normativa nacional de la responsabilidad social de la empresa. In: López Cumbre L (ed) Autonomía y heteronomía en la Responsabilidad Social de la Empresa. Granada, pp 105–106
Majoch AAA, Hoepner AGF, Hebb T (2017) Sources of stakeholder salience in the responsible investment movement: why do investors sign the principles for responsible investment? J Bus Ethics 140:723–741. https://doi.org/10.1007/s10551-016-3057-2
Malecki C (2009) L'investissement socialement responsable: quelques problématiques actuelles. Revue Lamy Droit des affaires 61:64
Malecki C (2018) Corporate social responsibility. Perspectives for sustainable corporate governance. Edward Elgar, Cheltenham, p 242. https://doi.org/10.4337/9781786433350
Miazad A (2023) D&O insurers as climate governance monitors. https://doi.org/10.2139/ssrn.4222100
Pugnetti C, Gebert T, Hürster M, Huizenga E, Moor M, Stricker L, Winistörfer H, Zeier Röschmann A (2022) Leading the green insurance revolution. ZHAW Zürcher Hochschule für Angewandte Wissenschaften, Winterthur
Rühmkorf A (2015) Corporate social responsibility, private law and global supply chains. Edward Elgar, Cheltenham, p 57
Rusconi G (2006) Il bilancio sociale: economia, etica e responsabilità sociale dell'impresa. Ediesse, Bergamo, p 120
Sánchez MR (2020) La Taxonomía UE: una regla de oro de las finanzas sostenibles. Revista de Derecho del Mercado de Valores 27:193–241
Scordis N, Suzawa Y, Zwick A, Ruckner L (2014) Principles for sustainable insurance: risk, management and value. Risk Manag Insur Rev 17(2):265–276. https://doi.org/10.1111/rmir.12024
Sievänen R, Rita H, Scholtens B (2013) The drivers of responsible investment: the case of European pension funds. J Bus Ethics 117:137–151. https://doi.org/10.1007/s10551-012-1514-0
Smith D (2002) Demonstrating corporate values: which standard for your company? Institute of Business Ethics, London, p 32
Sonnenberger D, Weiss GNF (2021) The impact of corporate social responsibility on firms' exposure to tail risk: the case of insurers. https://doi.org/10.2139/ssrn.3764041
Spence M (2002) Signaling in retrospect and the informational structure of markets. Am Econ Rev 92(3):434–459. https://doi.org/10.1257/00028280260136200
Stricker L, Pugnetti C, Wagner J, Zeier Röschmann A (2022) Green insurance: a roadmap for executive management. J Risk Financ Manag 15:221. https://doi.org/10.3390/jrfm15050221
Vaz Ogando N, Ruiz Blanco S, Fernandez-Feijoo Souto B (2018) El mercado de verificación de las memorias de sostenibilidad en España: un análisis desde la perspectiva de la demanda. Spanish Account Rev 21:248–262
Vercher-Moll J (2021) La verificación en la responsabilidad social empresarial. Revista Aranzadi de Derecho patrimonial 56:25–44
Vermiglio F (2005) Il bilancio sociale. In: Sacconi L (ed) Guida critica alla Responsabilità sociale e al governo d'impresa. Bancaria Editrice, Roma, p 656
Vives A (2019) La empresa privada y los objetivos de desarrollo sostenible: legitimidad o "greenwashing." Icade: Revista de la Facultad de Derecho núm. 108 (Ejemplar dedicado a: Objetivos de desarrollo sostenible: fortalezas y debilidades para alcanzar la Agenda 2030), Madrid, pp. 33–95
Viviani M (1999) Specchio mágico, Il bilancio sociale e l'evoluzione delle imprese. Il Mulino, Bologna, p 73

Javier Vercher-Moll is a Doctor of Law at the University of Valencia. He was awarded the extraordinary prize for a doctorate in law. His publications have focused on insurance companies' planning, supervision, and solvency. He also has several publications on the system of governance of insurance companies, the management of their risks, and the requirements of honesty and competence of the directors of insurance companies. He was also CEO of a mutual insurance company. Currently, his publications focus on the sustainability of insurance companies and assurance of non-financial information. This chapter is part of the Research Project whose reference is: IMPACTO DE LA RSE EN LAS SOCIEDADES MERCANTILES (CIGE/202/150/RSCOM) of the Generalitat Valenciana, Spain.

Sustainability Reporting Regulation: A Perspective on Insurance Market

Juan Bataller-Grau

1 An Initial Approach to Social Responsibility

1.1 A Notion of Social Responsibility

Social responsibility is a subject that is being analysed from different areas of knowledge. Thus, we can mention its ethical perspective, its penetration into the organisation of companies and public administrations, or the growing interest of those studying accounting in sustainability reports. Therefore, any aspiration to achieve a holistic explanation is currently unattainable in practice if the rigour that should be demanded of scientific knowledge is sought.

It is easy to understand that reaching an unambiguous definition is an extremely complex work. Synthesising so much content in a single sentence is a very difficult task. However, sometimes there are approaches that, with lesser explanatory pretensions, find certain support in the academia, as is the case in this field with that carried out within the European Union, where social responsibility (then corporate) was understood as *the voluntary integration, by companies, of social and environmental concerns in their business operations and in their relations with stakeholders.*[1] Without ignoring the fact that the time that has elapsed since its issuance deprives it of certain characteristics that have been gradually incorporated in the

[1] This is contained in the Green Paper of 18 July 2001, entitled "Promoting a European framework for Corporate Social Responsibility" COM (2001) 366 and has subsequently been reiterated in the Communications of the European Commission of July 2002, on "Corporate Social Responsibility: A Contribution to Sustainable Development" and March 2006, "Making Europe a Pole of Excellence on Corporate Social Responsibility."

J. Bataller-Grau (✉)
Mercantile Law 'Manuel Broseta Pont', University of Valencia, Valencia, Spain
e-mail: juan.bataller@uv.es

J. Bataller-Grau et al. (eds.), *Sustainability and the Insurance Market*, AIDA Europe Research Series on Insurance Law and Regulation 10,
https://doi.org/10.1007/978-3-031-72186-1_2

evolution of regulations, the influence that it has subsequently exerted on the current construction of social responsibility is unquestionable. Moreover, it has the virtue of emphasising the note of voluntariness that lies at the heart of social responsibility.

1.2 Shaping Features of Social Responsibility

It is appropriate to go a step further in this explanatory work, and we will therefore focus on identifying its most common elements. This approach, which is undoubtedly more efficient, provides us with six key features of social responsibility:[2]

Voluntariness Social responsibility must be assumed voluntarily beyond the norm. Mere compliance with the norm is not social responsibility. It has been stressed in some of the official documents that compliance with the norm is a prerequisite for social responsibility. It seems inconsistent for a company to want to take on new commitments when it does not even comply with those established by the regulations in force.

It is also a matter of pointing out that social responsibility projects itself where the legislator has not yet arrived. What is more, where perhaps the legislator should never go. In short, social responsibility implies the assumption of a legal duty not imposed by the legislator, which gives it a flexibility that the norm cannot and should not have.

Integration Social responsibility cannot be limited to the preparation of sustainability reporting. Transparency is certainly another of the elements that make up social responsibility, but its significance lies precisely in the fact that it must be imbricated in all decision-making processes within the entity in such a way that it permeates its functioning. It is not a mere addition, not even a question of doing more, but of doing differently.

Consistency Social responsibility cannot reside in isolated initiatives destined for ephemeral survival. The policies adopted by the entity require time for their implementation and, in turn, only continuous action can produce real effects. This is required for the credibility of the legal entity that has to justify its social licence to operate in the market. Consistency is not at odds with the advocated flexibility. It is one thing for policies to be sustainable, and quite another for the institution to enjoy full freedom to shape them.

Dialogue Social responsibility should be understood as obtaining a social licence to operate in the market, which gives the company the status of a social actor that is permanently obliged to legitimise itself. For this reason, the company must be willing to maintain fluid communication with its stakeholders. This note therefore has a bearing on the necessary complicity of the recipients of the policies

[2]On this point, we follow the work of Lozano (2011), pp. 82 et seq.

implemented. The legal entity's commitments can only be accommodated to the expectations of stakeholders through the existence of effective and efficient channels.

Transparency and Accountability This feature is currently a clear exponent of the regulatory development to which social responsibility is subject. This phenomenon cannot become a mere greenwashing of companies with the worst practices. Stakeholders must therefore be rigorously informed about the company's involvement in the different areas of materiality, as well as offering indicators that make it possible to accurately determine the degree of performance and, finally, be verified in order to provide certainty.

Surely it would be feasible to integrate some other feature as a conformer of social responsibility. However, we believe that the proposals outlined above are unavoidable, and at the same time allow us to fulfil the modest aim of this section, which is none other than to offer an initial perspective on the subject we propose to analyse.

1.3 Hard Law and Soft Law

Before continuing with the paper, a brief glossary should be included to ensure maximum precision, which is a requirement for any work that aspires to be minimally rigorous.

In the following sections, we will use the term *hard law* as a rule—or principle—of either national, EU or even international origin that can be directly imposed by a Court or directly applied by the Administration of a nation-state without requiring any declaration or action by the legal entity to which it is to be applied. In simplified terms, any rule that is directly enforceable by the Administration or by national Courts.

When we use the term *soft law,* we refer to those instruments that arise in the current stage of the development of legal systems that are situated between *hard law* and the absence of regulation. There are many names for *soft law*: standards, recommendations, codes of conduct, guidelines, principles, good practices, etc. The diversity shows the enormous amalgam of forms that *soft law* takes on, which leads to an enormous complexity when conceptualising this category.[3]

Finally, we will also use the term *self-regulation* to refer to the *soft law* of private origin. This is a familiar term, but at the same time, it allows me to distinguish it from the *soft law* of public origin.[4]

[3]Basedow (2021), p. 299.

[4]On this issue, more broadly Bataller Grau (2023a, b, c).

1.4 Stakeholders

A usual term in this area is "*stakeholders.*" This term, it should be made clear at the beginning, is not specific to legal science, but comes from *management*. The origin of the term within this discipline is not easy to determine, although it is commonplace in these early formulations of the concept that it should be understood as those groups without whose support the organisation would cease to exist.[5]

From a *management perspective,* stakeholders are divided into internal and external stakeholders. The former includes owners (shareholders), customers, employees and suppliers. External stakeholders include management, competitors, consumer advocates, environmentalists, social activists and the media.[6]

This construction is currently very widespread within *management,* even though different dogmatic currents have developed since its primitive design. Within this list, we can find a dogmatic construction that defends a specific configuration of social responsibility. This thesis considers that stakeholders have been considered as an externality from the point of view of the strategic direction and management procedures of organisations. However, this point of view must be abandoned. Stakeholders should seek and achieve active participation in the management of the organisation. It is therefore necessary to move from the influence of stakeholders to their participation in the management.[7]

From the point of view of this thesis focused on social responsibility, by stakeholders we understand those groups towards which the company has any moral obligation. Within these, the following agents can be mentioned: customers; suppliers; company staff and their families; partners; public administrations; civil society; local communities; and competitors. In addition, together with these stakeholders, it is necessary to point out the growing importance of environmental issues that transcend their inclusion as a stakeholder.

In addition, there is a duty to engage in dialogue with stakeholders when defining the risks and policies to be implemented by a company. Therefore, the stakeholder has significance in the management of social responsibility and is not subject to any legal consideration. However, this does not preclude the possibility of raising important legal questions such as, for example, who has the legal standing to enforce specific legal obligations.

---

[5] Freeman (2010), p. 31 and footnote 1, p. 49.

[6] On this point we follow Freeman (2010), pp. 4 ff. as it is one of the most complete and widely accepted.

[7] Dill (1975), pp. 57 ff.

1.5 From Corporate Social Responsibility to Sustainability

It is difficult to pinpoint a specific milestone as the birth of evolution.[8] When referring to the beginnings of social responsibility, the influence of Christianity, whether Catholic or Protestant, is sometimes mentioned.[9] However, the first common denominator in the literature on the subject lies in granting germinal value to the work published in 1953 by Bowen under the title *Social Responsibilities of the Businessman.*[10] It is also recurrent to refer to Carroll's pyramid[11] and Elkington's triple social bottom.[12]

This led to a series of green or white papers, opinions, etc. by various international organisations, but also by the EU institutions. The groundwork was thus being laid for the current regulatory development.

In this first stage, which lacked regulation, reference was made to an institution, corporate social responsibility, whose defining feature was voluntariness. In other words, by virtue of the principle of contractual freedom, companies were defining their policies and commitments in complete liberty.

A new step in the conceptual transmutation of the institution has been the pruning of the term "company" from its name. Corporate social responsibility is deprived of the hitherto mere epithet "company" to open up to other types of legal entities, especially those of a public nature. This is how social responsibility came into being. The institution can no longer be confined to the sphere of the company. Its expansive force makes it advisable to apply it to other types of legal entities. The corollary is the suppression of its pristine origin: the company thus disappears from the term as a result of the evolution of the concept itself.

The latest episode in this evolutionary series is the appearance of the term sustainability, the result of the regulatory frenzy in which we are currently immersed. Its epicentre is to be found in the regulation of the European Union, but not only.

Transmutation might seem not to harbour a conceptual evolution, which is why it might seem that we are dealing with synonyms, and this is defended in many forums that deal with the institution in question from different perspectives. The use of the term currently in vogue "Social Responsibility and Sustainability" responds more to an identifying intention that allows a link between the past and the present to be established than to a profound reflection on the possible new contours of the same.

A current view of the institution leads to the fact that we must point out that new shaping features have been introduced. The intensive regulatory work of the EU institutions has led to the introduction of a regime that is in many cases mandatory. This does not imply that there is still no room for corporate freedom. The implication is merely to state that this freedom begins with mandatory regulation.

---

[8] A broader approach to the non-legal literature can be found in Malecki (2018), pp. 19 et seq.

[9] On the beginnings, see Pasquero (2005), pp. 80 et seq.

[10] Bowen (1953).

[11] Carroll (1979), pp. 268–292.

[12] Elkington (1999).

For this reason, in this paper, we will refer to social responsibility on those occasions when we deal with commitments voluntarily assumed by companies. Likewise, when we use the term sustainability, we will be referring to the set of mandatory rules but also to those elements of social responsibility. In short, these are two concentric circles. Sustainability encompasses both.

One last caveat to be consistent with our thesis already defended on previous occasions: although sustainability reporting contains an imperative regulation, this does not prevent it from continuing to form part of social responsibility.[13]

2 The Legal Framework for Sustainability Reporting

2.1 Hard Law

Transparency is precisely one of the aspects of sustainability where the evolution that has taken place within the institution can be best appreciated. As with many changes in any aspect of evolution, the transition from one phase to another is not drastic or even reflexive. However, offering an approximation of its stages helps us to better understand how it has developed.

During the first phase in which social responsibility was outside EU legislation, companies began to publish sustainability reports. There was no obligation to publish any document, let alone a specific content to be respected, but as we have pointed out, transparency is among the elements that make up social responsibility. Therefore, the companies that have been pioneers in embracing social responsibility began to publish these reports, generally following the international standards that already existed at that time.

The next step in the evolution of the duty of transparency is the entry into force of Directive 2014/95/EU of the European Parliament and of the Council amending Directive 2013/34/EU as regards disclosure of non-financial information and diversity information by certain large undertakings and groups.

The next milestone was the Commission Communication on Guidelines on Non-Financial Reporting (Methodology for Non-Financial Reporting).[14] The development of Non-Financial Reporting Statements came hand in hand this time with public *soft law*.

The Directive restricts its scope of application to large undertakings that are public-interest entities and public-interest entities that are parent undertakings of a large group, in each case with an average number of employees exceeding 500, on a

---

[13] More broadly, Bataller Grau (2023a, b, c).

[14] DOUE 2017/C 215/01. This Communication is complemented by the Communication (2019/C 209/01): "Guidelines on non-financial reporting: Supplement on climate-related information" (OJEU, 20 June 2019).

consolidated group basis. It also focuses on improving the consistency and comparability of non-financial information disclosed in the Union.

As the Directive itself makes explicit, non-financial disclosure is essential for managing the transition to a sustainable global economy that combines long-term profitability with social justice and environmental protection. In this context, non-financial disclosure contributes to measuring, monitoring and managing the performance of companies and their impact on society. The European Parliament therefore called on the Commission to come forward with a legislative proposal on non-financial disclosure by companies, allowing for a high degree of flexibility in action to take account of the multidimensional nature of corporate social responsibility and the diversity of policies pursued by companies, while having a sufficient level of comparability to meet the needs of investors and other stakeholders, as well as the need to provide consumers with easy access to information on the impact of companies on society.

Thus, a decisive step in the consolidation of the institution was taken from the mere voluntarism of the initial sustainability reports to the Non-Financial Information Statements.

The latest stage in this evolution is the recent reform of transparency introduced by Directive (EU) 2022/2464 of the European Parliament and of the Council of 14 December 2022, amending Regulation (EU) No. 537/2014, Directive 2004/109/EC, Directive 2006/43/EC and Directive 2013/34/EU.[15]

The European Commission committed in the so-called "Green Deal" to review the non-financial disclosure provisions of Directive 2013/34/EU of the European Parliament and of the Council. The standard itself states that further progress was necessary as the Green Deal is the Union's new growth strategy and relevant, comparable and reliable sustainability information is unavoidable for the achievement of its objectives.

The Directive also noted the growing demand for sustainability information and therefore called for a reform to avoid a widening gap between the information needs of users and the sustainability information provided by companies, particularly to investors and civil society actors.

The reform introduced by Directive (EU) 2022/2464 extends to the following community rules:

- Regulation (EU) No. 537/2014 on specific requirements for the statutory audit of public interest entities;
- Directive 2004/109/EC on the harmonisation of transparency requirements in relation to information about issuers whose securities are admitted to trading on a regulated market;
- Directive 2006/43/EC on statutory audits of annual accounts and consolidated accounts;

[15] The Directive provides for a phased entry into force starting with accounting periods beginning on 1 January 2024, 1 January 2025 and 1 January 2026.

- Directive 2013/34/EU on the annual financial statements, consolidated financial statements and related reports of certain types of undertakings.

The material new features introduced by Directive (EU) 2022/2464 are significant and cross-cutting within existing community accounting law. In my view, the most noteworthy new features are those set out below.

First, the term "sustainability information" is adopted instead of "non-financial information," as the information referred to as such in Directive 2013/34/EU is increasingly relevant to financial aspects.

Second, the duty of transparency is extended, so that other categories of companies should be required to report sustainability information. Without claiming to be exhaustive, large companies and all companies, except for micro-undertakings, whose securities are admitted to trading on a regulated market in the Union, are required to report sustainability information. In addition, all companies that are parents of large groups are required to report sustainability information at the group level. Finally, third-country companies with significant activity in the EU territory are also required to provide sustainability information.

Third, the above-mentioned Directive (EU) 2022/2464 states that developments in this area require the establishment of mandatory common sustainability reporting standards to ensure that information is comparable and that all relevant information is disclosed. The content of the reports is therefore further refined and tightened based on existing experience with the implementation of Directive 2013/34/EU.

Fourth, this information is required to be provided in a pre-established digital format that facilitates computer processing.

Fifth, we must emphasise that one of the most noteworthy modifications takes place in the field of verification, going further than the current regime in the field of this activity, as well as in the requirements demanded of verifiers.

In this vein, a progressive approach is taken to improve the level of verification required for sustainability reporting, starting with the duty of the statutory auditor or audit firm to provide an opinion on the compliance of sustainability reporting with Union requirements on the basis of a limited assurance engagement. That opinion should express an opinion on the compliance of the sustainability reporting with Union standards for sustainability reporting, the process carried out by the company to determine the sustainability reporting in accordance with those standards and the compliance with the requirement to flag the sustainability reporting.

The auditor should also assess whether the company's reporting complies with the reporting requirements of Article 8 of Regulation (EU) 2020/852. To ensure a common understanding and expectations on what would constitute a reasonable assurance engagement, the statutory auditor or audit firm should be required to issue an opinion based on a reasonable assurance engagement on the compliance of sustainability reporting with EU requirements when the Commission adopts rules for the reasonable assurance of sustainability reporting by means of delegated acts no later than 1 October 2028, following an assessment as to whether reasonable assurance is feasible for auditors and companies.

In turn, independent verification service providers should be subject to compliance with requirements equivalent to those laid down in Directive 2006/43/EC of the European Parliament and of the Council as regards the verification of sustainability reporting, while adapting to the characteristics of independent verification service providers that do not carry out statutory audits.

Finally, it should be noted that the right of the shareholder (or minority shareholders) to request an audit of the accounting is now also extended to information on sustainability.

2.2 *Soft Law*

As I have been defending, transparency is a core requirement of social responsibility, there is a need to establish uniform criteria and global standards for the preparation of the main instrument of transparency in social responsibility: sustainability reports. Companies must provide objective and verifiable information on their impact on the *triple bottom line:* economic, social and environmental. Certainly, all companies are not the same, so it is not surprising that their social responsibility varies significantly. It seems clear that its approach in this area will not be the same if it is engaged in mineral extraction or financial services, nor will it be the same if it focuses its business on the European Union or is a company with a fully international presence. However, these divergences should not make us lose sight of the fact that the effectiveness of the duty of transparency requires a minimum standardisation that offers precise, comparable and verifiable information, even more so when we refer to the insurance market, as is the case in this paper.

In the following sections, we will offer a selection of the international standards that I consider to be the most important in the preparation of sustainability reports, and as regards material standards, we will limit ourselves to those specific to insurance companies.

2.2.1 General Standards

2.2.1.1 Global Reporting Initiative

In the field of sustainability reporting, the Global Reporting Initiative (GRI), founded in Boston in 1997,[16] has emerged strongly. Its objective is to create the

---

[16] Its promoters were the non-profit organisations Coalition for Environmentally Responsible Economies (CERES) and the Tellus Institute. The United Nations Environment Programme (UNEP) was also involved in the establishment of GRI.

Its objective was to create an accountability mechanism to ensure that companies follow the CERES Principles for Responsible Environmental Conduct. Investors were the original target audience of the framework.

conditions for a transparent and reliable exchange of information, for which it proposes a methodology for the preparation of reports, which has been widely used in practice. Indeed, the GRI standards are arguably the most widely used sustainability reporting methodology among multinational companies.

The GRI standards are designed to be used as a set by any organisation that wants to report on its impacts and how it contributes to sustainable development. The GRI standards are also a trusted reference for policymakers and regulators around the world; they encourage and enable credible non-financial reporting by companies under their jurisdictions.

The GRI system of standards for sustainability reporting is currently structured as an interrelated system in three distinct series: GRI Universal Standards; GRI Sector Standards; and GRI Topic Standards.[17]

In turn, the internal organisation of each of these groups of standards is composed of GRI 1: Fundamentals 2021 which specifies the requirements that the organisation that subscribes to use the standards must meet to report against the GRI Standards. The second group within this category, GRI 2: General Content 2021 includes content that the subscribing organisation will use to present information on its reporting practices and other organisational details, such as its activities, governance and policies. Finally, the third group, GRI 3: Material Issues 2021, provides guidance on how to identify material issues. It also includes content that the organisation uses to present information about its process for determining material topics, its list of material topics and how it manages each topic.[18]

In the case of Sectoral Standards, these are intended to provide information to the organisation on its potential material issues. The member company shall use the Sector Standards that apply to its business sectors to determine which material issues will be reported and the information to be reported in relation to each material issue.

Finally, the Topic Standards include content that each company uses to present information on the impact of its activities related to certain topics. Each company will use the Topic Standards according to the list of material topics included in GRI 3.

2.2.1.2 EFRAG

EFRAG is a private association established in 2001 with the encouragement of the European Commission to serve the public interest. EFRAG extended its mission in 2022 following the new role assigned to EFRAG in the CSRD, providing Technical Advice to the European Commission in the form of fully prepared draft EU Sustainability Reporting Standards and/or draft amendments to these Standards.[19]

[17] Rodes Paredes (2023).

[18] Rodes Paredes (2023).

[19] https://www.efrag.org/About/Facts.

EFRAG's activities are developing draft EU Sustainability Reporting Standards and related amendments for the European Commission. EFRAG's mission is to serve the European public interest in sustainability reporting by developing and promoting European views in the field of corporate reporting and by developing draft EU Sustainability Reporting Standards.[20]

2.2.1.3 International Auditing and Assurance Standard Board

The International Auditing and Assurance Standard Board (IAASB) is an independent standard-setting body that claims to serve the public interest by setting international auditing, quality assurance and review standards and facilitating international convergence. In doing so, the IAASB enhances the quality and consistency of accounting practice worldwide and strengthens public confidence in the auditing and assurance profession.[21]

Within its portfolio, we highlight the revised International Standard on Assurance Engagements (ISAE) 3000, as it is the standard used for the verification of sustainability reports. It describes the framework in which control is developed, a detailed description of the risk management system, and a matrix that specifies the risks established, the objectives for their control, and the control measures adopted.

2.2.1.4 AccountAbility

AccountAbility[22] is an NGO that works with companies, governments and multilateral organisations to promote responsible business practices and improve their long-term performance, with one of its aims being the promotion of international standards.

Within this facet, it has issued the AA1000 AS Standard as well as a set of documents for a better interpretation and implementation of the standard.

The purpose of the AA1000 assurance standard is to support reporting that follows specific standards, adapted by the reporting organisation. It is designed to be consistent with and promote the Global Reporting Initiative (GRI) Sustainability Reporting Guidelines and other related standards.

In addition, this set of standards is designed to complement the work of sustainability reporting specialists, including audits to verify compliance with labour standards or information related to employment diversity, environmental standards and carbon emissions, as well as to encourage the use of standards that can improve the company's accountability and sustainability.[23]

---

[20] https://www.efrag.org/About/Facts.

[21] https://www.iaasb.org/.

[22] https://www.accountability.org/.

[23] Rabanete Martínez (2023).

Organisations adopting any part of the AA1000 series commit to the practice of so-called "inclusivity," which implies a commitment to identify and understand their social, environmental and economic outcomes and impacts. It is a commitment to consider and respond consistently (whether negatively or positively) to the aspirations and needs of stakeholders with regard to the organisation's policies and practices, as well as to account for its decisions, actions and impacts. In addition, the principles outlined in the AA1000 series of standards form the basis on which an organisation ensures its credibility in relation to fulfilling its commitment to accountability.[24]

2.2.2 Material Standards Specific to the Insurance Sector

2.2.2.1 The Principles of Responsible Investment

In this section, we must begin with the Principles for Responsible Investment, as it is a widespread standard among companies operating in the financial markets, such as insurance companies. The Principles for Responsible Investment are an initiative of investors in collaboration with the United Nations Environment Programme Finance Initiative and the UN Global Compact.[25]

The Principles for Responsible Investment are addressed to institutional investors in a broad sense, including *asset owners*, *investment managers* and other investment service providers, irrespective of their size.[26]

Network members are committed, as institutional investors, to orient their activity towards the best interests of investors with long-term performance in mind. Crucial to this fiduciary role is the incorporation of environmental, social and corporate governance issues into the analysis of investment portfolios (to varying degrees across companies, sectors, regions, asset classes and over time). It is also believed that the application of the Principles for Responsible Investment can better align investors with broader societal goals. The international network of members aims to put the Principles for Responsible Investment into practice. It aims to understand the impact that environmental, social and corporate governance issues have on

---

[24] Rabanete Martínez (2023).

[25] Ban Ki-moon, in his tenure as UN Secretary-General, stated: "Sustainability is a global imperative. It is my top priority as Secretary-General and the UN believes that investors have an essential role to play in achieving it. Until recently, the implications of sustainability for investors and financial markets were little understood and largely overlooked. The UN-backed Principles for Responsible Investment have helped to address this gap by highlighting the financial relevance of environmental, social and governance (ESG) issues, as well as providing the global investment community with a framework to contribute to the development of a more stable and sustainable financial system."

https://www.unpri.org.

[26] Marimón Durá (2023).

investments and to advise members on how to integrate these issues into their investment and ownership decisions.

The Principles for Responsible Investment are specified in six maxims:

1. Integration incorporate ESG issues into investment analysis and decision-making processes.[27]

2. Engagement be active owners and incorporate ESG issues into ownership policies and practices.[28]

3. Transparency seek appropriate disclosure on ESG issues by the entities in which invest.[29]

4. Acceptance promote acceptance and implementation of the principles within the investment industry.[30]

5. Cooperation work together to enhance effectiveness in implementing the principles.[31]

6. Report each report on activities and progress towards implementing the principles.[32]

---

[27] Possible actions: Address ESG issues in investment policy statements; Support development of ESG-related tools, metrics, and analyses; Assess the capabilities of internal investment managers to incorporate ESG issues; Assess the capabilities of external investment managers to incorporate ESG issues; Ask investment service providers (such as financial analysts, consultants, brokers, research firms, or rating companies) to integrate ESG factors into evolving research and analysis; Encourage academic and other research on this theme; Advocate ESG training for investment professionals.

[28] Possible actions: Develop and disclose an active ownership policy consistent with the principles; Exercise voting rights or monitor compliance with voting policy (if outsourced); Develop an engagement capability (either directly or through outsourcing); Participate in the development of policy, regulation, and standard setting (such as promoting and protecting shareholder rights); File shareholder resolutions consistent with long-term ESG considerations; Engage with companies on ESG issues; Participate in collaborative engagement initiatives; Ask investment managers to undertake and report on ESG-related engagement.

[29] Possible actions: Ask for standardised reporting on ESG issues (using tools such as the Global Reporting Initiative); Ask for ESG issues to be integrated within annual financial reports; Ask for information from companies regarding adoption of/adherence to relevant norms, standards, codes of conduct or international initiatives (such as the UN Global Compact); Support shareholder initiatives and resolutions promoting ESG disclosure.

[30] Possible actions: Include principles-related requirements in requests for proposals (RFPs); Align investment mandates, monitoring procedures, performance indicators and incentive structures accordingly (for example, ensure investment management processes reflect long-term time horizons when appropriate); Communicate ESG expectations to investment service providers; Revisit relationships with service providers that fail to meet ESG expectations; Support the development of tools for benchmarking ESG integration; Support regulatory or policy developments that enable implementation of the principles.

[31] Possible actions: Support/participate in networks and information platforms to share tools, pool resources, and make use of investor reporting as a source of learning; Collectively address relevant emerging issues; Develop or support appropriate collaborative initiatives.

[32] Possible actions: Disclose how ESG issues are integrated within investment practices; Disclose active ownership activities (voting, engagement, and/or policy dialogue); Disclose what is required from service providers in relation to the principles; Communicate with beneficiaries about ESG issues and the principles; Report on progress and/or achievements relating to the principles using a

2.2.2.2 Principles for Sustainable Insurance

The initiative for the development of the Principles for Sustainability in Insurance began following a series of research studies conducted by the United Nations Environment Programme Finance Initiative (UNEP FI) between 2006 and 2009. The research focused on risks and opportunities in the insurance sector related to environmental, social and corporate governance issues. The development of the principles was overseen and managed by the UNEP FI insurance industry, observer institutions and the UNEP FI Secretariat.[33]

The Principles for Sustainable Insurance (PSI) aim to establish a cross-cutting framework that covers all aspects of the insurance company, both in its internal and external relations. A new long-term insurance business culture is thus advocated, not only from a financial point of view, but also from a non-financial point of view, i.e. according to the impact of its activity on the environment in which it operates. Therefore, these principles affect the company's relations with all stakeholders such as shareholders, customers, and governments, but also its internal development, whether through the integration of ESG issues in its management or the development of new types of risk management products and services.[34]

Sustainable insurance, it is advocated, is a strategic approach in which all activities in the insurance value chain, including interactions with all stakeholders, are conducted in a responsible and forward-looking manner by identifying, assessing, managing and monitoring risks and opportunities associated with environmental, social and governance issues. Sustainable insurance aims to reduce risk, develop innovative solutions, improve business performance and contribute to environmental, social and economic sustainability.[35]

The principles are:[36]

1. Embed environmental, social and corporate governance issues relevant to the insurance business into the decision-making process.
2. Work with clients and business partners to raise awareness of environmental, social and corporate governance issues, manage risk and develop solutions.
3. Collaborate with governments, regulators and other key stakeholders to promote widespread action across society on environmental, social and corporate governance issues.
4. Demonstrate accountability and transparency in regularly publicly disclosing progress in the implementation of the principles.

---

comply-or-explain approach; Seek to determine the impact of the principles; Make use of reporting to raise awareness among a broader group of stakeholders.

[33] https://www.unepfi.org/psi/wp-content/uploads/2013/06/PSI-document_Spanish.pdf.

[34] Vercher Moll (2023).

[35] https://www.unepfi.org/psi/wp-content/uploads/2013/06/PSI-document_Spanish.pdf.

[36] https://www.unepfi.org/psi/wp-content/uploads/2013/06/PSI-document_Spanish.pdf.

Finally, the Principles for Sustainable Insurance are stand-alone principles that can be adopted by any insurance company, but they are directly linked to the Principles for Responsible Investment, which focus on the risks and opportunities associated with ESG issues. Thus, as an institutional investor, insurance companies should compose a portfolio of investments that are ESG in nature, but without forgetting the levels of solvency required of them.[37]

3 Insurers as Public-Interest Entities

Directive 2013/34/EU of the European Parliament and of the Council of 26 June 2013 on the annual financial statements, consolidated financial statements and related reports of certain types of undertakings, amending Directive 2006/43/EC of the European Parliament and of the Council and repealing Council Directives 78/660/EEC and 83/349/EEC—Directive 2013/34/EU on the annual financial statements—differentiates in its Art. 3 between micro undertakings,[38] small undertakings,[39] medium-sized undertakings[40] and large undertakings.[41] This classification leads to greater accounting rigour as the size of the undertakings increases.

However, it is worth starting by explaining that from the point of view of accounting and auditing regulations, insurance entities are public-interest entities (Art. 2.1 Directive 2013/34/EU on the annual financial statements).

This qualification implies submission to the highest accounting standards regardless of the size of the company. In other words, insurance companies cannot be covered by the simplified regime even if their figures would allow such a classification. The legislator's mandate is fully consistent with the financial intermediation function they perform in the market.

---

[37] Vercher Moll (2023).

[38] Undertakings which on their balance sheet dates do not exceed the limits of at least two of the three following criteria: (a) balance sheet total: EUR 350,000; (b) net turnover: EUR 700,000; (c) average number of employees during the financial year: 10.

[39] Undertakings which on their balance sheet dates do not exceed the limits of at least two of the three following criteria: (a) balance sheet total: EUR 4,000,000; (b) net turnover: EUR 8,000,000; (c) average number of employees during the financial year: 50.

Member States may define thresholds exceeding the thresholds in points (a) and (b) of the first subparagraph. However, the thresholds shall not exceed EUR 6,000,000 for the balance sheet total and EUR 12,000,000 for the net turnover.

[40] Undertakings which are not micro-undertakings or small undertakings and which on their balance sheet dates do not exceed the limits of at least two of the three following criteria: (a) balance sheet total: EUR 20,000,000; (b) net turnover: EUR 40,000,000; (c) average number of employees during the financial year: 250.

[41] Undertakings which on their balance sheet dates exceed at least two of the three following criteria: (a) balance sheet total: EUR 20,000,000,000; (b) net turnover: EUR 40,000,000,000; (c) average number of employees during the financial year: 250.

Article 19a Directive 2013/34/EU on the annual financial statements is the regulatory provision for sustainability reporting. Article 19a.7 Directive 2013/34/EU on the annual financial statements establishes an important exception here by exempting small and medium-sized insurance undertakings from sustainability reporting before the financial year 2028. In such cases, the undertaking shall, nevertheless, briefly state in its management report why the sustainability reporting was not provided.

Captive insurance and captive reinsurance entities[42] also benefit from a simplified transparency regime. This is also a logical legislative option given that these entities are part of the risk management strategy of large corporate groups, and therefore it is the group that defines their sustainability policies.

The other inescapable precept under this heading is Art. 29 of Directive 2013/34/EU on the annual financial statements dedicated to consolidated sustainability reporting. Thus, parent undertakings of a large group shall include in the consolidated management report information necessary to understand the group's impacts on sustainability matters, and information necessary to understand how sustainability matters affect the group's development, performance and position.

Finally, the Directive itself provides for an exemption from sustainability reporting when certain subsidiaries or parent companies that are already included in the report of another entity also meet certain requirements.[43]

4 Sustainability Reporting Is a Duty

Directive 2014/95/EU of the European Parliament and of the Council of 22 October 2014 amending Directive 2013/34/EU makes the publication of sustainability reports *mandatory*. Consequently, the interpretation of the regulations in force leaves no doubt in this regard by requiring companies to draw up and subsequently communicate them. It is not a power, but a duty. This is clear from the literal wording of Articles 19a and 29a of Directive 2013/34/EU on the annual financial statements when it uses the expression "shall include."

However, this duty is not imposed *urbi et orbi,* as is usual in commercial law regulations. There are exceptions to the subjective scope, as described above.

In short, the above regime leads us to conclude that the community legal system imposes on certain insurance companies a duty of transparency that is fully imperative. For this reason, I cannot agree with the characterisation of the current regime as a *soft law* that some doctrine makes of it. The wording of Directive 2014/95/EU leaves no doubt in this regard. Consequently, the aforementioned precepts are fully mandatory with respect to companies that meet the aforementioned requirements.

---

[42] Article 13 Directive 2009/138/EC of the European Parliament and of the Council of 25 November 2009 on the taking-up and pursuit of the business of Insurance and Reinsurance (Solvency II).

[43] Articles 19 a.9 and 29 a.8 Directive 2013/34/EU on the annual financial statements.

5 The Areas and Content to be Included in Sustainability Reporting

Having affirmed the imposition of a duty of transparency, it remains to specify its content. The task is arduous and diverse because it requires tackling various problems, some of them intricate.

Beginning with the delimitation of the areas that make up the institution of social responsibility, it should be noted that companies enjoy very wide freedom to configure the commitments they intend to assume as a result of the primacy of voluntariness. However, it is no less true that not every activity can be classified as social responsibility. It is therefore necessary to define the boundaries of social responsibility.

UE legislator, when delimiting those matters that are included within sustainability, has opted to list certain areas, without subsequently demanding greater requirements for their qualification. Therefore, if the matter is within the areas listed by the UE legislator, its integration within sustainability is automatic, given that it is the regulator itself that grants it this nature.

However, the list of areas that form part of social responsibility must be formed from the integration of two regulatory blocks: the first is the aforementioned Directive 2013/34/EU on the annual financial statements and its implementing regulations, in which EFRAG is called upon to play a leading role, as the Directive itself anticipates; the second is Regulation (EU) 2019/2088 of the European Parliament and of the Council of 27 November 2019 on sustainability-related disclosures in the financial services sector[44] and its implementing regulations, where intense taxonomy work has been carried out.

The integration of Regulation (EU) 2019/2088 of the European Parliament and of the Council of 27 November 2019 on sustainability-related disclosures in the financial services within the regulatory block that defines social responsibility is convenient from the point of view of legislative policy, as it would be distorting to diverge the areas that make up the accountability of social responsibility and the areas to be considered to achieve the qualification of socially responsible investment. This has been understood in Art. 29b Directive 2013/34/EU on the annual financial

[44] Article 2.17 Regulation (EU) 2019/2088 of the European Parliament and of the Council of 27 November 2019 on sustainability-related disclosures in the financial services sector: 'sustainable investment' means an investment in an economic activity that contributes to an environmental objective, as measured, for example, by key resource efficiency indicators on the use of energy, renewable energy, raw materials, water and land, on the production of waste, and greenhouse gas emissions, or on its impact on biodiversity and the circular economy, or an investment in an economic activity that contributes to a social objective, in particular an investment that contributes to tackling inequality or that fosters social cohesion, social integration and labour relations, or an investment in human capital or economically or socially disadvantaged communities, provided that such investments do not significantly harm any of those objectives and that the investee companies follow good governance practices, in particular with respect to sound management structures, employee relations, remuneration of staff and tax compliance.

statements where an express reference is made to the aforementioned Regulation (EU) 2019/2088, and it is also included within its scope of application in Art. 1 Regulation (EU) 2020/852 of the European Parliament and of the Council of 18 June 2020 on the establishment of a framework to facilitate sustainable investment and amending Regulation (EU) 2019/2088.

Similarly, Article 29 b (5) of Directive 2013/34/EU on the annual financial statements calls for the implementing rules to take into account global standardisation initiatives relating to the presentation of information—the main ones discussed above—as well as other community standards and soft law instruments.

The list of contents that make up social responsibility is quite numerous—there are a large number of them—and complex—given that it is currently not possible to offer a unified methodology for their implementation. These contents are organised around the three areas that give socially responsible investment its name (ESG = environmental, social and governance), which allows at least a minimum of organisation.

However, the above list of contents is not exhaustive, as it admits the inclusion of any other content that the company considers relevant. We must therefore address a key question to provide a reliable answer to the object of our analysis: whether the mere inclusion in sustainability reporting allows the commitment to be classified as social responsibility.

An affirmative answer would mean adopting a formal criterion, which would imply that the mere inclusion per se of a matter in sustainability reporting would entail its qualification as social responsibility. In my opinion, this has not been the position of EU legislator, which, on the other hand, seems to be the most coherent thing to do. The absence of a closed structure in sustainability reporting, the preference for a management report that integrates non-financial information, the difficulties in the conceptual delimitation of social responsibility, and even the advocated flexibility that should shape the institution are decisive factors in refusing a merely formal qualification.

Having discarded this hermeneutic, in my opinion, it would have been advisable for the legislator to have adopted some criterion or criteria that would have allowed a clear decanting of the commitment independently of the interest group or area to which they are addressed. In my point of view, this omission can only be mitigated by the dogmatic construction of the concept of social responsibility. It is not by chance that we have directed our efforts to conceptualise the institution from a private law perspective, which allows us to refer to what has already been said.[45]

By way of conclusion, we can say that the classification of a commitment within social responsibility derives from its inclusion in the list of contents provided by EU regulations. However, these contents do not make up the entire perimeter of social responsibility, thus other matters can be included within sustainability reporting, without the regulator providing us with any requirement or element to guide the

[45] On the conceptual construction and its significance, more broadly, Bataller Grau (2017).

interpreter's work. This omission on the part of the legislator should not lead to its qualification being merely formally included in sustainability reporting but should be resolved by integrating it into the dogmatic concept of social responsibility.

6 The Information Is Not Financial

A relevant issue within transparency in social responsibility lies in the clear difference between financial and non-financial information. The former focuses on, without aspiring at this point to be exhaustive, "... a true and fair view of the undertaking's assets, liabilities, financial position and profit or loss" (Art. 4.3 Directive 2013/34/EU on the annual financial statements). Social responsibility, on the other hand, deals with policies, risk mitigation, stakeholder concerns and even values. It is therefore not surprising that how one and the other information should be presented should simply be different. A diverse subject matter should entail accountability tailored to the specificities of each. And all of this without pretending to deny the increasingly evident connection between the two.

Consequently, the regulation cannot be limited to providing us with a mere catalogue of contents. For this reason, the current regime on the duty of transparency takes a new step towards specifying its purpose: the main points that sustainability reporting must contain are introduced to specify the key performance indicators.

6.1 Main Points

The current legal regime on the subject is again to be found in Articles 19a and 29 of Directive 2013/34/EU on the annual financial statements. This is also where the main points are set out, without which the contents would be empty. The standard sets out the various milestones that must be reflected in all sustainability reporting:

(a) a brief description of the undertaking (or group)'s business model and strategy, including:

    1. the resilience of the undertaking (or group)'s business model and strategy in relation to risks related to sustainability matters;
    2. the opportunities for the undertaking (or group) related to sustainability matters;
    3. the plans of the undertaking (or group), including implementing actions and related financial and investment plans, to ensure that its business model and strategy are compatible with the transition to a sustainable economy and with the limiting of global warming to 1.5 °C in line with the Paris Agreement under the United Nations Framework Convention on Climate Change adopted on 12 December 2015 (the "Paris Agreement") and the objective of achieving climate neutrality by 2050 as established in Regulation

(EU) 2021/1119 of the European Parliament and of the Council, and, where relevant, the exposure of the undertaking to coal-, oil- and gas-related activities;
4. how the undertaking (or group)'s business model and strategy take account of the interests of the undertaking's stakeholders and of the impacts of the undertaking (or group) on sustainability matters;
5. how the undertaking (or group)'s strategy has been implemented with regard to sustainability matters;

(b) a description of the time-bound targets related to sustainability matters set by the undertaking (or group), including, where appropriate, absolute greenhouse gas emission reduction targets at least for 2030 and 2050, a description of the progress the undertaking (or group) has made towards achieving those targets, and a statement of whether the undertaking (or group)'s targets related to environmental factors are based on conclusive scientific evidence;
(c) a description of the role of the administrative, management and supervisory bodies with regard to sustainability matters, and of their expertise and skills in relation to fulfilling that role or the access such bodies have to such expertise and skills;
(d) a description of the undertaking (or group)'s policies in relation to sustainability matters;
(e) information about the existence of incentive schemes linked to sustainability matters which are offered to members of the administrative, management and supervisory bodies;
(f) a description of:

1. the due diligence process implemented by the undertaking (or group) with regard to sustainability matters, and, where applicable, in line with Union requirements on undertakings (or group) to conduct a due diligence process;
2. the principal actual or potential adverse impacts connected with the undertaking (or group)'s own operations and with its value chain, including its products and services, its business relationships and its supply chain, actions taken to identify and monitor those impacts, and other adverse impacts which the undertaking is required to identify pursuant to other Union requirements on undertakings to conduct a due diligence process;
3. any actions taken by the undertaking (or group) to prevent, mitigate, remediate or bring an end to actual or potential adverse impacts, and the result of such actions;

(g) a description of the principal risks to the undertaking (or group) related to sustainability matters, including a description of the undertaking (or group)'s principal dependencies on those matters, and how the undertaking (or group) manages those risks;
(h) indicators relevant to the disclosures referred to in points (a) to (g).

The main points, therefore, are the very core of the duty of transparency. Only by analysing them is it possible to gain an insight into the social responsibility actually practised by the company. The areas and content mark the playing field, but only the main points can provide transparency on the social responsibility of a particular entity or group of companies.

To this end, we have opted for a dynamic vision of social responsibility in which, from the necessary starting point, the business model, each of the steps taken is reflected in the results achieved and their subsequent verification. It is important not to lose sight of the fact that each business model poses very different challenges with regard to social responsibility. The risks to which an insurance company is subject differ from those of a petrochemical company or a real estate developer. But even within the same insurance companies, the possible variations are also significant, as not all of them deal with the same lines of business or even have the same products. If we add to these different structures in the value chain, intense internationalisation—or the lack of it—more or less contact with consumers, etc., we can clearly see that attempting an all-encompassing systematisation of all the possibilities is an unmanageable task.

However, as in any duty of transparency, results are a central element. The uniqueness of social responsibility is that the results come from the key performance indicators that are implemented in the process. We must therefore address them.

6.2 Key Performance Indicators

The key performance indicators (KPI) are those methodologies adopted by the company to measure the degree of compliance with the social responsibility policies, allowing them to be monitored and verified. This is a point to be included in sustainability reporting to obtain results that enable an evaluation of the social responsibility sponsored by the entity.

In my opinion, this is one of the most important issues in the definition of sustainability: the debate between flexibility and regulation.

Some would argue that flexibility should prevail, which means that it is easier for companies to determine their own KPI. The only obligation would then be to reflect them in sustainability reporting.

However, if this freedom extends to KPI, there is a clear weakness in the duty of transparency. The credibility of any reporting system depends on its ability to provide a true and fair picture. Therefore, the quality and adequacy of the results are a crucial element for its evaluation. This is where the importance of KPI emerges as the chosen method for obtaining results. Policy review requires the analysis of data that are created from the prior specification of indicators.

The corollary of the above is that the lack of an original normative specification of the methodology to be followed to achieve the results empowers the company to predetermine it. It is easy to deduce that an expert in the field can achieve the desired results for the image of a corporation if he can choose the methodology to be applied. If KPI can be freely defined, the danger of greenwashing is obvious.

The opposite option—prior regulation of KPI and the methodologies for their measurement—means curtailing—though not completely avoiding—the danger of greenwashing. However, it is also clear that it implies greater rigidity in an area that is otherwise very difficult to homogenise—each entity has its own idiosyncrasies, even if the corporate purpose is identical. This objection is compounded by its novelty, which poses major challenges to its standardisation.

Having said this, at this point, we must mention the important regulatory effort that has been made within the European Union. I will limit myself here to outlining the following implementing regulations, as I consider them to be the most relevant when it comes to specifying KPI:

1. Commission Delegated Regulation (EU) 2021/2139 of 4 June 2021 supplementing Regulation (EU) 2020/852 of the European Parliament and of the Council by establishing the technical screening criteria for determining the conditions under which an economic activity qualifies as contributing substantially to climate change mitigation or climate change adaptation and for determining whether that economic activity causes no significant harm to any of the other environmental objectives.

   Articles 10 and 11 Regulation (EU) 2020/852 of the European Parliament and of the Council of 18 June 2020 on the establishment of a framework to facilitate sustainable investment, and amending Regulation (EU) 2019/2088 required the Commission to adopt delegated acts establishing the technical selection criteria for determining the conditions under which a specific economic activity can be considered to contribute substantially to climate change mitigation or adaptation, respectively, and to establish, for each relevant environmental objective provided for in Art. 9 Regulation (EU) 2020/852, technical selection criteria for determining whether that economic activity does not cause significant harm to one or more of those environmental objectives.

   The technical selection criteria for determining whether an economic activity contributes substantially to climate change mitigation or adaptation should ensure that the economic activity has a positive impact on the climate objective or reduces the negative impact on the climate objective.

   These technical screening criteria should therefore relate to the thresholds or performance levels that the economic activity must reach in order to be considered as making a substantial contribution to one of these climate objectives. The technical selection criteria relating to the "do no significant harm" principle should ensure that the economic activity does not have a significant negative environmental effect.

   Accordingly, these technical selection criteria should specify the minimum requirements that the economic activity must meet in order to be considered environmentally sustainable.

   The technical selection criteria for determining under which conditions an economic activity can be considered as making a substantial contribution to climate change mitigation should reflect the need to avoid greenhouse gas emissions, to reduce greenhouse gas emissions or to enhance greenhouse gas removals and long-term carbon dioxide storage.

It is therefore appropriate to focus first on those economic activities and sectors that have the greatest potential to achieve these objectives. The choice of those economic activities and sectors should be based on their contribution to overall greenhouse gas emissions and on evidence regarding their potential to contribute to avoiding the generation of greenhouse gas emissions, reducing greenhouse gas emissions or contributing to the removal of greenhouse gases, or to facilitate avoidance, reduction, removal or long-term storage in other activities.

2. Commission Delegated Regulation (EU) 2021/2178 of 6 July 2021 supplementing Regulation (EU) 2020/852 of the European Parliament and of the Council by specifying the content and presentation of information to be disclosed by undertakings subject to Articles 19a or 29a of Directive 2013/34/EU concerning environmentally sustainable economic activities and specifying the methodology to comply with that disclosure obligation.

   The purpose of this Delegated Regulation is to implement Art. 8 of Regulation (EU) 2020/852 of the European Parliament and of the Council of 18 June 2020 on the establishment of a framework to facilitate sustainable investment and amending Regulation (EU) 2019/2088. Indeed, Art. 8.1 of the aforementioned Regulation (EU) 2020/852 requires companies obliged to issue sustainability reports to disclose how and to what extent the company's activities are associated with environmentally sustainable economic activities.

   In turn, Art. 8.2 Regulation (EU) 2020/852 requires non-financial companies to disclose information on the proportion of turnover, investments in fixed assets and operating expenses (KPI) of their activities related to assets or processes linked to environmentally sustainable economic activities. This provision, however, did not specify equivalent KPI for financial undertakings, i.e. credit institutions, asset managers, investment services firms and insurance and reinsurance undertakings.

It was therefore necessary to supplement Art. 8 of Regulation (EU) 2020/852 to specify KPI that apply to financial undertakings and to specify in more detail the content and presentation of the information to be disclosed by all undertakings, as well as the methodology for complying with such disclosure.

It was also necessary to ensure a uniform application of the disclosure requirements laid down in Article 8(2) Regulation (EU) 2020/852 by non-financial companies subject to sustainability reporting. Accordingly, rules should be laid down to further specify the content and presentation of the information provided in Art. 8 Regulation (EU) 2020/852, including the methodology for complying with those rules. To enable investors and the public to properly assess the proportion of environmentally sustainable economic activities ("taxonomy-compliant activities") of non-financial undertakings, non-financial undertakings should be required to disclose which of their economic activities comply with the taxonomy. In addition, it was necessary to disclose to which environmental objectives these activities contribute significantly. Therefore, non-financial companies were also required to provide a breakdown in KPI of the proportion of activities that conform to the taxonomy on the basis of each environmental objective to which those activities contribute substantially.

The standard establishes a series of annexes in which, on the one hand, KPI are developed and, on the other, the template for publishing the aforementioned results is provided for non-financial institutions, as well as for each type of financial institution (credit institutions, investment services institutions, insurance companies, etc.).

In short, the above regime has given rise to a treatment of KPI in which, in addition to those regulated by the aforementioned regulations, there may be others that the institutions adopt voluntarily in those areas where the primacy of freedom still prevails. On the latter, international standards will be called upon to play a leading role.

6.3 The Impossible Balancing Between Values

The title of this section seems obvious, but I believe it is pertinent to stress that reporting is about non-financial information. The intensity with which the conceptual construction generated around accounting permeates sustainability reporting is enormous. However, we must reiterate that despite their concomitance, their purposes and objects are different, so the methodology and therefore the results should present notable differences.

A clear exponent of our assertion lies in the impossible balancing of values. Indeed, accounting and financial information is ultimately centred on a fungible good: money. Consequently, its fungibility allows a balance between the different accounting records. In other words, a company's profits can come from an infinite number of combinations of accounting records. We are dealing with money, so it makes no difference in this context what combination results if it finally produces a distributable profit. The same conclusion applies to the reduction of share capital: it makes no difference which account in the balance sheet supports the required minimum balance between share capital and net book equity. If the figures respect the required minimum, the requirement is fulfilled, irrespective of possible mismatches between assets and liabilities in the balance sheet.

Social responsibility cannot be understood in the same way. We are talking about values that are neither compensable nor interchangeable. In my opinion, a company cannot aspire to be socially responsible for planting 1000 trees if it simultaneously allows child labour within its value chain. Similarly, we do not believe that a company that gives a book on women's day to its staff on women's empowerment, without at the same time adopting measures that avoid a high impact on the environment, should receive this qualification either.

Social responsibility is concerned with respecting values, beyond the fact that accountability through sustainability reporting requires the determination of indicators that can then be contrasted in most cases through quantitative results. The commitment that social responsibility demands in the fulfilment of values must be global, without the achievements in one country or area being able to compensate for the losses in other places or areas.

There is nothing to prevent an insurer from placing greater emphasis on some areas over others. For example, an insurer that focuses most of its branch on motor liability insurance may differ from an insurer that specialises in health insurance. It would come as no surprise that the motor insurance company would promote road safety campaigns, while the health insurer would support sports programmes.

Given the above, the balance that any entity must provide in each of the areas, indeed, in each of the contents, should respect minimum results. Affirmation that finds first support in the principle of "do no significant harm" of Art. 2a Regulation (EU) 2019/2088 of the European Parliament and of the Council of 27 November 2019 on sustainability-related disclosures in the financial services sector.

Furthermore, this thesis finds a new argument in the duty to prevent, mitigate, remedy and redress mentioned in Articles 19a f) and 29a f) of Directive 2013/34/EU on the annual financial statements.

7 Conclusions

The duty of transparency that sustainability entails has led to a paradigm shift in the information that companies provide to the market. However, its regulatory framework is still evolving. Only if we manage to give it credibility will sustainability become an efficient institution. It is therefore essential to be aware of both the hard law and soft law instruments that are shaping the legal regime of sustainability reporting.

Acknowledgements This work has been funded by the project "Responsabilidad social de la empresa: hacia un sistema financiero socialmente responsable" Programa Prometeo para grupos de investigación de Excelencia de la Conselleria de Innovación, Universidades, Ciencia y Sociedad Digital de la Generalitat Valenciana, (GVPROMETEO2021-013).

References

Basedow J (2021) EU private law. Anatomy of a growing legal order. Intersentia, Cambridge

Bataller Grau J (2017) Un concepto de Responsabilidad Social de la Empresa desde el Derecho Mercantil. Revista de Derecho mercantil 310:109–140

Bataller Grau J (2023a) Noción, objeto y fuentes de la Responsabilidad Social y la Sostenibilidad. In: Bataller Grau J, Boquera Matarredona J (eds) Responsabilidad Social y Sostenibilidad: una sistematización. Tirant Lo Blanch, Valencia

Bataller Grau J (2023b) El papel del Hard Law en la Responsabilidad Social. In: Bataller Grau J, Boquera Matarredona J (eds) Responsabilidad Social y Sostenibilidad: una sistematización. Tirant Lo Blanch, Valencia

Bataller Grau J (2023c) La autorregulación en la Responsabilidad Social. In: Bataller Grau J, Boquera Matarredona J (eds) Responsabilidad Social y Sostenibilidad: una sistematización. Tirant Lo Blanch, Valencia.

Bowen HR (1953) Social responsibilities of the businessman. Harper & Brothers, Iowa

Carroll AB (1979) A three-dimensional conceptual model of corporate social performance. Acad Manag Rev 4:497–523

Dill W (1975) Public participation in corporate planning: strategic management in a Kibitzer's world. Long Range Plann 8(1):57–72

Elkington J (1999) Cannibals with forks: the triple bottom line of 21st century business. Capstone, Gabriola Island

Freeman RE (2010) Strategic management: a stakeholder approach, 2nd edn. Cambridge University Press, Cambridge

Lozano JF (2011) Qué es la ética de la empresa. Proteus Editorial, Cànoves y Samalús

Malecki C (2018) Corporate social responsibility, perspectives for sustainable corporate governance. Elgar, Cheltenham

Marimón Durá R (2023) Los Principios de la Inversión Responsable auspiciados por Naciones Unidas Unidas (UN-PRI). In: Bataller Grau J, Boquera Matarredona J (eds) Responsabilidad Social y Sostenibilidad: una sistematización. Tirant Lo Blanch, Valencia

Pasquero J (2005) La responsabilité sociale de l'enterprise comme objet des sciencies de gestion: un regard historique. In: Turcotte MFB, Salmon A (eds) Responsabilité sociale et environnementale de l'entreprise. Presses de l'Université du Québec, Quebec, pp 80–111

Rabanete Martínez I (2023) Accountability AA1000 series of standards. In: Bataller Grau J, Boquera Matarredona J (eds) Responsabilidad Social y Sostenibilidad: una sistematización. Tirant Lo Blanch, Valencia

Rodes Paredes P (2023) La Global Reporting Initiative como elemento de la responsabilidad social de la empresa. In: Bataller Grau J, Boquera Matarredona J (eds) Responsabilidad Social y Sostenibilidad: una sistematización. Tirant Lo Blanch, Valencia

Vercher Moll J (2023) Principios para la Sostenibilidad en Seguros. In: Bataller Grau J, Boquera Matarredona J (eds) Responsabilidad Social y Sostenibilidad: una sistematización. Tirant Lo Blanch, Valencia

Juan Bataller-Grau is currently a full-time professor of Commercial Law at the Faculty of Law of the University of Valencia. His professional career has been recognised with different distinctions: Alfonso el Magnánimo Award – Diputación de Valencia (1997), L'Estimat Award – Colegio Profesional de Mediadores de Seguros de Valencia (2018), and Galicia Seguro Award for insurance research – INADE (2021).

He is currently director of the Revista de Derecho del Sistema Financiero, Chairman of the SEIDA Working Group on Insurance Supervisión Law, founding member of the European network of excellence "Restatement of European Insurance Contract Law" and member of the scientific committee of the Revista Española de Seguros. He has been a member of the group of experts of the European Commission for the study of insurance contracts in Europe, of the "Insurance & Reinsurance Stakeholder Group" of the European Insurance and Occupational Pensions Authority (EIOPA)—supervisor of insurance and pensions in the European Union—and of the Observatory of Civil Law of the Valencian Community.

His research work covers various areas of commercial law, which have resulted in various scientific publications, both national and international, with his main lines of research being insurance law, sustainability law, and the extinction and insolvency of companies. Furthermore, he has taught in several master's degrees and has given numerous conferences in Spain and other countries. He has been providing legal advice for the last 25 years to important economic corporations, prominent business associations and different public administrations.

Sustainability of the EU Insurance Markets and Adequacy of Insurance Regulations: Solvency II and ESG

Marcin Kawiński

1 Introduction

In most cases, defining the sustainability of insurance leads to different aspects of fulfilling insurance needs and contracts. Sophisticated risk-based regulations, like Solvency II [*Directive 2009/138/EC of the European Parliament and of the Council of 25 November 2009 on the taking-up and pursuit of the business of Insurance and Reinsurance* (SII)], or the U.S. equivalent, known as the "Insurance Financial Solvency Frame" (Lindberg & Seifert 2015; Zweifel & Eisen 2012, p. 335), provide numerous perspectives on insurance entities' challenges with sustainability. As regulators and supervisors rightly put solvency into a sustainability framework (Van Hulle 2019, p. 10), the sustainability analysis of particular markets can be narrowed to ratios based on micro-prudential-like ratios: solvency capital requirements, compositions of own funds or investment assets quality.

However, the concept of sustainability is now becoming even more complex with sustainable finance approaching. Financial markets are in the middle of a shift from CSR (Corporate Social Responsibility) to ESG (Environmental, Social and Governance). It is worth mentioning that the idea of CSR has not been widespread in less developed markets (Arraiano & Hategan 2019). That is why the concept of ESG is the first genuine attempt to introduce sustainable finance for such markets. ESG interferes considerably with insurance market sustainability within many planes, from both supply and demand perspectives. Regulations on ESG [i.e. CSRD (corporate sustainability reporting directive), 2022/2464/EU and NFRD (non-financial reporting directive), 2014/95/EU) are then necessary follow-up to insurance financial solvency-like rules.

M. Kawiński (✉)
Warsaw School of Economics, Department of Social Insurance, Warszawa, Poland
e-mail: mkawin@sgh.waw.pl

J. Bataller-Grau et al. (eds.), *Sustainability and the Insurance Market*, AIDA Europe Research Series on Insurance Law and Regulation 10,
https://doi.org/10.1007/978-3-031-72186-1_3

Risk-based regulations, like Solvency II, assume a particular level of market development (Van Hulle 2019, p. 9). It is necessary to match regulatory measures with market potential. From this perspective, the European Union regulations must satisfy very different markets. Although, regarding rules, it is possible to take a minimum harmonisation approach, maximum harmonisation is considered the only option for micro-prudential rules (Van Hulle 2019). The same applies to ESG regulations. However, the reasoning can be slightly different. However, regardless of this aspect, for some countries, the regulations can be overstated.

Within the EU insurance market, the countries that potentially lag in this regard can be identified based on fundamental insurance market development ratios (Outreville 1996; Prokopjeva et al. 2020; look also Born & Bujakowski 2022). In this chapter, this group has been identified as the CEE countries. The group of CEE countries has various typologies. For clarity in this text, the CEE countries are considered the so-called New Member States of the European Union: Bulgaria, Croatia, Czech Republic, Estonia, Hungary, Latvia, Lithuania, Poland, Romania, Slovakia, and Slovenia.

The sustainability of the EU insurance markets measured with the solvency ratios varies among Member States of the European Union, and the ESG issues are sometimes underdeveloped. This text aims to analyse two aspects of sustainability within the EU countries' insurance market, measured with solvency ratios and some unique features linked to ESG. Issues identified within solvency analysis are also eminent in examining ESG aspects. Both aspects of sustainability are confronted with regulations and their suitability.

2 The Overview of the EU Insurance Market

The overview of the EU insurance markets' main indicators shows a lower level of development among the CEE markets.[1] Gross written premium confronted with GDP reaches a smaller value than the other EEA countries, as demand for insurance depends on wealth (Table 1). Gross written premium per capita is also worse due to the low purchasing power.

Low spending on insurance suggests the dominance of basic, very often mandatory insurance products. Table 2 proves this guess. Within the EU market, the share of motor third-party liability insurance within non-life insurance is much higher in the CEE countries. This product used to be a stable base for local insurance products. However, due to safety developments, the number of car collisions and accidents is decreasing. On the other hand, the costs of repair are increasing. Overall, the importance of motor third-party liability insurance should fall in the long term (Deloitte 2016; McKinsey & Company 2022).

[1] CEE countries transformed from centrally planned economies into market-oriented ones during the 1990s, lagging in many areas of financial markets (Setiawan et al. 2021). The CEE financial markets have achieved many successes and still have room for potential growth. However, at the same time, there are still signs of the past.

Table 1 Gross written premium as % of GDP and per capita in 2021 [EUR, %]

	EEA	CEE	EEA without CEE
Gross written premium as % of GDP			
Mean	2.5	1.7	2.9
Median	2.5	1.7	2.2
Gross written premium per capita			
Mean	1238	89	1904
Median	370	88	831

Source: own calculations based on publicly available EIOPA's data
Note: level of significance for Mann-Whitney test (CEE vs EEA without CEE)—0.005 and <0.001

Table 2 Share of motor third-party liability insurance within non-life insurance [2021, in %]

	EEA	CEE	EEA without CEE
Mean	22.0	29.9	17.4
Median	23.2	31.1	15.0

Source: own calculations based on publicly available EIOPA's data
Note: level of significance for Mann-Whitney test (CEE vs EEA without CEE)—0.008

The following interesting pattern is the concentration of the insurance market. In the CEE countries, past monopolistic features are still visible. Monopolistic insurers were taken over by foreign capital or continued the activity within the market framework. Regarding capital origin, the outcome is quite clear. The concentration index for the first three non-life and life insurance undertakings is much higher in the CEE countries than in other EU markets (Figs. 1 and 2). It is also statistically significant (Mann-Whitney test—0.005 and 0.18). The difference in concentration index for the first five and ten insurance undertakings is not statistically significant.

Higher concentration in the CEE countries makes competition policy very needed (Koltay et al. 2022). Mergers and acquisitions are intense, significantly beyond the group of the most prominent entities (Deloitte 2020). At the beginning of the market opening, foreign capital used the opportunity to enter the new market. However, not all reached sufficient market share or found better opportunities elsewhere.

When monopolistic insurers continue the activity within a market framework, such markets can be more exposed to solvency issues. Local politicians distort governance standards in the past monopolies due to capital ties. Foreign capital sometimes took over the past monopoly, which has also influenced the concentration index. In both scenarios, the monopolistic past seems to be a load.

3 Effectiveness of Solvency II and ESG Regulations Within the EU Insurance Market

A simple analysis of primary insurance market ratios is just one of the possible analysis perspectives of development study (Kunreuther et al. 2009). This chapter, however, investigates the maturity of the CEE insurance market considering the

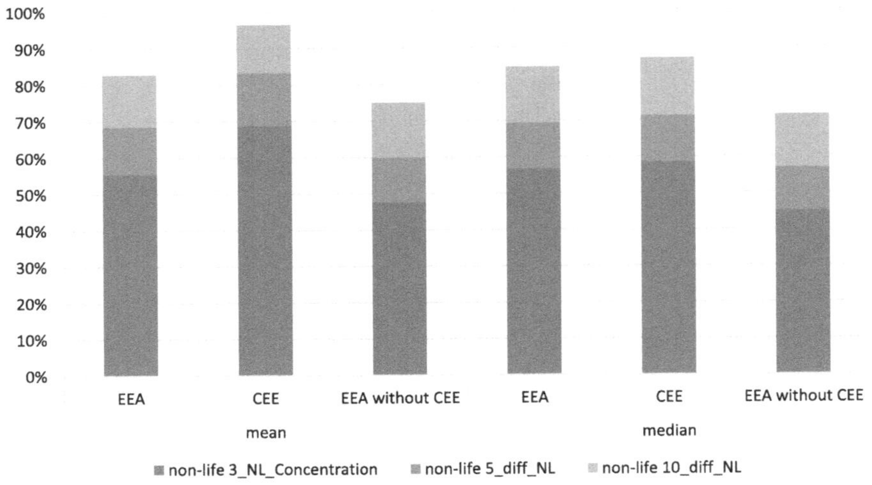

Fig. 1 Mean and median of concentration index for the first three, five, and ten non-life insurance undertakings in 2021 in EEA [in %] (Source: own calculations based on publicly available EIOPA's data)

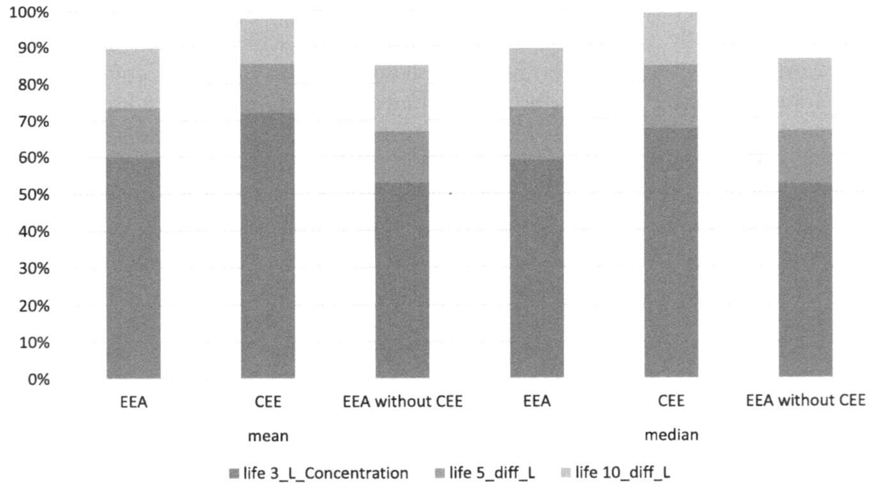

Fig. 2 Mean and median of concentration index for the first three, five, and ten life insurance undertakings in 2021 in EEA [in %] (Source: own calculations based on publicly available EIOPA's data)

adequacy of the Solvency II and ESG regulations compared to the rest of the EU. Generally, legal rules follow the market or try to shape future trends. European regulations are unique as they comprise regulatory needs. There is an assumption that European regulations adopt a specific standard of market development that could challenge some local markets and reveal sustainability issues. These challenges could speed up the overall development, consumer protection (Cyman 2021), etc., and lower sustainability risk, but other scenarios are also possible.

Various methods, both qualitative and quantitative, could be employed while examining the adequacy of regulations:

- the volume of adaptation, i.e. capital increase due to changes in capital requirements (quantitative);
- the value of demand and supply for particular products and changes (quantitative);
- regulatory and supervisory interventions (qualitative and quantitative);
- expert opinions (qualitative).

All of the above methods allow for assessing the actual maturity of the markets. However, not all of them are available in each case simultaneously, and this research should be considered exploratory.

3.1 Solvency II

The Insurance Financial Solvency Frame in the EU, which is laid down within Solvency II, is often presented as three pillars.

- Pillar I - the quantitative requirements, i.e. the assets and liabilities valuation and capital requirements.
- Pillar II - the qualitative requirements, including governance and risk management of the undertakings and the Own Risk and Solvency Assessment (ORSA).
- Pillar III - the supervisory reporting and public disclosure.

It takes both capital (pillar I) and governance (pillar II) perspectives. They are both essential—pillar I gives us a picture of financial soundness in a fixed reporting framework. Pillar II concentrates on risk management activity, business strategy and financial data interpretation. This is where all success and problems start. However, regarding the accessibility of information, there is very little information on pillar II. The primary documents of pillar II—ORSA (Own Solvency and Risk Assessment)—are not publicly available. Reporting, assured by the pilar III, gives mostly pillar I information. Although the average value is relatively high, the share of companies close to 100% is also remarkable. A few entities are also under 100% (EIOPA 2022a).

The primary ratio of pillar I is SCR (Standard Capital Requirement). The level of capital is enough to meet the losses that could happen on average once every 200 years (99.5% VaR). The level of 100% starts the safety zone. The particular level of SCR depends on the risk taken, risk appetite, and risk management techniques and instruments. The level above 200% should be considered very good.

Table 3 SCR with & without transitionary LTGs in 2021

NCA_CTR	SCR [a] (%)	SCR w/o Trans [b] (%)	SCR w/o LTGs [b] (%)
Mean			
EEA	217	211	212
CEE	199	197	199
EEA without CEE	227	219	220
Median			
EEA	210	205	209
CEE	196	186	196
EEA without CEE	221	212	215
Standard variation			
EEA	13.2	12.1	13.3
CEE	4.7	5.1	4.5
EEA without CEE	15.2	14.3	16.7

Source: own calculations based on publicly available EIOPA's data
[a] Difference CEE vs. EEA without CEE is statistically significant—level of significance for Mann-Whitney test 0.023
[b] Difference CEE vs. EEA without CEE is not statistically significant

SCR without transitionary measures (SCR w/o Trans) is the ratio that includes easing due to specific mechanisms (like the transitional measure on interest rates, the volatility adjustment and the matching adjustment), implemented by Omnibus II (Van Hulle 2019, p. 102) mainly after the financial crisis in 2007–2008. It allows using sophisticated algorithms within SCR calculations. Although the difference between CEE and EEA without CEE is not statistically significant (see Table 3), the market information will enable us to judge that there is minimal capacity to use this opportunity among the CEE countries. The same applies to SCR without long-term guarantees (SCR w/o LTGs). In the CEE countries, there are very few long-term liabilities and assets resulting from the level of insurance and financial market development.

The lower level of capital engagement in the CEE countries can be interpreted in many different ways. The first is lower capital available and/or needed. Most insurance entities have capital links to large international groups located outside CEE, and so is their capital. The second is the lower level of market development. Lack of long-term liabilities requires lower capital. The above ratios prove the above constatations of the CEE market development based on general market ratios. However, capital engagement should not be overestimated. The insurance business model is very different from the banking one. Capital requirements are just one of many safety measures, such as technical provision and reinsurance (Van Hulle 2019, p. 5). The regulator employs the formula of capital requirements to incentivise risk mitigation and risk management. From the insurance industry perspective, the critical factor is capital engagement efficiency compared to other economic areas.

Tiering of own funds (Table 4) represents a characteristic of capital engaged. The essential funds consist of excess assets over liabilities and subordinated liabilities. Paid-up share capital is classified as tier 1. Tier 1 – unrestricted is immediately

Table 4 Tiering of own funds in 2021

	Tier 1 – unrestricted [a] (%)	Tier 1 – restricted [b] (%)	Tier 2 [a] (%)	Tier 3 [b] (%)
	Mean			
EEA	93.8	1.1	4.4	0.6
CEE	96.8	0.6	2.1	0.4
EEA without CEE	92.1	1.4	5.8	0.7
	Median			
EEA	94.0	1.0	4.2	0.3
CEE	97.5	0.4	1.6	0.2
EEA without CEE	93.0	1.3	5.0	0.3
Standard deviation				
EEA	11.5	14.2	5.1	16.1
CEE	13.9	10.1	6.3	13.3
EEA-CEE	9.1	12.7	4.3	13.7

Source: own calculations based on publicly available EIOPA's data
[a] Difference CEE vs EEA without CEE statistically significant—level of significance for Mann-Whitney test 0.008 and 0.016 accordingly
[b] Difference CEE vs EEA without CEE not statistically significant

available to absorb losses. Ancillary own-funds are represented in tiers 2 and 3 and need the supervisory authority's prior approval to be considered own-funds. There are legal maximum thresholds for tiers other than tier 1 – unrestricted. A higher level of unrestricted tier 1 for the CEE countries is a matter of lower opportunity regarding other tiers and quite a conservative approach of local supervisors.

The composition of basic Solvency Capital Requirements gives more insight into the offer insurance market. Solvency II splits capital requirements between different risks, indicating different kinds of activity. The level of risk depends on the volume of risk. It can be lowered thanks to preventive measures. The overall implication can be reduced due to diversification. A higher share of capital engagement means just a higher volume of risk or a lower ability to cope with the risk. The CEE level is significantly higher in the non-life market than in the non-CEE market (Table 5). The opposite situation is observed for market risk. Both ratios are in line with the market characteristic. In the CEE countries, the introductory offer of the insurance market concentrates on the non-life market. In non-CEE countries, there is much higher exposure to insurance investment-like products.

Analysis of the above ratios shows that, although there are differences between CEE and non-CEE countries, the CEE countries do not fall behind in demanding Solvency II regime. However, it is fair to say that it has been the mother company's effort in most cases. Observed variances resulted from overall lower development of the insurance and financial market. Solvency II could be considered as exaggerated in the CEE countries, but on the other hand, it shapes the path of development in the future. Solvency II provides a very safe but costly regulatory environment due to a

Table 5 Basic solvency capital requirement composition in 2021

	Life underwriting risk [b] (%)	Non-life underwriting risk [a] (%)	Health underwriting risk [b] (%)	Market risk [a] (%)	Counterparty default risk [b] (%)	Intangible asset risk [a] (%)	Diversification [a] (%)
Mean							
EEA	22.4	32.4	10.6	58.4	8.4	0.0	−31.6
CEE	26.2	42.9	11.0	47.0	9.1	0.0	−36.2
EEA without CEE	20.2	26.3	10.3	65.0	8.0	0.0	−29.0
Median							
EEA	23.4	31.6	9.6	58.4	8.2	0.0	−31.0
CEE	23.6	47.0	10.4	40.7	8.5	0.0	−35.1
EEA without CEE	23.2	26.3	9.3	65.4	8.1	0.0	−28.7
Standard variation							
EEA	11.5	14.2	5.1	16.1	4.0	0.0	7.4
CEE	13.9	10.1	6.3	13.3	3.0	0.0	7.0
EEA-CEE	9.1	12.7	4.3	13.7	4.5	0.0	6.3

Source: own calculations based on publicly available EIOPA's data

[a] Difference CEE vs EEA without CEE statistically significant—level of significance for Mann-Whitney test 0.001, 0.005, 0.003, and 0.018 accordingly

[b] Difference CEE vs EEA without CEE not statistically significant

capital increase. However, international competition between different markets shows a space for cheap and safe offers. This would make the CEE countries' path of development also the path of growth.

Nevertheless, the best test for Solvency II is insolvencies. There have been several significant insolvencies of insurance entities after implementation:

- Denmark (avg. SCR 246.7% in 2021) - Alpha Insurance (2018), Gefion (2020).
- Ireland (avg. SCR 187.4% in 2021) - Quinn' Insurance (2023).
- Cyprus (avg. SCR 300.0% in 2021) - Olympic Insurance (2018), Prometheus Insurance (2021).
- Romania (avg. SCR 180.8% in 2021) - Carpatica (2016), City Insurance (2021), Euroins (2023).

It should be stressed that insolvencies have different legal statuses, and sometimes problems started before Solvency II was implemented (case of Ireland). The period after the implementation of Solvency II is relatively short, but there is no sign that it is a problematic framework for the CEE countries.

3.2 ESG and Insurance: Preliminary Considerations

The areas directly linked to sustainability and known under the acronym ESG (environmental, social, governance) are only growing in volume and importance. ESG dilemma is not entirely a new topic. For many years, the idea of CSR (corporate social responsibility) has been developed in business activities supporting general sustainability. CSR was also the answer to the consumers' needs and prepared regulators and other market participants for the sustainability-oriented shift in financial markets. CSR concept not only started earlier but is also broader and covers ESG. CEE economies almost missed CSR (Arraiano & Hategan 2019). Only the most advanced part of business implemented CSR, but it has stayed unknown for the majority. This is also why the ESG framework seems incomprehensible.

The theoretical framework of ESG within insurance allows structured analysis of particular areas. Table 6 proposes two perspectives. The first perspective is classical demand/supply. The second perspective is underwriting/investment, the main components of insurance activity.

The matrix of those perspectives gives insights into the crucial influence of ESG on insurance. Demand/underwriting perspectives show clients' perspectives. The ESG affects non-life insurance products, but the environmental risk is evident and, in most cases, already protected within existing policies. However, climate changes increase the risk of flood, drought and wildfire for all possible clients, households, farmers, companies and local authorities (EIOPA 2022b). The environmental part seems to be dominating; however, the accents can be significantly different from the business perspective. Third-party claims and associated liability are as crucial for companies as first-party claims. There is an increasing interest in products dedicated to companies and managers (D&O insurance) against liability due to ESG

Table 6 Perspective matrix of ESG within insurance

	Underwriting	Investment
Demand	• Catastrophic risk • Management liability of accusations and misdeeds concerning social and governance issues • Management liability concerning ESG reporting • Perception of ESG-friendly financial institutions (risk portfolio)	• Accessibility, profitability and risk of ESG-like IBIPs (investment-based insurance products) • Perception of ESG-friendly financial institutions (investment portfolio)
Supply	• ESG risk management • Capital requirements • Reputational risk	• Accessibility of ESG investments • Influences of ESG issues on UFR, solvency ratio, capital requirements

Source: own study

requirements passed by regulations and contracts with recipients within a production chain [The European Union Sustainability Reporting Standards (ESRS)]. Climate change also affects life assurance due to heat waves (Skotak et al. 2020). Finally, increasing ESG consciousness could result in consumers' choices, preferring insurance entities with green risk portfolios (Bethlendi et al. 2022).

Demand for ESG investment products is growing as institutional and retail investors start paying much more attention to this (Matos 2020; Petelczyc 2022). Investment perspective is associated with all three areas: environmental, social and governance issues. However, the accessibility of ESG investment varies (Adamska et al. 2016). The same applies to profitability (Giese et al. 2019). There is also more and more awareness regarding greenwashing (De Silva Lokuwaduge & De Silva 2022). All the above issues consist of challenges for investment-based insurance product providers. Insurance entities can be assessed on their own investment portfolio (matching liabilities) and also by clients and shareholders.

From the European single market perspective, the supply of ESG products is linked to the solvency framework in a particular way due to potentially catastrophic outcomes (Summerville & Leblanc 2022). The regulators, supervisors and other market entities still discuss if there is a need to single out climate risk or if it is enough to consider it within present submodules. But it is probably more important to implement this risk properly within the forward-looking projections employed under ORSA (EIOPA 2022b). Another vital area is the prevention and adaptation mechanisms to lower the impact of environmental hazards. The above-mentioned issues can be summarised as ESG risk management, which brings us to three important aspects. The first is the availability and quality of data and models. The second is the accessibility of reinsurance coverage, and finally, state engagements and partnerships. Capital requirements are a vital part of the solvency framework. The way ESG risks are incorporated into the standard formula is of great importance. Finally, any offer to entities not in line with ESG principles can be the subject of potential reputational risk (Karwowski & Raulinajtys-Grzybek 2021).

Asset liability management and proper risk mitigation require a sustainable investment portfolio. As the importance of ESG issues will probably grow, the accessibility of ESG investments is becoming critical. ESG would also affect macroeconomic features and consequently impact parameters such as UFR (Ultimate Forward Rate), solvency ratio, and capital requirements.

The following part of the article analyses ESG developments in the CEE countries mostly from a demand perspective; however, there are also elements of a supply perspective. ESG challenges of the CEE insurance market are almost neglected. No databases are dedicated to this area, and there is a very limited amount of research. If possible, ESG risks are confronted with other emerging risks, cyber and longevity.

3.3 ESG: Insurance Brokers' Perspective

Insurance brokers in Poland are intermediaries (distributors) that emerged after the transition to a market economy in 1990. Under the rules, they represent a client (policyholder) but can be renumerated by fee or commission. However, the latter method is much more popular. Brokers' clients are primarily companies and local authorities. Poland has 1429 (2023) active (with professional liability insurance) brokers.

Brokers' perspectives are unique as they contact the market cross-section. However, research based on brokers' opinions cannot be compared to a direct survey of companies and local authorities. The study below, the Fair Play survey, is limited to Poland, but it is the biggest insurance market within CEE countries and one of the most advanced regarding ESG.

Fair Play Survey (2022 and 2023)

Annually, an insurance broker congress gathers between 400 and 500 brokers, one of the most significant market events. Brokers taking part in the annual Congress are the employees of broker firms or individuals with their business activity. On average, they are more active or have better financial outcomes, allowing them to cover costs. The Congress is mainly used for networking and sharing professional knowledge. The Association of Polish Insurance and Reinsurance Brokers organises both Congress and Fair Play surveys.

Before Congress, a survey (CAWI) called Fair Play is provided to choose the best insurance companies, according to brokers' opinions. The Foundation Institute of Social Risk Management, an independent body, runs the survey. Data from the surveys are available under the permission of the Association of Polish Insurance and Reinsurance Brokers (https://www.spbuir.pl).

In 2022 and 2023, questions concerning ESG appeared in the questionnaires. Not all the brokers participating in the Congress filled out the questionnaire. The outcome of surveys cannot be considered representative. However, it has exploratory features that allow us to get a specific perspective. The difference between the

Table 7 Characteristic of respondents—Fair Play surveys of insurance brokers [% and years]

	6-28/04/2022 ($N = 214$ [a])	03/03/2023–15/04/2023 ($N = 383$ [a])
Gender		
Female	38.17	46.03
Male	59.16	52.61
No answer	2.67	1.36
Age		
18–24	1.1	1.0
25–34	19.1	13.1
35–44	28.6	26.1
45–54	30.5	30.2
55–64	13.4	15.8
65+	4.6	3.9
No answer	2.7	9.9
Experience as a broker		
0–5	16.4	15.4
6–10	18.3	15.6
11–15	21.0	18.9
16–20	16.4	12.3
21–25	14.5	16.2
26+	10.7	11.7
No answer	2.7	9.9

Source: Fair Play Survey (2022 and 2023)

[a] Number of respondents provided all answers within a questionnaire

2022 and 2023 groups concerning gender, age and experience as a broker is not statistically significant. 34.8% of respondents took part in both surveys. Table 7 presents the leading indicators of respondents.

In the Fair Play survey, there are two questions related to ESG. The first one tries to identify the frequency of environmental, social and governance issues reported by brokers' clients. It shows clearly that within three areas of ESG, G is the most important one for brokers' clients, E takes the second place, and the last is S. It is not surprising, considering their characteristics. However, concerning governance issues, there is also an eminent upward trend (Fig. 3). It should be noted that in 2022, the complexity of the Polish tax scheme increased considerably.

Figure 4 presents brokers' perspectives on the future importance of particular risks. In the case of climate risks, most opinions assume no changes. Here, the most stable is the risk of flood. The dynamic of draught is higher. Discrimination and mobbing are close to the flood. The highest dynamic of growth is perceived for cyber risk.

Based on the Polish Fair Play survey, insurance brokers' outlook suggests ESG has relatively low growth potential, except for governance risk. However, the run-on governance risk is probably due to the increasing complexity of legal surroundings.

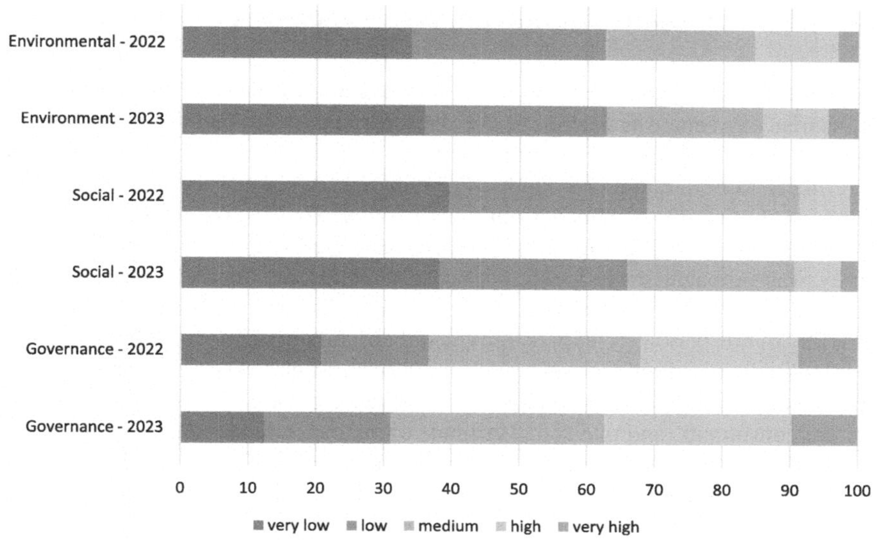

Fig. 3 Frequency of environmental, social and governance issues reported by Polish brokers' clients in 2022 and 2023 [Source: Fair Play Survey (2022 and 2023)]

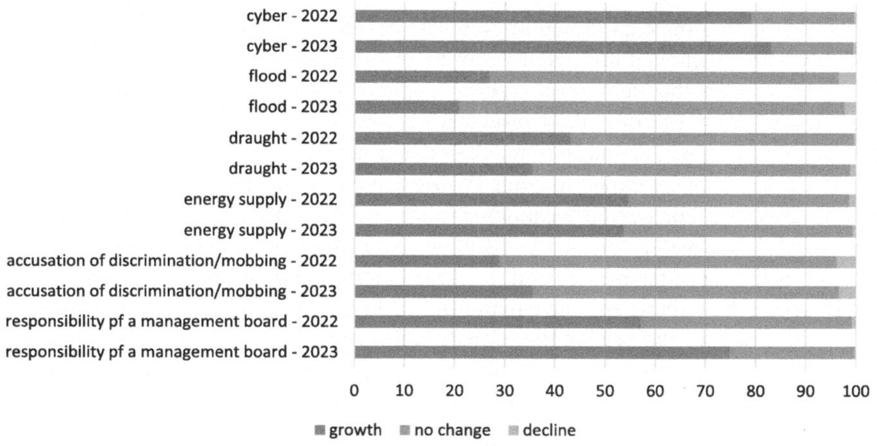

Fig. 4 The critical assessment of specific risks for insurance brokers' clients in the next three years [Source: Fair Play Survey (2022 and 2023)]

The situation could change in case of major catastrophic events, but for now, there is more interest in potential indirect consequences of climate change, like energy supply. Cyber risk has a much higher growth potential than ESG, showing what is considered a real issue for now.

3.4 ESG: Insurance Market Experts' Perspective

The Fair Play survey shows the indirect effects of ESG regulations based on demand for insurance coverage against particular risks. More in-depth and direct assessment requires a very high level of expertise, and due to a limited number of experts, it is more likely to be a qualitative study. The author carried out such a study, asking experts in the insurance market from the CEE countries to give their opinions on ESG regulations and offers from the perspective of the CEE insurance markets. The survey was propagated via local and European insurance market associations. It consisted of closed and open questions and was held between March 2 and April 13, 2023. In this period, 16 experts provided their opinions (nine from Poland, three from Bulgaria, one from Romania and one from Slovenia). They represent various provenance (five of them are employees of insurance entities, five are other experts, four are consultants, and one is a distributor of insurance products).

The survey starts with an inquiry into the influence of European rules on local markets concerning ESG issues (Fig. 5). Most of the experts estimate a considerable impact. The following parts allow us to present opinions on the utility of ESG regulations issued by the EU. The outcome suggests that the implementation effort is enormous. However, the local insurance market development adjustment is assessed with very high differentiation.

The analysis of solvency data suggests that the surroundings of the insurance market, including the capital market, limit its development. The existing articles on ESG investment showed limited offers of investment products in the CEE countries. The expert from the qualitative survey expresses a pessimistic opinion on the readiness to offer ESG-oriented products in the CEE countries. In their opinion, the average European situation is much better (Fig. 6).

The lack of opportunities to offer ESG-oriented insurance investment products corresponds to the perceived local demand for such products, which is low (Fig. 7). The non-life market is not very different, according to experts' opinions. The exceptions are large businesses and, to some extent, medium ones.

However, the experts see the capabilities of local insurers to offer ESG-oriented insurance products and predict the growth in this regard (Fig. 8). Specific questions on the ability to provide a meaningful cover linked to underwriting risk (i.e. coping with losses other than expected according to volume, type, etc.) reveal the potential difference between climate and cyber risk. Interestingly, experts estimate that covering against cyber risk is likely to be more challenging to offer. The next is longevity risk and then climate risk (Fig. 9). Experts' predictions regarding the near future (Fig. 10) show increased climate risk insurability.

In the qualitative survey of CEE insurance market experts (2023), respondents provided additional thoughts on the topic (open question). They mostly questioned European ESG regulations as inappropriate due to a lack of demand, additional barriers to the conclusion of insurance contracts, and a deficiency of public partnership. However, there was a voice in favour of such encouragement. All quotes below come from the qualitative survey of CEE insurance market experts (2023).

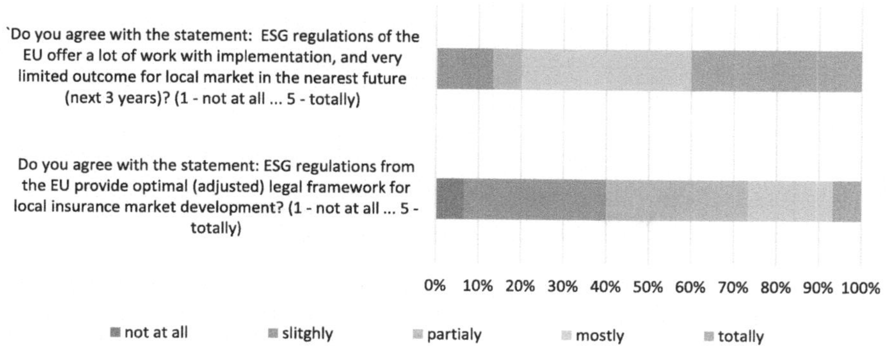

Fig. 5 Effectiveness and adjustment of EU regulations concerning ESG issues [Source: A qualitative survey of the CEE insurance market experts (2023)]

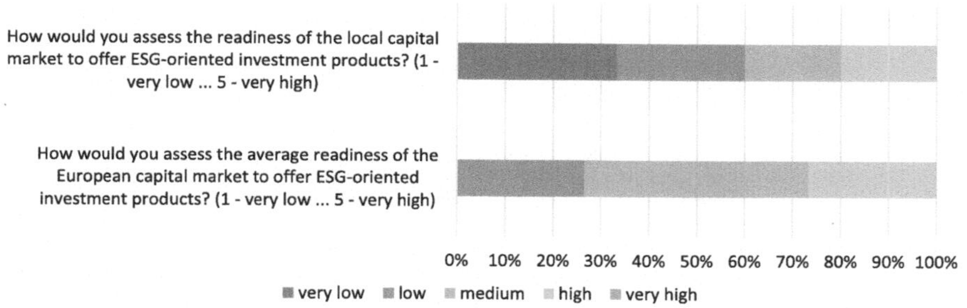

Fig. 6 Readiness of capital market to offer ESG-oriented investment products? [Source: A qualitative survey of the CEE insurance market experts (2023)]

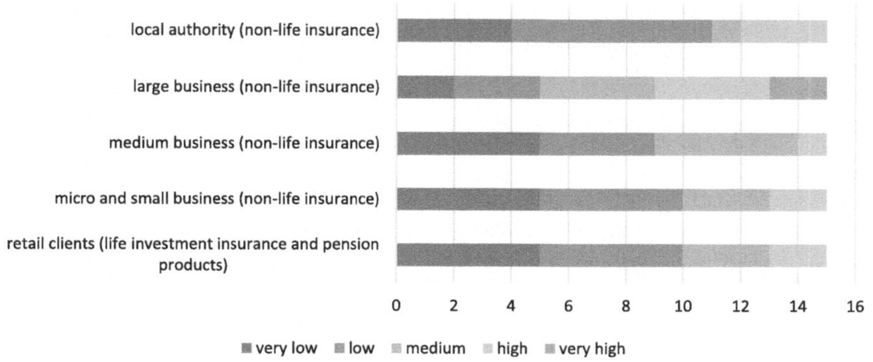

Fig. 7 Local demand for ESG-like products in certain CEE countries [Source: A qualitative survey of the CEE insurance market experts (2023)]

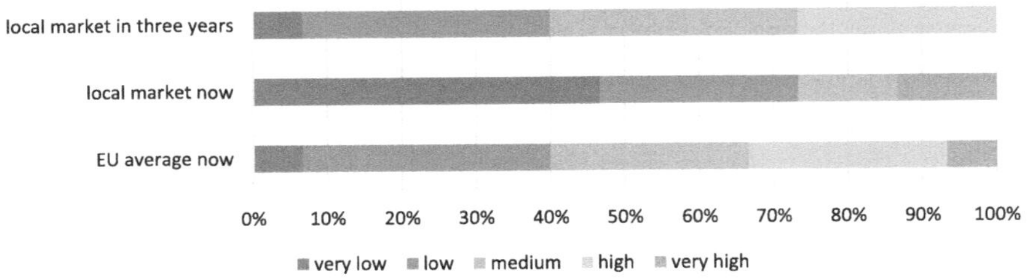

Fig. 8 Readiness of the insurance market to offer ESG-oriented insurance products in certain CEE countries [Source: A qualitative survey of the CEE insurance market experts (2023)]

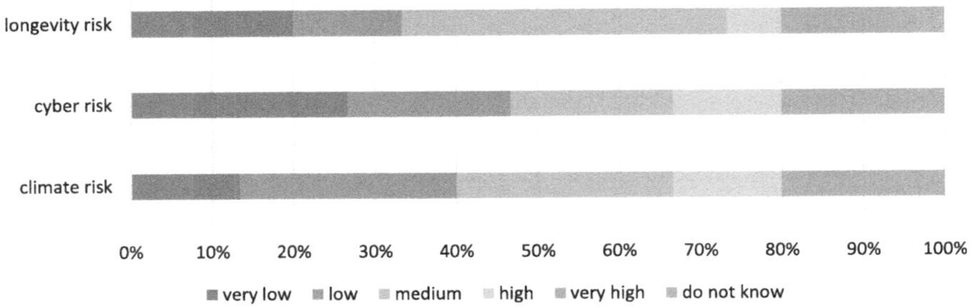

Fig. 9 Ability to provide a meaningful cover of particular risks linked to underwriting risk locally for certain CEE countries now [Source: A qualitative survey of the CEE insurance market experts (2023)]

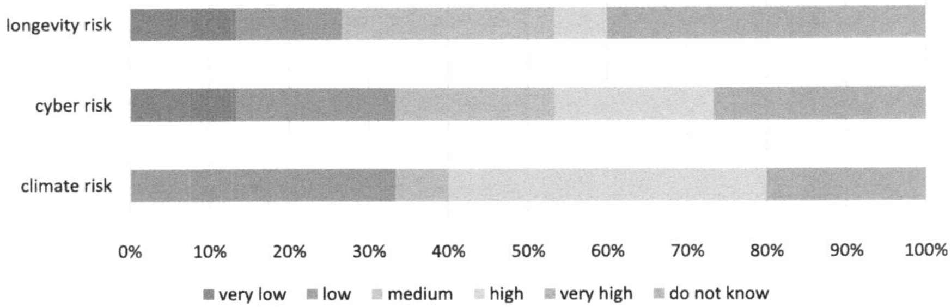

Fig. 10 Ability to provide a meaningful cover of particular risks linked to underwriting risk locally for certain CEE countries in three years [Source: A qualitative survey of the CEE insurance market experts (2023)]

> There is no demand for ESG products, and there will not be in the nearest future. – an employee of the insurance company

> Not appropriate for this moment, introducing another red tape on the table of concluding an insurance contract. – an employee of an insurance company

> Too extensive and too strict reporting obligations do not encourage the creation of green insurance products; lack of data necessary to create green products; the Polish government does not help in the development of the green economy, for example, the act on wind farms, the so-called 10H. – consultant

> In my opinion, Europe and the legal assessment encourage companies to take environmental action. Conscious corporations like my own with a focus on non-regulated social responsibility. – an employee of an insurance company

4 Conclusions

Sustainability provides context to reach research angles of insurance companies. Comparison between the CEE and other EEA countries proves some vital differences. The lower level of overall financial market development can be easily seen in the data. At the same time, the main solvency regulatory framework (Solvency II) is the same. The CEE countries cannot fully employ mechanisms available under Solvency II. However, those differences do not comprise the security of policyholders. Solvency II is not fully adequate to the CEE insurance market development level, but remains workable. It also determined future developments due to regulatory frameworks and capital links.

ESG provide additional plain, but also underlines and widens specific characteristics of risk known to the insurance industry before. Especially future trends bring some challenges. However, the most significant present issues result from the shift in the economy and especially the capital market. The matrix of two perspectives, demand/supply and underwriting/investment, gives a useful framework for further analysis.

CEE countries are underdeveloped concerning ESG topics. Fair Play's quantitative survey of Polish insurance brokers gives informative insight. They have proved low interest of Polish firms and local authorities in ESG, remarkably compared to cyber risk. The only exception is the governance (G) area, primarily due to D&O-like insurance. Interest in those insurance is imposed by ESG reporting regulation for a non-financial sector of the EU.

A qualitative survey of experts of the CEE insurance market echoes market data analysis, suggesting low capital market development. Furthermore, it copies the outcome of the Fair Play survey on low demand for ESG products, excluding big companies. According to expert opinion, the ability of insurance entities to supply ESG products is low but should increase within three years to the European average. Experts are unanimous regarding the insurability of three significant risks, climate, cyber and longevity. They are challenging now and will remain such in the near future.

References

Adamska A, Dabrowski T, Grygiel-Tomaszewska A (2016) Socially responsible investment in post-Communist and developed European countries. Revue d'études Comparatives Est-Ouest 47(3):7–43

Arraiano IG, Hategan CD (2019) The stage of corporate social responsibility in EU-CEE countries. Eur J Sustain Dev 8(3):340–340. https://doi.org/10.14207/ejsd.2019.v8n3p340

Bethlendi A, Nagy L, Póra A (2022) Green finance: the neglected consumer demand. J Sustain Finance Invest, 1–19. https://doi.org/10.1080/20430795.2022.2090311

Born P, Bujakowski D (2022) Economic transition and insurance market development: evidence from post-communist European countries. Geneva Risk Insur Rev 47:201–237. https://doi.org/10.1057/s10713-021-00066-3

Cyman D (2021) The customer as a subject of protection on the financial market in European Union. Financ Law Rev 24(4):43–54. https://doi.org/10.4467/22996834FLR.21.031.15398

De Silva Lokuwaduge C, De Silva K (2022) ESG risk disclosure and the risk of green washing. Aust Account Bus Finance J 16(1):146–159. https://doi.org/10.14453/aabfj.v16i1.10

Deloitte (2016) Future of automotive insurance in the new mobility ecosystem. https://www2.deloitte.com/us/en/pages/consulting/articles/automotive-insurance-future-mobility-ecosystem.html

Deloitte (2020) CEE Insurance M&A Outlook. https://www.google.com/search?q=CEE+insurance+M%26A+outlook+Despite+general+headwind+M%26A+activity+continues+to+rise+November+2020+zotero&rlz=1C1GCEA_enPL1039PL1039&oq=CEE+insurance+M%26A+outlook+Despite+general+headwind+M%26A+activity+continues+to+rise+November+2020+zotero&aqs=chrome..69i57.3097j0j4&sourceid=chrome&ie=UTF-8

EIOPA (2022a) Financial Stability Report. https://www.eiopa.europa.eu/publications/financial-stability-report-december-2022_en

EIOPA (2022b) Application guidance on climate change materiality assessments and climate change scenarios in ORSA. EIOPA-BoS-22/329. https://www.eiopa.europa.eu/publications/application-guidance-climate-change-materiality-assessments-and-climate-change-scenarios-orsa_en

Giese G, Lee LE, Melas D, Nagy Z, Nishikawa L (2019) Foundations of ESG investing: how ESG affects equity valuation, risk, and performance. J Portfolio Manag 45(June):69–83. https://doi.org/10.3905/jpm.2019.45.5.069

Karwowski M, Raulinajtys-Grzybek M (2021) The application of corporate social responsibility (CSR) actions for mitigation of environmental, social, corporate governance (ESG) and reputational risk in integrated reports. Corp Soc Responsib Environ Manag 28(4):1270–1284. https://doi.org/10.1002/csr.2137

Koltay G, Lorncz S, Valletti TM (2022) Concentration and competition: evidence from Europe and implications for policy. CESifo working paper, no. 9640. https://www.cesifo.org/en/publications/2022/working-paper/concentration-and-competition-evidence-europe-and-implications

Kunreuther HC, Michel-Kerjan EO, Doherty NA, Grace MF, Klein RW, Pauly MV (2009) At war with the weather. The MIT Press, Cambridge. http://www.jstor.org/stable/j.ctt5hhn3h

Lindberg DL, Seifert DL (2015) Risk management in the insurance industry: a comparison of solvency II to U.S. insurance regulations. J Insur Issues 38(2):233–243

Matos P (2020) ESG and responsible institutional investing around the world: a critical review. SSRN Scholarly Paper. Rochester. https://doi.org/10.2139/ssrn.3668998

McKinsey & Company (2022) Autonomous mobility: the future of auto insurance. https://www.mckinsey.com/industries/financial-services/our-insights/connected-revolution-the-future-of-us-auto-insurance#/

Outreville JF (1996) Life insurance markets in developing countries. J Risk Insur 63(2):263–278. https://doi.org/10.2307/253745

Petelczyc J (2022) The readiness for ESG among retail investors in Central and Eastern Europe. The example of Poland. Glob Bus Rev 23(6):1299–1315. https://doi.org/10.1177/09721509221114754
Prokopjeva E, Kuznetsova N, Kalayda S (2020) Insurance market development and economic growth indicators: the study of relationship in the world. Economic Annals-XXI (blog), 21 November 2020. http://ea21journal.world/index.php/ea-v185-05/
Setiawan B, Saleem A, Nathan RJ, Zeman Z, Magda R, Barczi J (2021) Financial market development and economic growth: evidence from ASEAN and CEE region. Pol J Manag Stud 23(2):481–494. https://doi.org/10.17512/pjms.2021.23.2.29
Skotak K, Orych I, Piekarska K, Zacharczuk K, Chmielewski T, Fiecek B, Pancer K et al (2020) Raport końcowy zawierający trendy i prognozy umieralności i chorobowości z powodu chorób klimatozależnych, a także wnioski i rekomendacje dla jednostek systemu ochrony zdrowia w zakresie adaptacji do zmian klimatu. PZH
Summerville EF, Leblanc K (2022) Financial condition of the residential property insurance market. Louisiana Department of Insurance
Van Hulle K (2019) Solvency requirements for EU insurers: solvency II is good for you. Intersentia, Cambridge. http://lib.ugent.be/catalog/rug01:002773890
Zweifel P, Eisen R (2012) Insurance economics, Springer texts in business and economics. Springer, Berlin. https://doi.org/10.1007/978-3-642-20548-4

Marcin Kawiński is the Head of the Department of Social Insurance at the Warsaw School of Economics. His scientific interest focuses on the management of social risk, with particular attention paid to insurance for households, the insurance market and insurance regulations, insurance distribution, new technologies, over and underperformance of insurance contracts, behavioural aspects of annuity and insurance literacy, guarantee schemes in basic pension schemes, benchmarks for pension funds, and equity release in Poland.

Kawiński has a background in consumer affairs, participating in many public hearings. Marcin Kawiński is a member of the Insurance and Reinsurance Stakeholder Group at the EIOPA (the European Insurance and Occupational Pensions Authority) as a representative of academia. In the past, he was also a member of the Occupational Pensions Stakeholder Group at the EIOPA, and the Banking Stakeholder Group at the EBA (the European Banking Authority). From 2010 to 2016, Kawiński, as an independent expert, was a member of FSUG (Financial Services User Group at the European Commission), advising on consumer issues within financial services. He was a member of FIN-USE (Forum of User Experts in Financial Services at the European Commission, 2007–2010), and participated in the Steering Committee of the FIN-NET (Financial Dispute Resolution Network at the European Commission, 2006–2008). Kawiński was also an expert in PHARE and TAIEX (the Technical Assistance and Information Exchange at the European Commission) and for many years, had worked for the Insurance Ombudsman in Poland.

The Multiple Functions of Insurers in the Blue Economy

Lucrezia Anzanello

1 Our Common Future

1.1 The Brundtland Report

The first attempt to provide an accomplished definition for the concept of sustainable development is dated 1987, specifically with the United Nations-World Commission on Environment and Development Report of 20 March 1987 signed in Oslo by Norwegian Minister Gro Harlem Brundtland, who chaired its drafting.

The report called precisely "Our Common Future," starts from the assumption that although the contingent situation at the time reflected a situation of increasing environmental degradation, the future could have been different, and it also could have led to further economic growth.

But this WAS believed to be possible only in the presence of economic policies able to protect, on one side, environmental resources, and, on the other side, support development and enable human progress, thus recalling the dual meaning of sustainability—derived from the Latin origin of the term (*sustinentia*)—of the interrelationship between support and resistance.

Not only that. The concept of sustainability, thus understood, is also projected toward the protection of future generations:[1]

[1] This concept is taken up, in a rather accentuated way, in some constitutional texts: Art. 66, c. 2, lett. D of the Portuguese Constitution where reference is made to the principle "da solidariedade entre gerações"; Art. 24, c. 1 of the Greece Constitution "The protection of the natural and cultural environment constitutes a duty of the State and a right of every person. The State is bound to adopt special preventive or repressive measures for the preservation of the environment in the context of

L. Anzanello (✉)
University of Milan-Bicocca, Milan, Italy
e-mail: lucrezia.anzanello@unimib.it

J. Bataller-Grau et al. (eds.), *Sustainability and the Insurance Market*, AIDA Europe Research Series on Insurance Law and Regulation 10,
https://doi.org/10.1007/978-3-031-72186-1_4

27. Humanity has the ability to make development sustainable to ensure that it meets the needs of the present without compromising the ability of future generations to meet their own needs. The concept of sustainable development does imply limits - not absolute limits but limitations imposed by the present state of technology and social organization on environmental resources and by the ability of the biosphere to absorb the effects of human activities. But technology and social organization can be both managed and improved to make way for a new era of economic growth. The Commission believes that widespread poverty is no longer inevitable. Poverty is not only an evil in itself, but sustainable development requires meeting the basic needs of all and extending to all the opportunity to fulfil their aspirations for a better life. A world in which poverty is endemic will always be prone to ecological and other catastrophes.

So, it is a dynamic concept that does not aspire to a permanent state of harmony but involves an ongoing evolutionary dynamic that has to conform to present needs, and it has to shape itself for future needs.

It is of immediate evidence that this notion takes its cue from the natural sciences by seeking the balance of the three Es: ecology, equity, economics. This presupposes the carrying capacity of the environment[2] which measures the maximum level of crowding, as well as the need to use the planet's natural resources in such a way as to meet the needs of present generations without jeopardising the ability of future generations to meet their own, in compliance with intergenerational equity.[3]

The Brundtland Report, in addition to exemplifying virtuous behaviours, ends with concrete action consisting of the enactment of legal principles for environmental protection and sustainable development among which, of particular interest, are the following:

- *Inter-Generational Equity - 2. States shall conserve and use the environment and natural resources for the benefit of present and future generations.*

---

the principle of sustainability"; Art. 7 of the Czech Republic Constitution "The state shall see to it that natural resources are used economically and natural wealth is protected"; Art. 72 of the Slovenian Constitution "Everyone has the right in accordance with the law to a healthy living environment. The state shall promote a healthy living environment"; Art. 45 of the Spanish Constitution "Todos tienen el derecho a disfrutar de un medio ambiente adecuado para el desarrollo de la persona, así como el deber de conservarlo. Los poderes públicos velarán por la utilización racional de todos los recursos naturales, con el fin de proteger y mejorar la calidad de la vida y defender y restaurar el medio ambiente, apoyándose en la indispensable solidaridad colectiva"; Arts. 5, 74 and 86 the Polish Constitution "The Republic of Poland shall (...) ensure the protection of the natural environment pursuant to the principles of sustainable development (...) Public authorities shall pursue policies ensuring the ecological security of current and future generations. Protection of the environment shall be the duty of public authorities. Everyone shall have the right to be informed of the quality of the environment and its protection. Public authorities shall support the activities of citizens to protect and improve the quality of the environment (...) Everyone shall care for the quality of the environment and shall be held responsible for causing its degradation. The principles of such responsibility shall be specified by statute"; and Art. 56 of the Turkey Constitution "Everyone has the right to live in a healthy, balanced environment. It is the duty of the state and citizens to improve the natural environment, and to prevent environmental pollution."

[2]La Camera (2003).

[3]Silvestri (2015).

- *Conservation and Sustainable Use - 3. States shall maintain ecosystems and ecological processes essential for the functioning of the biosphere, shall preserve biological diversity, and shall observe the principle of optimum sustainable yield in the use of living natural resources and ecosystems.*
- *Sustainable Development and Assistance - 7. States shall ensure that conservation is treated as an integral part of the planning and implementation of development activities and provide assistance to other States, especially to developing countries, in support of environmental protection and sustainable development.*

Resilience, protection and future. These are the key themes in which the above principles can be summarised.

1.2 New Perspectives on Sustainability

Subsequently, the concept of sustainability was expanded and acquired a multidimensional meaning by including issues on both environmental protection and preservation of natural resources and concerning also of economic development and social progress as the right to development of the poorest countries with an active participation of the signing states.

The new conception of this term—together with precise behavioural action intended for the signing states—was first affirmed in 1992 during the Earth Summit of the First United Nations Conference on Environment and Development which resulted in the Rio Declaration on Environment and Development and in the local implementation tool called Agenda 21.

Particularly:

- *Principle 1 - Human beings are at the centre of concerns for sustainable development. They are entitled to a healthy and productive life in harmony with nature.*
- *Principle 3 - The right to development must be fulfilled so as to equitably meet developmental and environmental needs of present and future generations.*
- *Principle 25 - Peace, development and environmental protection are interdependent and indivisible.*

The Rio Declaration reaffirms many principles from the Declaration of the United Nations Conference on the Human Environment, adopted in Stockholm on 16 June 1972.

The Stockholm Declaration represents, indeed, a first taking stock of the global human impact on the environment, an attempt at forging a basic common outlook on how to address the challenge of preserving and enhancing the human environment.

But, as a result, the Stockholm Declaration espouses mostly broad environmental policy goals and objectives rather than detailed normative positions.[4]

The Stockholm Declaration identifies 26 principles on human responsibilities in relation to the environment, among them one of the most important principles is that of intergenerational equity meant as the right of access to natural resources by all human communities and responsibility to future generations.[5]

This is an ethical principle that proceeds in parallel with that of sustainable development and introduces the theme of the rights of future generations, highlighting the close link between poverty and environmental degradation.

The multidimensional character of sustainability was reaffirmed during the World Summit on Sustainable Development in Johannesburg in 2002 through the Declaration on Sustainable Development and particularly in the Plan of Action in which emerges more clearly the meaning of the triangle of (1) environmental sustainability as protection of the ecosystem, (2) economic sustainability as productive growth of resources, and (3) social sustainability as defence of human rights, fight against poverty, distributive equity of resources and safeguarding health.

Sustainable development is the only way to achieve growth taking into account both economic, social and environmental aspects and to constitute a more equitable social structure for future generations:

- *5. Accordingly, we assume a collective responsibility to advance and strengthen the interdependent and mutually reinforcing pillars of sustainable development—economic development, social development and environmental protection—at the local, national, regional and global levels.*
- *11. We recognize that poverty eradication, changing consumption and production patterns and protecting and managing the natural resource base for economic and social development are overarching objectives of and essential requirements for sustainable development.*
- *26. We recognize that sustainable development requires a long-term perspective and broad-based participation in policy formulation, decision-making and imple-*

---

[4]Handl (2012). Of the same author see also—Handl (1995). See also Marchisio (1992); Panjabi (1993).

[5]"Every generation receives a natural and cultural legacy in trust from its ancestors and holds it in trust for the future descendants."

Thus Weiss (1989), the leading exponent of intergenerational equity theory, summarises its essence; each generation receives an inheritance, in cultural and natural terms, which it preserves in a trust for future descendants. This means that in the head of each generation arise both rights relating to receiving as an inheritance an environment (and a cultural complex) preserved in its resources, and duties to protect these riches for future generations; however, the theory of intergenerational equity argues that the aforementioned duties and rights are not individual, but collective, referring to generational classes and not to individuals' part of society. For a further analysis —Brunnée, (2008).

mentation at all levels. As social partners, we will continue to work for stable partnerships with all major groups, respecting the independent, important roles of each of them.

In the community dimension of the European Union, the Single European Act of 1986 gives the European Community shared competence in environmental matters and, while it does not yet mention the concept of sustainable development, entrusts it with the task of "ensuring the prudent and rational utilization of natural resources."

An initial and new definition of the term occurred with the 25/26 June 1990 Dublin Declaration of the European Council through which Member States:

> As Heads of State and Government of the European Community, we recognise our special responsibility for the environment both to our own citizens and to the wider world. We undertake to intensify our efforts to protect and enhance the natural environment of the Community itself and the world of which it is part. We intend that action by the Community and its Member States will be developed on a coordinated basis and on the principles of sustainable development and preventive and precautionary action.

With the 1992 Maastricht Treaty, the aim "to promote balanced and sustainable economic and social progress" is included under B among the objectives of the European Union, while in the Treaty of the European Community reference is made in Article 2 to the promotion of "sustainable and non-inflationary growth which respects the environment."

The principle of sustainable development, in the 1997 Treaty of Amsterdam, qualifies as definitively a "legal principle" and foundation for Community policies and actions, thus not only as a guiding principle of an ethical nature.

In the preamble, it states that the Member States are "determined to promote the social and economic progress of peoples, taking into account the principle of sustainable development in the context of the completion of the internal market and the strengthening of cohesion and environmental protection" and in Article 2 the Treaty reaffirms that the primary objective of the European Union is to promote economic and social progress, a high level of employment and to achieve balanced and sustainable development.

Finally, in 2007, the Treaty of Lisbon specified that the Union's action is to "foster the sustainable development of developing countries in economic, social and environmental terms, with the primary aim of eradicating poverty" as well as "contribute to the development of international measures to preserve and improve the quality of the environment and the sustainable management of the world's natural resources in order to ensure sustainable development."

However, the transition from the declaration of principles to the assumption of precise obligations to implement environmentally preservative behavioural patterns has taken several years in both the EU and international context.

At the international level, in December 2015, the Paris Agreement was signed by 195 countries and then entered into force in November 2016. This agreement assigns precise environmental goals to the signatory states:

> This Agreement, in enhancing the implementation of the Convention, including its objective, aims to strengthen the global response to the threat of climate change, in the context of

> sustainable development and efforts to eradicate poverty, including by: (a) Holding the increase in the global average temperature to well below 2 °C above pre-industrial levels and to pursue efforts to limit the temperature increase to 1.5 °C above pre-industrial levels, recognizing that this would significantly reduce the risks and impacts of climate change; (b) Increasing the ability to adapt to the adverse impacts of climate change and foster climate resilience and low greenhouse gas emissions development, in a manner that does not threaten food production; (c) Making finance flows consistent with a pathway towards low greenhouse gas emissions and climate resilient development. 2. This Agreement will be implemented to reflect equity and the principle of common but differentiated responsibilities and respective capabilities, in the light of different national circumstances.

From a programmatic standpoint, the certainly most concrete action is that represented by the Agenda2030 for Sustainable Development, which highlights seventeen global goals and no less than 169 targets ("a call for action") to be achieved by 2030.

The document is the result of a complex preparatory process, where the goals achieve universal character, they are addressed to both developing and advanced countries, and are based on the integration of the three dimensions of sustainable development (environmental, social and economic) as a prerequisite for eradicating poverty in all its forms.

The Agenda consists of four parts [(1) Declaration, (2) Goals and targets, (3) Implementation instruments, (4) Implementation monitoring and review] and touches on several, interconnected areas that are fundamental to ensuring the well-being of humanity and the planet: from combating hunger to eliminating inequality, from protecting natural resources to urban development, from agriculture to consumption patterns.

Of particular interest is Goal No. 14 called "Conserve and sustainably use the oceans, seas and marine resources for sustainable development."

Specifically, it highlights the essentiality of marine and coastal biodiversity for human life as well as for the environment due to the ability of the oceans to absorb carbon dioxide produced by humans without considering the number of people employed thanks to fishing industries.

It is of immediate evidence; therefore, how proper management of the oceans and seas is fundamental to sustainable development.

1.3 The Link Between Sustainability and the Environment

The very strong connection between environmental protection and the fulfilment of duties of environmental solidarity, in the past years, was made explicit through the various principles that govern EU and international environmental policy, precisely from the goal of sustainable development.

However, the two aspects—environmental solidarity and sustainable development—always maintain their specific physiognomy, finding their essential point of contact in the circumstance that the duty of environmental solidarity also addresses and is addressed to future generations, "beyond the horizon of present generations"[6] to "ensure the continuity over time of economic and social development, with respect for the environment, without compromising the natural resources indispensable to human activity."[7]

The link between sustainable development and the benefits of the present and future generations and the environment is strengthened by the social idea that the latter is no longer the object of individual appropriation, but the interest of the collective.[8]

Therefore, the present generation has the duty to not unreasonably use environmental resources, in order to remove all obstacles that prevent the full development of the human person with respect to the environment and to preserve the right of future generations to see the natural heritage reasonably used.

Then, the foundation of ethicality that distinguishes the duty of environmental solidarity and that requires the "global renunciation of continuing to contend for the earth's limited riches in unbridled competition,"[9] or that, more modestly, leads to the protection of the plant even if it does not serve economic or social purposes and even if, in an ecocentric view of the environment, it is not used to satisfy a material human need, highlights the content of that duty that is not economic, political or social in nature.[10]

And this although the characteristic of international environmental law has been, since its origin in the early 1970s, to deal with environmental problems in a very sectoral way.

It has dealt with air and marine pollution, trade in protected animals, hazardous waste, and protection of certain geographical areas from nuclear damage....

In more recent times, this sectoral approach has been followed by a comprehensive approach to problems affecting the environment as a whole. In this context, the principle of sustainable development can serve to give unity on the substantive level to environmental governance that on the formal level remains sectoral and fragmented mainly because of its origin in treaty norms that, however important, remain unenforceable against third states.

As for the gap between theoretical enunciations of the principle of sustainable development and the actual arrangements for economic development, it is due to the circumstance that states put the value of environmental sustainability before the need to sustain the economic growth and consumption of their citizens.[11]

[6] Frumento E, Lo stato ambientale e le generazioni future: per una tutela del diritto fondamentale all'ambiente, www.ambientediritto.it.

[7] Fifth Environmental Action Programme.

[8] Maddalena (1990).

[9] Jonas (2000).

[10] Grasso (2003), p. 581.

[11] This is evident in the 2005 UNDP (United Nations Development Programme) Report in which it is reported that more than 60% of countries consider environmental protection to be an obstacle to development rather than a component of it. This is not surprising when one considers that 60% includes poor countries that certainly do not look favourably at environmental protection policies whose costs fall on their shoulders. But despite this, it is precisely economic and consumption

It is in this search for a unity of action, overcoming the old environmental sectionalism, and for coherence between abstract proclamations and the real economic policy choices of states that the principle of sustainable development can play a unifying role with respect to already established or emerging principles of international environmental law.[12]

1.4 Intergenerational Equity and Jurisprudential Approach

In the judgments of the International Courts, it is difficult to discern a situation in which the rights related to intergenerational responsibility have been individually or collectively acted upon.

However, the issue was first dealt with by Judge Weeramantry's dissenting opinion, within the discussion on the use of nuclear weapons.

Indeed, he also includes among the effects of the possible use of nuclear weapons the harm to future generations:

> This Court, as the principal judicial organ of the United Nations, empowered to state and apply international law with an authority matched by no other tribunal must, in its jurisprudence, pay due recognition to the rights of future generations. If there is any tribunal that can recognize and protect their interests under the law, it is this Court.
>
> It is to be noted in this context that the rights of future generations have passed the stage when they were merely an embryonic right struggling for recognition. They have woven themselves into international law through major treaties, through juristic opinion and through general principles of law recognized by civilized nations.
>
> Among treaties may be mentioned, the 1979 London Ocean Dumping Convention, the 1973 Convention on International Trade in Endangered Species, and the 1972 Convention Concerning the Protection of the World Cultural and Natural Heritage. All of these expressly incorporate the principle of protecting the natural environment for future generations and elevate the concept to the level of binding State obligation.

---

growth that is dramatically accelerating environmental degradation and now posing the question of the sustainability of economic development in terms of "global security." This new relationship between environmental sustainability and collective security is the basis for initiatives to reform the United Nations system. It emerges in the Report of the High-Level Panel on Threats, Challenges and Change, which insists on the need for new initiatives to go beyond the Kyoto Protocol, which is deemed insufficient to counter the global climate change crisis, and especially in Secretary-General Kofi Annan's March 2005 report, which proposes measures targeted at specific areas such as desertification, biodiversity protection and atmospheric warming.

[12] This is especially in application of the principles developed by the Working Group on Environmental Law of the European University Institute (1) the principle of prevention, (2) the principle of responsibility of non-state actors, particularly multinational corporations, with respect to compliance with international environmental standards, (3) the precautionary principle, (4) the principle of equity in the distribution of benefits derived from the exploitation of natural resources, (5) the principles of information and participation of affected populations in decisions affecting important environmental issues.

> Juristic opinion is now abundant, with several major treatises appear in upon the subject and with such concepts as intergenerational equity and the common heritage of mankind being academically well established.
>
> Moreover, there is a growing awareness of the ways in which a multiplicity of traditional legal systems across the globe protects the environment for future generations. To these must be added a series of major international declarations commencing with the 1972 Stockholm Declaration on the Human Environment.
>
> When incontrovertible scientific evidence speaks of pollution of the environment on a scale that spans hundreds of generations, this Court would fail in its trust if it did not take serious note of the ways in which the distant future is protected by present law. The ideals of the United Nations Charter do not limit themselves to the present, for they look forward to the promotion of social progress and better standards of life, and they fix their vision, not only on the present, but on "succeeding generations."
>
> This one factor of impairment of the environment over such a seemingly infinite time span would by itself be sufficient to call into operation the protective principles of international law which the Court, as the pre-eminent authority empowered to state them, must necessarily apply.[13]

As for other Courts—such as the European Court of Justice or the European Court of Human Rights—they have not expressed directly about intergenerational equity.

Notwithstanding, the Courts, both international and EU, carry out their role in protecting the environment from the perspective of future generations also through the application of the principle of sustainable development.

An emblematic case in which there was a reference to the principle of sustainable development, also related to future generations, is Gabčíkovo-Nagymaros.

The facts consisted of the suspension of a pact between Czechoslovakia and Hungary, concerning the construction of a hydroelectric power plant, by the latter, due to concerns about the environmental impact of the project, which had been followed by unilateral actions by Czechoslovakia.

Once again, it is the knowledgeable opinion of Judge Weeramantry that needs to be taken into consideration.

First, Judge Weeramantry declares that the principle of sustainable development is an integral part of modern international law[14] and it could be used to settle the proceeding, as accepted by both states involved in the dispute.

> This case offers a unique opportunity for the application of that principle, for it arises from a Treaty which had development as its objective and has been brought to a standstill over arguments concerning environmental considerations.
>
> The people of both Hungary and Slovakia are entitled to development for the furtherance of their happiness and welfare. They are likewise entitled to the preservation of their human right to the protection of their environment. Other cases raising environmental questions have been considered by this Court in the context of environmental pollution arising from

[13] Separate Opinion of Vice President Weeramantry.

[14] "The principle of sustainable development is thus a part of modern international law by reason not only of its inescapable logical necessity, but also by reason of its wide and general acceptance by the global community."

> such sources as nuclear explosions, which are far removed from development projects. The present case thus focuses attention, as no other case has done in the jurisprudence of this Court, on the question of the harmonization of developmental and environmental concepts.[15]

Furthermore, Judge Weeramantry traces some historical major steps in environmental protection[16] showing the idea of the rights of future generations being served through the harmonisation of human developmental work with respect for the natural environment and concluding that "Sustainable development is thus not merely a principle of modern international law. It is one of the most ancient of ideas in the human heritage."

On the outcome of the dispute, the International Court of Justice concluded that both parties committed internationally wrongful acts, and it has noted that those acts gave rise to the damage sustained by the parties; consequently, Hungary and Slovakia are both under an obligation to pay compensation and are both entitled to obtain compensation and the issue of compensation could satisfactorily be resolved in the framework of an overall settlement if each of the parties were to renounce or cancel all financial claims and counterclaims.

Another paradigmatic and domestic case to be mentioned is Minors Oposa v. Secretary of the Department of Environmental and Natural Resources[17] argued before the Supreme Court of the Philippines and having as an instrument cited the constitution of the Philippines.

The plaintiffs' complaint concerns the ongoing deforestation in the country. A group of children, including those of renowned environmental activist Antonio Oposa, brought this lawsuit in conjunction with the Philippine Ecological Network, Inc. (a non-profit organisation) to stop the destruction of the fast-disappearing rain forests in their country.

The plaintiff children based their claims on the 1987 Constitution of the Philippines, which recognises the right of people to a "balanced and healthful ecology"[18] and the right to "self-preservation and self-perpetuation" (see Section 16, Article II). Oposa also raised the idea of "intergenerational equity" before the court, which is the idea that natural resources belong to people of all ages and that if adults were to harvest all of a country's resources, they would be stealing from their children, their children's children, and all future generations.

---

[15] Separate Opinion of Vice President Weeramantry.

[16] Brohier (1934) and Masao (1974).

[17] G.R. No. 101083 July 30, 1993.

[18] As a result of scientific research, the need was identified to maintain a balance between the use of environmental areas as free forests (in the majority) and for industrial, housing or any exploitation purposes (in the minority). The alteration of this balance, which the plaintiffs complain about, would lead to major consequences for both local and planetary ecosystems; there could be "environmental tragedies." The plaintiffs attach documentary, photographic and satellite evidence that would show how the administration was not concerned with the maintenance of resources, but rather disrupted them by licensing various companies for logging instrumental to the acquisition of timber.

The Supreme Court ruled in favour of the children, and made several ground-breaking and powerful statements, finding:

- The right to a clean environment, to exist from the land, and to provide for future generations are fundamental.
- There is an intergenerational responsibility to maintain a clean environment, meaning each generation has a responsibility to the next to preserve that environment, and children may sue to enforce that right on behalf of both their generation and future generations.
- The Philippine Constitution requires that the government "protect and promote the health of the people and instill health consciousness among them."

The uniqueness of this case is clearly related to the fact that the plaintiffs were minors representing their generation as well as generations yet unborn,[19] and this allowed for the extension of the time limit relating to the damage that the actions complained of had created and were creating to the environment and to the circumstance whereby the Court acknowledged that the class of members represented not only their own interests, but also those of future generations.

There is no lack of jurisdiction over the minors, indeed the action is admissible.[20] This is justified by the same by referring precisely to intergenerational responsibility, arguing on the one hand on the right to a balanced and healthy environment and, on the other hand, that each generation must respect such, it is said, "rhythm and harmony" of nature; in essence, it is not only affirmed that the claim of the minor class members consisted in the exercise of their prerogative, but also the fulfilment of their duty, to future generations.

The Court's reasoning is also based on the citation of some direct references to future generations in Philippine law itself; particularly, the text of a 1977 Presidential Decree forming the so-called Philippine Environment Code is cited, which expresses itself with respect to the responsibilities of each generation by defining them as

---

[19] This case, however, has a special and novel element. Petitioners' minors assert that they represent their generation as well as generations yet unborn. We find no difficulty in ruling that they can, for themselves, for others of their generation and for the succeeding generations, file a class suit. Their personality to sue on behalf of the succeeding generations can only be based on the concept of intergenerational responsibility insofar as the right to a balanced and healthful ecology is concerned. Such a right, as hereinafter expounded, considers the "rhythm and harmony of nature." Nature means the created world in its entirety. Such rhythm and harmony indispensably include, inter alia, the judicious disposition, utilisation, management, renewal and conservation of the country's forest, mineral, land, waters, fisheries, wildlife, off-shore areas and other natural resources to the end that their exploration, development and utilisation be equitably accessible to the present as well as future generations. Needless to say, every generation has a responsibility to the next to preserve that rhythm and harmony for the full enjoyment of a balanced and healthful ecology. Put a little differently, the minors' assertion of their right to a sound environment constitutes, at the same time, the performance of their obligation to ensure the protection of that right for the generations to come.

[20] "Plaintiffs have a clear and constitutional right to a balanced and healthful ecology and are entitled to protection by the State in its capacity as the *parens patriae*."

"responsibilities [...] as trustee and guardian of the environment for succeeding generations."

It clearly echoes the theory of intergenerational equity by defining present generations as trustees of the environment for succeeding generations.

2 Blue Economy: A Terminological Investigation

2.1 A New Business Model

The Italian Treccani dictionary defines the Blue Economy as "An economic form in which production techniques aim to create a sustainable ecosystem, characterized by total absence of carbon emissions, through the use of energy sources and natural resources, eliminating the traditional cycle leading from product to waste, whether polluting or recyclable."

It is therefore and foremost an economic model that, aware of the primary role of oceans and seas in terms of sustainability and progress and natural heritage, aims to research and apply new techniques that can generate a positive and long-term impact.

The author who coined the terminology Blue Economy is Gunter Pauli, a Belgian economist.

In his book,[21] Pauli highlights the potential benefits of linking and combining seemingly disparate environmental problems with open-source scientific solutions based on common physical processes in the natural world to create solutions that have environmental, economic and social benefits. The book suggests that we can change the way we manage our industrial processes and address the resulting environmental problems by moving away from the use of rare, high-energy cost resources and instead seeking solutions based on simpler, cleaner technologies. It also proposes to focus on generating more value instead of blindly cutting costs. Finally, he aims to inspire entrepreneurs to adopt their own insights, demonstrating ways in which this can create economic benefits through job creation and reduced energy consumption.

In a further moment, Pauli proposed some examples of virtuous blue economy such as producing edible mushrooms from coffee waste and making natural surfactants from orange peels. Or the construction of buildings designed on the basis of termite mounds for better thermal management.

Again, global intentions have been well identified in guiding principles first enunciated in 2018[22] that are the subject of a United Nations initiative involving the global community "Sustainable Blue Economy Finance Initiative."

---

[21] Pauli (2010).

[22] Sustainable Blue Economy Finance Principles: (1) Protective: We will support investments, activities and projects that take all possible measures to restore, protect or maintain the diversity,

Obviously, they, and especially number 8, are extremely connected to Agenda's goal 14 above (Conserve and sustainably use the oceans, seas and marine resources for sustainable development) by promoting its implementation and setting standards specific to oceans, enabling the financial sector to integrate sustainability of ocean-based sectors.

The Blue Economy has gained traction in international and regional scenarios and governance throughout the past decade.[23] Despite the prominence of the term in

---

productivity, resilience, core functions, value and the overall health of marine ecosystems, as well as the livelihoods and communities dependent upon them. (2) Compliant: We will support investments, activities and projects that are compliant with international, regional, national legal and other relevant frameworks which underpin sustainable development and ocean health. (3) Risk-aware: We will endeavour to base our investment decisions on holistic and long-term assessments that account for economic, social and environmental values, quantified risks and systemic impacts and will adapt our decision-making processes and activities to reflect new knowledge of the potential risks, cumulative impacts and opportunities associated with our business activities. (4) Systemic: We will endeavour to identify the systemic and cumulative impacts of our investments, activities and projects across value chains. (5) Inclusive: We will support investments, activities and projects that include, support and enhance local livelihoods, and engage effectively with relevant stakeholders, identifying, responding to, and mitigating any issues arising from affected parties. (6) Cooperative: We will cooperate with other financial institutions and relevant stakeholders to promote and implement these principles through sharing of knowledge about the ocean, best practices for a sustainable Blue Economy, lessons learned, perspectives and ideas. (7) Transparent: We will make information available on our investment/banking/insurance actives and projects and their social, environmental and economic impacts (positive and negative), with due respect to confidentiality. We will endeavour to report on progress in terms of implementation of these Principles. (8) Purposeful: We will endeavour to direct investment/banking/insurance to projects and activities that contribute directly to the achievement of Sustainable Development Goal 14 ("Conserve and sustainably use the oceans, seas and marine resources for sustainable development") and other Sustainable Development Goals especially those which contribute to good governance of the ocean. (9) Impactful: We will support investments, projects and activities that go beyond the avoidance of harm to provide social, environmental and economic benefits from our ocean for both current and future generations. (10) Precautionary: We will support investments, activities and projects in our ocean that have assessed the environmental and social risks and impacts of their activities based on sound scientific evidence. The precautionary principle will prevail, especially when scientific data is not available. (11) Diversified: Recognising the importance of small to medium enterprises in the Blue Economy, we will endeavour to diversify our investment/banking/insurance instruments to reach a wider range of sustainable development projects, for example in traditional and non-traditional maritime sectors, and in small and large-scale projects. (12) Solution-driven: We will endeavour to direct investment/banking/insurance to innovative commercial solutions to maritime issues (both land- and ocean-based), that have a positive impact on marine ecosystems and ocean-dependent livelihoods. We will work to identify and to foster the business case for such projects, and to encourage the spread of best practice thus developed. (13) Partnering: We will partner with public, private and nongovernment sector entities to accelerate progress towards a sustainable Blue Economy, including in the establishment and implementation of coastal and maritime spatial planning approaches. (14) Science-led: We will actively seek to develop knowledge and data on the potential risks and impacts associated with our investment/banking/insurance activities, as well as encouraging sustainable finance opportunities in the Blue Economy. More broadly, we will endeavour to share scientific information and data on the marine environment.

[23] Mulazzani and Malorgio (2017) and Patil et al. (2016).

international and national programs the blue economy as a concept remains poorly defined and largely under-implemented at a national level.[24] This renders the blue economy at risk of becoming a political tool rather than a tool to achieve practical objectives and advance ocean health, economic development, and social equity.[25]

Today's Blue Economy transcends traditional sectors, with the exponential growth in recent years of new innovative and emerging sectors, such as wind energy and biotechnology. These sectors offer significant potential for growth and employment, especially in renewable energy. Pollution of the seas could have disastrous consequences through not only the impact on climate change and rising costs to mitigate its consequences, but already on marine litter on the surface and seabed. Indeed, these already generate lost costs and revenues in sectors such as fisheries, aquaculture and tourism, in an estimated amount of nearly 11 billion euros per year. The Blue Economy is interconnected with many other activities in the economy and its impact goes beyond the sectors mentioned above.

Given the increasing urgency of addressing the decline in ocean health, and the continued growth of ocean industries, translating high-level conceptualisations of the blue economy into operational implementation and reviewing this implementation for future adaptation should be a high priority.

2.2 *From Blue to Ocean Economy*

> Protecting our oceans is not a luxury. It is a necessity that contributes to our economy, our climate and our way of life. Working together, we can change the current course and chart a sustainable future.[26]

A new common definition of "Blue Economy" stressed the promotion of economic benefits of "good for the ocean" industries and activities, while ensuring truly sustainable development.

Blue Economy evolves in Ocean Economy.

There is still no universally accepted definition of the ocean economy.

For example, the ocean economy is defined by the OECD as the sum of the economic activities of ocean-based industries, together with the assets, goods and services provided by marine ecosystems. These two pillars are interdependent, in that much activity associated with ocean-based industry is derived from marine ecosystems, while industrial activity often impacts marine ecosystems.

For the European Commission "the maritime economy consists of all the sectoral and cross-sectoral economic activities related to the oceans, seas and coasts. This includes the closest direct and indirect supporting activities necessary for the

[24] Voyer et al. (2022), p. 5. For a further analysis—Colgan (2018).

[25] Brent et al. (2020) and Louey (2022). See also - Voyer et al. (2018); European Commission (2022).

[26] US Secretary of State, John Kerry (2014).

functioning of these economic sectors, which can be located anywhere, including in landlocked countries."[27]

A similar definition is suggested by the doctrine[28] after conducting a meta-study about the different worldwide existing definitions of the ocean economy: "The ocean economy are the economic activities that take place in the ocean, receive outputs from the ocean, and provide goods and services to the ocean. In other words, the ocean economy can be defined as the economic activities that directly or indirectly take place in the ocean, use the ocean's outputs, and put the goods and services into the ocean's activities."

Although there is not a univocal definition, it is possible to observe that, nowadays, the human relationship with the ocean is changing, and the old ocean economy is adapting to respond to new demands, ecological needs, and the dynamics of global climate change.

Global awareness of the climate and biodiversity crises continued to rise, with commitments from numerous governments raising hope for progress towards goals contained in the Paris Agreement and the post-2020 Global Biodiversity Framework and to fulfil the commitments made in 2015 across the 17 SDGs.

As mentioned above, Goal 14—"Conserve and Sustainability Use the Oceans, Seas and Marine Resources for Sustainable Development"—outlines seven targets and three means of implementation relating to the sustainable use of the ocean.

Particularly noteworthy in this context is target 14.7, which declares, "By 2030 increase the economic benefits to small island developing states and least developed countries from the sustainable use of marine resources, including through sustainable management of fisheries, aquaculture and tourism." This focus on economic development is starting to create a shift in the management and protection of marine resources and their social and economic impact.

Furthermore, it has to be mentioned also target 14.c focused on "Enhance the conservation and sustainable use of oceans and their resources by implementing international law as reflected in United Nations Convention on the Law of the Sea,[29] which provides the legal framework for the conservation and sustainable use of oceans and their resources."

The interdependency of ocean-based industries and marine ecosystems combined with increasingly severe threats to the health of the ocean, have led to a growing recognition of the need for an integrated approach to ocean management.

The blue economy is so about unsustainable versus sustainable. Are there traditional ocean activities that generate economic returns but that are benign or regenerative for our coasts and ocean?

---

[27] Wolters et al. (2013). See also Davis and Gartside (2001).

[28] Park and Kildow (2014).

[29] The UN Convention was adopted in 1982. It lays down a comprehensive regime of law and order in the world's oceans and seas establishing rules governing all uses of the oceans and their resources.

Many new emerging technologies designed to address climate change through the development of alternative sources of energy are increasingly being deployed in marine ecosystems even if the private sector and industry engagement in investment for a sustainable ocean economy transition remains a challenge, and innovative incentives and measures to minimise risks are needed.

The new "ocean economy" is so driven by a combination of population growth, rising incomes, dwindling natural resources, responses to climate change and pioneering technologies.

2.3 *Concrete Application of a New Model*

Coastal flooding is one of the major challenges of global climate change for humanity. It is estimated that by 2070, approximately 150 million people and $35,000 billion of assets will be exposed to a 1 in 100-year flood event.[30] Storm surges and oceanic waves are the major cause of extreme sea levels and devastating coastal impacts along many coastlines around the world with significant human and economic costs.

To improve the ability to assess the potential change of storm surge, it is critical to have a well-established baseline of the storm surge climate, based on consistent techniques.

The sciences-based products developed in this use case will help to enhance the safety of coastal communities by supporting the decision-making process related to planning coastal defences and emergency response to severe coastal flooding.

They could also be used by insurers.

The insurance industry and insurers have, indeed, a critical role to play in finding solutions to some of the world's biggest challenges both as risk managers and risk carriers protecting society's assets as well as institutional investors funding the economy.

Climate change is clearly having an impact on the insurance industry and is causing an increase in the frequency and severity of claims. The financial impact has worsened by the fact that there is more wealth concentration, therefore claims are costlier, and insurers are more exposed. In 2022, the insurance sector has paid out over $120 billion to cover losses from natural catastrophes.[31]

The future needs to develop insurance-led solutions to risks caused by a changing ocean, with a focus on using nature to build resilience.

---

[30] Wenhai et al. (2019).

[31] Source Munich Re.

3 The Positive Impact of Insurance

3.1 Sustainable Insurance

Sustainable insurance could be considered as a strategic approach where all activities in the insurance value chain, including interactions with stakeholders, are done in a responsible and forward-looking way by identifying, assessing, managing and monitoring risks and opportunities associated with environmental, social and governance issues.[32]

> Sustainable insurance aims to reduce risk, develop innovative solutions, improve business performance, and contribute to environmental, social and economic sustainability.[33]

Nowadays, the impacts of climate change are causing warmer temperatures, rising sea levels, and erratic rain patterns, as well as other extreme weather conditions. The disasters that may occur can lead to losses in the socio-economic sector. These risks cannot be avoided, especially if they are exacerbated by the occurrence of climate change. Insurance plays an important role in the event of a disaster or as a means of economic recovery. The existence of insurance guarantees the availability of funds for economic recovery.[34] Thus, with insurance, the large-scale, planned, timely, and targeted sustainable financing needs can be met, which are managed transparently to protect state finances.

Well-designed insurance products help to reduce the economic impact of and facilitate quick recovery after natural catastrophes.[35] In turn, it can help protect livelihoods from catastrophic events and in combination with mitigation and risk prevention measures, risk transfer can help to strengthen resilience to climate change.

Insurers need to act for three reasons: (1) as good citizens given the magnitude of the impact of climate change on the economy and society, (2) given the insurance industry's significant role in mitigating impact and fostering transition and (3) also due to their manifold exposure to climate change risks.

Insurance is an intangible product: there are no direct emissions attached to its production. The "greenness" of an insurance product is therefore linked to the object or activity that is insured. Thus, the fulfilment of the promise, the claims handling, becomes much more material. Taking into account the life cycle of an insured object or activity, and the choices consumers make along the way, the roadmap for green insurance products consists of four major aspects and one overarching dimension:

1. Cover of green insurance objects with specific tariffs to promote eco-friendly objects.

---

[32] For a further analysis, in this volume, see Vercher-Moll.

[33] Principles for Sustainable Insurance, UNEP, 2012.

[34] Kaushalya et al. (2014).

[35] Churchill (2006).

2. Adding green insurance features to conventional objects or activities, as part of the core product or related service, or as independent service. Products or services can cater to specific sustainability themes or related risks.
3. Support the sustainability transition after a claim with ecological repair, replacement, or upgrades.
4. Set up incentives, ecosystems and communication to promote environmentally friendly behaviour, characteristics and transition outside a claim.
5. Lead regular dialogue with customers on critical issues, and provide incentives and risk advice to support their risk mitigation and efforts of transition.

3.2 Climate Risk Management

Managing the risks from climate change requires urgent action to adapt to the changes in climate at a local level to minimise risks and maximise potential opportunities. Once again, the role of the insurance industry is crucial.

Adaptation, or lack thereof, is particularly critical to the insurance industry as it directly affects the risk landscape that they insure and the concept of "insurability" itself. The insurance industry has traditionally based its view of risk on historical records of hazard occurrences. Insurability depends on several criteria, including actuarial, market-based and societal factors, many of which may potentially be affected by climate change.

An increase in the magnitude or frequency of weather hazards with future climate change could also lead to an increase in the risk of correlated losses, for instance from coastal or inland flooding.

Adaptation (or risk mitigation) can have significant benefits in terms of helping existing private insurance markets to continue to function. The insurance industry has an opportunity not only to contribute to the formulation of public policy on adaptation, but also to directly influence adaptation through its business practices.[36]

Insurers can harness their competencies in climate risk management and risk transfer to develop a variety of services that help businesses, investors and the public sector to adapt to climate change. Potential services include assessments of the physical risks from climate change, identification of priorities for risk mitigation, advice on risk transfer options and business continuity or disaster response planning.

Insurers can also play a significant role in informing and educating customers about the risks of climate change that they face, and, importantly, about how best to reduce them. The Insurance industry can play a leading role in guiding society's adaptation to the impacts of climate change with a constructive relationship with policy-makers, regulators, public sector organisations and other stakeholders in the private sector.

---

[36] Herweijera et al. (2009).

3.3 Ocean Risk

As seen, a diverse array of ocean-related phenomena occurs today and more are expected to emerge in the future as ocean risk evolves in response to the observed and accelerating warming, acidification, oxygen depletion and other man-made threats to the ocean.

The ocean and the many ecosystem services it provides are key natural resources for the Blue Economy. The rise of the Blue Economy is being driven by rapid growth of marine transport and tourism, industrial use of coastal and seashore areas and extraction of resources from the ocean and marine environments. Since insurance penetration covers only minor parts of today's blue economy this presents a significant business opportunity for the insurance industry.[37]

The ocean and the marine ecosystems that support the blue economy are shifting. The ocean is showing a sustained and accelerating upward trend in sea-surface temperature, ocean heat content and sea levels in almost all ocean basins and, at the same time, ocean acidity is increasing, and oxygen concentrations are decreasing. The changes in the ocean have the potential to trigger catastrophic consequences, which can be termed as "ocean risk."

Ocean risk is a function of exposure and vulnerabilities to hazards arising from ocean change, which may or may not be avoided, reduced or adapted to through pre-emptive action. Ocean risk encompasses well-known phenomena, such as storm surge from tropical and extra-tropical cyclones, or other extreme weather events strongly influenced by oceanic modes of variability. But ocean risk also encompasses lesser-known and potentially surprising phenomena that are associated with the observed regime shifts in marine ecosystems such as outbreaks of marine-mediated diseases or economic shocks and/or food security crises due to sudden changes in marine ecosystems.

Ocean investments often have high risks but the enabling regulatory environment for attracting investors is not in place. Overcoming the higher risk profile associated with the ocean sector will require addressing a number of challenging enabling conditions to attract investments and new forms of finance. These challenges include human capacity constraints, data challenges and higher risk of operation. In addition, structural challenges related to the ocean make scale and replication more complex than in more familiar terrestrial sectors (notably related to tenure and ownership, monitoring, and enforcement). To attract large-scale investments, it is critical to find ways to de-risk the enabling environment associated with ocean-based sustainable development projects and activities. While traditional marine insurance is a strategy for managing commercial risks for shipping, aquaculture, fishing, and other offshore industrial activities, it does not cover all risks to the ocean economy (e.g. blue carbon and nature-based infrastructure investments).

---

[37] Insurance has always been concerned with water and the seas. In fact, insurance began as a form of protection against the dangers of the sea.

The impact of ocean risk on the insurance industry has three main components: (1) increasing loss potentials for many property and casualty (P&C) lines due to sea-level rise, increasing precipitation extremes and changing ocean-atmosphere modes; (2) changing loss potential in various insurance lines such as health, aquafarming, political risk or product liability; and (3) an implied asset risk that could potentially strand entire regions and global industries, leading to direct and indirect impacts on investment strategies and liabilities. Quantifying the financial impacts and managing emerging ocean risk requires new risk modelling solutions that go beyond the better representation of the effects of ocean warming and climate change into traditional risk models of extreme weather events.[38]

In addition, there is a need for risk models that quantify the probability and economic impact of losing marine ecosystem services. Such ecosystem risk models would have the potential to unlock new insurance markets in the space spanned by ocean risk, international development programs and the blue economy. Business opportunities for the insurance industry will arise in the form of new insurance solutions to transfer ocean risk.

Another relevant measure for the insurance industry could be to reduce or delete pirate fishing or illegal, unreported & unregulated (IUU) fishing which costs the global economy USD 10 to 23.5 billion yearly. In fact, IUU fishing contributes to overfishing and destruction of marine habitats and ecosystems, and marine pollution. Furthermore, the proliferation of illegal activities related to fishing leads to heightened risks for insurers in relation to other insured parties. There is also a problem of possible linkage with other crimes and consequently, two main critical issues arise. The first criticality coincides with an increased risk of fraud against insurers. The second criticality concerns the exposure of the insurers themselves to strict legal liabilities also in relation to the violation of international standards.

Insurance could be also useful in improving the viability of insurance in coastal regions through a mechanism of coordination across governments and insurers.

Governments around the world are increasingly searching for innovative solutions to effectively manage the growing financial exposures and damages resulting from natural disasters. Residents of coastal regions are particularly prone to the economic and financial damages of extreme weather events, such as hurricanes, floods, winter storms and climate change-driven sea-level rise and storm surges. The expansion of property insurance has been identified as a key strategy for strengthening pre- and post-disaster management.[39]

Coastal communities face significant challenges that limit the deployment of insurance. Research on flood insurance, for example, identifies risk concentration as a factor that increases uncertainty within insurance markets and can limit the availability and affordability of coverage.[40] Risk concentration is intrinsic to coastal areas since risk increases in relation to the proximity to the coastline. The closer

[38] Ocean Risk and the Insurance Industry, (2018), AXA Report.

[39] Krieger and Demerrit (2015).

[40] Botzen and Van Den Bergh (2008).

properties are to the coastline, the more at risk they are of suffering damages from coastal flooding, storm surges and high winds. Federal government policy, however, can play a significant role in reducing insurance uncertainty and expanding its role in local risk mitigation and disaster recovery acknowledging the insurers' strategic role in the present blue/ocean economy.

4 Conclusions

Sustainability is a key point of the action "Agenda2030 for Sustainable Development" which highlights seventeen global goals and no less than 169 targets to be achieved by 2030.

Particularly, the Agenda takes into consideration, from the perspective of sustainable development, the use of oceans, seas and marine resources.

This provision reflects the present idea of a link between sustainable development and the environment in order to preserve the benefits of the present and future generations.

As said, the present generation has the duty to not unreasonably use environmental resources to remove all obstacles that prevent the full development of the human person with respect to the environment and to preserve the right of future generations to see the natural heritage reasonably used.

The relationship between sustainable development and the environment also related to future generations has been also promoted by Courts, such as in the analysed cases Gabčíkovo-Nagymaros or Minors Oposa v. Secretary of Department of Environmental and Natural Resources.

The environmental issues concerning the use of oceans, seas and marine resources inspired the reflections on the blue economy and its evolution in the Ocean Economy.

Whereas there is no universally accepted definition of the ocean economy, the Ocean Economy concerns the economic activities of ocean-based industries, together with the assets, goods and services provided by marine ecosystems.

In this context, the insurance industry has the potential to play three important roles risk managers, risk carriers and investors.

As risk managers, insurers can communicate recommendations for more sustainable practices to their clients and within the communities they serve. As risk carriers, insurers can choose to exclude or restrict access to insurance to clients or projects that engage in unsustainable or illegal practices. Finally, insurers are also major institutional investors, and in this role, they can elect to support only those clients or projects that contribute to a sustainable ocean economy and divest from those that do not. There is also an opportunity for all levels of government—local, national or international—to work with the insurance industry to promote the development of a sustainable ocean economy. At the local level, this could involve making improvements in risk modelling, and at national or international levels, policy and regulatory frameworks could be reshaped to incentivise responsible and sustainable maritime industry practices.

Sitography

https://eur-lex.europa.eu
https://www.un.org/en/conferences/environment/stockholm1972
https://www.un.org/en/conferences/environment/rio1992
http://www.un-documents.net/jburgdec.htm
https://www.consilium.europa.eu/media/20562/1990_june_-_dublin__eng_.pdf
https://www.un.org/en/conferences/SDGSummit2023
https://sustainabledevelopment.un.org/content/documents/5987our-common-future.pdf
https://www.undp.org/
https://www.icj.org/
https://ec.europa.eu/environment/archives/action-programme/env-act5/pdf/5eap.pdf
https://lawphil.net/judjuris/juri1993/jul1993/gr_101083_1993.html
https://oecd.org

References

Bennett NJ, Cisneros-Montemayor AM, Blythe J, Silver JJ, Singh G, Anews N et al (2019) Towards a sustainable and equitable blue economy. Nat Sustain 2(11):991–993. https://doi.org/10.1038/s41893-019-0404-1

Botzen WJ, Van Den Bergh JC (2008) Insurance against climate change and flooding in the Netherlands: present, future, and comparison with other countries. Risk Anal 28(2):413–426. https://doi.org/10.1111/j.1539-6924.2008.01035.x

Brent ZW, Barbesgaard M, Pedersen C (2020) The blue fix: what's driving blue growth? Sustain Sci 15(1):31–43. https://doi.org/10.1007/s11625-019-00777-7

Brohier RL (1934) Ancient irrigation works in Ceylon. Ceylon Government Press, Ceylon

Brunnée J (2008) The Stockholm Declaration and the structure and processes of international environmental law. In: Chircop A, Dorman TL, Rolston SJ (eds) The future of ocean regime building: essays in tribute to Douglas M. Johnston. Martinus Nijhoff

Chiaramonte L, Dreassi A, Paltrinieri A, Piserà S (2020) Sustainability practices and stability in the insurance industry. Sustainability 12(14):5530

Churchill C (2006) What is insurance for the poor? In: Churchill C (ed) Protecting the poor: a microinsurance compendium. Geneva and Munich, ILO and Munich Re Foundation, pp 12–24

Colgan CS (2018) The blue economy: theory and strategy. In: Attri VN, Bohler-Mulleris N (eds) The blue economy handbook of the Indian ocean region. Africa Institute of South Africa

Davis D, Gartside DF (2001) Challenges for economic policy in sustainable management of marine natural resources. Ecol Econ 36(2)

European Commission (2022) The EU blue economy report 2022. Publications Office of the European Union, Luxembourg. https://doi.org/10.2771/793264

Golnaraghi M (2021) Climate change risk assessment for the insurance industry: a holistic decision-making framework and key considerations for both sides of the balance sheet. Technical report. The Geneva Association, Zurich

Grasso G (2003) Solidarietà ambientale e sviluppo sostenibile tra Costituzioni nazionali, Carta dei diritti e progetto di Costituzione europea. Politica del diritto 4:581–608

Handl G (1995) Sustainable development: general rules vs. specific obligations. Sustainable Development and International Law, p 35

Handl G (2012) Declaration of the United Nations conference on the human environment (Stockholm declaration), 1972 and the Rio declaration on environment and development. United Nations Audiovisual Library of International Law
Herweijera C, Rangerb N, Wardb R (2009) Adaptation to climate change: threats and opportunities for the insurance industry. Geneva Papers 34:360–380. https://doi.org/10.1057/gpp.2009.13
Jambeck J et al (2020) Pollution and a regenerative economy: municipal, industrial, agricultural, and maritime waste, its impacts, and solutions Blue Paper 5. World Resources Institute
Jonas H (2000) Sull'orlo dell'abisso. Conversazioni sul rapporto tra uomo e natura. Einaudi, Torino
Kaushalya H, Karunasena G, Amarathunga D (2014) Role of insurance in post disaster recovery planning in business community. Procedia Econ Financ 18:626–634
Krieger K, Demerrit D (2015) Limits of insurance as risk governance: market failures and disaster politics in German and British flood insurance. Discussion paper. Centre for Analysis of Risk and Regulation, October
La Camera F (2003) Sviluppo Sostenibile. Origini, teoria e pratica. Editori Riuniti, Roma
Louey P (2022) The pacific blue economy: an instrument of political maneuver. Mar Policy 135. https://doi.org/10.1016/j.marpol.2021.104880
Maddalena P (1990) Il diritto all'ambiente e i diritti dell'ambiente nella costruzione della teoria del risarcimento del danno pubblico ambientale. Rivista Giuridica dell'Ambiente 5(3):469–484
Marchisio S (1992) Gli atti di Rio nel diritto internazionale. Rivista di diritto internazionale:581
Masao FT (1974) The irrigation system in Uchagga: an ethno-historical approach. Tanzania Notes Records 75
Mulazzani L, Malorgio G (2017) Blue growth and ecosystem services. Mar Policy (85):17–24
Nogueira FG, Lucena A, Nogueira R (2018) Sustainable insurance assessment: towards an integrative model. Geneva Papers Risk Insur Issues Pract 43:275–299
Panjabi RKL (1993) From Stockholm to Rio: comparison of the declaratory principles of international environmental law. Denver J Int Law Policy 21:215
Park QS, Kildow JT (2014) Rebuilding the classification system of the ocean economy. J Ocean Coastal Econ (1), Article 4
Patil PG, Virdin J, Diez SM, Roberts J, Singh A (2016) Toward a blue economy: a promise for sustainable growth in the Caribbean. https://openknowledge.worldbank.org/handle/10986/25061
Pauli G (2010) The blue economy. Paradigm Publications, Taos
Pfeifer D, Langen V (2021) Insurance business and sustainable development. In: Sarfraz M, Ivascu L (eds) Risk management. IntechOpen. https://doi.org/10.5772/intechopen.91067
Sheppard SRJ, Shaw A, Flanders D, Burch S, Wiek A, Carmichael J, Robinson J, Cohen S (2011) Future visioning of local climate change: a framework for community engagement and planning with scenarios and visualisation. Futures 43(4):400–412. https://doi.org/10.1016/j.futures.2011.01.009
Silvestri M (2015) Sviluppo sostenibile: un problema di definizione. Gentes - Rivista di Scienze Umane e Sociali (2):215–219
Thistlethwaite J, Minano A (2016) Managing climate change risk in coastal Canadian communities through sustainable insurance. Centre for International Governance Innovation, CIGI policy brief no. 93
Voyer M, Quirk G, McIlgorm A, Azmi K (2018) Shades of blue: what do competing interpretations of the blue economy mean for oceans governance? J Environ Policy Plann 20:595–616. https://doi.org/10.1080/1523908x.2018.1473153
Voyer M, Benzaken D, Rambourg C (2022) Institutionalizing the blue economy: an examination of variations and consistencies among commonwealth countries. Philos Trans R Soc 377:1854. https://doi.org/10.1098/rstb.2021.0125
Weiss EB (1989) In fairness to future generations: international law, common patrimony and intergenerational equity. Hotei Publishing

Wenhai L, Cusack C, Baker M, Tao W, Mingbao C, Paige K, Xiaofan Z, Levin L, Escobar E, Amon D, Yue Y, Reitz A, Neves AAS, O'Rourke E, Mannarini G, Pearlman J, Tinker J, Horsburgh KJ, Lehodey P, Pouliquen S, Dale T, Peng Z, Yufeng Y (2019) Successful blue economy examples with an emphasis on international perspectives. Front Mar Sci 6:261. https://doi.org/10.3389/fmars.2019.00261

Wisner B, Blaikie P, Cannon T, Davis I (2003) At risk: natural hazards, people's vulnerability and disasters. Routledge, London. https://doi.org/10.4324/9780203428764

Wolters HA, Gille J, de Vet JM, Molemaker RJ (2013) Scenarios for selected maritime economic functions. Eur J Futures Res 1(11)

Lucrezia Anzanello is a researcher at the University of Milan-Bicocca.

Lucrezia's main areas of research and practice are comparative and commercial law with a focus on sustainable development and ESG criteria.

She is a legal counsel specialising in commercial law and she has been enrolled in the Milan Bar Association since 2016.

Lucrezia is a co-leader of the Jean Monnet Module in Private Comparative Law: Animal Law in Comparative and Global Perspective.

She graduated full votes in Law at the Catholic University of Milan and she holds a PhD in Private Comparative Law from the University of Milan-Bicocca.

Lucrezia has been a visiting scholar at the Università Paris IX-Dauphine and the UConn School of Law, and she has been a visiting lecturer at the Université de Toulon.

She is a member of the scientific association SIRD (società italiana per la ricerca nel diritto comparato).

Author of academic papers in Italian and English on comparative private law.

Part II
Sustainability and Insurers' Governance

The Relevance of Governance in the Insurance Sector Within the Framework of Sustainable Investments

Jaume Llorca Galiana

1 Introduction

The necessary regulation of insurance companies' products following the 2008 crisis has led to regulation at the European level, whose purpose is to offer certain guarantees of investor protection through so-called product governance. The aim, from the moment the product is developed and approved, is that the target market is determined, and its interests and objectives are taken into consideration, guaranteeing a series of product tests that allow more information to be provided on their characteristics, and establishing controls on the distribution of these products. Likewise, the undoubted importance of the insurance sector has led it to become an essential agent for the reorientation of the financial system towards sustainability. For this reason, Regulation 2020/852, known as the European Sustainable Activities Taxonomy Regulation, aims to establish a classification of environmentally sustainable economic activities to facilitate investments in these activities and, in turn, to extend the obligations regarding the disclosure of information on the sustainability of financial products. This had a clear impact on product governance in the insurance sector, modifying the regulations governing product governance requirements and introducing the obligation to consider the investor's sustainability preferences and inform them of the different options for investing in environmentally sustainable activities. This is a matter of recent regulation, but it represents a paradigm shift in

This paper has been carried out within the scope of the National Project: Ministry of Science and Innovation. PID2020-118006RB-I00. M.J.P.T.S.E.D., awarded by the Ministry of Science and Innovation within the framework of its R+D+i 2020 programme.

J. Llorca Galiana (✉)
University of Alicante, Alicante, Spain
e-mail: jaume.llorca@ua.es

J. Bataller-Grau et al. (eds.), *Sustainability and the Insurance Market*, AIDA Europe Research Series on Insurance Law and Regulation 10,
https://doi.org/10.1007/978-3-031-72186-1_5

the insurance sector, and it is already clear that it will be of unquestionable practical relevance in the coming years.

2 Product Governance

2.1 Concept

The growing complexity in the functioning of financial markets has given rise to the need to configure instruments to improve the regulatory framework with the aim of guaranteeing adequate investor protection, reinforcing transparency, and thus offering greater confidence to all those involved in the financial system. The crises experienced in recent years and the situations of abuse by certain market participants have led to the creation of a regulatory framework that allows the gradual adoption of measures to balance these positions to the benefit of investors and to offer greater security in the market.[1] In this context, product governance should be highlighted as an instrument for improving the functioning of the financial system. International regulators have gradually established criteria for the application of a new function of investment institutions that allows for greater control over the process of product design, issuance, marketing, and distribution. The European Securities and Markets Authority (ESMA)[2] issued an opinion on best practices for the implementation of financial product governance obligations[3] to provide the other EU regulators with homogeneous and uniform criteria. This laid the foundations for a system that strengthens the financial system, improves transparency, and protects investors.[4]

Product governance aims to reflect this improvement in the system by offering financial products that have passed certain internal processes within the institution. First, institutions must bear in mind a series of considerations from the initial design of the product.[5] In this respect, the financial needs of the investor will be relevant, and, for this reason, a prior analysis of the potential target market must be carried out. Hence, it will be essential to determine the specific target customer, the knowledge and experience they may have of this type of product, as well as of the financial system in general, the possibility of bearing losses in accordance with their financial situation, risk tolerance, as well as the aims and needs of the investors. Conversely, this analysis is also useful to identify the target audience for whom the product should not be intended, and it is objectively unsuitable. To this end, the specific characteristics of the product, its liquidity, its risk in relation to its profitability and its

---

[1] Marano (2019), pp. 59–96.

[2] Pursuant to the power provided under Article 29.1.a) of Regulation 1095/2010. On ESMA's technical guides, Palá Laguna (2019), pp. 5–7.

[3] ESMA (2014), p. 332.

[4] Canalejas Merín (2019), p. 3.

[5] Fernández Pérez (2019), p. 258; Moya Ballester (2019), p. 687.

complexity should be considered. Second, the product should be analysed by assessing, if possible, the development of similar products on the market and in any case, by subjecting it to simulations of future scenarios to determine its adaptation to crisis situations and its profitability under different scenarios. This makes it possible to gather information on the specific characteristics of the product and all the relevant information about it, which will be necessary to offer greater guarantees in the market and so that the investor can choose the product with full knowledge of it. If this analysis yields a different result than expected, the target market must be re-evaluated.

Investor information is an essential element of product governance. Therefore, the institution must offer complete and detailed information on the target public, the characteristics of the product, its profitability, its risk, its past performance, if any, the cost of disinvestment, as well as all those issues that are relevant to guarantee adequate investor protection. The aim is to overcome the insurers' exclusive search for greater profits by offering adequate information to the insured, which will be of benefit to them. In this sense, it is convenient to avoid confusing denominations that do not reflect the reality of the product and should be offered following those that adjust to the nature of the product and avoid confusion with it.

Likewise, one of the issues that must be addressed from the beginning is the product's distribution strategy. To this end, it will be advisable to establish the distribution channels through which the product is to be offered and to assess the need to prioritise a channel according to the type of product or the potential customer for whom it is designed.

Appropriate measures should also be taken to ensure constant monitoring of product development by establishing thresholds to which the product must conform, thus making it possible to know whether it is developing as planned and, where appropriate, to take measures to correct any deviation that could have a negative impact on the investor, and the distributors and investors concerned should be informed of the adoption of such measures.

2.2 Regulatory Framework Applicable to the Insurance Sector

The implementation of Directive 2004/39/EC of the European Parliament and of the Council of 21 April 2004 on markets in financial instruments (MiFID) initiated the process of establishing a European-wide regulatory framework for protection in the financial system. Subsequently, Directive 2009/138/EC of the European Parliament and of the Council of 25 November 2009 on the taking up and pursuit of the business of Insurance and Reinsurance (Solvency II Directive) contemplated, in relation to corporate governance, a series of duties to promote appropriate risk management by improving internal management and promoting self-monitoring measures for insurance companies.[6] Following this, Directive 2014/65 of the European Parliament and of the Council of 15 May 2014 on markets in financial instruments (MiFID II Directive) consolidated the regulations on this matter, the impact of which is unquestionable for the insurance sector.[7] A few months later, Regulation 1286/2014 of the European Parliament and of the Council of 26 November 2014, on key information documents relating to PRIIPs and insurance-based investment products was adopted. Directive 2016/97 of the European Parliament and of the Council of 20 January 2016 on insurance distribution sets out product governance criteria for insurance distribution, covering product governance requirements in the insurance sector, as well as establishing a legal regime for the insurance intermediary.

This legislation is further developed by delegated Regulations and Directives. Delegated Directive 2017/593 implements MiFID II by setting out product governance obligations for investment firms producing financial instruments and distributors. Similarly, Directive 2016/97 is implemented by Commission Delegated Regulation 2017/2358 of 21 September 2017 as regards control and product governance requirements for insurers and insurance distributors as well as Commission Delegated Regulation 2017/2359 as regards disclosure requirements and conduct of business rules applicable to the distribution of insurance-based investment products. These latter Delegated Regulations, among others, have been subsequently amended to adapt to sustainability factors, risks and preferences and, due to their importance, will be considered in another chapter of this paper.

Finally, it is worth noting the technical guidelines established, inter alia, by the European Securities and Markets Authority (ESMA),[8] the European Banking Authority (EBA)[9] and the European Insurance and Occupational Pensions Authority (EIOPA)[10] on governance and oversight procedures for these products.

All this makes up a regulatory framework that has progressively advanced in strengthening the financial system in general, the investor's protection and, in particular, in improving management by financial institutions and insurance companies.

[6]Paragraph 1.8 of the EIOPA Guidelines (2016). On this, Hernández Barros and Martínez Torre-Enciso (2010), pp. 75–91; Pérez Frutuoso and Gragera Cubero (2018), pp. 219–245.

[7]Peñas Moyano (2020b), p. 883 with quote from Marano (2017), p. 417 expose that the EU is considered to have adopted a process of "mifidisation" in the field of insurance.

[8]ESMA (2014), p. 332.

[9]BDE (2016).

[10]EIOPA (2016).

2.3 *Product Governance in the Insurance Sector*

2.3.1 Entities Obliged and Excluded from the Application of the Regulation

The insurance industry has been forced in recent years to adopt constant changes to adapt to new regulations on insurance products.[11]

Product governance implies an improvement in the governance of insurance companies and thus aims to offer investor protection in various ways. Therefore, these measures should be implemented globally for all insurance and investment products.

First, it should be recalled that insurance producers can be insurance undertakings on the one hand and insurance intermediaries on the other hand. The latter are divided into intermediaries who are insurance preparers or producers and intermediaries who are only insurance distributors. Delegated Regulation 2017/2358 makes a clear distinction in terms of duties between producers, which may be insurance undertakings or producer intermediaries, and distributors, which are non-producer intermediaries.[12]

The obligation to implement product governance measures rests with insurers and insurance intermediaries insofar as they are responsible for the development of products offered for sale to customers.[13] Producers are responsible for the product approval process and the choice of distribution channels. As far as insurance distributors are concerned, they are responsible for obtaining from the producer the necessary information on insurance products in order to offer it to customers in an appropriate manner, and for informing the producer when the product is not in line with the defined target market, its interests or objectives. This is intended to ensure comprehensive investor protection, irrespective of the method of contracting, thus guaranteeing that any party involved in the product design, development and distribution process complies with product governance processes.[14] In those cases where insurance companies or insurance distributors play a key role in the design and development of the product, they will be considered producers.

Therefore, the producer will be considered to be the person in charge of designing the insurance product and responsible for maintaining, managing, and reviewing its

---

[11] Peñas Moyano (2020a), p. 9, "There is, in principle, no exclusion regarding the application of product governance to any particular type of insurance contract. The regulation is applicable both to newly created insurance products because they have not yet been marketed and to those which have been substantially modified after a period of marketing, as provided for in Art. 1 of the Delegated Regulation. It is also applicable to all types of products, from the simplest to the most complex."

[12] On insurance distributors, Vercher Moll (2021), pp. 179–195.

[13] Zunzunegui (2021b), p. 90, "we are facing a transition of the sector towards financialisation, which is reflected in the actions of supervisors."

[14] Peñas Moyano (2020a), p. 6, understands that insurance comparators are included as a distribution activity when they allow the direct or indirect conclusion of an insurance contract at the end of the process.

approval process, and must carry out this task individually and before the marketing or distribution of the product, taking into consideration the nature of the product.[15] Specifically, it is considered that to interpret the relevance of the role of the insurer or distributor, the independent determination of the essential elements of the product, such as the target market, coverage, costs, price, risk, and guarantee rights must be taken into consideration, provided that the insurance company offering the coverage for this product does not modify the above elements in a relevant manner, i.e. that the conditions initially foreseen are maintained.[16]

In the case of producers, an insurer and an insurance intermediary shall agree on a protocol providing for the method of defining the target market for the product and the roles of each in the approval of the product.

In any case, large exposure insurance[17] and all those that are personalised products are excluded from the application of the product governance rules, as it is considered that in this case, it is not necessary to offer such intensive investor protection.

2.3.2 Product Governance Requirements in the Insurance Sector

The need to provide investors in insurance-based products with certain guarantees has led to the imposition of certain obligations on producers.[18]

First, as mentioned above, the target market must be determined. However, in the case of the insurance sector, due to its particularities, the potential clients whose profile fits the product must be determined in detail, taking into consideration the risk, nature, characteristics, and complexity of the insurance product, as well as the financial culture of the selected market and the information available to them.[19] To ensure that the product design complies with these requirements, producers should ensure that the personnel responsible for the design and configuration of the insurance product are properly trained and have the necessary experience and knowledge to be able to understand the insurance products and the potential target market.

Once the target market has been determined, the market behaviour of the target market should be checked beforehand, without prejudice to the subsequent control described below, by testing it in different scenarios.[20] This has two purposes. On the one hand, knowing the product considers the variability of the market and, therefore, being able to offer this information to the investor. On the other hand, if the tests are

[15] Article 3 of Delegated Regulation 2017/2358.

[16] Tapia Hermida (2018), p. 6.

[17] Article 25.4 Directive 2016/97.

[18] De Polis (2020), pp. 4–7.

[19] Hernández Barros (2015), pp. 61–70.

[20] Zunzunegui (2021a), pp. 413–428.

not favourable, to rule out a certain target market and be able to readapt it according to the test result.[21]

In any case, producers should set a specific deadline for reviewing insurance products once they have been introduced on the market. The timeframe will vary depending on the characteristics of the product and the market situation. Such monitoring should ensure that the insurance product continues to meet the objectives envisaged from the outset and that the essential features are maintained after introduction into the financial system, with particular attention to the target market. It will have to be monitored whether it is being distributed to the originally intended market or whether it has been diverted to other unintended markets. If these controls detect any anomaly not foreseen in the product tests indicated, all necessary measures must be taken by the producers to avoid any circumstance detrimental to the investor, and these facts must be brought to the attention of the insurance distributors and the investors who may have been affected. On the contrary, but with the same purpose, if the distributors detect that the insurance product does not in practice meet the objectives of the target market or that any cause that could adversely affect the investor is noticed, they shall inform the producer and where appropriate, cease distribution of the product.[22]

In the distribution of the product, producers must select the distribution channels, which must be adjusted to the needs of the target market according to its own characteristics. Likewise, producers must inform distributors in a complete, clear, and detailed manner about the target market, the characteristics of the product, the risks, the costs, and the proposed distribution strategy to enable them to properly understand the insurance product and to identify customers who might be interested in the product.[23] In this regard, insurance distributors should ensure that they obtain all necessary information from the producer and ensure that they understand the nature and complexity of the product adequately.[24] This is to protect the investor by ensuring that their objectives and interests are considered and to ensure that they have the necessary information to take out the product.

Distributors must update the distribution mechanisms of the product to ensure that, after a certain period on the market, the product continues to be aligned with the objectives of the target market and is being distributed to the target market as indicated by the product.[25] In this respect, the producer must check on a regular basis that the distributor is in line with the distribution strategy and is distributing to the target market.

---

[21] Canalejas Merín (2019), p. 5.

[22] Almarcha Jaime (2016).

[23] On the information to be provided by insurance intermediaries under Directive 2002/92, Bataller Grau (2007), p. 77.

[24] On this, Armour et al. (2016), p. 57.

[25] Marano (2020), p. 868.

The aim is to ensure that the agents involved in the insurance sector strengthen their governance[26] and offer protection to investors from the very moment the product is designed, taking into account their objectives and interests from the initial stages of product development, which allows the product to be adapted to their needs, thus ensuring that the investor has adequate guarantees to carry out the investment.

3 Sustainable Investments

3.1 Concept

Sustainability is a multi-faceted concept that, in recent years, has become increasingly important in a wide variety of areas. The financial sector has not been oblivious to this reality,[27] and is increasingly involved, either voluntarily or by legal obligation in the implementation of sustainable measures.[28] The Environmental, Social and Governance (ESG) criteria have brought about a gradual but significant change in the financial sector, seeking an orderly transition towards a process of neutral environmental impact and decarbonisation[29] in the financial sector, given the detrimental effects that this can have on the environment.[30]

The European Union is committed to combat climate change and environmental issues on a number of fronts, through different avenues that directly and indirectly affect the financial sector. Support for the Paris Agreement and the UN's 2030 Agenda for Sustainable Development and the development of the European Green Pact, which contains ambitious environmental commitments, demonstrate the EU's interest in tackling climate change.[31] Particularly, the Commission's Communication on the Action Plan: Financing for Sustainable Development 2018 sets out concrete targets that aim, among other things and in different ways, to boost sustainable investment in order to increase financing for sustainable development and thus achieve European and international goals for improving the environment.

---

[26] On this, Gallego Sánchez (2019), p. 211 and Spainsif (2021), p. 20, "Governance as the backbone of the company is a tool that facilitates the achievement of the environmental and social objectives of the entities and, therefore, of the higher state or European plans."

[27] Sjafjell (2019), pp. 163–165.

[28] Siri and Shanshan (2020), pp. 3–5.

[29] In this regard, the Commission communication "Stepping up Europe's climate ambition for 2030: Investing in a climate-neutral future for the benefit of our people," SWD (2020). In this case, decarbonisation means the process of achieving reductions in greenhouse gas emissions, primarily those in the form of carbon dioxide.

[30] A reference on the impact of the market on the environment is the report by Stern (2007).

[31] Siri and Zhu (2019).

3.2 Measures Taken by the EU

3.2.1 European Taxonomy of Sustainable Activities

One of the main challenges for the EU is to facilitate the raising of capital to support sustainable growth and decarbonisation of the European economy to meet EU and international climate targets. To this end, the European taxonomy of sustainable activities is the basis on which the European Sustainable Finance Standard is being developed. This standard is essential to reduce the fragmentation caused by different classifications in different EU countries and to reduce transaction costs in the markets.

Regulation 2020/852 of the European Parliament and of the Council of 18 June 2020 on establishing a framework to facilitate sustainable investments provides a common classification system for economic activities whose contribution to achieving environmental objectives is relevant[32] according to scientific criteria. This implies that the market has a common definition of sustainability and makes it possible to identify concrete objectives that can be met through economic activity. These environmental objectives are the sustainable use and protection of water and marine resources, the transition to a circular economy, the prevention and control of pollution, and the protection and restoration of biodiversity and ecosystems. This will also combat the so-called “greenwashing,” as this common definition, based on scientific criteria, will prevent products from being offered as environmentally friendly if they do not meet the criteria set out in European legislation.[33]

This regulation seeks to establish the requirements that economic activity must meet to be considered sustainable and to be able to provide information on the impact of investments on the environment.[34] It is understood that economic activity is environmentally sustainable when it meets four requirements, namely: the activity makes a substantial contribution to one or more of the six environmental objectives set out in the Regulation, does not cause significant damage to any of these objectives,[35] is carried out in accordance with the procedures of the OECD, the UN and other international conventions, and complies with the technical criteria established by the Commission in implementation of the Regulation.

This ensures that there are standard criteria throughout the EU that allow, without specific technical knowledge, to know and apply the necessary measures to be able to classify products as sustainable.[36] At the same time, it also makes it easier for

---

[32] As foreseen in the Regulation, the relevance of the contribution is determined by the specific objective pursued.

[33] Murillo García (2020), p. 16.

[34] Recalde Castells (2022), p. 17.

[35] The aim is to prevent an investment that is considered environmentally sustainable from causing more damage than the contribution it makes.

[36] LMA, APLMA (2021).

investors to find out quickly and easily what criteria have been used to qualify the product in this way, offering confidence and security in the market.[37]

Undoubtedly, regulation at the European level makes it possible to homogenise the criteria for classifying activities, given that, if each state were allowed to set its own taxonomy, it would generate a disincentive for investors to carry out cross-border operations by having a regulation with different criteria. This would also mean that actors in the financial sector would be forced to adapt their products according to the interests of each state, and a certain product could be labelled as sustainable in one state and not be so in a neighbouring state due to the different classifications of each of them. This would generate a fragmentation of the market that would be contrary to the purpose of the EU itself.

To clarify the specific aspects of Regulation 2020/852, Delegated Regulation 2021/2139 has been adopted, as amended by Delegated Regulation 2022/1214, which establishes the technical selection criteria for considering that an economic activity makes a substantial contribution to climate change mitigation and does not cause significant harm to environmental objectives. This Delegated Regulation sets out the regulatory technical standards (RTS) that implement Articles 10 and 11 of the Taxonomy Regulation and harmonise the criteria for screening, disclosure, and verification of market activities so that they can be considered environmentally sustainable.

In any case, we are at an early stage in the implementation of the taxonomy of sustainable activities. There are many issues that this taxonomy must overcome to be successful and to fulfil the functions envisaged by the EU. The truth is that for the moment, this regulation is difficult to apply to small and medium-sized enterprises, which make up the majority of the social fabric, as well as to companies from outside the EU due to the high cost of verifying compliance with the requirements. Likewise, it is still necessary to have a greater business culture on the subject, given that the lack of adequate and complete information on the product makes it difficult to qualify it, which can lead to it not being considered sustainable even though it is in fact complying with European regulations. So far only a small percentage of listed companies have sustainable revenues according to the European taxonomy, limiting the possibilities for sustainable investment in the EU.[38]

It is therefore an undoubtedly positive measure, but one that is still in its infancy and will need to be further developed and promoted in the coming years.

3.2.2 Product Information Disclosure Duties

Information on environmental data is essential to establish the sustainability of investments. It is therefore necessary to provide investors with information on sustainability risks, sustainable investment objectives and the environmental

[37] Calvo Vérgez (2021), pp. 119–144.

[38] Romo González (2021), p. 16.

characteristics of a product to be able to make a fully informed, rigorous, and consistent choice from the wide range of products available on the market.[39]

Directive 2013/34 of the European Parliament and of the Council of 26 June 2013 established a number of transparency obligations in the disclosure of non-financial information relating to social, environmental and governance issues. However, this regulation was not as effective as expected because the format and presentation required meant that such information was not usually passed on to the end investor.[40] Regulation 2019/2088 of the European Parliament and of the Council of 27 November 2019 aims to set harmonising rules on transparency in financial markets regarding sustainability risks, adverse impacts at the entity level, remuneration policies, integration of sustainability risks, transparency of environmental characteristics of sustainable investments in pre-contractual information, websites, and periodic reports.

Regulation 2020/852 intensively strengthens the regulation of disclosure obligations in the financial sector. It establishes the obligation to provide certain information on the sustainability of financial products in accordance with the taxonomy established by the regulation itself. Specifically, where a financial product targets sustainable investments, it shall specify which of the objectives set out in the regulation the investment underlying the financial product contributes to, and shall describe how and to what extent the investments are directed towards economic activities that are considered environmentally sustainable, including information on the proportion of enabling and transitional activities and the total percentage of the investments selected for the financial product.[41]

Furthermore, in the case of financial products that aim to promote environmental features, they must additionally disclose in a statement whether or not the investment in question complies with the requirements set out in the Regulation in relation to the concept of "not causing significant harm to the environment," compliance with which is necessary to qualify an economic activity as sustainable. The statement to be included states that "the principle of 'no significant harm' applies only to investments underlying the financial product that meet the EU criteria for environmentally sustainable economic activities." The investments underlying the rest of the financial product do not take into account the EU criteria for environmentally sustainable economic activities.

In terms of pre-contractual information and periodic reports, for those products that are not subject to Article 8 or 9 of Regulation 2019/2088, but are required to comply with non-financial disclosure obligations, they are required to include a statement indicating that "the investments underlying this financial product do not

[39] Mínguez Prieto (2022), pp. 8–15.

[40] As stated in recital 2 of Directive 2014/95 of the European Parliament and of the Council of 22 October 2014.

[41] This is without prejudice to other information to be included, e.g. for products with a carbon emission reduction target, a detailed explanation of how the low carbon emission target is ensured to meet the long-term global warming objectives as foreseen in Article 9(3) of Regulation 2019/2088.

take into account the EU criteria for environmentally sustainable economic activities."

Similarly, on the transparency of companies in non-financial statements, the regulation requires companies to disclose in their non-financial statement or consolidated non-financial statement information on how and to what extent the company's activities are associated with economic activities that are considered sustainable. Particularly, it shall indicate the proportion of its turnover that comes from products or services related to sustainable economic activities, as well as the proportion of its total fixed assets and the proportion of its operating expenses related to assets or processes associated with sustainable economic activities. Compliance with these requirements must be carried out by the competent authorities in each sector in relation to the financial intermediary.

In any case, to harmonise Regulation 2019/2088 and Regulation 2022/852, Article 25 of the latter regulation provides, as a final provision, for Regulation 2019/2088 to be amended to draw up detailed regulatory technical standards on the content and presentation of the information. The result is Commission Delegated Regulation 2022/1288 of 6 April 2022, which supplements Regulation 2019/2088 and lays down regulatory technical standards determining the content and presentation of information on the "no significant harm" principle[42] and establishes and supplements the methods and presentation of information on sustainability indicators and the identification of specific sustainable investment targets in pre-contractual documents. This facilitates the work of stakeholders in the financial sector and supervisors by providing templates that structure the information, the benefit of which will also accrue to the investor as the information can be compared in a more comprehensive and user-friendly way.[43]

This provision is therefore intended to ensure that those involved in the financial sector can be fully, comprehensively, and detailedly informed of all information on financial products and their relationship with environmentally sustainable activities.

4 Product Governance Applied to Sustainable Investments

4.1 Relevance of the Issue to the Insurance Sector

The Commission's 2018 Action Plan: Financing sustainable development indicates that insurance companies are an important source of external financing for the European economy but that they may be affected by risks related to unsustainable economic development.[44] The Commission understands that risks related to climate and other environmental factors may lead to a lack of credibility and effectiveness of

[42] Known as the DNSH (Do No Significant Harm) principle.

[43] On this, Iñiguez Ortega (2022); Palá Laguna (2022); Llopis Blanque (2023).

[44] On this, Internacional Association of Insurance Supervisors, (2018).

the EU prudential framework and its risk-based nature. However, it recognises that insurance distributors can play a key role in reorienting the financial system towards sustainability.[45] The UN through the Environment Programme Finance Initiative and specifically in the Principles for Sustainable Insurance states that sustainable insurance aims to reduce risk, develop innovative solutions, improve business performance, and contribute to environmental, social, and economic sustainability.

The 2021 Social Report on Insurance[46] stresses that the important role of insurance as an institutional investor allows it to act as an instrument for change in the financial system. Thus, three quarters of the sector in Spain consider ESG criteria in the configuration of its investment portfolio. In turn, a quarter of the entities that market savings products have some product that complies with the environmental or social characteristics set out in EU sustainability regulations.

The importance of the insurance sector in promoting a shift in the financial market towards investments in environmentally sustainable activities is therefore undeniable.

4.2 Impact of Sustainable Investments on the Governance of the Product

The product governance regulations discussed above are complemented by Delegated Regulation 2021/1257 which amends Delegated Regulations 2017/2358 and 2017/2359 mentioned above to include sustainability factors, risks and preferences in the control and governance requirements for investment products of insurance undertakings and establishes conduct of business and advisory rules for these insurance-based investment products.

Considering the importance of the sector in achieving sustainable economic growth, there is an obligation to take sustainability factors into account in product governance requirements from the time of design and approval for a market that is interested in sustainable insurance products.

During the process of developing and approving the insurance-based investment product, the target market should be defined in sufficient detail, taking into account, in addition to the product features, risk profile, complexity and other product circumstances described earlier in this paper, the sustainability factors. Sustainability factors in this respect are understood to include information on environmental and social issues, employee issues, respect for human rights, and anti-corruption.[47] Therefore, a general classification of the product as sustainable is insufficient, but it should be designed and marketed with the sustainability objectives of the target

[45] Cousy (2009), p. 245, considers that insurance has traditionally been neglected in financial regulation.

[46] UNESPA (2022).

[47] Seventh recital of Directive 2022/2464.

market in mind, always taking into account the level of information of the customers and their financial literacy. Product developers should be qualified to understand the sustainability objectives and characteristics of the target market.[48]

On product testing, sustainability factors should be taken into consideration in terms of how the product will perform in the market during its life cycle and whether it would meet the sustainability objectives and the objectives of the target market throughout its life cycle. Thus, products that after testing are found not to meet the sustainability objectives and the needs of the target market, cannot be placed on the market. In any case, it must be ensured that customers' sustainability concerns are duly taken into account. Therefore, if the insurance distributor detects that a product is not in line with the sustainability interests of the established target market, it should bring this to the attention of the producer to modify the distribution strategy of the product.[49]

Therefore, this regulation establishes that sustainability must be taken into consideration throughout the product development, approval, and distribution process to ensure that environmentally sustainable products reach the target market after having been developed for this purpose, having undergone a detailed and complete analysis of the customer profile and having passed product testing and that there is a control process for compliance with the provisions of the product approval for the protection of the investor.

4.3 *Impact of Sustainable Investments on Information Requirements in Product Distribution*

Delegated Regulation 2017/2359 on information requirements and conduct of business rules for the distribution of insurance-based investment products is amended by Delegated Regulation 2021/1257 to introduce sustainability preferences.

Investors must be informed of their sustainability preferences, i.e. whether they wish to include a sustainable financial product in their investment to a greater or lesser extent. To this end, in the product selection process and the investor's suitability assessment, investors must be asked whether they have sustainability preferences and, if so, what percentage of their investment they wish to allocate to sustainability. The client should then be offered a threefold possibility to realise these sustainability preferences. First, the investor may choose investments that are considered sustainable under the criteria and requirements of Regulation 2020/852 as set out above. Second, the investor may invest in products that are sustainable under Regulation 2019/2088. Finally, the option should be offered to invest in products that take into consideration the main adverse impacts on sustainability

[48] Zunzunegui (2021a, b).

[49] On the consideration and protection of investors as consumers, Gimeno Beviá (2015), pp. 312–314.

factors, i.e. that manage the negative impacts that the investment may have on climate issues, with the qualitative or quantitative elements being determined by the investor.

The favouring of environmentally sustainable activities is gradual in these options, with the first option being more favourable to sustainable economic activities because of the type of activities invested in under Regulation 2020/852, and the last option being less favourable to sustainable economic activities because it is only investments in products that take into consideration the adverse effects of the activity. Insurance intermediaries should be able to explain the different degrees of sustainability to the investor in such a way that the investor can understand the difference between the different types of sustainability.

In any case, it should be pointed out that, at present, taking into account that this is a relatively recently approved regulation, few investment products comply with the strict requirements of Regulation 2020/852, and the investor has limited choice, with greater variety in the case of the third option, which does not have the same sustainability requirements. In any case, this is a good start for investors to begin to be aware of the different sustainability preferences available, and a greater culture in the financial sector on this type of product is needed to broaden the offer of environmentally sustainable products, which will undoubtedly allow investors to choose the option that best suits their interests.

It should be made clear that the suitability assessment will comprise a series of questions to enable recommendations to be made based on their financial objectives and sustainability preferences. In any case, to avoid any potential for abuse in the distribution of these products, the investment objectives and the specific situation of each investor should be assessed first, followed by questions on their sustainability preferences. In addition, clients who have already completed the suitability assessment prior to this regulatory provision should be able to express their preferences on sustainability factors in the next periodic update of the suitability assessment.

Insurance intermediaries shall not recommend products where there is a conflict of interest and products that do not match the customer's expressed sustainability preferences and shall explain the reasons for this to the customer and keep a record of this. If the customer decides to adapt their sustainability preferences when no product is in line with their preferences, the decision, and the reasons for it must be recorded to avoid mis-selling and greenwashing.

4.4 Integrating Sustainability Risks into Governance

Sustainability has also affected insurers in terms of integrating sustainability risks into the governance of insurers. Commission Delegated Regulation 2021/1256 of 21 April 2021 amends Delegated Regulation 2015/35 and integrates these sustainability risks. The Commission aims to ensure that the governance system of insurance undertakings and the assessment of overall solvency needs reflect sustainability risks. To this end, it defines sustainability risk as any environmental or governance event or condition that, if it were to occur, could have an actual or potential negative effect on the value of the investment or the value of the liability.

It provides for the need to review and adapt risk management policies to integrate sustainability risks in the terms expressed. Likewise, information on how the integration of sustainability risks into the risk management system is taken into consideration should be included in the remuneration policy, given the importance of remuneration policies in ensuring that the risks identified by the risk management system are effectively managed by the insurer's personnel. Similarly, the actuarial function should consider sustainability risks when reviewing the underwriting policy of the insurer.

Finally, the integration of sustainability risks into the principle of prudence is foreseen, whereby sustainability risks should be taken into consideration when determining, managing, and monitoring the risks arising from investments,[50] considering the potential long-term impact of their investment strategy on sustainability factors, and the sustainability preferences of investors should be reflected in these strategies and decisions.

5 Conclusions

The European Union's 2018 Action Plan for Financing Sustainable Development marked a starting point for a significant structural shift in the financial system. To redirect financial investments towards activities that address climate change and achieve environmental objectives, the Regulation on the Taxonomy of Sustainable Activities was approved. The objective of this regulation is to set common criteria for what should be considered environmentally sustainable activities. The EU is aware that the volume of investment to meet environmental objectives requires the financial system to develop instruments of a private nature. This will allow the necessary savings and monetary resources to be channelled to transformative sustainable investments that will help meet the objectives of a circular economy and respond to current environmental needs.

Product governance has become one of the main factors in facilitating this investment by providing security to investors in the product. The aim is to offer financial products that have been previously created by the entity following specific internal processes. The interests and objectives of the potential target market will be taken into consideration from the very beginning of the product's design, and the specific client for whom it is intended will be established. Likewise, the product is subjected to certain tests to obtain complete and detailed information on the charac-

[50] On the incorporation of environmental, social and corporate governance issues into investment analysis processes, Bataller Grau and Córdoba-Mochales (2020), pp. 21–47.

teristics of the product, its response in future scenarios, its adaptation to crisis situations, its possible profitability, etc. All this information will be provided to the investor, who will be able to select the investment product with the best guarantees and with full information on the product, a key element being the information offered to the investor.

The insurance sector has a key role to play in realigning investments towards sustainable activities. Therefore, insurance-based investment products should be designed taking into consideration the governance obligations of the product to ensure the investor. In any case, recent EU legislation sets out a number of obligations on producers and distributors of insurance products to include sustainability factors, risks, and preferences in the governance requirements of investment products. Sustainability factors must be taken into consideration in the governance requirements from the initial design and approval of the product, as well as in its distribution. On product testing in the governance framework, it should be analysed whether the originally envisaged sustainability objectives would be met over the estimated life of the product. In addition, investors should be informed about sustainability preferences and may include a financial product in their investment. Investors should be offered a triple investment choice of sustainable products, which will vary according to their objectives and interests. The investor will be able to select products that meet the sustainability requirements under Regulation 2020/852 (Taxonomy Regulation), products that are considered sustainable under Regulation 2019/2088 (Disclosure Regulation) or products that take into consideration the main issues on sustainability factors. The choice of one option or the other will depend on the interests of the investor, taking into account that the former option offers higher guarantees of sustainability of the products due to the higher requirements to be met, and the latter option offers lower guarantees of sustainability. Distributors of insurance products should provide all the information provided by the producers to the investors on the different products so that they can choose the option they consider most appropriate. However, it cannot be overlooked that at this initial stage of regulation, taking into consideration that the regulations establishing these obligations are recent, the reality is that the options for investors seeking to invest in environmentally sustainable economic activities are still limited. In any case, the paradigm shift is inexorable and still a long way off, so that in the coming years the options for investors will increase, fulfilling the objective of offering a variety of products and extensive information on them.

In conclusion, product governance plays a crucial role in the investment in environmentally sustainable activities within the insurance sector, as it helps overcome the traditional hesitations of investors towards such products. This is achieved through a strict product design, development, and distribution process that takes into account the interests of the target market. Additionally, it provides comprehensive and detailed information about the products, thereby offering security and confidence to the investors.

References

Almarcha Jaime J (2016) La nueva Directiva sobre la distribución de seguros: hacia la MiFID del sector asegurador. GA_P, Madrid

Armour J, Awrey D et al (2016) Principles of financial regulation. Oxford University Press, Oxford

Bataller Grau J (2007) La incesante reforma del derecho del seguro: ¿Último acto? In: Cuñat Edo V, Bataller Grau J (eds) Comentarios a la ley de mediación de seguros y reaseguros privados. Aranzadi Thomson Reuters, Navarra

Bataller Grau J, Córdoba-Mochales I (2020) Capital riesgo y la responsabilidad social de la empresa. Revista Española de Capital Riesgo , 1/2020

BDE (2016) Directrices sobre procedimientos de gobernanza y vigilancia de productos de banca minorista. EBA/GL/2015/18.

Calvo Vérgez J (2021) La delimitación del concepto de "inversión financiera sostenible." El papel de los llamados "bonos verdes.". Revista Aranzadi de derecho ambiental, 50

Canalejas Merín JF (2019) Las obligaciones de gobernanza de producto en la MiFiD II y su transposición al Derecho español. Revista de Derecho del Mercado de Valores, 24

Cousy H (2009) Le secteur des assurances será-t-il mifidisé. Bulletin des Assurances, 89

De Polis S (2020) Dalle regole alla vigilanza di condotta. La product oversight governance dei prodotti assicurativi Profili giuridici e operative. Istituto per la vigilanza sulle assicurazioni.

EIOPA (2016) Directrices preparatorias relativas a los procedimientos de gobernanza y vigilancia de productos para las empresas de seguros y los distribuidores de seguros, Bos-16/071.

ESMA (2014) Structured retail products – good practices for product governance arrangements. 332.

Fernández Pérez N (2019) Instrumentos financieros complejos y su tratamiento jurisprudencial. In: Castillo Martínez C (ed) Jurisprudencia sobre hipotecas y contratos bancarios y financieros: Análisis de la jurisprudencia reciente sobre préstamos, créditos, cláusulas de préstamos hipotecarios, contratos bancarios, tarjetas, productos financieros y usura. Tirant lo Blanch, Valencia

Gallego Sánchez E (2019) El derecho de la sociedad emisora a conocer la identidad de los accionistas. In: Rodríguez Artigas F et al (eds) Sociedades cotizadas y transparencia en los mercados. Aranzadi Thomson Reuters, Navarra

Gimeno Beviá V (2015) La tutela de inversores y consumidores frente a la contratación de productos financieros complejos. In: Demetrio Crespo E et al (eds) Corrupción y delincuencia económica. Ediciones Jurídicas Castillo de Luna, Madrid

Hernández Barros R (2015) Los riesgos de las entidades aseguradoras en el marco del Enterprise Risk Management (ERM) y el control interno. Innovar, edición especial.

Hernández Barros R, Martínez Torre-Enciso MI (2010) La nueva regulación europea de seguros privados: Solvencia II. Boletín de estudios económicos, 65

Iñiguez Ortega P (2022) Perspectivas actuales del sistema de clasificación unificado europeo: hacia un inversor catalizador de productos financieros verdes. Revista de Derecho del Mercado de Valores 31

Internacional Association of Insurance Supervisors (2018) Issues paper on climate change risks to the insurance sector.

Llopis Blanque A (2023) La incidencia de las tecnologías de registro distribuido y criptoactivos y su normativa de desarrollo sobre los sistemas multilaterales de negociación y los inversores minoristas. Revista de Derecho del Sistema Financiero, 5

LMA, APLMA (2021) Green loan principles. Supporting environmentally sustainable economic activity. Loan Market Association.

Marano P (2017) La "mifidización": el atardecer de los seguros de vida en la normativa europea de seguros? Revista Española de Seguros:171–172

Marano P (2019) The product oversight and governance: standards and liabilities. In: Marano P, Rokas I (eds) Distribution of insurance-based investment products. Springer, Cham

Marano P (2020) La contribución de la supervisión y gobernanza de productos (POG) al mercado único: un conjunto de reglas organizativas para la conducta empresarial. In: Vega Copo AB (ed) Retos y desafíos del contrato de seguro: del necesario aggiornamento a la metamorfosis del contrato. Aranzadi, Navarra

Mínguez Prieto R (2022) El impacto del marco normativo ESG en las operaciones de financiación crediticia bancaria y en las de los mercados de renta fija. Revista de Derecho del Mercado de Valores 30

Moya Ballester J (2019) Deberes de información de las entidades emisoras de valores distintos de las acciones admitidos a negociación en mercados secundarios oficiales. In: Rodríguez Artigas F et al (eds) Sociedades cotizadas y transparencia en los mercados. Aranzadi Thomson Reuters, Navarra

Murillo García UE (2020) Reglamento de taxonomía de la UE de actividades económicas sostenibles. Boletín Económico de ICE, 3126

Palá Laguna R (2019) La aplicación de la MIFID II y la teoría del caos. Revista de Derecho del Mercado de Valores 24

Palá Laguna R (2022) Desarrollo normativo del Reglamento sobre la divulgación de información relativa a la sostenibilidad en el sector de los servicios financieros. GA_P, Madrid

Peñas Moyano MJ (2020a) De la información al cliente a la gobernanza del producto: una evolución necesaria en el sector asegurador. Revista de Derecho del Mercado de Valores, 26

Peñas Moyano MJ (2020b) Gobernanza de producto y distribución de seguros. In: Vega Copo AB (ed) Retos y desafíos del contrato de seguro: del necesario aggiornamento a la metamorfosis del contrato. Aranzadi, Navarra

Pérez Frutuoso MJ, Gragera Cubero J (2018) Análisis y gestión del riesgo operacional en las entidades financieras y aseguradoras. Una comparativa. Revista Ibero-Latinoamericana Seguros, 49

Recalde Castells A (2022) La obligación de las sociedades de identificar, reducir y reparar los efectos adversos sobre el medioambiente y los derechos humanos (Notas a la propuesta de directiva sobre "diligencia debida"-"due diligence" en materia de sostenibilidad). Revista de Derecho Mercantil, 326

Romo González LA (2021) Una taxonomía de actividades sostenibles para Europa. Banco de España, Documentos Ocasionales 2101.

Siri M, Shanshan Z (2020) L'integrazione della sostenibilità nel sistema europeo di protezione degli investitori. Banca Impresa Società

Siri M, Zhu S (2019) Will the EU Commission successfully integrate sustainability risks and factors in the investor protection regime? A research agenda. Sustainability, 11 6292

Sjafjell B (2019) Integrating sustainability into the duties of the corporate board. In: Martínez-Echevarría A (ed) Interés social y gobierno corporativo sostenible: deberes de los administradores y deberes de los accionistas. Aranzadi Thomson Reuters, Navarra

Spainsif - Foro español de inversión socialmente responsable (2021) La gobernanza en las finanzas sostenibles. Ministerio de Trabajo y Economía Social.

Stern N (2007) The economics of climate change: the Stern review. Cambridge University Press, Cambridge

Tapia Hermida AJ (2018) El retraso en la aplicación de la Directiva 2016/97 de distribución de seguros y su impacto en el Derecho español. La Ley Unión Europea 59.

UNESPA (2022) Memoria Social del Seguro 2021. Una visión de la gestión del seguro desde una perspectiva ambiental, social y de gobernanza. Madrid.

Vercher Moll FJ (2021) Insurance distribution carried out by insurers in Spain. In: Marano P, Noussia K (eds) Insurance distribution directive. AIDA Europe research series on insurance law and regulation, vol 3. Springer, Cham.

Zunzunegui F (2021a) La financiarización de la distribución de seguros. Revista española de seguros 185-186

Zunzunegui F (2021b) La MiFID entra de lleno en la distribución del seguro. Asesores Financieros

Jaume Llorca Galiana is an Assistant Professor at the Department of Commercial Law at the University of Alicante. He completed his Law Degree and a Master's in Law at the University of Alicante, followed by a Master's in Taxation at the Universitat Oberta de Catalunya. He has practised as a lawyer for over four years, serving as a partner in a firm specialised in civil-commercial law.

He specialises in commercial contracting, insurance law, and intellectual property. He is a member of the Research Networks at the University of Alicante. Llorca Galiana is a bi-monthly contributor to the digital magazine La Ley, analysing themes such as digital contracting, blockchain, and smart contracts. He has numerous publications in collective works and journals concerning his research area in Commercial Law. He has been a part of the evaluation and accreditation committee for university degrees within the social and legal sciences field. He also serves on Scientific and Organisational Committees for various seminars and conferences in the realm of commercial law. Additionally, he has participated in various national and international conferences. He is a member of the Spanish Section of the International Insurance Law Association (SEAIDA).

He teaches commercial law across various degree programmes at the University of Alicante, as well as in the Master's in Intellectual Property and Digital Innovation, Magister Lvcentinvs, at the same institution.

Sustainable Investment Challenges from the Perspective of Insurance Companies in the European and Polish Market

Marianna Cicirko

1 Introduction

The latest IPCC report confirmed that climate change is a strategic topic. Therefore, environmental, social and governance (ESG) measures have become a decisive factor in business analyses and investment strategies. Recent studies have pointed in different directions, some indicate that green investments are associated with lower financial returns and others argue in favour of superior returns from ESG endeavours. Although the experience of investors with ESG principles is still shallow, some of them see ESG as a business opportunity.

The relevance of the issue prompted the author to undertake research aimed at determining the condition of sustainable investment in the insurance sector and identifying the challenges faced by insurance companies in the field of sustainable investments with a focus on the Polish market. The article aims to present the concept of sustainable investments and ESG in Europe and Poland to indicate the opportunities and obstacles to their development. The research problem formulated for the study is the perception of sustainable investment development by experts in the Polish insurance sector. The research is qualitative exploratory, and the selected research method is individual in-depth interviews, and for its needs questions were formulated: Is the insurance sector in Europe and Poland vulnerable to climate change and to what extent?; Are the investment activities of the insurance sector particularly vulnerable to climate change?; How investment market towards sustainable investment affects the insurance sector?; What obstacles do insurance companies identify in sustainable investment?; Do the investment activities of the insurance sector require the implementation of new regulations or changes to the

M. Cicirko (✉)
Warsaw School of Economics, Department of Social Insurance, Warsaw, Poland
e-mail: marianna.cicirko@sgh.waw.pl

J. Bataller-Grau et al. (eds.), *Sustainability and the Insurance Market*, AIDA Europe Research Series on Insurance Law and Regulation 10,
https://doi.org/10.1007/978-3-031-72186-1_6

currently applicable ones? The research group was selected to present various perspectives and needs of the insurance sector. The respondents are people with many years of experience in the insurance market and having substantive knowledge about it. The study complements the research gap for Poland in terms of sustainable investment challenges from the perspective of insurance companies in the European and Polish markets.

2 Climate Change Influence, ESG Aspects and New Regulation

Global warming is the highest economic priority according to the latest IPCC report titled "Climate Change 2021" (IPCC 2021), therefore it is forcing transformation of the entire economy. The impact depends on the extent to which the economic activity relies on natural resources. The food and energy sectors are the most vulnerable channels. Companies relying on suppliers located in the most exposed regions to extreme weather events may face delays or price increases affecting their bottom line (Wolters Kluwer 2015). The impact on the financial sector will be twofold, on the one hand directly through climate change, and on the other indirectly by the non-financial sector. Economic losses due to natural disasters are increasing (IAIS & SIF 2018; ESRB 2020). Since the 1980s, the number of events increased more than twice, but the estimated global value of those losses increased almost 3.5 times (FSB 2020). This means that such events have become more likely and more severe (IPCC 2014, 2018). Some studies suggest that potential impacts could reduce global GDP by 2–3% annually by 2060, but other analysis suggests that the frequency and intensity of extreme weather events may increase non-linearly and become increasingly correlated with each other over time (OECD 2015).

According to EIOPA (2019), there can be two types of climate-change-related risks, also called climate risks. Those arising from specific weather events such as heatwaves, floods and rising mean temperatures are defined as physical risk. It can occur as financial assets depreciation which results in losses for asset owners or from a sharp increase in risk premium due to uncertainty about future repayments. Credit losses, in turn, can occur as reduced income or profitability of borrowers (Stenek et al. 2011) and reduction of the assets' market value, that were used as collateral. Those risks may also be concentrated in certain sectors and regions of the real economy. Estimates of the impact of physical risk on asset prices depend on the degree of global warming expectation according to the results of the studies from 2015 (EIU 2015) and 2016 (Dietz et al. 2016). In the scenario where the rise of global mean temperature is 2°C above pre-industrial level, the global financial assets will fall from 0.7% to 4.2% ($1–6 trillion). In the "baseline" scenario, where the 2010 mitigation policies are extended indefinitely, but there are no additional actions to reduce CO_2 emissions, the temperature rise will be around 4°C, the value of assets will fall from 2, 9.7% to 9.7% ($ 4–14 trillion), depending on the selected rates. The uncertainty of the climate change direction and its impact on asset prices is large and carries significant tail risk.

The second risk identified is transitional risk, which refers to government and regulatory activities, which mainly include laws on carbon emissions. Late government action which materialises in a short time will increase transitional risk for all market participants (EIOPA 2019). The transition risk materialisation may disrupt the structure of the economy including a significant reallocation of investments (FSB 2020). This can have a big impact on fossil fuel companies as well as other sectors whose business models are fossil or energy-intensive, such as heavy industry and transport (Bank of England 2018). Changes in asset prices due to economic transition do not necessarily pose a threat to financial stability, rather, they will reflect an adjustment of a properly functioning financial system by directing investments towards more climate-neutral investments (NGFS 2019). Moving to a low-carbon economy may reduce the ability of some borrowers to generate sufficient income to service and pay off their debts (Monnin 2018). Particularly, the depreciation of certain assets may also be offset by the positive effects of growth in less-emitting sectors and firms. In addition, climate policy aimed at achieving the structural economic change described above can also stimulate innovation and investment, including in low-carbon technologies (NGFS 2019). Furthermore, a shift into a low-carbon economy will jeopardise the viability of business models relying on customers in high-carbon sectors. On the other hand, it can create opportunities for the development and design of new insurance products targeted at emerging economic sectors (EIOPA 2021).

Climate risk is considered currently in three ways: as a key business problem, as an issue of sustainable development that becomes a core business or as a matter of sustainable development and environmental protection (Golnaraghi 2018). The idea of sustainable development is crucial for business strategies in terms of adjusting the economy to climate change. In the latest regulations in the European Union appeared the idea of ESG, which refers to three factors that are analysed by investors:

- an environmental factor (e.g. assets invested in green bonds)
- a social factor (e.g. investments only in companies that respect human rights)
- a corporate governance factor (e.g. pursuing a transparent information policy about its corporate governance).

Climate risk is no longer only about ESG discussion. Since the 1972 United Nations conference in Stockholm, many principles were adopted that started an international dialogue on the link between economic growth and environmental pollution. The latest important step was the adoption in 2015 by the United Nations of the global framework for economic transformation, i.e. the 2030 Agenda with defined 17 sustainable development goals. A year later, the European Commission decided to link those goals to EU policy (European Commission 2016). The year 2015 was also important due to the adoption of the first legally binding climate agreement, i.e. the Paris Agreement, the aim of which was to ensure the consistency of financial flows, lower greenhouse gas emissions and climate-resilient development. However, the financial sector was not covered by any regulations regarding the disclosure of information in the field of sustainable development. The lack of transparency and the lack of legal ESG regulations stood in the way of the full implementation of the goals of the 2030 Agenda.

Recent years have opened the way to greater transparency of disclosed information by enterprises. Regulation (EU) 2019/2088 of the European Parliament and of the Council of 27 November 2019 on sustainability-related disclosures in the financial services sector called Sustainable Finance Disclosure Regulation (SFDR) imposes transparency obligations on financial institutions regarding sustainability reporting within their investment processes. The purpose is the standardisation of published information on financial products that promote environmental and social factors or contribute to the achievement of a sustainable goal. The new regulations apply to investment products, including insurance products and pension funds. The SFDR aims at protecting final investors and improving the financial information to investors and other financial market participants. In practice, this means that market participants will have access to data such as investment volumes involved in non-renewable energy and fossil resources, deforestation, poor water and energy management, lack of respect for human rights, corruption, arms trade, etc. Financial institutions are required to publish information, including ESG risk management strategy, information about the negative impact of investment decisions, and transparency of the remuneration policy in the field of sustainable development.

According to SFDR, sustainable investment means an investment in an economic activity that contributes to an environmental objective or social objective and such investments do not significantly harm any of those objectives and that the investee companies follow good governance practices, particularly sound management structures, employee relations, remuneration of staff and tax compliance. Articles 8 and 9 of the Directive precisely define the three-tier system for dividing the products. Their distinction is important from the perspective of their appropriate adjustment to the customer's preferences in terms of supporting sustainable development. Article 8 distinguishes the so-called light green/ESG products, that can be sold as sustainable in the European Union. Disclosures about this product are based on an investment process incorporating a mix of social or environmental factors. In turn, Article 9 specifies the requirements for products referred to as dark green. These products are targeted at sustainable investors striving to achieve sustainable investment results. If the product includes investments related to ESG, but does not qualify as environmentally sustainable according to the Taxonomy (a framework to facilitate sustainable investment within the meaning of regulation 2020/852), then it will be a light green product. The investment must pursue a sustainable goal, not just avoid harming such goals. If a given product cannot be classified as light or dark green, then it is called a brown product. Importantly, SFDR does not directly regulate the issue of product nomenclature, and the name should result from the actual characteristics of the product.

Interest in investing in line with sustainable development is growing around the world. Investors notice that related issues are becoming more and more important. ESG integration can potentially affect the long-term performance of an investment. Holding companies may use different approaches to integrating ESG into their investment processes. The way ESG aspects are considered in investment strategies depends primarily on the motivations that already drive managers when deciding between traditional and sustainable market stalls.

3 ESG Investing

3.1 ESG Investment Integration

Each investor has specific goals and strategies. Consequently, responsible investing does not have a single motivation, single strategy or set of approaches that are widely used (Dimson et al. 2013). The most common motivation for considering ESG aspects is related to investment performance, followed by customer demand, product strategy, and then ethical considerations. A significant obstacle so far was the lack of reporting standards (Armel-Zadeh & Serafeim 2018, pp. 87–103). Investment managers and rating agencies can give scores to the potential investments. However, it is important to prioritise each aspect, identify the relevant factors and interpret the ESG performance in relation to the financial indicators. Investors can allocate capital to companies with a positive impact on enterprises whose development is constrained by external financing conditions. Incentives for firms to adopt ESG grow with investor participation, so screening approaches should be pursued in a large coalition of investors and include stocks and bonds (Kölbel et al. 2020, pp. 554–574).

Investors are also motivated by risk management. The risk aspect is naturally a major concern of insurance companies and other low-risk investors. However, some investors also see ESG as an investment opportunity, looking for "alpha." For example, ESG analysis can improve your understanding of long-term trends. Some investors even find new investment targets in the green and social space. The UN Principles for Responsible Investment, in turn, has created six principles of responsible investment:

1. Incorporate ESG issues into investment analysis and decision-making processes.
2. Be active owners and incorporate ESG issues into ownership policies and practices.
3. Seek appropriate disclosure on ESG issues by the entities in which you invest.
4. Promote acceptance and implementation of the principles within the investment industry.
5. Work together to enhance your effectiveness in implementing the principles.
6. Report on your activities and progress towards implementing the principles.

The ESG analysis should be based on external ESG information, preferably reports, obtained directly from entities or institutional sources. For this purpose, the investment fund should establish a dedicated ESG team. The result of the work of such a team would be the integration of financial valuation and ESG factor assessment. In pursuit of increasing returns and optimal risk management, while achieving the expected social and environmental outcomes. Investors use several methods to integrate ESG considerations into their decision-making. Moreover, different ESG approaches can be implemented with active or passive investment styles (Inderst & Stewart 2018):

- Negative/Exclusionary Control—This strategy excludes certain activities or industries (e.g. controversial weapons, tobacco, fossil fuels) found to be unacceptable. The problem with exclusions is the potential reduction in the investment universe.
- Positive selection/selection of the best in class—This is a positive selection or weighting of companies or countries with better ESG scores over similar sectors. It can be implemented both at the level of ESG measures and their potential for change. The problem with this method is the potential reduction in the investment universe.
- Active Ownership/Voting/Engagement/Governance—This refers to the practice of engaging in dialogue with companies or countries on ESG issues and the use of both property rights (including voting) and a "vote" (especially important in cases where investors do not have voting rights, such as bondholders) to implement changes.
- ESG Integration—This is the systematic integration of ESG risks and opportunities into investment analysis, portfolio construction and risk management.
- Thematic Investments—Investment themes are based on ESG considerations, including clean technology, renewable energy, energy efficiency, sustainable forestry and agriculture, water, education, health and diversity.

ESG reporting requirements and green investment strategies can also create opportunities for insurers, as they account for a large part of the investment market. Particularly, life insurers can invest in long-term assets such as environmentally sustainable infrastructure and renewable energy projects, which fit well with their investment strategies given their long-term horizon. They pay more attention to shareholder rights, risk, opportunity management, and reputation. They could also benefit from the higher returns that may be available on long-term assets (Fitch Wire 2021). The combination of sustainable investment and the application of an ESG strategy in insurance has many other benefits, which include attracting more consumers interested in ESG, as well as the possibility of obtaining positive financial returns on their investments. By effectively integrating ESG factors into risk assessment and insurance processes, insurers may be able to mitigate their losses due to the growing number and scope of climate risks. From an underwriting perspective, failure to include all ESG factors in the underwriting risk assessment will result in a misunderstanding of the scope of possible events and associated risks covered by the policy. This is likely to lead to an increase in policy claims, which can significantly reduce the profitability of insurers. However, profits and market values are declining as a result of incidents such as oil spills and weather-related supply chain disruptions. If an insurer invests in companies by seeing a decline in the value of their shares, this may reduce the return on investment. Over the long term, some companies may eventually fail to face threats from long-term trends such as climate change. Failure to do so may impact the value of institutional investment portfolios and insurance returns (Debevoise & Plimpton 2021).

3.2 *ESG Investing: Global Market Perspective*

ESG investing is gaining popularity in the mainstream not only in business but also among asset managers (Orsato et al. 2015, pp. 161–170). The increase in the value of balanced assets from 2005 to 2013 on average increased by 30.7% annually. What is more, all forms of ESG integration practices in Europe have grown by 65% between 2011 and 2013, making this one of the fastest-growing investment strategies. Looking from a broader perspective, according to the US SIF study from 2020 (US SIF 2020) on sustainable investment in the United States (Fig. 1), in 1995, the size of sustainable investments in the US was $ 639 billion, assets grown more than 25 times since then. The fastest growth has taken place since 2012. Between 2018 and 2020, it increased by 42% from USD 12.0 trillion in early 2018 to USD 17.1 trillion in early 2020.

Practitioners have identified difficulties in implementing sustainable investment in funds related to the development of long-term strategies that could generate value without sacrificing financial return (Sievänen 2014, pp. 309–326). ESG development accelerates every year, so it motivates managers to undertake such investments. There are many conducted research among private investors on ESG. Most studies confirm that ESG is most prevalent in listed stocks. According to the CFA Report from 2017 (CFA 2017), 45% of global fixed-income investors integrate ESG

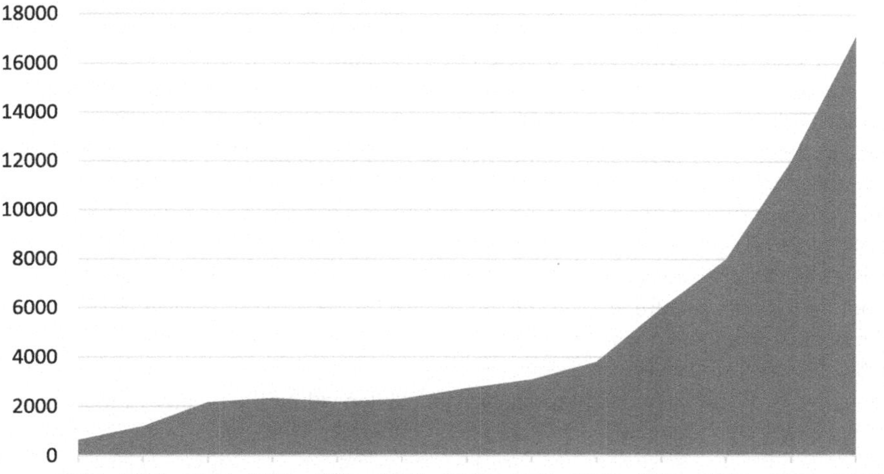

Fig. 1 Sustainable investing in the United States 1995–2020 in billions USD (own assessment on US SIF 2020)

analysis compared to 76% for listed stocks. The main reasons for the shift towards ESG investments, according to the conducted research, are stakeholder preferences; higher investor awareness about climate change; social and political problems; legal and regulatory changes and reputation risk (Inderst & Stewart 2018). Empirical evidence on institutional investors' ESG strategies shows that financial incentives are becoming a more important factor in driving social and environmental performance (Dyck et al. 2019, pp. 693–714). Full integration of ESG into investments seems to be a good business strategy. Firms that deal well with relevant ESG issues tend to perform better (Khan et al. 2016, pp. 1697–1724). This is in line with the idea that strong ESG management gives you a competitive advantage. A study from 2015 (Friede et al. 2015, pp. 210–233) found that around 90% of studies show a non-negative relationship between ESG and a company's bottom line, while most studies show a positive relationship. According to other studies, 88% of firms with sound sustainability practices show improved operational performance which ultimately translates into cash flow, and 80% of the analysed studies confirm that firms with good ESG scores also perform well on traditional financial ratios (Hill 2020).

According to a non-institutional global survey among institutional investors (Eccles et al. 2017, pp. 125–133), the widely recognised barriers to ESG integration were not as high as was universally believed. These barriers were: the belief that ESG integration requires sacrifice of profits, a fiduciary duty to prevent it, and the unrealistic short-term expectations that ESG will perform better. An OECD study from 2020 (Boffo & Patalano 2020) shows that environmental, social, and corporate governance aspects can affect long-term results and should therefore be properly considered when making investment decisions. Research suggests that investors seek to use ESG primarily to compete for better risk-adjusted returns and risk management. What is the most important the biggest barrier is the lack of high-quality data on companies' performance in terms of relevant ESG factors, which results from the scarcity of standards for measuring ESG performance and the statistics on ESG performance reported by companies.

According to the Halbritter and Dorfleitner (2015, pp. 25–35) studies from 2015 on the data from 2000–2012, ESG portfolios do not show significant differences in returns between companies with high and low ESG ratings. This applies to both the overall score and the individual pillars. While ESG portfolios are unable to detect a link between social and financial performance, the regressions of Fama and MacBeth (1973, pp. 607–636) suggest an influence of some ESG variables across the board. Nevertheless, the impact is highly dependent on the ESG rating provider. In addition, there is not identified a systematic pattern for each ESG dimension. However, the results provide evidence of a diminishing impact of ESG variables on returns, which is consistent with the results of Carhart's four-factor model (Carhart 1997, pp. 57–83). Perhaps the results of these studies depend on the quality of these ESG ratings and the time horizon. The very conclusion that there is no significant difference in returns between more or less green entities is positive because entities with ESG strategies are competitive with traditional ones. The results of the subsequent studies provided indicate differences between green and non-green entities.

According to research from 2009, the markets are heavily influenced by social norms, namely investing in shares that do not meet ESG standards, e.g. alcohol, tobacco and gambling companies listed on the stock exchange. There is a significant price effect of 15–20% from large institutional investors avoiding unsustainable equities. For these stocks at least, the neglect of these stocks by large institutions has had a significant impact on their cost of capital. Unfortunately, these researched non-green firms had a higher return than acceptable firms by around 2% per year, but still, the green investors are more risk-tolerant than neutral investors (Hong & Kacperczyk 2009, pp. 15–36). On the other hand, a study conducted two years later shows that companies with a high level of employee satisfaction (social aspect) generate better long-term returns. These results suggest that the market does not fully account for intangible assets in equity valuation. Moreover, the study's findings are in line with the theories of interpersonal relationships, which claim that employee satisfaction leads to better company results through better recruiting, retention and motivation (Edmans 2011, pp. 621–640). In addition, research suggests that higher CSR leads to higher goodwill, higher returns on capital and lower risk. Earnings surveys provide mixed evidence on the link between issuer ESG performance and bond prices and return characteristics: bonds issued by issuers with both excellent and very poor ESG performance tend to underperform those of issuers that do not perform very well or not (Gerard 2019, pp. 61–83). Market analysis shows that ESG investments can offer higher returns compared to more traditional investments. Including ESG factors may also reduce portfolio risk. Insurers that incorporate ESG risk into their investment processes may also be more competitive.

Many academic and investor studies in recent years have found historically lower risk and even better mid- to long-term performance for portfolios that combined key ESG factors with rigorous financial analysis (Guido 2017). However, many studies from 2005 to 2022 are influenced by various market events, including the growing number of natural disasters. It is also worth analysing the results of research from later years.

The study conducted by Bennani et al. (2018) examined the impact of ESG investing on the valuation of assets on the stock exchange in the period 2010–2017 and it was repeated in 2020 by the Drei et al. (2019). ESG investing generated better results both in Europe and North America and ESG preferences change asset prices (Pastor et al. 2019).

The European regulatory environment continues to increase the interest in sustainable investments, which means that the availability of data on ESG investment return rates will increase. The research conducted shows that the belief in lower financial returns from ESG investments compared to traditional ones is wrong (Jain et al. 2019). There are significant ESG excess returns in the US and Japan (Berg et al. 2023).

It is worth emphasising that both empirical observations and theoretical studies confirm the existence of a positive correlation between the rate of return and the level of risk incurred (Feder-Sempach 2012). This means that ESG investments, which were encouraged by potentially high rates of return, were not attractive enough due to the equally high investment risk. The results show that the vulnerability of funds to contagion decreases as the level of compliance with ESG increases. ESG investing offers a new diversification opportunity that makes the system more immune to contagion (Cerqueti et al. 2022). However, faced with rating uncertainty, investors are less likely to invest in ESG and are actively involved in corporate ESG issues. This can increase the cost of capital for green businesses and further limit their ability to make socially responsible investments and generate real social impact (Avramov et al. 2022).

ESG investing is very unique and cannot be compared to other styles of investing. Indeed, usually, the first motivation of investors when implementing a specific investment strategy is purely financial, and in the case of ESG there is also a non-financial element (Andersson et al. 2016, pp. 13–32). For this reason, ESG investing cannot be compared to styles of investing based on low volatility, value or trend-following (Bennani et al. 2018). Recent global analysis of the weighting of sub-criteria found that investors with a strong long-term investment propensity, such as pension funds and insurance companies, paid more attention to shareholder rights, risk and opportunity management and reputation. On the other hand, investors with a higher propensity for short-term investments, such as securities and asset management companies, have been found to place greater emphasis on customer satisfaction and environmentally-friendly products and strategies (Park & Jang 2021).

However, investors' motivations for the choice of green and investments differ depending on the market studies, and from the perspective of the analysis of this study, the most important are the two European and American markets.

3.3 ESG Investment Strategies in the USA and Europe

American investors are more patient with the timeframe to see better ESG performance (Eccles et al. 2017). Sustainable investment in North America is based on a different strategy than in European countries. For US companies, the risk-mitigating effect of ESG operations is enhanced by overall market volatility. The environmental factor plays an important role in reducing risk, while for European companies it appears to be the social component (Bannier et al. 2019). According to the research from 2018 (Bennani et al. 2018) and another research from a longer time horizon 2003–2017 (Bannier et al. 2019). ESG is the second chosen factor in North America, so it is important in building a multi-factor portfolio. ESG has a high proportion in a low-diversification portfolio but is redundant in an already well-diversified portfolio. The situation is different in the case of the Eurozone. Also, ESG may be a risk factor in the euro area, but not in North America. Looking backwards, ESG seems not to be a new risk factor in North America whereas ESG could improve the diversification of multi-factor portfolios in the Eurozone. This shows that ESG strategies remain the alpha strategy in North America.

While the European and American ESG investment markets are developed, the Polish market is still developing. It can be assumed that it will advance in the direction of Europe, due to the financial connections of the countries and the direction of the policy development of the Eurozone.

3.4 Poland Market Perspective

Currently, in Poland, there are serious barriers limiting investments around sustainable development, due to the lack of incentives for pro-ecological activities. From the financial market perspective, an important moment was the launch of the WIG-ESG index in 2019 replacing the RESPECT Index, which included companies from WIG20 and WIG40 (Respect Index 2019). This drew the attention of potential investors to ESG criteria. Since then, the Polish market has become more aware of the environmental factors. According to a study from 2021, the goals related to environmental protection are considered urgent for most of the surveyed companies. Economic incentives are the most important factor motivating Polish companies to invest in solutions in sustainable development. However, a serious barrier limiting ESG investments are problems with their financing (Laurisz 2021).

The SFDR had a significant impact on the development of ESG reporting in Poland and undoubtedly contributed to the increase in the amount of ESG data published by companies. At the same time, a huge challenge for the market is not only the adaptation to international reporting standards, but most of all the transformation of market processes in line with the goals of sustainable development. It is a multidimensional challenge that represents legal, strategic and operational changes. Polish enterprises are increasing the scope of investments for sustainable development, but the main reason for that is pressure from regulators, shareholders and parent companies (mostly from Western Europe) in capital groups. Additionally, another barrier is the high dependence on coal of the energy industry. Despite the agreement to stop coal mining by 2049, employment in this sector is a sensitive political issue.

Poland is highly dependent on coal, therefore potentially many economic entities of the country will be threatened by the phenomenon of "stranded assets." They are defined as assets that are written off unexpectedly or prematurely, devalued or converted into liabilities (Caldecott et al. 2013). However, in the context of environmental concerns and climate change, this purely financial definition is rather insufficient to cover a complex reality. Consequently, all natural resources, investment in infrastructure and means of production and distribution, as well as other tangible or intangible assets that may become obsolete as a result of a greener economy transition or physical damage, are classified as "lost" (Parker & Krustins 2021) Therefore, to achieve the goals of transformation and sustainable development, a clever set of actions must be taken to reach the goal of carbon neutrality and environmental protection, without endangering economic growth and human capital. Additionally, the implementation of this policy will require high investment outlays in the energy sector, as well as a deep transformation of the Polish mining industry (Karpa & Grginović 2021). Market experts agree that this will allow both to reduce

Table 1 Poland's green bonds (Ministry of Finance Republic of Poland 2017, 2019, 2020; IntelliNews 2019)

	2016 issue	2018 issue		2019 issue
Tenor (years)	5	8	10	30
Maturity	20.12.2021	07.08.2026	07.03.2029	08.03.2049
Amount issued (EUR)	0.75 billion	1.0 billion	1.5 billion	0.5 billion
Yield	0.634%	1.153%	1.057%	2.017%
Allocation to green investors	61%	41%	47%	43%

emissions—to support clean transport and to increase the share of renewable energy sources—which has been growing rapidly since 2017 according to GUS data.

What seems to be surprising, Poland was the first country in the world to issue green treasury bonds in 2016, and this was not a one-time event (Climate Bonds Initiative 2016) The Polish Ministry of Finance has issued green bonds on the EUR market four times so far. In 2016, a five-year green bonds (Ministry of Finance Republic of Poland 2017), two years later eight-year green bonds (Ministry of Finance Republic of Poland 2019) and in 2019 issuance of two tranches: ten-year and 30-year green bonds (Ministry of Finance Republic of Poland 2020) (Table 1).

In Poland, the largest institutions focusing on sustainable investing are publicly owned and the best known are BOŚ Bank and NFOŚ. In the private sphere, there are several initiatives focused mainly on the Warsaw Stock Exchange, under which ESG-related indexes are created. However, available research shows that currently there are only four funds in Poland that consider ESG criteria for investment purposes. Some available products are based on the US or Western European ESG indexes but do not include local assets (Dmuchowski 2021, pp. 44–53). Despite the agreements concluded and international actions taken, Polish market practice shows that investment companies are still focused on increasing sales and profits—they do not focus on environmental elements. Such action may result from the belief that the rates of return on ESG investments are not higher than the returns on classic products (Stanilewicz 2019). This is the greatest threat to investments in Poland from the perspective of the ESG economic transformation. Currently, the main emphasis in the public space as well as in scientific studies is on strengthening the awareness of sustainable internet access in Poland as well as the beneficial consequences of their implementation.

Poland has a chance to gain economically from the green transformation. It will be one of the main beneficiaries of EU funds from the European Green Deal. Poland is listed in the top 10 countries in the world with the most qualified workforce for "green technologies." In addition, Poland faces a massive energy transformation program that can be seen as a great investment opportunity (Dmuchowski 2021, pp. 44–53). However, the market lacks data confirming practical interest. The survey numbers indicate interest, but this is not reflected in sales. It can then be assumed that the problem is the availability of these products. As mentioned, few entities deal with the issue of green products. To identify the prospects and needs of the Polish market, interviews with experts from the insurance sector were conducted, as the insurance entities are the biggest participants in the investment market. Setting the right course of action is extremely important for the next ten years. The results of this study are presented in the next chapter.

4 Research Results: Individual In-Depth Interviews

The study was conducted at the turn of March and April 2022 in the form of in-depth interviews with a group of five experts from the insurance sector, whose identity remains anonymous for the purposes of the study. Each of the interviewees gave informed consent to participate in the study and to record the interviews. The target group was selected to cover various sectoral perspectives and to best present the needs of the entire industry. The respondents are people with many years of experience in the insurance market and with substantive knowledge about it. In addition, experts hold management positions in various insurance institutions (insurance companies, supervision and regulators), so they are an authority in their industry. What is also important, the key dimension of the sample selection strategy was to include those institutions that are involved in the work on the implementation of ESG requirements in the Polish insurance market.

In-depth interviews were conducted in accordance with the prepared 11-question scenario (Table 2). Answering the questions, the respondents expressed only their opinions, which cannot be directly identified with any sectoral institution. However, due to the positions held, these are professional opinions.

Table 2 In-depth-interview scenario

No.	Area
1.	Is climate change a particular risk for the insurance sector?
2.	How do you think the climate risk affects the area of investment?
3.	How do each of the climate risks—physical or transition—affect the investment area?
4.	Does the insurance sector have tools to mitigate climate risk? What are these measures for the investment area?
5.	Do insurance regulators and supervision play a role in climate risk management?
6.	Is the current regulation of the insurance sector sufficient to manage climate risk?
7.	How do you think the new regulations will affect the investment area of insurance companies, and how to insure?
8.	Will the new regulations, i.e. Taxonomy, affect the quality of climate risk management in insurance companies?
9.	Do you see changes in the Polish investment market towards sustainable investment?
10.	What obstacles may insurance companies face when investing sustainably in the Polish market?
11.	In your opinion, will the currently observed war situation affect the plans for sustainable development of Europe and Poland?

Source: own assessment

The research problem formulated for the study is the perception of sustainable investment development by experts in the Polish insurance sector. The analysis of the research includes results for questions:

- Is the insurance sector in Europe and Poland vulnerable to climate change and to what extent?
- What do insurance companies have to pay attention to in order to invest sustainably?
- How investment market towards sustainable investment affects the insurance sector?
- What obstacles do insurance companies identify in sustainable investment?
- Do the investment activities of the insurance sector require the implementation of new regulations or changes to the currently applicable ones?

There were more questions for the interview than research questions and some of them were more extensive. Greater detail concerned the area of impact of climate change on the insurance sector and the regulations introduced for the insurance sector. This approach resulted from the desire of the author to supplement the conclusions of the cited research in the previous part of the article to give the reader a full picture of the situation. The author believed that both climate change and regulations are such complex issues that it is necessary to pay more attention to them in questions to respondents. It allowed us to get more specific answers from market experts. Such distinction between interview questions and research questions still made it possible to draw adequate conclusions and formulate answers to research questions.

The results of the survey showed that, according to respondents, climate change affects insurance. All respondents indicated that climate change affects insurance companies directly compared to other sectoral institutions, the others are indirectly threatened primarily by natural disasters.

> These changes will also be related to natural disasters, floods, hailstorms, fires. [...] there is no one big catastrophe and peace for 20–30 years, now these catastrophes are much more frequent and this period of return [...] is much shorter. The most significant risk is the climate change resulting from natural disasters. And yet the risk I see is the risk of passing. It may not be related to climate change, but it is such a risk that it will be difficult to insure the risks associated with difficult energy. It is also such a big risk that no one will want to take on. (R1)

Experts agree that climate risk will affect both the assets and liabilities area, but experts have had difficulty pinpointing which one is more. It mainly depends on the strategy chosen by a given insurance company, so the final impact is an individual matter. According to the respondents, the four most important areas of change towards ESG and thus generating the highest risk are underwriting, reinsurance, investments, and regulations.

> From the investment side, there may also be such emphasis on investing in securities that will be green. Companies may lose if they have in their portfolios companies that invest in dirty energy. [...] energy companies will have higher risk weights, [...] those securities will

> not be as attractive. Insurance companies may be punished for having investment papers related to this dirty energy. (R1)

For climate risk management, respondents indicated two types—physical and transition risks. However, they had difficulties with indicating which is the most important for insurance companies. One of the experts explained that their significance depends on the time horizon being analysed. Experts agree that the insurance sector is equipped with tools to mitigate climate risk. They can use a positive approach to investment decisions investing in green and negative approach—excluding brown products. As for the portfolio, the tools are valuation expertise by obtaining data on portfolio exposures. For the investment area, these are the same tools that companies use now, and in the future, derivative instruments will probably be created to hedge against the risk associated with the so-called dirty energy or state treasury guarantees.

> On the investment side, insurance companies have investments in various coal-related projects in their assets, the valuation of which may drop significantly in the future.[...] They must fill this gap with something. These risks on the investment side are simply a decline in the valuation of assets. (R2)

The main issue is developing products that will protect customers from climate change. Certainly, insurance companies will develop in this direction in the future. There is currently such a self-promotion of insurers in the sector, because, for example, in promotional newspapers, they boast the ESG strategy and have a product offer planned for a few years in advance, so it is visible.

> Insurance companies must consider the prudent principle when investing. They must take on those risks that they can correctly evaluate. [...] Nor can it be that they will focus only on ungreen bonds, which have high risk and high capital requirement and do not have a capital base for it. It is the same as now [...]. Supervisory authority cannot define what and how insurance companies invest their funds, and that is why this prudent investor principle is invoked. They must measure and manage this risk. Bonds should be profitable, safe and liquid—these are features that must be met by a financial instrument. If the bonds do not meet these criteria, the supervision [...]would act. (R1)

When asked how the prudent investor principle relates to ESG investments, the interviewers indicated that it still applies to insurance companies primarily in terms of the level of risk assumed at the time of investment and the valuation of this risk. They should provide liquidity and should be profitable. It also cannot happen that the company will focus only on high-risk debt bonds but will not have a sufficient capital base for this. Investing itself does not change. Just like now, when insurers invest in some risky paper, they follow the prudent investor principle. For example, now (April 2022), hardly anyone would decide to invest in Russian bonds, precisely considering factors such as valuation, capital requirement, liquidity and high-risk weight. They increase the capital requirement and do not meet the regulations related to a prudent investor. According to the respondents, insurance companies must be aware that this risk must be measured and managed. Bonds should be profitable, safe and liquid—these are features that must be met by a financial instrument. If the bonds do not meet these criteria, the insurance company should not invest in them.

Of course, if such an investment was made, the supervision would act. Certainly, the BION assessment would not be favourable if the supervision saw that the company invests in such securities. Experts noted that the source of the development of climate risk management by the insurance sector can be seen in the image pressure, including matching services to clients. This trend is more visible in Western EU countries than in Poland and is driven by a bottom-up initiative of young clients who are interested in green investment products. Insurance companies, wanting to attract new customers, or remain attractive and retain the older ones, will follow the path of transformation while improving their image on the market.

> In the financial dimension, there are risks related to the valuation of assets. [. . .] If we have in the portfolio a company that has invested in coal, it will be more difficult e to exit this investment. (R2)

The current changes in macroeconomic conditions in the financial markets should not affect the sustainable development plans of Europe and Poland. As for the economic side, this situation has already influenced the market risk, mainly the increase in inflation, interest rates and costs of all economic entities. From the reinsurance side, it is certainly reflected in the elimination of reinsurance from Russia on the European market or at least their significant reduction. However, from the regulatory side, there are no changes, and everything is proceeding according to plan. At the European level, the timetable has remained the same and work is progressing on it, and all documents have been issued without delay. There is also no tendency to deviate from ESG. The impact may, of course, be local, and the demand response will be visible in a longer period.

> You can see such changes in the insurance sector, some life insurance companies have eco-friendly companies in their portfolio because they invest in green investments. [. . .] companies are promoting themselves in this way and encouraging to buy because there are green products. And as I said before, these products will protect customers from climate change, and this is a field for the future where insurance companies can develop. We also see such self-promotion, e.g. in the campaign boast that they have an ESG strategy and have a product offer planned for a few years ahead, so it is visible. (R1)

What the current market turmoil may have an impact on in the long term is data quality. ESG indicators will be created based on the time series of data, so disturbing their current situation may contribute to a different shape of these indicators. From the investment side, the assets of those plants that have funds invested in projects related to coal are exposed. From the perspective of green transformation, there is a potential risk that the assets of such entities will fall into the category of stranded assets or they will not be manageable for some time. A solution to mitigate risk would be reinsurance, but there are already declarations to limit coal-related reinsurance. There are still coal-fired power plants in Poland that must be insured, so there is a potential risk of problems with the reinsurance of such entities soon.

> We are not leading [here: Poland against the European background] when it comes to green products, but this also results from the environment where we live. Such domestic products will be more expensive, because we do not have strictly green investments, although there were plans for the government to Polish issued such green bonds. We also don't have such incentives for insurance companies [. . .] the European market has not yet decided what the

> colour of nuclear energy is, whether it is brown or green [..]. But also cutting off these investments will cause turbulence on the European market in terms of investment. It's hard to say about the competition, we are not the leader. However, we are developing these products, or the insurance companies are developing themselves. (R1)

> Poland is main coal producer. So, the problem for the insurance market is unique. [. . .] The transition problem is infrastructure – the centralized place where the energy is produced. So, the question for the future is about how to distribute the energy. (R3)

Unprepared insurance companies will find it difficult to implement the new climate agenda. Experts also pointed to the problem of setting a strategy related to sustainable development by entities so that they would be consistent with the strategy of Poland. Unfortunately, there is no designated direction for the market in terms of ESG activities on a domestic basis. Therefore, entities cannot precisely plan the direction of their activities for the next ten years, therefore the strategies of entities and ESG strategies are often not combined.

> Insurance companies identify similar problems on the Polish market as those on the European one. It also results from belonging to capital groups. Very often companies must follow the strategies developed by the Groups and the group says more than once that you can invest in brown bonds, but only in such and such amount they have some limits, so this is also an aspect. The activity is changing, and this is also due to how the group changes in terms of investing. If we have countries where this coal is important, then they have the same problems as we do with reinsurance[. . .] And above all, data, [. . .] is a general European problem with access to adequate data and with forecasting this risk and creating appropriate scenarios. Therefore, EIOPA publishes this publication on ORSA to help and indicate how this climate risk can be stressed and a document showing how these scenarios can be created. (R2)

According to the respondents, changes on the Polish investment market towards sustainable investment are already noticeable. You can see that some life insurance companies have eco-friendly companies in their portfolio and are investing in green investments. This is not a significant market impact yet in terms of the number of green products. Insurance companies promote themselves in this way and encourage them to buy them. Compared to Europe, Poland is not a leader in terms of the availability of green products. The reason for this situation is, of course, the slow process of any changes in the EU, and usually it arrives in Poland later. In the case of green products, it also results from the environmental conditions of Poland, as shown by climate forecasts, and the risk of climate change is not as high as in southern and western Europe. Additionally, such reduced availability increases the price.

One of the respondents emphasises that:

> there is a problem of the availability of green products on the Polish market—sustainable investments—even if we wanted to invest in a sustainable manner, there are no such products as on the Polish market, there are no such products, and when they appear, they are won by the biggest players. (R4)

What is important is that there are no strictly green investments in Poland, although there were plans for the Polish government to issue such green bonds. There are also no market incentives for insurance companies to be even more confident in implementing sustainable strategies. The European market is still discussing the classification of nuclear energy and gas to the group of the so-called brown or green. Waste or the entire infrastructure associated with it is not environmentally friendly, but it must be remembered that the complete cut-off of these investments will cause turbulence on the European market in terms of investment. So far, it cannot be said that Poland is a competition because Western countries are at a further stage of implementing ESG.

> No more reporting obligations should be imposed on financial institutions, because they have to obtain data (usually buy it). This green product will then be more expensive. If I am to be able to offer such a product, I must have information, yet I cannot find such information on the company's website. Since it is difficult, it will not offer such products. You should not introduce new reporting regulations, but only bring those that are. (R2)

When investing sustainably in the Polish market, insurance companies identify problems like those in the European market. The respondents agreed that in the Polish market, many insurance companies operate within larger capital groups, where parent companies are companies in Western Europe. Adaptation to the ESG regulations and implementation of sustainable development in the strategies of the daughter companies result from the adaptation to the strategy of the entire capital group. If we are to indicate any source of pressure on insurers to offer green products, these are the parent companies, not the Polish market or the state.

It also results from belonging to capital groups, insurance companies must follow the strategies developed by the groups and, for example, they cannot invest in brown bonds or have designated limits for such investments. The activity is changing, and this is also due to how the group changes in terms of investing. As part of consultations with European supervision, they report similar problems and doubts about Poland, especially problems related to risk placement. For example, if there are countries where coal is as important as in Poland, then the insurance sector has the same problem with reinsurance. Or if we have a market where green securities are not very popular, we have a problem later with the diversification of such risk.

Yet another important issue for the whole of Europe is the availability of adequate data and forecasting climate risk and creating appropriate scenarios. Therefore, EIOPA publishes this publication on ORSA to help and indicate how this climate risk can be stressed and how to create these scenarios. According to experts, supervision plays an important role in managing climate risk in the sector. Three experts indicated that European supervision, i.e. EIOPA, has a special role in this. On the one hand, it acts in accordance with the current work of the European Commission and its recommendations, and on the other hand, it also creates its own guidelines. Apart from EIOPA, the EBA and ESBA are also equally important for the entire financial sector. Among others, joint committees of these three bodies are organised, which allows for combining works and applying supervisory convergence. The respondents agreed that the role of both the European and Polish regulators is important in managing the climate risk in the insurance sector. The quality of the legislation should, however, be improved. They also emphasised the positive aspects of the new regulations. The SFDR and taxonomy aim to reduce greenwashing and provide transparency to stakeholders.

> It seems that regulations are being still created, because we are waiting for information whether brown energy will have higher capital requirements or not, but it seems to me that it is not for now. [...] the trend is good, but do not create any new regulations, there are too many of them, let's finish what is planned. Certainly, the new regulations will influence the quality of climate risk management, because they will structure the existing ones, will give clarity on how this ESG management system will look like in the future and what risks the insurance companies will bear on the investment side. (R1)

> New regulations will only affect investments. For now, these regulations have an impact on the reporting side. However, there is no such thing as the EU does not prohibit investment. New regulations will generally have a positive effect. First, we are waiting for the CFDR revisions. (R2)

For the supervision and the market, the most important thing is currently cooperation, and from the side of the regulator, ensuring legislative stability by introducing new regulations also as such support for the financial market. The biggest challenge currently facing the market is the availability of adequate data. An important role in this market transformation will also be played by consulting, auditors and insuretechs, as support for financial institutions, whether in regulatory interpretations or the implementation of processes adapted to sustainable strategies and legislation.

> SFDR, taxonomy are the aim to do two things. 1) to avoid greenwashing – try to make more objective measure about what different corporates are doing and 2) be transparent to stakeholders. [...] if they are comparable enough, they van decide whether to invest in which insurance company. [...]. In the beginning everything that comes from regulator is seen as an obligation. You must create a system to report. In the asset side you will show a movement. At the beginning is a low expectations taxonomy-compliant matching the requirements, but next year you need to show some improvements, which means you will ally with taxonomy related investments and therefore you will have an impact as well. (R3)

Insurance companies face the challenge of adapting the distribution and underwriting area to climate change on the one hand, and the investment portfolio on the other. The important point is that the first area is covered by them themselves, but the content of the portfolio is also influenced by the availability of appropriate products. There is a lack of sustainable investments in Poland, and if their pace of entering the market does not increase, a major problem may arise not only for the insurance sector, but also for the entire financial sector.

5 Conclusion

Climate change is one of the greatest civilisational challenges we have ever faced, and climate issues are beginning to play a key role in building the economic, social and political order in the world. The transformation in line with sustainable development brings many opportunities, also for the financial market. Therefore, monitoring and forecasting its evolution become the most important element of an effective development and adaptation strategy.

Regulatory and legislative changes put pressure on banks and insurance companies to counter climate threats, and current analyses of the finance sector are carried out in terms of responsible goals related to their insurance and investment activities. The transformation will put pressure on investment strategies focused on brown products and will threaten the viability of business models based on these sectors, which may lead to a decline in the value of some entities' assets but will also create opportunities for the development and design of new products aimed at conscious market participants.

The profitability of sustainable investments is one of the concerns of the market, but from the insurance view, it is a more complicated matter. Insurers need to consider other perspectives, such as ESG products adaptation or readjustment of risk measurement. Compliance with sustainable requirements may also offer opportunities for insurer companies, such as attracting a growing number of green-minded stakeholders. For the company, customer retention is as crucial as attracting investors from the market and raising capital. By integrating ESG factors into risk assessment and underwriting processes, insurers may be able to mitigate their losses from the growing number of climate-related risks.

The results of the study show that the impact of climate risk on the activities of insurance companies is particularly significant. The study allowed us to obtain answers to the research questions posed. Respondents confirmed that climate change poses a particular threat to the operations of insurance companies. Climate risk will affect both the area of assets and liabilities, and the most important areas of change towards ESG and thus generating the highest risk are underwriting, reinsurance, investments and regulations. Experts agree that the insurance sector is equipped with tools to mitigate climate risk. They can use a positive approach to investment decisions investing in green and negative approach—excluding brown products. Insurance companies identify the same problems as the European market. The main issue is developing products that will protect customers from climate change. Certainly, insurance companies will develop in this direction in the future. According to the respondents, insurance companies must be aware that this risk must be measured and managed. Bonds should be profitable, safe and liquid—these are features that must be met by a financial instrument. Unprepared insurance companies will find it difficult to implement the new climate agenda. Experts also pointed to the problem of setting a strategy related to sustainable development by entities so that they would be consistent with the strategy of Poland. Unfortunately, there is no designated direction for the market in terms of ESG activities on a domestic basis. Therefore, entities cannot precisely plan the direction of their activities for the next ten years, therefore the strategies of entities and ESG strategies are often not combined.

According to the respondents, changes on the Polish investment market towards sustainable investment are already noticeable. You can see that some life insurance companies have eco-friendly companies in their portfolio and are investing in green investments. This is not a significant market impact yet in terms of the number of green products. Insurance companies promote themselves in this way and encourage them to buy them. Compared to Europe, Poland is not a leader in terms of the availability of green products. The reason for this situation is, of course, the slow process of any changes in the EU, and usually it arrives in Poland later. In the case of green products, it also results from the environmental conditions of Poland, as shown by climate forecasts, and the risk of climate change is not as high as in southern and western Europe. Additionally, such reduced availability increases the price. When investing sustainably on the Polish market, insurance companies identify problems like those on the European market. The respondents agreed that on the Polish market, many insurance companies operate within larger capital groups, where parent companies are companies in Western Europe. Adaptation to the ESG regulations and implementation of sustainable development in the strategies of the daughter companies result from the adaptation to the strategy of the entire capital group. The biggest obstacle seems to be the availability of correct data that makes it possible to invest in a sustainable manner. A significant problem in the Polish market is the lack of availability of sustainable products. New regulations will oblige non-financial companies to public ESG information, but the cost of producing such data will affect the entire financial market.

The results show that market experts consider new European regulations to be complicated and challenging for both Europe and Poland. There is no need to introduce new regulations currently, so market participants must organise themselves and learn to operate with the present ones. For the supervision and the market, the most important thing, currently, is cooperation. The impact assessment of regulatory changes and the economic transformation towards sustainable development on the activities of insurance companies and the entire financial sector leaves a gap to be filled by future scientific work.

References

Andersson M, Bolton P, Samama F (2016) Hedging climate risk. Financ Anal J 72(3):13–32

Armel-Zadeh A, Serafeim G (2018) Why and how investors use ESG information: evidence from a global survey. Financ Anal J 74(3):87–103

Avramov D, Cheng S, Lioui A, Tarelli A (2022) Sustainable investing with ESG Rating Uncertainty, 2021. J Financ Econ 145(2)

Bank of England (2018) Transition in thinking: the impact of climate change on the UK banking sector. https://www.bankofengland.co.uk/-/media/boe/files/prudential-regulation/report/transition-in-thinking-the-impact-of-climate-change-on-the-uk-banking-sector.pdf

Bannier CE, Bofinger Y, Rock B (2019) Doing safe by doing good: ESG investing and corporate social responsibility in the U.S. and Europe. CFS working paper series (621). Center for Financial Studies, Universitätsbibliothek Johann Christian Senckenberg

Bennani L, Guenedal T, Lepetit F, Ly L, Mortier V, Sekine T (2018) The Alpha and Beta of ESG Investing. Working paper, Cross Asset Investment Strategy, Amudi. https://research-center.amundi.com/article/alpha-and-beta-esg-investing

Berg F, Lo AW, Rigobon R, Singh M, Zhang R (2023) Quantifying the returns of ESG investing: an empirical analysis with six ESG metrics. MIT Sloan research paper no. 6930-23

Boffo R, Patalano R (2020) ESG investing: practices, progress and challenges. OECD Paris. https://www.oecd.org/finance/ESG-Investing-Practices-Progress-Challenges.pdf

Caldecott B, Howarth N, McSharry P (2013) Stranded assets in agriculture: protecting value from environment-related risks. https://www.smithschool.ox.ac.uk/sites/default/files/2022-03/stranded-assets-agriculture-report-final.pdf

Carhart MM (1997) On persistence in mutual fund performance. J Financ 52(1):57–82

Cerqueti R, Ciciretti R, Dalò A, Nicolosi M (2022) Mitigating contagion risk by ESG investing. Sustainability 14(7)

CFA Institute (2017) Environmental, Social and Governance (ESG) survey. https://www.cfainstitute.org/-/media/documents/survey/esg-survey-report-2017.ashx

Climate Bonds Initiative (2016) Poland wins race to issue first green sovereign bond. A new era for Polish climate policy? https://www.climatebonds.net/2016/12/poland-wins-race-issue-first-green-sovereign-bond-new-era-polish-climate-policy

Debevoise&Plimpton (2021) ESG in the insurance sector: growth, opportunities and risks. https://www.debevoise.com/-/media/files/insights/publications/2021/01/20210106-esg-in-the-insurance-sector.pdf

Dietz S, Bowen A, Dixon C, Gradwell P (2016) Climate value at risk of global financial assets, Climate value at risk of global financial assets. Nat Clim Chang 6:676–679

Dimson E, Kreutzer I, Lake R, Sjo H, Starks L (2013) Responsible investment and the Norwegian Government Pension Fund Global. Norwegian Ministry of Finance, Oslo

Dmuchowski P (2021) Zrównoważone inwestowanie – trendy globalne i perspektywy dla Polski in ed. Ludwik Kotecki, Zielone Finanse w Polsce 2021, UN Global Compact, Centrum Myśli Strategicznych, pp 44–53

Drei A, Le Guenedal T, Lepetit F, Mortier V, Roncalli T, Sekine T (2019) ESG investing in recent years: new insights from old challenges. https://doi.org/10.2139/ssrn.3683469

Dyck A, Lins K, Roth L, Wagner H (2019) Do institutional investors drive corporate social responsibility? International evidence. J Financ Econ 131(3):693–714

Eccles RG, Kastrapeli MD, Potter SJ (2017) How to integrate ESG into investment decision-making: results of a global survey of institutional investors. J Appl Corp Financ 29(4):125–133

Economist Intelligence Unit (2015) The cost of inaction. https://impact.economist.com/sustainability/net-zero-and-energy/the-cost-of-inaction?utm_medium=cpc.adword.pd&utm_source=google&ppccampaignID=18151738051&ppcadID=&utm_campaign=a.22brand_pmax&utm_content=conversion.direct-response.anonymous&gclid=Cj0KCQjwwtWgBhDhARIsAEMcxeBunfwccbgtQNqg2xdq0TatnQ7vZ3MFsmM7RObwK9STYn_q6S9k4XUaAhxwEALw_wcB&gclsrc=aw.ds

Edmans A (2011) Does the stock market fully value intangibles? Employee satisfaction and equity prices. J Financ Econ 101(3):621–640

EIOPA (2019) Opinion on sustainability within Solvency II (EIOPA-BoS-19/241)

EIOPA (2021) Opinion on the supervision of the use of climate change risk scenarios in ORSA

ESRB (2020) Positively green: measuring climate change risks to financial stability. https://www.esrb.europa.eu/pub/pdf/reports/esrb.report200608_on_Positively_green_-_Measuring_climate_change_risks_to_financial_stability~d903a83690.en.pdf

European Commission (2016) Sustainable development: EU sets out its priorities. https://ec.europa.eu/commission/presscorner/detail/en/IP_16_3883

Fama EF, MacBeth JD (1973) Risk return and equilibrium: empirical tests. J Polit Econ 81(3):607–636

Feder-Sempach E (2012) Ryzyko inwestycyjne. Analiza polskiego rynku akcji, CeDeWu

Financial Stability Board (2020) The implications of climate change for financial stability. https://www.fsb.org/wp-content/uploads/P231120.pdf

Fitch Wire (2021) European insurers to boost ESG investments on Solvency II Reform. https://www.fitchratings.com/research/insurance/european-insurers-to-boost-esg-investments-on-solvency-ii-reform-23-09-2021

Friede G, Busch T, Bassen A (2015) ESG and financial performance: aggregated evidence from more than 2000 empirical studies. J Sustain Financ Invest 5(4):210–233

Gerard B (2019) ESG and socially responsible investment: a critical review. Beta: Scand J Bus Res 33(1):61–83

Golnaraghi M (2018) Climate change and insurance industry: taking action as risk managers and investors perspectives on risks and opportunities from insurance industry's C-level executives. The Geneva Association, Tokyo

Guido G (2017) Has ESG affected stock performance? MSCI. https://www.msci.com/www/blog-posts/has-esg-affected-stock/0794561659

Halbritter G, Dorfleitner G (2015) The wages of social responsibility - where are they? A critical review of ESG investing. Rev Financ Econ 26:25–35

Hill J (2020) Environmental, social, and governance (ESG) investing: a balanced analysis of the theory and practice of a sustainable portfolio. Elsevier

Hong H, Kacperczyk M (2009) The price of sin: the effects of social norms on markets. J Financ Econ 93(1):15–36

IAIS and SIF (2018) Issues paper on climate change risks to the insurance sector. https://www.insurancejournal.com/research/app/uploads/2018/08/IAIS_and_SIF_Issues_Paper_on_Climate_Change_Risks_to_the_Insurance_Sector_-1.pdf

Inderst G, Stewart F (2018) Incorporating environmental, social and governance (ESG) factors into fixed income investment. World Bank Group Publication

IntelliNews (2019). https://www.intellinews.com/poland-places-2bn-worth-of-green-bonds-157278/

IPCC (2014) AR5 Synthesis Report. https://www.ipcc.ch/report/ar5/syr/

IPCC (2018) Special report: global warming of 1.5 °C. https://www.ipcc.ch/sr15/

IPCC (2021) Climate change 2021. The physical science basis, working group i contribution to the sixth assessment report of the intergovernmental panel on climate change. https://www.ipcc.ch/report/ar6/wg1/downloads/report/IPCC_AR6_WGI_FullReport.pdf

Jain M, Sharma GD, Srivastava M (2019) Can sustainable investment yield better financial returns: a comparative study of ESG indices and MSCI indices. Risks 7(1):15

Karpa W, Grginović A (2021) (Not so) stranded: the case of coal in Poland. Energies 14(24)

Khan M, Serafeim G, Yoon A (2016) Corporate sustainability: first evidence on materiality. Account Rev 91(6):1697–1724

Kölbel JF, Heeb F, Paetzold F, Busch T (2020) Can sustainable investing save the world? Reviewing the mechanisms of investor impact. Organ Environ 33(4):554–574

Laurisz M (2021) Zrównoważony rozwój wkracza do strategii polskich firm, według badania "Smart Industry Polska 2021." https://itreseller.com.pl/zrownowazony-rozwoj-wkracza-do-strategii-polskich-firm-wedlug-badania-smart-industry-polska-2021/

Ministry of Finance Republic of Poland (2017) Green Bond report on the use of proceeds. https://www.gov.pl/web/finance/issues-international-bonds

Ministry of Finance Republic of Poland (2019) Green Bond report on the use of proceeds. https://www.gov.pl/web/finance/issues-international-bonds

Ministry of Finance Republic of Poland (2020) Green Bond report on the use of proceeds. https://www.gov.pl/web/finance/issues-international-bonds

Monnin P (2018) Integrating climate risks into credit risk assessment current methodologies and the case of central banks corporate bond purchases. Council on Economic Policies

NGFS (2019) A call for action climate change as a source of financial risk. https://www.ngfs.net/sites/default/files/medias/documents/ngfs_first_comprehensive_report_-_17042019_0.pdf

OECD (2015) The economic consequences of climate change. https://www.oecd.org/env/the-economic-consequences-of-climate-change-9789264235410-en.htm

Orsato RJ, Garcia A, Mendes-Da-Silva W, Simonetti R, Monzoni M (2015) Sustainability indexes: why join in? A study of the 'Corporate Sustainability Index (ISE)' in Brazil. J Clean Prod 96: 161–170

Park SR, Jang JY (2021) The impact of ESG management on investment decision: institutional investors' perceptions of country-specific ESG criteria. Int J Financ Stud 9(3):48

Parker E, Krustins K (2021) Special report climate change 'Stranded Assets' are a long-term risk for some sovereigns. Fitch Ratings
Pastor L, Stambaugh RF, Taylor LA (2019) Sustainable investing in equilibrium. NBER working paper series. Working paper 26549
Respect Index (2019). http://respectindex.pl/aktualnosci?ph_main_content_start=show&ph_main_content_cmn_id=1141
Sievänen R (2014) Practicalities bottleneck to pension fund responsible investment? Bus Ethics Eur Rev 23(3):309–326
Stanilewicz R (2019) Inwestycje ESG to szansa na wyższe zyski, wywiad z B. Pawłowskim, analizy.pl. https://www.analizy.pl/analizy-player/24509/b-pawlowski-inwestycje-esg-to-szansa-na-wyzsze-zyski
Stenek V, Amado J, Connell R (2011) Climate risk and financial institutions: challenges and opportunities. World Bank Group. https://firstforsustainability.org/media/IFC%20Climate%20Risk%20and%20FIs.pdf
US SIF (2020) Report on US sustainable and impact investing trends. https://www.ussif.org/files/Trends%20Report%202020%20Executive%20Summary.pdf
Wolters Kluwer (2015) Do you know your operational risks from climate change? https://www.wolterskluwer.com/en/expert-insights/do-you-know-your-operational-risks-from-climate-change

Marianna Cicirko, M.Sc. assistant at the Department of Social Insurance at the Warsaw School of Economics. A graduate of Quantitative Methods in Economics and Information Systems as well as Finance and Accounting at the Warsaw School of Economics. For several years, she has been a risk management specialist in the largest insurance company in Poland. Co-organiser of a series of seminars entitled "New technologies in the insurance sector" and "Climate seminars."

Her professional interests focus on risk management in insurance companies, modern technologies in the insurance sector and sustainable investments (ESG) (mainly in pension security).

Recently, she has conducted or is continuing research in the area of: EIOPA Consumer Research—research on information on ESG financial products (as part of the cooperation of SGH with the European supervisory body EIOPA), perception of ESG investments by SGH students, "PPK in Polish universities" (boundary conditions for investments in ESG) and qualitative and quantitative exploratory research among insurance sector experts covering Poland and Central and Eastern Europe. Author and co-author of several publications on challenges for the insurance sector related to climate change and new technologies in the financial sector.

Rating "Social" Within the EU Law the ESG Factors: Relevance for the Insurance Industry and the Risk of "Social Washing"

Pierpaolo Marano and María del Val Bolívar Oñoro

1 The EU Proposal for a Regulation on the Transparency of ESG Rating Activities and the Need for a Social Taxonomy

The expression "environmental, social, and governance" (ESG) was coined in the first "Who Cares Wins" Report in the year 2004.[1] The report provided several recommendations for integrating ESG aspects in asset management, securities brokerage services, and the associated buy-side and sell-side research functions. The term "ESG" throughout that report "is a way of highlighting the fact that these areas are closely inter-linked",[2] but the term is not provided with any definition.

[1] United Nations, The Global Compact (2004).

[2] United Nations, The Global Compact (2004), p. 2, where the rationale of this choice is explained as follows: "Sound corporate governance and risk management systems are crucial pre-requisites to successfully implementing policies and measures to address environmental and social challenges."

P. Marano (✉)
Department of Insurance and Risk Management, University of Malta, Msida, Malta
e-mail: pierpaolo.marano@unicatt.it

M. del Val Bolívar Oñoro
University of Alcalá, Alcalá de Henares, Spain
e-mail: val.bolivar@uah.es

J. Bataller-Grau et al. (eds.), *Sustainability and the Insurance Market*, AIDA Europe Research Series on Insurance Law and Regulation 10,
https://doi.org/10.1007/978-3-031-72186-1_7

The United Nations Principles for Responsible Investment (PRI) includes a list of examples,[3] but no explicit definition was set for each component of ESG.[4] This uncertainty is inevitably reflected in the perception and subsequent application of these factors.[5] The continuing regulatory uncertainties are an obstacle to the progressive alignment of the recipients of these provisions towards the objectives pursued with the introduction of ESG. This uncertainty leaves wide margins for discretion, which risks frustrating these objectives.

Policymakers are (slowly) designing the global regulatory framework that should alleviate the uncertainties reported, and the European Union (EU) is particularly active in completing its regulation on ESG.

In this context, the European Commission (Commission) issued a Proposal for a Regulation on the transparency of ESG rating activities on 13 June 2023.[6] Such a proposal intends to introduce transparency requirements related to ESG ratings and rules on the organization and conduct of ESG rating providers. It aims to contribute to the smooth functioning of the internal market while achieving high consumer and investor protection and preventing greenwashing or other types of misinformation, including social washing.[7] To this end, the proposal regulates rating agencies established in the EU and the provision of ESG ratings in the Union by third-country ESG rating providers.

This proposal comes at the end of a process started when the Commission commissioned a Study on Sustainability Related Ratings, Data, and Research issued in 2021.[8] The study highlighted the need for more transparency and accuracy in ESG rating methodologies and the lack of clarity over the operations of ESG rating providers. The International Organization of Securities Commissions (IOSCO) reached the same conclusion as the Commission coeval with the Final Report on Environmental, Social and Governance (ESG) Ratings and Data Products Providers.[9] Such a report revealed little clarity and alignment on definitions, including

---

[3] The Report pointed out that "examples of environmental, social and governance (ESG) factors are numerous and ever shifting". Environmental factors include "Climate change, Resource depletion, Waste, Pollution, Deforestation"; social factors include "Human rights, Modern slavery, Child labour, Working conditions, Employee relations"; and governance factors include "Bribery and corruption, Executive pay, Board diversity and structure, Political lobbying and donations".

[4] The Principles for Responsible Investment are available at https://www.unpri.org/download?ac=10948.

[5] This definition problem preceded the introduction of the term ESG as it also concerned the predecessor, corporate citizenship, i.e., a company's overall role in society. See World Economic Forum, Values and Value. Communicating the Strategic Importance of Corporate Citizenship to Investors, at 13, reporting the findings of a 2003 CEO Survey of the World Economic Forum Global Corporate Citizenship Initiative, which is available at https://docplayer.net/96430975-Values-and-value-communicating-the-strategic-importance-of-corporate-citizenship-to-investors.html.

[6] The proposal is available at https://eur-lex.europa.eu/legal-content/EN/TXT/?uri=CELEX:52023PC0314.

[7] See Article 1.

[8] European Commission (2021).

[9] The Final Report is available at https://www.iosco.org/library/pubdocs/pdf/IOSCOPD690.pdf.

what ratings or data products intend to measure, and there needs to be more transparency about the methodologies underpinning these ratings or data products.[10]

Since ESG ratings are produced using both quantitative models and qualitative analysis and are accompanied by analyst reports to explain the ratings, they may incorporate an element of analytical judgment or opinion.[11]

The EU Proposal for a Regulation on the transparency of ESG rating activities acknowledged that ESG ratings play an enabling role in the functioning of the Union's sustainable finance market by providing necessary information for investment strategies, risk management, and disclosure obligations by investors and financial institutions.[12] Moreover, ESG ratings have a significant impact on the operation of the markets and the trust and confidence of investors and consumers. To ensure that ESG ratings used in the Union are independent, objective, and of adequate quality, the principles of integrity, transparency, responsibility, and good governance must be used in conducting ESG rating activities.[13]

To achieve these outcomes, the Proposal mirrors the Recommendations set forth by the IOSCO Final Report. Therefore, the Proposal does not provide any definition of "social" but emphasizes the integrity and reliability of ESG rating activities through (*i*) the provision of organizational requirements, processes, and documents concerning the governance of such entities;[14] (*ii*) transparency requirements related to the disclosure of the methodologies, models, and key rating assumptions used in ESG rating activities to the public and subscribers of ESG ratings and rated entities;[15] (*iii*) and organizational measures to ensure the independence and avoidance of conflicts of interest.[16]

This approach should neutralize or mitigate the critical issues that have emerged regarding the role of rating agencies and the conflicts to which they are exposed. Also, disclosing the methodologies, models, and critical rating assumptions used in ESG rating activities can be appreciated as it allows a better understanding of the outcomes embedded in the ratings.

---

[10]The Final Report also revealed that (*i*) while there is wide divergence within the ESG ratings and data products industry, there is an uneven coverage of products offered, with certain industries or geographical areas benefitting from more coverage than others, thereby leading to gaps for investors seeking to follow certain investment strategies; (*ii*) there may be concerns about the management of conflicts of interest where the ESG ratings and data products provider or an entity closely associated with the provider performs consulting services for companies that are the subject of these ESG ratings or data products; and (*iii*) better communication with companies that are the subject of ESG ratings or data products was identified as an area meriting further attention given the importance of ensuring the ESG ratings or other data products are based on sound information.

[11]See IOSCO (2021).

[12]See Recital No. 11 of the Proposal for a Regulation on the transparency and integrity of Environmental, Social and Governance (ESG) rating activities.

[13]See Recital No. 10 of the Proposal for a Regulation on the transparency and integrity of Environmental, Social and Governance (ESG) rating activities.

[14]See Articles 14–20.

[15]See Articles 21–22.

[16]See Articles 23–25.

The European Securities and Markets Authority (ESMA) reported that the predominant business model is investor pays. At the same time, the provision of ESG ratings on an issuer-pay basis was indicated in around a third of the responses from providers.

To the Proposal established a clear distinction between rating activities and other business operations to prevent conflict of interests and introduced[17] the duty to take all the necessary steps to ensure that any ESG rating provided is not affected by any existing or potential conflict of interest or by any business relationship, either from the ESG rating provider itself or from their shareholders, managers, rating analysts, employees, or any other natural person whose services are placed at the disposal or under the control of the ESG rating providers or any person directly or indirectly linked to them by control.[18] Meanwhile, ESMA may require the ESG rating provider to take measures to mitigate that risk.[19]

The harmonization pursued by the European Union through the legislative proposal under consideration ultimately concerns the conduct of business by rating agencies. Their integrity and reliability depend on the transparency of the rating methodologies and the effective management of conflicts of interest.[20]

This harmonization, therefore, refers to the rating processes. It does not define the substantial profiles of these processes, i.e. the meaning of each of the components included in the definition of ESG that rating agencies must consider.

This approach presupposes that some regulations already defined these substantial profiles, which must be sufficiently detailed to avoid (too) discretionary choices by rating agencies. In this way, the risk of these agencies emphasizing aspects favourable to their customers in their analysis while underestimating or ignoring the less favourable ones is mitigated.

However, the current European Union regulations still need to be suitable to integrate the provisions intended to be introduced with the legislative proposal under consideration.

The EU Regulation (EU) 2020/852 of 18 June 2020 (Taxonomy Regulation) established the basis for the EU taxonomy by setting out the overarching conditions that economic activities must meet to qualify as environmentally sustainable,

---

[17] A list of prohibited activities is provided under Article 15 of the Proposal, which also sets forth that rating agencies must ensure that activities/services not included in such list do not create risks of conflicts of interest within its ESG rating activities.

[18] See Article 23, para. 2, of the Proposal. See also Article 24, which is related to the management of potential conflicts of interest from employees.

[19] See Article 23, para 3, of the Proposal. Such measures may include the establishment of an independent oversight function representing stakeholders, including users of the ESG ratings and contributors to such ratings, in a balanced manner.

[20] Ermokhin et al. (2023), p. 10. This statement is coherent with the one reached by these authors: "In this regard, the development of basic recommendations in terms of methodological problems, including the definition of a minimum set of factors and their weights, rating scales, etc., as well as requirements for transparency of methodologies, definitions and terms, may be the best option to increase the degree of correlation of ESG ratings at the moment." Escrig-Olmedo et al. (2019), p. 14.

allowing the Commission to come up with the actual list of environmentally sustainable activities by defining technical screening criteria for each environmental objective through delegated and implementing acts.[21]

While the Taxonomy Regulation aims to provide a common language of green and sustainable, such Regulation specifies that "further guidance on activities that contribute to other sustainability objectives, including social objectives, might be developed at a later stage".[22]

Nonetheless, the Taxonomy Regulation set down the criteria for environmentally sustainable economic activities, including the notion that economic activity is carried out in compliance with the minimum safeguards, and established the Platform on Sustainable Finance (Platform) with several tasks, including advising the Commission on applying the minimum safeguards.[23]

The Platform published its final report on a social taxonomy in February 2022,[24] proposing a structure for a social taxonomy. The report identifies three objectives for a social taxonomy mainly based on the Universal Declaration of Human Rights, the European Convention of Human Rights, and the UN Sustainable Development Goals: (*i*) decent work (including value chain workers),[25] (*ii*) adequate living standards and well-being for end users,[26] (*iii*) inclusive and sustainable communities and societies.[27]

---

[21] See Article 23 on the exercise of delegation. An updated list of these acts is available at https://finance.ec.europa.eu/regulation-and-supervision/financial-services-legislation/implementing-and-delegated-acts/taxonomy-regulation_en.

[22] See Recital No. 6. For an explanation of the relevant concepts used in the Taxonomy, see Busch (2021), pp. 12–14.

[23] See Article 20, para 2, let. k).

[24] The Report is available at https://finance.ec.europa.eu/system/files/2022-08/220228-sustainable-finance-platform-finance-report-social-taxonomy_en.pdf.

[25] It applies to all value-chain workers. Thus, it is not confined to organizations' immediate employees, nor is it confined within the EU. This objective includes the following sub-objectives: (*i*) promoting decent work, (*ii*) promoting quality and non-discrimination at work, and (*iii*) ensuring respect for human rights and rights of affected workers by conducting risk based due diligence.

[26] It focuses on people and end users of certain products and services that either pose heightened health or safety risks or that have the potential to help people meet basic human needs. This objective includes the following sub-objectives: (i) ensuring healthy and safe products and services, (ii) designing products to be durable and repairable and offering services that allow for a smooth multimodal experience, (iii) providing for cybersecurity and the protection of personal data and privacy, (iv) engaging in responsible marketing practices, and (v) ensuring access to quality healthcare products and services, healthy and highly nutritious food of good quality, good-quality drinking water, good-quality housing, and education and lifelong learning.

[27] It emphasizes respect and support for human rights through paying attention to the impact of economic activity on communities and the wider society. This will be achieved by addressing and avoiding negative impacts on communities and societies and by making basic economic infrastructure available to certain target groups. This objective includes the following sub-objectives: (i) promoting equality and growth, (ii) supporting sustainable livelihoods and land rights, and (iii) ensuring respect for the human rights of affected communities by conducting risk based due diligence.

In addition, the Platform published its final report on minimum safeguards in October 2022 and identified four substantive topics from the OECD guidelines for multinational enterprises, the UN Guiding Principles on Business and Human Rights, the International Labour Organization core conventions, and the International Bill of Human Rights: (*i*) human rights (including labour and consumer rights); (*ii*) bribery, bribe solicitation, and extortion; (*iii*) taxation; and (*iv*) fair compensation.

The Platform's report also considers these provisions as part of the EU's broader regulatory landscape and how these provisions link to the obligations set down in the Sustainable Finance Disclosures Regulation,[28] the Corporate Sustainability Reporting Directive,[29] and the draft Corporate Sustainability Due Diligence Directive.[30]

However, the Commission's feedback to the Sustainable Finance Reports is still awaited, so introducing prescriptive rules does not appear imminent. Notwithstanding, a social taxonomy is needed to limit the risk of embedding opinions in the rating, which are based on discretionary assumptions. The absence of harmonization concerning the objective of these processes, i.e. the rating of the "social" component of the activity/products of the rated companies, can nullify or limit the benefits of the harmonization of the rating processes.

The current lack of a prescriptive taxonomy of the "social" component within the acronym ESG and, at the same time, the release of ratings on this component outline the research question of this essay, which aims to assess how the rating agencies' criteria identify and evaluate the "social" component of ESG.

The expected results consist of ascertaining whether the current practice of rating agencies is misaligned with the current and future regulatory frameworks of the European Union on the consideration of the "social" factor in the ESG context and can affect upcoming EU laws.

Although the result of this analysis does not pertain to a particular industry, the discussion will refer specifically to the insurance industry due to its importance in achieving the objectives underlying the introduction of ESG.

Therefore, the chapter will flow as follows: the next paragraph outlines the importance of the "social" factor for the insurance market and the international and European regulatory framework relevant to assessing this factor. The following paragraph illustrates the empirical research on social rating based on analysing the

[28] Regulation (EU) 2019/2088 of the European Parliament and of the Council of 27 November 2019 on sustainability-related disclosures in the financial services sector. A list of the related implementing and delegated acts is available at https://finance.ec.europa.eu/regulation-and-supervision/financial-services-legislation/implementing-and-delegated-acts/sustainable-finance-disclosures-regulation_en.

[29] Directive (EU) 2022/2464 of the European Parliament and of the Council of 14 December 2022 amending Regulation (EU) No 537/2014, Directive 2004/109/EC, Directive 2006/43/EC, and Directive 2013/34/EU as regards corporate sustainability reporting.

[30] Proposal for a Directive of the European Parliament and of the Council on Corporate Sustainability Due Diligence and amending Directive (EU) 2019/1937.

information released by six relevant rating agencies. A final paragraph provides the conclusions.

2 The Relevance of "Social" for the Insurance Market

The insurance industry is crucial in transitioning to a sustainable economy. Insurance undertakings can drive change through responsible operations and asset allocation[31] and incentivize other businesses and individuals to change by considering ESG factors in underwriting and product design activities.[32]

The economic dimension of the insurance industry unequivocally highlights its driving capacity towards compliance with sustainability objectives behind the ESG factors. The worldwide insurance industry collected, in 2021, a total premium volume of $6.9 trillion, and the amount is projected to grow to $7.3 trillion in 2022.[33] As of Q1 2023, only European Economic Area (EEA) (re-)insurers held €8.57 trillion in assets.[34]

Furthermore, the mentioned drivers for change are consistent with the insurance industry's evolution. This sector does not limit itself to offering products that allow damages to be compensated but, with ever-greater awareness, stimulates conduct to prevent its occurrence. It has been sharply observed how the problem is no longer so much to multiply the responsibility for risk and to organize the solvency of those liable through insurance but rather to prevent certain risks from being taken.[35]

The UN Environment Programme (UNEP) acknowledges the role the insurance industry can play in driving change to a sustainable economy by stating that "Environmental, social and governance (ESG) issues—also known as sustainability issues—pose a shared risk to insurers, communities, businesses, cities, governments, and society at large, providing a strong incentive for innovation and collaboration".[36]

Developed by the UN Environment Programme's Finance Initiative, the Principles of Sustainable Insurance (PSI) were launched at the 2012 UN Conference on

[31] Systematically integrating ESG benchmarks into investment portfolios aims to generate a positive impact on investment performance. Improving risk-adjusted return profiles and reducing downside risks make sense for long-term investors such as insurers: see Munich Re, *Sustainable Insurance*, available at https://www.munichre.com/en/company/sustainability/sustainability-in-insurance-business.html, and Swiss Re, *Responsible Investing in Practice*, available at https://www.swissre.com/our-business/managing-our-assets/responsible-investing-in-practice.

[32] Flückiger and Carbone (2021); Bhattacharya-Craven et al. (2020).

[33] See Swisse Re Institute, Sigma No. 4/2022, p. 13.

[34] See EIOPA (2023).

[35] See Ewald (2007), p. 296, where it was also noted that "Not only is prevention taking precedence over the compensation, but we are also trying to anticipate and prevent risks whose existence has not been proven".

[36] UN Environment Programme (UNEP). All information is available at https://www.unep.org/.

Sustainable Development (Rio+20) and led to the largest collaborative initiative between the UN and the insurance industry. As a result, the UNEP and PSI issued a guide for non-life insurance in 2020[37] with the aim to:

(i) Provide optional guidance to insurance industry participants in developing approaches to assess ESG risks in non-life insurance business transactions, particularly industrial and commercial insurance businesses,
(ii) support clients, intermediaries, and other stakeholders in facilitating ESG-related information which might be required during the ESG due diligence of transactions, highlight the materiality of ESG risks to various lines of business and economic sectors, including characteristics that might affect the ability to assess and mitigate such risks,
(iii) address growing concerns by stakeholders across society (e.g., NGOs, investors, governments) on ESG risks and articulate the peculiarities of the insurance business, and
(iv) demonstrate the insurance industry's valuable role in the global economy and society and strengthen the industry's contribution to sustainable development.

Political reasons push for using "sustainability" in documents with a global vision of the topic,[38] while the EU still emphasizes the acronym "ESG".[39] However, the Commission Delegated Regulation (EU) 2021/1257 of 21 April 2021 amending Regulation (EU) 2017/2358 and Regulation 2017/2359 as regards the integration of sustainability factors, risks and preferences into the product oversight and governance requirements for insurance undertakings and insurance distributors and into the rules on conduct of business and investment advice for insurance-based investment products mention customers' "sustainability preferences"[40] to be investigated in the case of selling insurance-based investment products and "sustainability factors"[41] to consider in the product approval process.[42]

---

[37] UNEP PSI (2020).

[38] See, e.g., Expansión (2024).

[39] See European Commission (2022).

[40] Article 2, point 4, of the amended Delegated Regulation (EU) 2017/2359 provides that '"sustainability preferences" means a customer's or potential customer's choice as to whether and, if so, to what extent, one or more of the following financial products should be integrated into his or her investment: (a) an insurance-based investment product for which the customer or potential customer determines that a minimum proportion shall be invested in environmentally sustainable investments as defined in Article 2, point (1), of Regulation (EU) 2020/852 of the European Parliament and of the Council; (b) an insurance-based investment product for which the customer or potential customer determines that a minimum proportion shall be invested in sustainable investments as defined in Article 2, point (17), of Regulation (EU) 2019/2088 of the European Parliament and of the Council; (c) an insurance-based investment product that considers principal adverse impacts on sustainability factors where qualitative or quantitative elements demonstrating that consideration are determined by the customer or potential customer.'

[41] Article 2, point 5, of the amended Delegated Regulation (EU) 2017/2359 refers to the sustainability factors as defined in Article 2, point 24, of Regulation (EU) 2019/2088; i.e. they mean "environmental, social and employee matters, respect for human rights, anti-corruption and anti-bribery matters".

[42] See Recitals No. 4 and 5 and Article 5 of the amended Delegated Regulation (EU) 2017/2358.

Such political choice ultimately adds a layer of uncertainty to the meaning of each component embedded in the ESG as the social factors included in the sustainability factors do not coincide with those mentioned in the minimum safeguards identified under the Platform on Sustainable Finance Report of October 2022.[43]

In any case, the insurance industry must clearly understand the sustainability/ESG factors to embed them in its products and promote insureds' behaviours coherent with those factors. As the Geneva Association[44] pointed out, "without reliable, comparable, and meaningful sustainability disclosure from companies, investors and banks will struggle to incorporate long-term sustainability risks and opportunities into their decision-making".[45]

In the context of the ESG factors, in particular, there is agreement in noting that the "social" component is the most evanescent, lending itself to multiple meanings that make a common understanding and uniform application of such factors particularly difficult.[46] While climate change is a top agenda item for ESG investors, a substantial minority of investors think the focus on climate change is distracting from other issues.[47]

Although "social" sounds almost similar in several languages,[48] its meaning varies in the common language.[49] Based on these multiple meanings, e.g., an

---

[43] The Report mentioned (*i*) human rights (including labour and consumer rights); (*ii*) bribery, bribe solicitation, and extortion; (*iii*) taxation; and (*iv*) fair compensation. On the other hand, the sustainability factors refer to environmental, social, and employee matters; respect for human rights; and anti-corruption and anti-bribery matters.

[44] The Geneva Association was founded in 1973 as the International Association for the Study of Insurance Economics to make an original contribution to the progress of insurance through objective studies of the interdependencies between the economic environment and insurance activities. Members of the association include over 70 insurance and re-insurance companies based in 26 countries worldwide, which manage assets worth $21 trillion and have 2.6 billion insured persons.

[45] Schanz (2022), p. 15.

[46] Schanz (2022), pp. 13 ff.

[47] Ground (2022): she also added that "Four in 10 (41%) think social issues are being overlooked in the climate change debate. And climate change is still proving a politically charged issue for some".

[48] Such as Croatian: socijalan, Danish: social, Dutch: social, Finnish: sosiaalinen, French: social, German: sozial, Italian: sociale, Norwegian: sosial, Portuguese: social, Romanian: social, Russian: социальный (sociál′nyj), Swedish: social, and Turkish: sosyal.

[49] According to the Oxford Dictionary, "social" means, in its second meaning, "Connected with society and the way it is organised". However, the Royal Academy of the Spanish Language, in its dictionary, gathers the following meanings: "1. adj. Pertaining or relating to society. 2. adj. Pertaining or relating to a company or partnership, or to the partners or partners, allies, or confederates. 3. adj. Pertaining to the economically disadvantaged social classes". In Italian, the Treccani Institute provides several meanings, the first as follows: "a. Who lives in society; b. Pertaining to human society, bearing on man's life as a participant in a community in which he has, or should have, substantial right of equality with other members; c. Pertaining to the environment in which one lives, the people with whom one is in contact: life s.; relationships, relations s.; social conventions.; d. In the language of politics and economics, it is used mainly regarding programs and aspirations tending toward an improvement in the living conditions of society and especially of workers." In French, the Larousse dictionary provides the following meanings: "1.

Anglo-Saxon insurer might understand that everything related to society should be included under the heading "social", while a Spanish insurer could confine that part only to action taken to help "economically disadvantaged social classes". That might impact the work insurers are doing under the heading of "social" and the identification of those actions while analysed by third parties.

The international research literature does not help in providing uniformity in the meaning of "social" within ESG factors as the approaches are different,[50] and synthesis is far from achieved. Given this cacophony of approaches, some reports provide their definition of "social",[51] multiplying the uncertainty about definitions and their link to sustainability or ESG.

As pointed out in the previous paragraph, the EU regulatory framework does not provide a social taxonomy, but several laws applying to insurance undertakings should lead to understanding the meaning of "social".

The EU Regulation (EU) 2019/2088 of 27 November 2019 on sustainability-related disclosures in the financial services sector (SFDR) defines sustainable investment and deals with the issue of cornering the meaning of "social" because such investment definition includes "an investment in an economic activity that contributes to a social objective, in particular, an investment that contributes to tackling inequality or that fosters social cohesion, social integration, and labor relations, or an investment in human capital or economically or socially disadvantaged communities".[52]

The Directive (EU) 2022/2464 of 14 December 2022 concerning corporate sustainability reporting (CSRD) requests insurance undertakings to include in the management report information necessary to understand the undertaking's impacts on sustainability matters and information necessary to understand how sustainability matters affect the undertaking's development, performance, and position.

Which relates to a society, a human community considered as its entity: Social organisation. Social phenomena; 2. Which concerns the relationship between an individual and other members of the community: Have a highly developed social life; 3. Which concerns the relations between the members of society or the organisation of its members into groups, into classes: Social inequalities; 4. Refers to trades, organisations, and activities concerned either with the relationships between individuals and groups in society or with the economic and psychological conditions of members of society: Social worker; 5. Concerning improving the living conditions and, in particular, the material conditions of the members of society: The social policies of the State".

[50] See Eccles and Viviers (2011), pp. 389 ff.; Ting-Ting et al. (2021); Clément et al. (2023).

[51] Schanz (2022), p. 13, proposed a dual definition of social sustainability: "From an activity perspective, we view social sustainability as the process of identifying and managing both positive and negative business impacts on key constituencies such as employees, value-chain workers, customers and affected local communities. From an outcome perspective, social sustainability can be defined as the capacity of current and future generations to live, learn, and work in healthy and liveable conditions which promote diversity and equal opportunities."

[52] See Article 2, No. 17. For a commentary on the implications of this Directive for financial actors, see Bengo et al. (2022).

Meanwhile, sustainability matters mean "environmental, social and human rights, and governance factors, including sustainability factors".[53]

Further details on the "social" factor can arise from the Proposal for a Directive on Corporate Sustainability Due Diligence issued by the Commission on 23 February 2022,[54] at least regarding human rights.[55] Likewise, the Proposal for a Directive amending Directives 2005/29/EC and 2011/83/EU as regards empowering consumers for the green transition through better protection against unfair practices and through better information intends to amend Directive 2005/29/EC on unfair commercial practices by inserting a reference to misleading information on the social characteristics of the products or suppliers of those products,[56] where the meaning of social follows a case-by-case assessment and can be understood in a broad sense.[57]

Based on the above, "social" can be related to inequality, socially disadvantaged communities, labour relations, human rights, anti-corruption, and anti-bribery. At the same time, it is questionable that the above elements embed factors such as taxation, health, or solidarity. In addition to the uncertainty related to the components of the "social" factor within the ESG, the relevant regulatory framework lacks details on the different elements related to this factor. So the risk of "social washing" is still relatively high.[58]

---

[53] Sustainability factors are those "defined in point (24) of Article 2 of Regulation (EU) 2019/2088", i.e. "environmental, social and employee matters, respect for human rights, anti-corruption and anti-bribery matters".

[54] The due diligence process set out in this Directive should cover the six steps defined by the OECD Due Diligence Guidance for Responsible Business Conduct, which include due diligence measures for companies to identify and address adverse human rights and environmental impacts. These measures encompass integrating due diligence into policies and management systems, identifying and assessing adverse human rights (and environmental impacts), and preventing, ceasing, or minimizing actual and potential adverse human rights (and environmental impacts). See Recital No. 16, which adds the following steps: assessing the effectiveness of measures, communicating, and providing remediation.

[55] The Proposal identifies the adverse human rights impact, which means "an adverse impact on protected persons resulting from the violation of one of the rights or prohibitions listed in the Annex, Part I Section 1, as enshrined in the international conventions listed in the Annex, Part I Section 2", that is, the human rights considered in all the Human Rights and Fundamental Freedoms Conventions signed at EU and international levels.

[56] See the text of the European Parliament adopted at first reading on 17 January 2024, retrieved at https://www.europarl.europa.eu/doceo/document/TA-9-2024-0018_EN.html.

[57] Recital No. 3 states that "Information provided by traders on the social characteristics of a product throughout its value chain can relate, for example, to the quality and fairness of working conditions of the workforce involved, such as adequate wages, social protection, the safety of the work environment and social dialogue. Such information can also relate to respect for human rights, to equal treatment and opportunities for all, including gender equality, inclusion, and diversity, to contributions to social initiatives or to ethical commitments, such as animal welfare. The environmental and social characteristics of a product can be understood in a broad sense, encompassing the environmental and social aspects, impact, and performance of a product."

[58] For further analysis, see Fichtner et al. (2023), pp. 493–494: "Subsequently, mandatory minimum standards could be developed to ensure asset owners that their investments actually create

Despite the reported uncertainties, insurance companies have adopted a "bottom-up" market approach in pursuing the "social" objective as rating agencies assess them for the adherence of their activities to the "social" component of the ESG.

The definition of "social" as conveyed by the rating is of critical importance in the relationship between insurers (and intermediaries) and their customers and, ultimately, in achieving the objectives underlying the introduction of ESG factors. As mentioned, in fact, Commission Delegated Regulation (EU) 2021/1257 of 21 April 2021 amending Regulation (EU) 2017/2358 and Regulation 2017/2359 expressly requires considering sustainability factors in the product approval process, investigating customers' sustainability preferences, and advising customers on the most suitable product matching such preferences.

Therefore, ratings that measure the "social" component of sustainability preferences are likely to influence insurance market practices and customer choices. The following paragraph empirically analyses how rating agencies measure this component and its distinctive value.

3 The Meaning of "Social" in the Rating Agencies' Reports

3.1 The Role Played by ESG Rating Agencies

The ESG dimension has suffered a significant development in the investment industry over the last decade.[59] In 2020, the Global Sustainable Investment Review (GSIR) revealed that the industry has grown to US$35.3 trillion, an increase of 15% in 2 years.[60]

The inevitable consequence of the former is twofold. First is the rise of ESG rating agencies, which scrutinize businesses and assess their corporate sustainability. Second, the surge of these rating companies is a key reference for all actors (financial markets, academia, lawyers, parliaments, etc.).[61]

Scholars pointed out that ESG rating agencies play a crucial role in constructing "calculative standards designed to institutionalize the field".[62] What is more, "investors, shareholders, governments, and firms have benefitted from this since they request accurate information not only regarding financial performance but also about environmental, social and governance (ESG) aspects, which has become part of their competitive strategy".[63]

---

meaningful impact via these mechanisms. This would also address concerns of greenwashing which is harmful to investors and asset managers alike."

[59] Escrig-Olmedo et al. (2019).

[60] Global Sustainable Investment Alliance (2020).

[61] Escrig-Olmedo et al. (2019).

[62] Elbasha and Avetisyan (2018), pp. 38–46.

[63] Escrig-Olmedo et al. (2019).

However, the approaches towards the meaning of ESG ratings collide between the ESG rating agencies and their clients.[64] Raters might believe that their ratings are purely about financial risk management. Meanwhile, for their clients, the promise of ESG ratings goes beyond a real investment in sustainability. This mismatching is worrisome because either social impact is internalized by all actors or "the messages launched by rating agencies about what could a sustainable company be or how corporate sustainability performance could be measured might be misrepresented".[65]

Another concern has been raised as to the rater's tendency to give "higher ESG ratings to sister firms owned by the same large shareholders (...) provides evidence that conflicts of interest in market practices can undermine the integrity of ESG ratings".[66] As extracted from the European Commission's "Targeted consultation on the functioning of the ESG rating market in the EU and the consideration of ESG factors in credit ratings", 91% of the respondents considered that there are significant biases with the methodology in ESG rating.[67]

In any case, it cannot be forgotten that the investment in sustainability exists for many reasons, such as pressure groups, different regulations, the organization's competitive position, etc.[68] This money injection could be a game changer for the entire world. As mentioned before, insurance companies can drive change through responsible operations and asset allocation, as well as incentivizing other businesses and individuals to change by considering ESG factors in underwriting and product design activities.[69]

What is more, insurance companies will obtain benefits from those actions. One clear example is Sustainable Development Goal (SDG) number 6, clear water, and sanitization. Investing in sewage treatment plants could help eradicate diseases related to the consumption of contaminated water all around the world. This will decrease insurance claims related to these health conditions worldwide. However, for that to happen, regulatory frameworks must ensure that investors use their resources to build a world where SDG concerns have been considered. Otherwise, we bear the risk that they could be disguising their old investments with new slogans.

As some authors have highlighted after performing an appropriate analysis, "the results suggest a linear relationship between the sentiments towards ESG and greenwashing, i.e., greenwashing is significantly growing at the rate of ESG".[70]

Considering the role of ESG rating agencies, biased ESG provides misleading information about corporate sustainability, which "can affect the social legitimacy

[64] DDQ Invest (2022).

[65] Escrig-Olmedo et al. (2019).

[66] Tang et al. (2021), p. 29.

[67] European Commission (2022).

[68] Mackenzie et al. (2013), pp. 495–512.

[69] For instance, many SDGs require, for their realization, infrastructure and training, and many insurance companies—money-wise and knowledge-wise—are in the position to provide them.

[70] Biju et al. (2023).

and trust of both companies and ESG rating agencies".[71] Moreover, this could trigger various adverse consequences. For instance, rating disagreement could reduce the incentives to improve ESG performance as there is no commercial logic behind spending resources that will end up on useless ratings.[72] This inevitability ends with fewer resources spent on ESG objectives. Thus, expectations held by stakeholders—as referred to before, e.g. NGOs, investors, and governments and rating agencies about sustainability and sustainable development—should be matched to avoid these issues.[73]

However, each ESG rating agency uses its own definitions and methodology, posing several challenges, such as the lack of transparency, commensurability, trade-offs among criteria, the lack of an overall score, and the lack of consideration of stakeholders' preferences.[74]

To solve this issue, scholars proposed that "greater quantitative ESG disclosure may bring about lower ESG rating divergence".[75] Nonetheless, to achieve a standardized quantitative disclosure, companies should be able to work with the same concepts because they are at the heart of all methodologies. Therefore, the solution to this scenario starts by shedding light on what ESG rating agencies understand to be fitted within the "S" dimension of ESG. Then it should be determined whether the EU regulation analysed in the previous part matches or will match the above-mentioned needs in this field.

3.2 ESG Ratings Reports

According to Deloitte, no one-fits-all methodology exists to analyse ESG data used by rating agencies. More than 600 agencies are currently operating on the market and often issuing different ratings concerning the same entity.[76]

ESMA addressed a Letter on ESG Rating Call for Evidence to the Directorate General for Financial Stability, Financial Services and Capital Markets Union at the

[71] Escrig-Olmedo et al. (2019).

[72] Liu (2022), p. 2.

[73] Escrig-Olmedo et al. (2019).

[74] Escrig-Olmedo et al. (2019).

[75] Liu (2022), p. 2.: "Standardized quantitative disclosure, following sustainable reporting instruments and standards developed by regulators or non-governmental organizations, is conducive to the rating convergence among agencies for the following reasons: (1) rating agencies tend to incorporate the indicators required by reporting instruments or standards into their assessment process, which greatly narrows the differences between agencies' evaluation systems and then converge rating outcomes; (2) when horizontal comparisons between companies are easily implementable, different rating agencies would choose similar companies' portfolio as highly rated companies."

[76] See Deloitte, *ESG Ratings: do they add value? How to get prepared?*, available at https://www2.deloitte.com/ce/en/pages/about-deloitte/articles/esg-ratings-do-they-add-value.html.

European Commission on 22 June 2022,[77] which reported that the number of providers currently active in the EU is 59. The market structure among providers is split between a small number of huge non-EU entities on one hand and many significantly smaller EU entities on the other. As mentioned earlier, the predominant business model is investor pays. However, the provision of ESG ratings on an issuer-pays basis is more prevalent than anticipated and was indicated in around a third of the responses from providers.

Based on evidence from academic papers,[78] consulting firms,[79] and the UN Principles for Responsible Investment (PRI),[80] the following rating agencies should be the most preeminent: Sustainalytics, MSCI Inc., RepRisk, Moody's Corporation, Fitch Group, and S&P Global ESG. All these firms provide ESG ratings, but the last three also offer credit ratings and ESG indicators enhancing credit rating transparency. These three ratings are different, as defined by PRI.[81] Indeed, ESG ratings "provide a synthetic indicator of an issuer's ESG characteristics or exposure to ESG risks". Credit ratings "assess the credit risk of an issuer or one of its debt instruments". ESG indicators "highlight how ESG factors affect credit ratings".

Full information concerning the indicators these companies use for ESG rating is generally not made available to the public. On the contrary, the definition and materiality test used in credit rankings are consistent across rating agencies and are made available to the public.[82] These differences could be triggered because there is only a lack of uniform ESG rating regulation; credit rankings have been widely regulated in the same or similar way all around the world.[83]

This lack of uniformity could have made the methodology used a competitive advantage. However, this could lead to a "customized" ESG rating, which could not show the real ESG impact of the companies according to the ESG regulatory framework.

As addressed by Walter,[84] creating the kinds of social impact metrics needed for S-scoring is difficult because credibility requires that highly granular (even interpersonal) welfare comparisons must be defended as legitimate. However, communities are different, and comparisons are challenged. The EU Proposal for a Regulation on the transparency of ESG rating activities could solve this issue, but

---

[77] The Letter is available at https://www.esma.europa.eu/sites/default/files/library/esma80-416-347_letter_on_esg_ratings_call_for_evidence_june_2022.pdf.

[78] Khovrak (2020), p. 45. Tayan et al. (2022).

[79] See Deloitte, https://www2.deloitte.com/ce/en/pages/about-deloitte/articles/esg-ratings-do-they-add-value.html and ERM https://www.erm.com/news/new-erm-report-ranks-esg-ratings-agencies-and-urges-action-to-maintain-business-and-investor-trust/.

[80] See UNPRI (2023).

[81] Ibid.

[82] See UNPRI (2023).

[83] In the EU, Regulation (EU) No. 462/2013 of the European Parliament and of the Council of 21 May 2013 amending Regulation (EC) No. 1060/2009 on credit rating agencies.

[84] Walter (2020).

the question is whether the definitions used by ESG ratings to measure the "S" are that different.

Therefore, this essay aims not to analyse the methodology used by these agencies to calculate their ratings as this information is private, and some analyses have already been performed in this area.[85] The objective is to infer how each rating agency understands the term "social" based on what they comprise under that category. This understanding is critical as the lack of uniform definitions will lead to a more significant divergence among results and, consequently, less comparability among ratings. A lower degree of comparability makes these instruments less useful for determining the real ESG impact of companies.[86] In addition, the risk of social washing, conflicts of interest, and unfair commercial practices increases.[87]

3.3 *The Methodology Used for the Empirical Analysis of the Rating Agencies' Approach to the "Social" Factor*

To answer the question of how each rating agency understands the term "social", the empirical analysis will illustrate the consulted indications regarding the performance of the ESG analysis provided by these companies. It will summarize the most relevant data and classify the information into similarities and differences. Moreover, it will re-conduct the similarities into broad categories brought from the different instruments analysed in the previous parts; i.e. labour management and human capital would both fit within the broad category labelled "labour". At the same time, it will reunite the most prominent differences within the "others" category.

Half of the selected rating agencies offer only ESG ratings, and the rest provide ESG indicators enhancing credit rating transparency. As explained before, the degree of opacity of companies only offering ESG ratings is more significant due to the lack of consistent regulation in the field. Therefore, by adding companies subject to a higher degree of disclosure, more accuracy of this analysis is expected.[88] For instance, ESG rating companies could refrain from publishing the parts in which they divide their analysis, so no/less accurate deduction can be performed on the meaning of "S".

[85] Chatterji et al. (2016).

[86] AFM, *Position Paper: Call for a European Regulation for the provision of ESG data, ratings, and related services*, pp. 4–5, available at https://www.afm.nl/~/profmedia/files/rapporten/2020/amf-afm-paper-call-european-regulation-esg-data-ratings.pdf?la=en.

[87] Ibid. That is to say that two companies can be rated quite differently in two ratings and undergo the same investment in ESG or that one company could do good or bad in two different ratings with the same actions.

[88] As to the differences between those categories, see Cash (2021).

However, as publishing some data regarding credit rating is compulsory, it is possible to transfer the basic definitions, such as "S", to ESG ratings. For example, Fitch Group provides extensive explanations on different aspects of credit ratings, and some of these documents touch upon aspects related to "S".[89] This approach is coherent with the preexisting literature in the field.[90] Moreover, it will allow determining whether specializing in both tasks makes the rating agencies converge on the meaning of "S".

Finally, it is important to highlight that not all companies selected have specific ESG criteria for insurers. Therefore, the information provided below forms part of their general ESG criteria. However, if publicly available and relevant, specific data regarding the insurance sector is provided.

3.4 *An Empirical Analysis of Rating Methodologies on "Social" Factor in the ESG*

A commented summary of the most relevant public indications used by the selected ESG rating agencies is reported as follows.

Sustainalytics

In the case of Sustainalytics, its public information explains that "the ESG Risk Ratings are composed of three building blocks that contribute to a company's overall rating. These building blocks include Corporate Governance, material ESG issues (MEIs), and idiosyncratic ESG issues (...) material ESG issues (MEIs): For example, the topics of employee recruitment, development, diversity, engagement, and labour relations are all-encompassed by the material ESG issue of Human Capital because they are all employee-related and require Human Resources initiatives and oversight. (...) Occupational Health and Safety also concerns employees, but the common thread here is to ensure the health and safety of employees at their workplace."[91] However, it also explains that "these material ESG issues may have a pure environmental, social, or governance character. Typically, however, they are mixed bags or combinations of two or all three of these."[92] Therefore, from this

[89] Fitch Ratings, available at https://www.fitchratings.com/search?expanded=research&filter.language=English&filter.reportType=Rating%20Criteria&filter.tag=Active%20Criteria&filter.tag=Exposure%20Draft&sort=recency.

[90] Gargantini and Siri (2022), p. 5: "The services offered by traditional CRAs consist of assessing the creditworthiness of a debtor or of a financial obligation, quantified through a system of symbols that ranks the result of the evaluation (Article 3(1)(a) Regulation (EC) 1060/2009 on credit rating agencies—CRA Regulation). As we mentioned, this exercise can hardly ignore the risks stemming from ESG factors (High-Level Expert Group on Sustainable Finance 2018). For this reason, CRAs stress they include ESG factors in their methodologies (S&P Global Ratings 2022), although with few details on the assessment criteria."

[91] Sustainalytics (2019), p. 5.

[92] Sustainalytics (2019), p. 12.

information, it can be inferred that Sustainalytics does not work with an autonomous meaning of the term "social" within the ESG.

This outcome is confirmed by looking at the report prepared by Sustainalytics for the Santander group because under the heading "Overall Assessment of Social Use of Proceeds", the following categories are mentioned: affordable basic infrastructure (energy, transport, water and waste management, and communication and technology), access to essential services (education, human healthcare and related activities, social housing, and the owner living in housing), employment generation, and programs designed to prevent and/or alleviate unemployment stemming from socio-economic crises, including through the potential effect of small and medium-sized enterprise (SME) financing and microfinance (financial and insurance activities). Therefore, here, categories that usually fit within the E in the trinomial ESG, e.g. waste management, are covered under the heading "social".

MSCI Inc.

MSCI informs that under the heading social, the following issues are studied: labour management, health and safety, human capital development, supply chain labour standards, product safety and quality, chemical safety, consumer financial protection, privacy and data security, responsible investment, community relations, controversial sourcing, access to finance, access to health care, and opportunities in nutrition and health. Besides the distribution of categories, the company offers industry-specific ESG ratings and company-specific ones. Regarding industry specific, the explanation is as follows:

> An evaluation of weight-setting schemes found that the industry-specific weight setting methodology used by MSCI ESG Ratings outperformed equal-weighted and optimized weight setting methodologies over a 13-year study period. The weights displayed in the ESG Industry Materiality Map represent the average Key issue Weight for companies in an industry. Key Issue Weights are determined through a combination of two factors: 1) how much each industry contributes to the main externality connected to the issue as compared to other industries (for instance, how carbon-intensive the industry is relative to other industries) and 2) the time horizon within which the externality may materialize.[93]

Regarding company specific, this approach is justified as follows:

> The foundation for the ESG Industry Materiality Map is an industry-specific evaluation of key ESG risks and opportunities. However, the ESG Industry Materiality Map also reflects company-specific nuances that may not be captured by the industry classification. The lines of business, production processes used, and regions where a company operates are among the determinants of ESG risk. Rules-based model variants take these nuances into account, meaning that not all companies in a given industry are necessarily rated on all the same highlighted Key Issues. Because the ESG Industry Materiality Map includes company-specific Key Issues, issues that are only applied to a small proportion of the industry will appear to have a low "average" weight.[94]

[93] Sustainalytics (2019).

[94] MSCI, ESG Industry Materiality Map Engine, available at https://www.msci.com/our-solutions/esg-investing/esg-industry-materiality-map.

The "ESG Industry Materiality Map" can be consulted in an engine generated by the company.[95] In the publicly available information provided by this engine, the components of social remain the same, but weight is only assigned to certain parts. For instance, the life and health insurance industry, within the heading "Social", has been assigned with the following criteria and percentages: human capital development—19.9%, responsible investment—14.9%, privacy and data security—14.9%, access to finance—9.9%, and product safety and quality—0.1%, whereas the data for oil and gas drilling is health and safety, 18.5%, and community relations, 6.9%. These data are quite impressive as one could have thought that among the general criteria used by MSCI to analyse "S", "access to healthcare", "health and safety", and "opportunities in nutrition and health" are key for health and life insurance. The same applies to oil and gas drilling as it is difficult to understand why "chemical safety" is left behind. However, further information would be needed to analyse that data.

RepRisk

This rating agency does not declare to have an ESG rating. However, there are rather four different instruments to assess ESG obligations: RepRisk Index (RRI), RepRisk Rating (RRR), UN Global Compact (UNGC) Violator Flag, and UNGC Violator Index. Moreover, the company explains that "the RRI does not have any E, S, or G components. What is available, however, is a breakdown of each RRI by the number of associations a company has with the aggregate E, S, or G issues. The ESG breakdown should not be used for company-to-company comparisons, but rather to see how a company's E, S, or G exposure has developed over time." Additionally, within the index, there is no weighting of the ESG issues, e.g., by sector or country.[96] This information can be completed with the document entitled "An Introduction to RepRisk: The Leading Research Tool to Help You Flag, Assess, and Monitor ESG Risks in Your Business".[97]

According to this document, the research scope of RepRisk comprises 28 ESG issues, which are in line with key international standards. Within "social", the following components are gathered: community relations (human rights abuses and corporate complicity, impact on communities, local participation issues, and social discrimination) and employee relations (forced labour, child labour, freedom of association and collective bargaining, discrimination in employment, occupational health and safety issues, and poor employment conditions). Moreover, the following issues are considered "cross-cutting": controversial products and services,

---

[95] Ibid.

[96] RepRisk, Methodology, available at https://www.reprisk.com/news-research/resources/methodology#:~:text=What%20is%20the%20RepRisk%20Rating,conduct%20risks%20into%20business%20processes.

[97] RepRisk, An Introduction to RepRisk: The leading research tool to help you flag, assess, and monitor ESG risks in your business, available at https://iseb3-site.s3.amazonaws.com/columbia-ws2/reprisk-2018-fgv-b3-ise.pdf.

violation of national legislation, products (health and environmental issues), violation of international standards, and supply chain issues.

Moody's Corporation

If looking at the information provided by the UN PRI, this company offers credit rankings, ESG indicators enhancing credit rating transparency, and ESG rankings. However, when looking at their webpage, the boundaries between the two last categories appear somehow blurry. Moreover, the publicly available information refers to ESG in credit ratings. Hence, the following information will touch upon that category.

The document entitled "ESG Scores Explained: Quantifying the Degree of Credit Impact",[98] which was produced by Moody's, refers, various times, to the meaning of "social" in the same manner as containing the following: for the private sector, customer relations, demographic and societal trends, human capital, health and safety, and responsible production and, for the public sector, access to basic services, demographics, education, health and safety, housing, labour, and income.

It is also important to highlight that the company refers to "adaptable ESG solutions". The explanation is that they leverage their "deep domain expertise and industry knowledge as well as innovative technologies to help you address evolving business needs".[99]

Fitch Group

According to the company, when asked what external data sets are provided for users, they refer to "social" for entities. Then "social" is divided into the following categories: grade, community and customer grade, diversity grade, human rights grade, labour rights grade, risk and incident treatment grade, and target and supply chain grade.[100] No concrete explanation has been found as to the definition of these items or the methodology used to calculate them.[101]

S&P Global ESG

S&P shows four items under "social": workforce and diversity, safety management, customer engagement, and communities.[102] Moreover, the company has created an "Atlas" to provide "a view of relative environmental, social, and governance (ESG)

---

[98] Moody's Investor Service (2022).

[99] Moody's, ESG rating, available at https://www.moodys.com/web/en/us/capabilities/esg-risk.html.

[100] Fitch Group (2023).

[101] For instance, the information provided for human rights is as follows: "We investigate whether the issuer has a human rights policy and, if so, analyse its quality. We also look into whether the entity has signed up to the UN Global Compact or similar or left it up to the local legislation. We also take into consideration whether those policies and commitments have actually been implemented."

[102] S&P, evaluation, available at https://www.spglobal.com/ratings/en/products-benefits/products/esg-evaluation.

risks we see around the world". The Atlas reflects the various ESG risks faced by different sectors and geographies. For insurance, the document informs as follows:

> Social exposure for the insurance sector reflects its exposure to consumer behaviors, human capital management, and demography. Insurers face high reputational risks that could damage their customer franchise. For instance, data privacy and security problems or mis-selling can also cause reputational damage and large fines. In addition, as a collector of risks, the insurance industry could face significantly more claims in a mass litigation (e.g., asbestos), which could tarnish their reputation. Insurers also have exposure to human capital management, as a large productive workforce is at the core of their business model. Finally, longer life expectancy could hit life insurers by affecting products covering longevity risk.

From all the information provided by the companies, it is possible to conclude that for them, the components of "social" are not unified. Moreover, the terms comprised within "social" are too broad to achieve a consensus as regards its scope; for instance, the terms communities and diversity could be defined in multiple ways.

Nevertheless, to better discuss the EU Proposal for a Regulation on the transparency of ESG rating activities, it is possible to re-conduct some of the information gathered by these rating agencies into the following categories: equality/non-discrimination, solidarity, labour rights/workers, health, and security.

Table 1 shows the classification of the information into the former categories.

From the above analysis, one can conclude that the meaning of "social" managed by ESG rating agencies is not homogeneous. Only the components "work" and "solidarity" are common to the above rating agencies. The components "health", "equality", and "safety" are considered by some agencies but not by others, while additional factors to those mentioned above can be found, albeit heterogeneous. This finding only partially matches the pre-existing literature on the matter:

> Regarding the social pillar criteria, the aspects that have been mainly considered in the assessment process of ESG rating agencies analyzed in 2008 were human capital development and training (100%), human rights (87.5%), and community relations (87.5%). On the contrary, the aspects incorporated into the assessment process of all ESG rating agencies in 2018 were labor management, human rights and quality working conditions, health, and safety. After the definition of Sustainable Development Goals (SDGs), aspects related to the improvement of health and education, the reduction of inequalities, and the necessity to spur economic growth seem to be crucial to measure how companies contribute to sustainable development.[103]

Indeed, factors such as health, safety, and equality are not yet a common standard for all rating agencies when rating the "social" component of ESG.

Furthermore, a significant difference can be found in the used data. This difference led to the difficulty of comparing information from one rating agency to another.[104] Authors have highlighted that "rating divergence is not merely a matter

[103] Escrig-Olmedo et al. (2019).

[104] Zumente and Lace (2021). They outlined that "a correlation of 0.58 is found between the two most comparable ESG ratings (RobecoSAM and Sustainalytics) implying that the ESG rating divergence is high even among those European companies".

Table 1 Classification of information into categories

Categories (→) / Rating Agency (↓)	Equality	Solidarity	Labour	Health	Security	Others
Sustainalytics	Diversity	Affordable basic infrastructure Access to essential services	Employee recruitment Labour relations	Occupational health	Occupational security	
MSCI		Community relations	Labour management Human capital Supply chain labour standards	Health Access to healthcare Opportunities in nutrition and health	Safety Product safety and quality Chemical safety Privacy and data security	Development Consumer financial protection Responsible investment Controversial sourcing Access to finance
RepRisk	Social discrimination Discrimination in employment	Impact on communities Local participation issues	Forced labour Child labour Freedom of association and collective bargaining Poor employment conditions	Occupational health and safety issues		Human rights abuses and corporate complicity Controversial products and services Violation of national legislation Violation of international standards Supply chain issues
Moody's Corporation		Access to basic services (public sector)	Human capital Labour and income (public sector)	Health	Safety	Customer relations Demographic and societal trends Responsible production Education (public sector) Housing (public sector)

Fitch Group	Diversity	Community	Labour rights		Risk and incident	Grade Customer grade Human rights grade Target and supply chain grade
S&P Global ESG	Diversity	Communities	Workforce		Safety management	Customer engagement

of varying definitions but a fundamental disagreement about the underlying data".[105] Also, those rating agencies dedicated to ESG and credit ratings refer to broader categories. For instance, while Sustainalytics refers to "affordable basic infrastructure and access to essential services" that undoubtedly affect the whole community, Fitch group only refers to "community".

Therefore, these ratings might still be helpful for some stakeholders, but they cannot be used for comparisons. This gap has been read to mean that ESG rating agencies are not fully integrating sustainability principles into the corporate sustainability assessment process.[106]

At the same time, heterogeneity in the criteria could lead rating agencies' clients to expect an assessment "a la carte". The client could pick the rating agency with the "right" criteria to assess that client as "social". Alternatively, some rating agencies could approach the client, mentioning that their methodology does not include criteria that are less favourable to the client.

4 Conclusions

From the information collected in the empirical analysis provided by ESG rating agencies, it is possible to conclude that they do not work with the same components when assessing the "social" component. Moreover, the concepts used are too broad to have a uniform definition; this can be observed, for instance, when using the words "communities", "supply chain", or "diversity".

Nevertheless, the analysis makes it possible to infer that they are not conceptually that far. Still, the lack of transparency regarding definitions and methodologies makes it impossible for all stakeholders to compare the results of different ESG rating agencies.

This gap could trigger various adverse consequences, such as reducing incentives to improve ESG performance due to the lack of repercussions from a commercial point of view. Moreover, the observed heterogeneity in selecting the components could stimulate the offering/searching of ratings "a la carte" as they are predetermined or interpreted in favour of the client's need rather than an objective assessment.

The Proposal for a Regulation on the transparency of ESG rating activities can be appreciated for the organizational requirements, processes and documents concerning governance, as well as the transparency requirements it aims to introduce. This set of rules will harmonize the ESG rating activities regardless of where the rating agency is based, including those providers established in a third country.[107]

---

[105] Berg et al. (2022).

[106] Escrig-Olmedo et al. (2019).

[107] See Articles 9–13 of the Proposal.

The obligation to disclose on the agencies' websites the methodologies, models, and key rating assumptions they use in their ESG rating activities[108] can help stakeholders understand this information, reduce agencies' discretion and opacity and, ultimately, appreciate the distinctive value of the ESG rating.

If the Proposal for a Regulation on the transparency of ESG rating activities could handle issues arising from opaque methodologies and conflicts of interest, the rating agencies' criteria to identify and evaluate the "social" component of ESG need to be harmonized.

Adopting a social taxonomy covering the gaps in this matter appears compulsory if ESG objectives are to be fulfilled. Some evidence suggests that investors will include sustainability if they have better data and clarity on the elements of sustainability that translate into superior financial performance.[109] Therefore, a social taxonomy should limit the risk of embedding opinion in the ratings and neutralize social washing risk.

Although the taxonomy is necessary to recognize a distinctive value in the social rating, more is needed. Table 2 compares the meaning of "social" from the European Union regulatory framework set out in paragraph 2 and the results from the empirical analysis of the ESG rating methodologies carried out in paragraph 3.

The results of the empirical analysis do not pertain to a particular industry. Thus, they can be referred to the insurance industry, too. However, the relevance of such an industry in achieving the objectives underlying the introduction of ESG requires some further considerations.

Scholars have highlighted that the current and proposed regulatory framework in the EU will be successful in catering to investor preferences but not in promoting sustainable finance as a tool to accelerate the sustainability transition.[110]

This misalignment must be avoided because, if it occurred, it would encourage social washing and, in general, unfair practices towards customers and expose insurers to operational and reputational risks.

The Commission Delegated Regulation (EU) 2021/1257 of 21 April 2021 requires the integration of sustainability factors, risks, and preferences into the product oversight and governance requirements for insurance undertakings and insurance distributors and into the rules on the conduct of business and investment advice for insurance-based investment products.

Manufacturing products that incorporate the ESG factors, including the social one, requires that insurers can rely on the ESG ratings of the companies in which they invest the premiums collected. If so, insurers (and insurance intermediaries) will be able to market products that genuinely satisfy the sustainability preferences of their customers.

The EU Proposal for Regulating the transparency of ESG rating activities could help solve this problem as it aims to avoid a social rating "a la carte".

---

[108] See Article 21.

[109] Esty and Cort (2017), p. 42.

[110] Ramos Muñoz and Smoleńska (2023).

Table 2 Comparison of the meaning of "social" from the EU regulatory framework and the results from the empirical analysis performed in this paper

Instrument	Objective	Instruments	Shortcomings
EU Proposal for a Regulation on the transparency of ESG rating activities	Integrity and reliability of ESG rankings	1) Transparency of the rating methodologies 2) The effective management of conflicts of interest	It does not define the substantial profiles of these processes, i.e. the meaning of each of the components included in the definition of ESG that rating agencies must consider.
EU Regulation (EU) 2020/852 of 18 June 2020 (Taxonomy Regulation)	Overarching conditions that economic activities must meet to qualify as environmentally sustainable	1) List of environmentally sustainable activities by defining technical screening criteria for each environmental objective 2) Safeguards (Art.18)—Report Oct. 2022—HR (incl. labour and consumer rights, bribery, and taxation) 3) Established the Platform on Sustainable Finance with several tasks 4) Common language of green and sustainable	Further guidance on activities that contribute to other sustainability objectives, including social objectives, might be developed at a later stage.
Directive (EU) 2022/2464 of 14 December 2022 concerning corporate sustainability reporting (CSRD)	Sustainability reporting	Requests insurance undertakings to include in the management report: 1) Information necessary to understand the undertaking's impacts on sustainability matters 2) Information necessary to understand how sustainability matters affect the undertaking's development, performance, and position	Sustainability is understood as a whole, in particular: "environmental, social and human rights, and governance factors, including sustainability factors".
Proposal for a Directive on Corporate Sustainability Due Diligence	Due diligence measures to identify and address adverse HR and environmental impacts (six steps	1) Integrating due diligence into policies and management systems 2) Identifying and	Adverse human rights impact is defined by reference to HR conventions. Even among instruments from the

(continued)

Table 2 (continued)

Instrument	Objective	Instruments	Shortcomings
	defined by the OECD Due Diligencia Guidance for Responsible Business Conduct)	assessing adverse human rights (and environmental impacts) 3) Preventing, ceasing, or minimizing actual and potential adverse human rights (and environmental impacts)	same continent (ECHR and Charter of the Fundamental Rights of the EU), there are wider disagreements regarding some definitions.
Social Taxonomy (as in the Final Report of the Platform on Sustainable Finance) [a]	Based on the UNDHR, ECHR, and SDGs: 1) Decent work 2) Adequate living standards and well-being 3) Inclusive and sustainable communities	Not yet determined by the Platform, but as in the Taxonomy—Art. 18—it is suggested to consider UNGPs and OECD	The absence of harmonization concerning the objective of these processes, i.e. the rating of the "social" component of the activity/products of the rated companies, can nullify or limit the benefits of the harmonization of the rating processes.
ESG ratings under analysis	Provide information about "work" and "solidarity" Some about "health", "equality", and "safety"	Various (examples): S&P Global ESG—created an Atlas MSCI Inc.—ESG Industry Materiality Map Moody's—ESG Scores	Lack of homogeneous definition of "S" and the components measured under "S". No comparisons are possible without an in-depth analysis.

[a] The Report is available at https://finance.ec.europa.eu/system/files/2022-08/220228-sustainable-finance-platform-finance-report-social-taxonomy_en.pdf

However, more unification concerning the objective of the EU regulatory framework on the ESG is needed. The components of the social factor to be considered should be the same, regardless of the purposes of the regulations that refer to it. It would be highly questionable to differentiate the legal meaning of the social factor within the ESG factors depending on the purpose and scope of the legislation.

The emphasis (and uncertainties) on human rights as a social component considered in the Proposal for a Directive on Corporate Sustainability Due Diligence and the difference between human rights and the social factor in the EU Regulation (EU) 2020/852 of 18 June 2020 (Taxonomy Regulation) Directive (EU) 2022/2464 of 14 December 2022 concerning corporate sustainability reporting (CSRD) needs to be clarified.

The unification of meaning would benefit stakeholders as it clarifies the objectives underlying this definition and their achievement. Furthermore, standardization would (also) help the insurance industry to incorporate this factor into its value chain, avoiding unnecessary costs to comply with different, non-coinciding legal meanings of "social".

If social "a la carte" must be avoided, "social by purpose" must be avoided, too.

References

Bengo I, Boni L, Sancino A (2022) EU financial regulations and social impact measurement practices: a comprehensive framework on finance for sustainable development. Corp Soc Responsib Environ Manag 29(4):809–819. https://doi.org/10.1002/csr.2235

Berg F, Ko JF, Rigobon R (2022) Aggregate confusion: the divergence of ESG ratings. Rev Financ 26(6):1315–1344. https://doi.org/10.1093/rof/rfac033

Bhattacharya-Craven A, Cohen AB, Ghafur S (2020) Digital health – is the euphoria justified? The Geneva Association, December 2020. https://www.genevaassociation.org/sites/default/files/digital_health_web.pdf

Biju AVN, Kodiyatt SJ, Krishna PPN (2023) ESG sentiments and divergent ESG scores: suggesting a framework for ESG rating. SN Bus Econ 3:209. https://doi.org/10.1007/s43546-023-00592-4

Busch D (2021) Sustainability disclosure in the EU financial sector. European Banking Institute working paper series 2021 - n. 70. https://doi.org/10.2139/ssrn.3650407

Cash D (2021) Sustainability rating agencies vs credit rating agencies: the battle to serve the mainstream investor. Palgrave Macmillan

Chatterji AK, Durand K, Levine DI, Touboul S (2016) Do ratings of firms converge? Implications for managers, investors and strategy researchers. Strateg Manag J 37(8). https://doi.org/10.1002/smj.2407

Clément A, Robinot E, Trespeuch L (2023) The use of ESG scores in academic literature: a systematic literature review. J Enterprising Commun People Places Glob Econ (ahead-of-print). https://doi.org/10.1108/JEC-10-2022-0147

DDQ Invest (2022) ESG v sustainability: are we heading in the right direction? https://ddqinvest.com/esg-v-sustainability-are-we-heading-in-the-right-direction/

Eccles NS, Viviers S (2011) The origins and meanings of names describing investment practices that integrate a consideration of ESG issues in the academic literature. J Bus Ethics 104(3): 389–402

EIOPA (2023) Factsheet on EEA insurer's investments at the end of Q1 2023, September 2023. https://www.eiopa.europa.eu/publications/factsheet-eea-insurers-investments-end-q1-2023_itat

Elbasha T, Avetisyan E (2018) A framework to study strategizing activities at the field level: the example of CSR rating agencies. Eur Manag J 36(1):38–46. https://doi.org/10.1016/j.emj.2017.02.001

Ermokhin I, Burhanova Y, Levashenko A (2023) The problem of divergence of ESG ratings awarded by persons providing services for the assessment of sustainable development. The main trends in the field of legislative regulation of the ESG rating Institute in Russia and in the world. Int Organ Res J 18(3):186–204. https://doi.org/10.17323/1996-7845-2023-03-10

Escrig-Olmedo E, Fernández-Izquierdo M, Ferrero-Ferrero I, Rivera-Lirio J, Muñoz-Torres M (2019) Rating the raters: evaluating how ESG rating agencies integrate sustainability principles. Sustainability 11(3):915. https://doi.org/10.3390/su11030915

Esty D, Cort T (2017) Corporate sustainability metrics: what investors need and don't get. J Environ Invest 8(1) (Special issue State of ESG Data and Metrics)

European Commission (2021) Directorate-General for Financial Stability, Financial Services and Capital Markets Union, Study on sustainability-related ratings, data and research, Publications Office of the European Union. https://data.europa.eu/doi/10.2874/14850.

European Commission (2022) Targeted consultation on the functioning of the ESG rating market in the EU and the consideration of ESG factors in credit ratings. https://finance.ec.europa.eu/regulation-and-supervision/consultations/finance-2022-esg-ratings_en

Ewald F (2007) The return of Descartes's malicious demon: an outline of a philosophy of precaution. In: Baker T, Simon J (eds) Embracing risk. The changing culture of insurance and responsibility. The University of Chicago Press, Chicago

Expansión (2024) Wall Street destierra para siempre las siglas ESG. https://amp.expansion.com/directivos/2024/02/02/65bd17eee5fdeab5018b458a.html

Fichtner J, Jaspert R, Petry J (2023) Mind the ESG capital allocation gap: the role of index providers, standard-setting, and "green" indices for the creation of sustainability impact. Regul Gov 18:479–498. https://doi.org/10.1111/rego.12530

Fitch Group (2023) ESG rating methodology. https://your.fitch.group/rs/732-CKH-767/images/2023_12_20_ESG-Ratings-Methodology-Sustainable-Fitch.pdf?mkt_tok=NzMyLUNLSC03NjcAAAGQSQ87kDFKWk0WuBKtjy3oBnQHxMchYG_ePtnTQ99dBT3pnC2ZDblW-Oe_PvPZ1yoC48Po7NNVfK3aJZX1JnhevQvzWyQOmk_Ekp15p-LXv3n5rzN0rIHp

Flückiger I, Carbone M (2021) From risk transfer to risk prevention. How the Internet of Things is reshaping business models in insurance. The Geneva Association, May 2021. https://www.genevaassociation.org/sites/default/files/iot_insurance_research_report.pdf

Gargantini M, Siri M (2022) Information intermediaries and sustainability ESG ratings and benchmarks in the European Union. ECMI working paper no 15, November 2022. https://www.ecmi.eu/publications/working-papers/information-intermediaries-and-sustainability-esg-ratings-and-benchmarks

Global Sustainable Investment Alliance (2020) Report 2020. https://www.gsi-alliance.org/

Ground J (2022) ESG Global Study 2022. Harvard Law School Forum on corporate governance, June 17, 2022. https://corpgov.law.harvard.edu/2022/06/17/esg-global-study-2022/

IOSCO (2021) Environmental, social and governance (ESG): ratings and data products providers, final report. https://www.iosco.org/library/pubdocs/pdf/IOSCOPD690.pdf

Khovrak I (2020) ESG-driven approach to managing insurance companies' sustainable development. Insur Markets Companies 11(1):42–52. https://doi.org/10.21511/ins.11(1).2020.05

Liu M (2022) Quantitative ESG disclosure and divergence of ESG ratings. Front Psychol 13: 936798. https://doi.org/10.3389/fpsyg.2022.936798

Mackenzie C, Rees W, Rodionova T (2013) Do responsible investment indices improve corporate social responsibility? Good's impact on environmental management. Corp Gov Int Rev 21(5): 495–512. https://doi.org/10.1111/corg.12039

Moody's Investor Service (2022) ESG scores explained: quantifying the degree of Moody's, ESG rating. https://www.moodys.com/web/en/us/capabilities/esg-risk.html

Ramos Muñoz D, Smoleńska A (2023) The governance of ESG ratings and benchmarks (infomediaries) as gatekeepers: exit, voice and coercion. EBI working paper series, 04/08/2023

Schanz KU (2022) The role of insurance in promoting social sustainability. The Geneva Association, November 2022. https://www.genevaassociation.org/sites/default/files/2022-11/social_sustainability_report.pdf

Sustainalytics (2019) The ESG risk ratings methodology-abstract-version 2.0, November 2019. https://red-advertising.com/file/3051

Tang DY, Yan J, Yao CY (2021) The determinants of ESG ratings: rater ownership matters. Working paper

Tayan B, Larcker D, Watts E, Pomorski L (2022) ESG ratings: a compass without direction. The Harvard Law School Forum on corporate governance. https://corpgov.law.harvard.edu/2022/08/24/esg-ratings-a-compass-without-direction/

Ting-Ting L, Wang K, Sueyoshi T, Wang DD (2021) ESG: research progress and future prospects. Sustainability 13(21):11663. https://doi.org/10.3390/su132111663

UNEP PSI (2020) PSI ESG guide for non-life insurance: managing environmental, social and governance risks in non-life insurance business, June 2020. https://www.unepfi.org/psi/wp-content/uploads/2020/06/PSI-ESG-guide-for-non-life-insurance.pdf
United Nations, The Global Compact (2004) Who cares wins: connecting the financial markets to a changing world? https://d306pr3pise04h.cloudfront.net/docs/issues_doc%2FFinancial_markets%2Fwho_cares_who_wins.pdf
UNPRI (2023) ESG in credit ratings and ESG ratings. https://www.unpri.org/credit-risk-and-ratings/esg-in-credit-ratings-and-esg-ratings/11071.article
Walter I (2020) Sense and nonsense in ESG ratings. J Law Financ Account 5(2):307–336. https://papers.ssrn.com/sol3/papers.cfm?abstract_id=3568104
Zumente I, Lace N (2021) ESG rating—necessity for the investor or the company? Sustainability 13(16):8940. https://doi.org/10.3390/su13168940

Pierpaolo Marano is an esteemed law professor specializing in insurance regulation at the University of Malta and the Catholic University of Milan. He obtained his law degree from the Catholic University and holds a PhD in Banking Law and Regulation from the University of Siena. Professor Marano is an academic member of the Insurance and Reinsurance Stakeholders Group at EIOPA and chairs the Scientific Committee of AIDA Europe, where he spearheads research and scholarly initiatives in insurance law. Moreover, he leads the Working Party on the Distribution of Insurance Products at AIDA World, focusing on the legal aspects of insurance product distribution. With over 140 academic papers in English, Italian, and Spanish, Professor Marano also serves as the director of the AIDA Europe Research Series on Insurance Law and Regulation.

María del Val Bolívar Oñoro is a Professor of Constitutional Law at the University of Alcala (Spain). She holds a Ph.D. in Law from the universities of Alcala (Spain) and Maynooth (Ireland). Her work focuses primarily on the intersection between the right to health, equality and non-discrimination, and freedom of enterprise. She currently brings a human rights perspective to projects related to disability, dignity, insurance, and sustainable development goals.

Part III
Sustainability and Insurance Products

Precontractual ESG Disclosure on Insurance-Based Investment Products

Isabel Rodríguez Martínez

1 ESG Criteria, Sustainability Risks, and Suitability of Insurance-Based Investment Products

1.1 The Integration of ESG Criteria into Insurance Investments

The weight of investment portfolios allocated to insurance-based investment products and, most obviously, unit-linked life insurance has progressively increased its share of the volume of life investments in recent years in the insurance sector.[1]

Weak confidence in the pension system and, on the other hand, the disincentive caused by low or moderate interest rates have diverted the channeling of savings and the interest of nonprofessional investors from traditional savings products to other

This paper is within the framework of the reference research project PID2020-116423RB-I00 under the title "Corporate Governance: Sustainability, ESG/ESG Factors and Reputation," awarded by the Spanish Ministry of Science and Innovation within the framework of its R+D+i 2020 program.

[1] In Spain, from 8% in 2017 to 12.7% at the end of the third quarter of 2021. If what we take as a reference is the insurance industry's investments as a whole, its weight has grown from 6% to almost 8%, according to the latest available data (2020). The trend is good, and the growth potential is very high. In any case, this last percentage (8%) is still much lower than the average for the eurozone, which stands at around 16.5% of total insurance investments (source: Mapfre Economics, Ahorro Inversiones, https://documentacion.fundacionmapfre.org/documentacion/publico/es/media/group/1115683.do. Accessed 21. April 2024.

I. Rodríguez Martínez (✉)
Universidad Nacional de Educación a Distancia (UNED), Madrid, Spain
e-mail: irodriguez@der.uned.es

J. Bataller-Grau et al. (eds.), *Sustainability and the Insurance Market*, AIDA Europe Research Series on Insurance Law and Regulation 10,
https://doi.org/10.1007/978-3-031-72186-1_8

more profitable financial products.[2] In this context, the general boom in insurance-based investment products, and particularly the so-called unit-linked insurance contracts, can be seen and explained.[3] These are characterized as life insurance policies through which policyholders can plan their retirement savings with a good return on their investments and with the tax advantages derived from this type of product but in which the function of covering the social welfare needs they are intended to offer implies the full assumption of a series of investment risks for the policyholders.

This growing evolution of portfolios allocated to insurance-based investment products has also been accompanied by new demands and requirements on the part of the insurance industry to incorporate, evaluate, and report financial risks in their investment policies and to seek to integrate ESG or sustainability criteria as quality criteria for the insurers themselves and for the quality and profitability of the products, as well as to inform policyholders, as final investors, of the social and environmental impacts of such products, decisions, and investment policies within the framework of their marketing and distribution policies.

1.2 ESG Risks and Sustainability of Investments: Rationale for the Precontractual Duty to Disclose Sustainability Information

It is not difficult to understand and analyze how deficiencies in the disclosure of financial information (financial risks) can affect the decisions of retail investors and have an impact on the volume of transactions in the financial markets and also in the insurance sector. The EU legislator has mitigated its negative effects and addressed this need for transparency and investor protection by regulating information and

[2] The flexibility offered by this financial product seems to be catching on with savers and/or investors. What is a fact is *that contributions to pension plans continue to fall*, while unit-linked plans are showing steady growth. Moreover, as we published in *this article*, unit-linked insurance is an ideal vehicle not only for implementing the more well-known situations of pension commitments or retirement plans but also for implementing deferred remuneration schemes.

[3] According to ICEA figures released by UNESPA, with 19,763 million euros at the end of 2021, unit-linked products accounted for 10.46% of the assets under management (technical provisions) of all savings insurance products in Spain. Although it might seem a small percentage, in perspective, the data undoubtedly reflect the unstoppable rise of these products. Thus, in 2018, 4 years earlier, the weight of these insurances was 6.74%, even though they were currently showing difficulty in fitting into the profile of the Spanish saver. At the end of 2019, these instruments already represented 7.58% of the finalist savings managed by life insurers. And in 2020, in the year of the pandemic, their share was already 8.54%.

disclosure tools for the knowledge of key data on retail investment products and insurance-based products[4] (IBIPs) as well as the associated risk factors.[5]

However, it is not only the information affecting financial risks that has an impact on decision-making and on the assessment of the suitability of investment products and, in particular, of those based on insurance. The social and environmental impacts generated by each investment also affect the assessment of the quality and suitability of those decisions and are not exempt from financial relevance.[6] An investment is sustainable when it does not cause significant environmental or social harm and respects good governance practices. It is generally accepted that insurance companies generate significant positive and negative social and environmental impacts through their investment and underwriting activities and therefore have a key role to play in the transition to a fully sustainable economic and financial system in line with the Green Pact.[7]

Sustainability risk is a nonfinancial risk that includes the environmental, social, and governance aspects of investments (ESG aspects). In the same way that financial risks can generate losses in the value of investments, sustainability risks would be associated with those environmental, social, or governance circumstances that, if occurring, could have a negative impact on the value of the investment.[8]

In general terms, and since the adoption in 2015 of the Paris Agreement on Climate Change and the 3030 Agenda for Sustainable Development,[9] the sustainability of investment decisions as an element of information to be provided to the final investor interested in its social impact has occupied and occupies a central place in the project of the European Union, after warning and recognizing that the financial

---

[4]The need to strengthen transparency and customer protection through the consequent information obligations has been addressed by the EU legislator. Of particular note are EU Regulation 1286/2014 on key information documents relating to linked retail investment products and insurance-based products, which aims to ensure a certain duty of information through the key product information document in order to facilitate the understanding and comparison of the key features and risks of such products, and later the approval of Directive (EU) 2016/97 of the European Parliament and of the Council, of January 20, 2016, on insurance distribution (hereinafter Distribution Directive or DDS), whose transposition into Spanish law was articulated by Royal Decree-Law 3/2020, of February 4 (hereinafter RDL 3/2020) and which regulates in its Chapter VI the additional requirements in relation to IBIPs (see Mayorga Toledano (2015)). See also Esty DC, Karpillow Q (2019) Harnessing Investor Interest in Sustainability: The Next Frontier in Environmental Information Regulation. Yale Journal on Regulation 36: 625–692. Available at SSRN: https://ssrn.com/abstract=3809880.

[5]On the scope and application of ESMA guidelines on investment risk factors and their inclusion in prospectuses, see Martinez Lopez (2019) and Palá Laguna (2019).

[6]See Recital 8 of Directive (EU) 2022/2464 of the European Parliament and of the Council of 14 December 2022 amending Regulation (EU) No 537/2014, Directive 2004/109/EC, Directive 2006/43/EC and Directive 2013/34/EU as regards corporate sustainability reporting.

[7]See Recital 27 of Directive (EU) 2022/2464 of the European Parliament and of the Council of 14 December 2022 amending Regulation (EU) No. 537/2014, Directive 2004/109/EC, Directive 2006/43/EC, and Directive 2013/34/EU as regards sustainability reporting by companies.

[8]Di Marco et al. (2022).

[9]https://sdgs.un.org/2030agenda. Accessed 21 Apr 2024.

system plays a key role and as a protagonist in a more sustainable and ecological-economic model.[10] Beyond channeling the financing of economic activities, employment, and growth, the financial system must encourage investment decisions to incorporate new ESG criteria (ecological, social, and governance)[11] and introduce into its analysis not only financial risk factors but also those related to environmental and social considerations.[12] The aim is not only to make the system and investment decisions more efficient but also to improve them and broaden their scope in order to achieve a sustainable environment.[13]

In order to ensure adaptation to the new ESG/ESG criteria and their proper functioning, the new EU financial system is based, inter alia, on the transparency legal framework for the disclosure of sustainability information in the markets.[14] This legal framework, established by Regulation (EU) 2019/2088 of 27 November 2019 and amended and implemented by Regulation (EU) 2020/852 of the European Parliament and of the Council of 18 June 2020 on establishing a framework to facilitate sustainable investment and amending Regulation (EU) 2019/2088 (also known as the Sustainable Investment Regulation (SIR)), has clear implications for the EU financial sector. More specifically, it has obvious implications for the insurance sector in relation to the marketing of insurance-based investment products, such as unit-linked products, understood as life insurance products in which the policyholder (end investor) "decides in which assets to be held by the insurer (and which will make up the technical provisions) must invest his/her savings premium, assuming exclusively the risks of such investment.[15]

The legal framework imposes a duty of prior disclosure and transparency on financial sector participants trading in financial products regarding investment policy and informed decision-making and reoriented to nonfinancial objectives. Specifically, it establishes a series of duties in order to facilitate the assessment of the

[10] On investors' growing interest in ESG factors in decision-making, see Eccles and Klimenko (2019). See also, Leipziger D (2010) The Corporate Responsibility Code Book, revised second edition, The author provides a comprenhesive guide to corporate responsibility frameworks, focusing on best practices for integrating sustainability into business strategies.

[11] Environment: climate change, GHG emissions, resource depletion, waste, and pollution; social: working conditions, health and safety, employee relations and diversity, and local communities; governance: executive compensation, bribery and corruption, board diversity, and tax strategy.

[12] The aim is to turn the financial system into the engine and architect of change, into another channel for sustainable economic growth that guarantees stability and promotes greater transparency and long-termism in the economy. For the causes, issues at stake, and adverse effects of short-termism in company law and corporate governance, see Tapia Hermida (2019).

[13] See *A new start for Europe: Agenda for jobs, growth, equity and democratic change—Policy orientations for the next European Commission*, Strasbourg, 15 July 2014 (https://commission.europa.eu/document/download/ad3f4ceb-aed8-4cc5-b6bb-4c60f448a5f2_en?filename=juncker-political-guidelines-speech_en.pdf, accessed 21 Apr 2024), which highlights the EU's commitment to adapt its policies to achieve smart investments aimed at achieving specific objectives.

[14] On the incidence of transparency and nonfinancial information as a strategic factor of sustainability, see Enciso Alonso-Muñumer (2020).

[15] Maldonado Molina (2000).

sustainability of an investment, which requires a complex analysis based on the knowledge of a series of elements and factors, such as (1) sustainability risks, understood as any environmental, social, or governance event or condition that, if it were to occur, could cause a material negative impact on the value of the investment; (2) adverse sustainability impacts, such adverse impacts being understood as any significant negative impact on the environment or society that could occur as a result of investing in a given economic activity; and, finally, (3) sustainable investment objectives.

1.3 The Process of Integrating ESG Criteria into Investments in the Insurance Sector

More specifically, in the insurance sector, the process of integration of ESG/ESG criteria has its antecedent in March 2018, when the Commission published its Action Plan "Financing Sustainable Growth,"[16] establishing an ambitious and comprehensive strategy related to sustainable finance and among whose set objectives stands out that of redirecting capital flows toward sustainable investments in order to achieve sustainable and inclusive growth. Immediately afterward, in May of the same year, the integration process began when the importance and need for insurance and reinsurance companies to take sustainability factors into account as part of their obligations to investors was documented.[17] This justified the mandate for insurance and reinsurance undertakings to assess not only all relevant financial risks on an ongoing basis but also all relevant sustainability risks, as referred to in Regulation (EU) 2019/2088 of the European Parliament and of the Council,[18] that, if occurring, could have an actual or potential material adverse effect on the value of an investment or liability.

The incorporation of ESG/ESG criteria into investments in the insurance sector has occurred in two dimensions.

---

[16] COM (2018) 97 final.

[17] Commission Staff Working Document Impact Assessment, Accompanying the document Proposal for a Regulation of the European Parliament and of the Council on the establishment of a framework to facilitate sustainable investment and Proposal for a Regulation of the European Parliament and of the Council on disclosures relating to sustainable investments and sustainability risks and amending Directive (EU) 2016/2341 and Proposal for a Regulation of the European Parliament and of the Council amending Regulation (EU) 2016/1011 on low carbon benchmarks and positive carbon impact benchmarks (SWD (2018) 264 final).

[18] Regulation (EU) 2019/2088 of the European Parliament and of the Council of 27 November 2019 on sustainability disclosures in the financial services sector (OJ L 317, 9.12.2019, p. 1).

1.3.1 In the Area of Transparency and Disclosure to End Investors of Insurance-Based Investment Products

In a first dimension, and in line with the objectives of the European Union promoting sustainable and competitive growth, on the occasion of the entry into force of the aforementioned Regulation (EU) 2019/2088 on March 10, 2021, insurance entities offering insurance-based investment products—as financial market participants—must integrate sustainability risks into their investment or advisory decision-making processes and comply with the duty to disclose information regarding how they assume and internalize ESG criteria in their organizational structure and business model.[19]

Regulation (EU) 2019/2088 of the European Parliament and of the Council of 27 November 2019 (also known as the Disclosure Regulation) is intended to serve as a reinforcement to the initial protection of end investors in financial products[20] and also for insurance-based investment products, such as the policyholders of unit-linked insurance contracts, insofar as it allows prior information on investment policy and informed decision-making redirected to nonfinancial objectives, thereby contributing to the better functioning of the system.[21]

The necessary EU harmonization of the duty to disclose information on the integration of sustainability risks to end investors was operationalized and implemented by Regulation (EU) 2020/852 of the European Parliament and of the Council of 18 June 2020 on establishing a framework to facilitate sustainable investments and amending Regulation (EU) 2019/2088, also known as the Sustainable Investment Regulation (RIS). The RIS complements the transparency rules on precontractual disclosure and periodic reporting under Regulation (EU) 2019/2088 and sets out the general framework for determining whether an economic activity

[19] At this stage and until August 2, 2022, however, the regulation of ESG criteria in the insurance sector was still at an incipient stage as it had no impact on the capital charges of Directive 2009/138/EC of the European Parliament and of the Council of November 25, 2009 on life insurance, access to and pursuit of the business of insurance and reinsurance (hereinafter Solvency II), although insurance companies were not oblivious to the growing social demand for specific and more demanding parameters of diligence and good practices in the sector, precisely because of their greater reputational value and regulatory compliance. See García Giménez y González-Palenzuela (2021) Nueva normativa de divulgación de información relativa a la sostenibilidad en el sector de los servicios financieros. In: López Jiménez JM, Zamarriego A (eds) La sostenibilidad y el nuevo marco institucional y regulatorio de las finanzas sostenibles. Thomson Reuters Aranzadi, Pamplona, p 950.

[20] In this regard, see Recital 4.

[21] Indeed, its regime focuses on those disclosure duties to *end investors* that have not yet been harmonized because they refer to the sustainability of investments and, therefore, relate to (1) the inclusion in investments of sustainability risks, understood as any environmental, social, or governance event or condition that, if it were to occur, could have a material adverse impact on the value of the investment; (2) the analysis of adverse sustainability impacts, understood as any significant negative impact on the environment or society that could occur as a result of investing in a particular economic activity; and (3) sustainable investment objectives or the promotion of environmental or social characteristics.

can be considered environmentally sustainable for the purpose of setting the degree of environmental sustainability of an investment.

1.3.2 In Terms of Governance Obligations for Insurers

In a second dimension affecting governance, there is both a consolidation of ESG/ESG criteria in the different procedures, businesses, and governance within the insurance sector and an integration of sustainability risks in the underwriting and reservation of policies, in asset and liability management, in risk management policies and procedures associated with investment portfolios, in the calculation of technical provisions of the actuarial function, and, finally, also in remuneration policy systems.

In the first phase, while insurance entities were called, under the prudent person principle, to invest only in assets whose risks they were able to identify, measure, monitor, manage, control, and duly report,[22] it became urgent to materialize the obligation to effectively manage climate and environmental risks by insurance and reinsurance companies, taking into account the sustainability risks and reflecting the sustainability preferences of their clients in their investment process. Therefore, the European Commission adopted Delegated Regulation (EU) 2021/1256 of 21 April 2021 amending Delegated Regulation (EU) 2015/35 as regards the integration of sustainability risks in the governance of insurance and reinsurance undertakings[23] in order to ensure that the system of governance of insurance and reinsurance undertakings and the assessment of their overall solvency needs, which should reflect sustainability risks, are correctly observed and applied. It specifically provides that insurance undertakings that disclose principal adverse impacts in sustainability factors in accordance with the aforementioned Regulation (EU) 2019/2018 shall also adapt their processes, systems, and internal controls with respect to such disclosure.

The second phase started in August 2021, when the European Union began the process that has culminated in the adaptation of the Markets in Financial Instruments Directive II (MiFID II),[24] Insurance Distribution Directive

---

[22] Commission Delegated Regulation (EU) 2015/35 of 10 October 2014 supplementing Directive 2009/138/EC of the European Parliament and of the Council on the taking-up and pursuit of the business of insurance and reinsurance (Solvency II) (OJ L 12, 17.1.2015, p. 1) did not explicitly refer to sustainability risks.

[23] Commission Delegated Regulation (EU) 2015/35 of 10 October 2014 supplementing Directive 2009/138/EC of the European Parliament and of the Council on the taking-up and pursuit of the business of Insurance and Reinsurance (Solvency II) (OJ L 12, 17.1.2015, p. 1).

[24] Commission Delegated Regulation (EU) 2021/1253 of 21 April 2021 amending Delegated Regulation (EU) 2017/565 as regards the integration of sustainability factors, risks and preferences into certain organizational requirements and operating conditions of investment firms and Commission Delegated Directive (EU) 2021/269, of 21 April 2021 amending Delegated Directive (EU) 2017/593 as regards the integration of sustainability factors into product governance obligations. See Martínez MT, Sánchez Calero Guilarte J (eds) (2019) Nuevas tendencias de Derecho

(IDD),[25] Solvency II,[26] Undertakings for Collective Investment in Transferable Securities (UCTIS),[27] and Alternative Investment Fund Managers Directive (AIFMD),[28] which require financial institutions to integrate, respectively, environmental, social, and governance factors (ESG factors) and sustainability risks in their internal procedures, in investment management, and, where appropriate, in the *assessment of the suitability of* customers.

In the insurance sector, however, the incorporation of the new sustainability obligations into Solvency II took place, as of August 2, 2022, through Commission Delegated Regulation (EU) 2021/1257 of April 21, 2021, which amends the Insurance Distribution Directive (IDD).[29] Such duties are aimed at imposing the

---

Europeo y del Derecho español en las sociedades cotizadas, vol 7. Servicio de Publicaciones Facultad de Derecho. Colección "Actas y Homenajes". The autor explores recent developments in European and Spanish law concerning publicly traded companies and highlights new regulatory trends, including the evolving role of corporate governance, shareholder rights, and the integration of sustainability factors into corporate practices. The book also examines the impact of EU regulations on Spanish corporate law, focusing on how these legal changes influence market practices and corporate behavior, particularly regarding transparency, accountability, and investor protection.

[25] Commission Delegated Regulation (EU) 2021/1257 of 21 April 2021 amending Delegated Regulations (EU) 2017/2358 and (EU) 2017/2359 as regards the integration of sustainability factors, risks and preferences in the product control and governance requirements applicable to insurance undertakings and insurance distributors, and in the conduct of business and investment advice rules relating to insurance-based investment products.

[26] Commission Delegated Regulation (EU) 2021/1256 of 21 April 2021 amending Delegated Regulation (EU) 2015/35 as regards the integration of sustainability risks in the governance of insurance and reinsurance undertakings.

[27] Commission Delegated Directive (EU) 2021/1270 of 21 April 2021 amending Directive 2010/43/EU as regards sustainability risks and sustainability factors to be taken into account in relation to undertakings for collective investment in transferable securities (UCITS).

[28] Commission Delegated Regulation (EU) 2021/1255 of 21 April 2021 amending Delegated Regulation (EU) No. 231/2013 as regards sustainability risks and sustainability factors to be taken into account by alternative investment fund managers.

[29] Specifically, Commission Delegated Regulation (EU) 2021/1257 of 21 April 2021 amends Delegated Regulations (EU) 2017/2358 and (EU) 2017/2359 as regards the integration of sustainability factors, risks and preferences into the product control and governance requirements applicable to insurance undertakings and insurance distributors, and into the conduct of business and investment advice rules relating to insurance-based investment products. According to these rules, "sustainability preference" means a customer's decision as to whether and to what extent the recommendation made by the entity should include IBIP with any of the following characteristics: (a) that a minimum proportion is invested in sustainable activities according to the Taxonomy Regulation, (b) that a minimum proportion is invested in sustainable activities according to the Disclosure Regulation, or (c) that it takes into account the principal adverse sustainability impacts (PIAS) according to the qualitative and quantitative elements to be selected by the customer. See Muñoz Pérez AF (2019) Los mercados de capitales y el impulso de las finanzas sostenibles. Revista de Derecho del Mercado de Valores 25, digital edition. The author highlights how the integration of environmental, social, and governance (ESG) factors is reshaping investment decisions and regulatory frameworks. The author emphasizes the importance of legislation and incentives in facilitating the transition to a sustainable economy, promoting transparency and corporate accountability, especially for publicly listed companies.

following obligations on insurance companies and insurance distributors. Firstly, it imposes the duty to consider the "sustainability preferences" of customers in product governance procedures. In this regard, the European Insurance and Occupational Pensions Authority (EIOPA) published the final version of the guidelines on the integration of sustainability in the assessment of suitability under the Insurance Distribution Directive (IDD). These recommendations provide guidance to intermediaries and insurance companies when offering and/or advising in relation to insurance-based investment products (IBIPs) on how to consider the sustainability preferences of clients.[30] Secondly, it establishes the obligation to integrate sustainability risks into underwriting and reserving policies, asset and liability management, risk management policies and procedures associated with investment portfolios, the calculation of technical provisions of the actuarial function, and remuneration policy systems. Finally, the principle of prudence establishes the obligation to incorporate in the company's strategy and investment decisions the possible long-term effects as well as to take into account and reflect individual sustainability risks and preferences in the product approval process.[31]

[30]These guidelines establish the following orientations on prior actions: (1) the duty to explain to the customer in a clear and nontechnical way the concept of "sustainability preferences" and the different types of products within this definition. (2) It allows the use of the wording of the margin notes of the standardized models of precontractual and periodic information of the Delegated Regulation 2022/1288, which implements the SFDR Regulation (SFDR Regulation). (3) Institutions may use these explanations as an introduction to questions about the client's sustainability preferences. However, more detailed information should be provided at the client's request.

It also establishes the approach of asking the client about their sustainability preferences. Thus, (a) regarding the sequence of questions, a decision tree is introduced, whereby the following is clarified: (1) if the client has sustainability preferences, it will first ask whether he/she is interested in sustainable investments, principal adverse sustainability events (PIAS), or a combination of them; (2) if he/she opts to have sustainable investments, the client will be asked if he/she wants them to be aligned with taxonomy as a second step; and (3) finally, it maintains the obligation to ask both for the minimum proportion of sustainable investment, according to the Taxonomy and Disclosure Regulations and the specific indicators, by PIAS families, if he/she has preferred this approach. (b) As of January 1, 2023, entities are required to report and inquire about the two key performance indicators (KPIs) used to calculate the proportion of environmentally sustainable investment under the taxonomy.

[31]Similar novelties have been introduced in terms of ESG/ESG requirements in the UCITs and AIFMD collective investment regulations. In CII management companies, sustainability risks will be taken into account (1) in the identification and management of conflicts of interest, (2) in risk management procedures and other internal control systems, and, finally, (3) in investment *due diligence* processes. In the case of alternative funds, (1) direct responsibility is imposed on senior management for the integration of sustainability risks in the entity and in investment management, and (2) resources with the necessary expertise in sustainability factors and risks are required.

2 The Precontractual Disclosure Legal Framework Relating to the Sustainability of Insurance-Based Investment Products

2.1 General Aspects of EU Regulation 2019/2088 on Transparency Related to Sustainable Investments and Sustainability Risks

2.1.1 Scope and Objectives

In terms of disclosure of information related to ESG/ESG criteria, it is EU Regulation 2019/2088 or the Disclosure Regulation, which amends Directive (EU) 2016/2341[32] and is directly applicable, on a general basis, from March 10, 2021,[33] that establishes the harmonized transparency legal framework regarding how financial market participants and financial advisors are to integrate sustainability risks and adverse sustainability impact analysis into their investment decisions and investment or insurance advice (Article 1).

On the other hand, it also aims to shape the mandatory sustainability information, i.e. sustainability factors, understood as all information related to environmental and social issues, personnel matters, human rights, and the fight against corruption and bribery (Article 2.24). Thus, both insurers and distributors of insurance-based investment products, in their capacity as financial market participants and/or financial advisors, are required not only to continuously assess the financial risks associated with their investments but also to provide an analysis of all "sustainability risks" that have negative effects on the financial performance of their investments and/or, where appropriate, to advise in this regard, meaning concerning "any environmental, social or governance event or condition that, if it occurs, could have an actual or potential material adverse effect on the value of the investment" (Article 2.22).[34]

2.1.2 Objective Scope of Application

2.1.2.1 A First Approach to Sustainable and Responsible Investment

The trend toward socially responsible investment selection has its origins in Anglo-Saxon countries, where the notion of socially responsible investment (SRI) arises to refer, in general terms, to that which incorporates ethical, social, or environmental

[32] Directive (EU) 2016/2341 of the European Parliament and of the Council of 14 December 2016 on the activities and supervision of institutions for occupational retirement provision.

[33] See Sect. 2.1.4.

[34] On climate-related financial risks, see Campiglio et al. (2018).

considerations, beyond strictly financial ones, in investment decision-making[35] and, therefore, in the study, analysis, and selection of securities in an investment portfolio.[36] It is common to include aspects other than social, environmental, and ethical ones, such as issues related to corporate governance.[37]

Thus, in general terms, it should be noted that the concept of socially responsible investment (sustainable, ethical, social investment) is a nonunivocal notion that, by combining the fundamental financial analysis associated with an investment (profitability risk) with extrafinancial analysis (ESG criteria),[38] takes into consideration the function of the nature and objectives of the economic activities of the *target* company.[39] In the analysis of all SRIs, a fourth criterion (commitment) is added to the traditional three investment criteria (liquidity, profitability, and risk), which requires the measurement of the social and environmental impact of the company in which the investors finally place their savings. However, the difficulty of this analysis lies precisely in homogenizing the measurement criteria that allow an investment to be coined as socially responsible.

Community regulations have been shaping a notion that, derived from that of socially responsible investment, has been specified in order to delimit its scope of application and, therefore, its efficiency.

2.1.2.2 The Broad Concept of Sustainable Investments in EU Regulation 2019/2088

2.1.2.2.1 Requirements

EU Regulation 2019/2088 establishes a broad concept of "sustainable investments" for the purposes of the transparency legal framework it institutes to cover various sustainable development goals or objectives,[40] namely:

---

[35] See Asociación Española de Contabilidad y Administración de Empresas (AECA, 2004). "Marco Conceptual de la Responsabilidad Social Corporativa. Madrid". This document outlines guidelines for corporate social responsibility (CSR), emphasizing transparent management practices and a balanced focus on economic, social, and environmental aspects. It has been referenced in multiple contexts related to CSR and corporate governance studies.

[36] See, SPAINSIF (2018) "La inversión sostenible y responsable en España"; EUROSIF (2018b) "European SRI Study 2018,"; Global Sustainable Investment Alliance (GSIA, 2018), *Global Sustainable Investment Review*,, US SIF Foundation. (2019). Moving Forward with Sustainable Investing: A Roadmap for Asset Owners. Washington, D.C.: US SIF Foundation.

[37] Eurosif (2006) European SRI Study 2006.

[38] On the impact of ESG criteria on corporate governance, see Landi and Sciarelli (2019).

[39] SRI strategies focus on investing in companies listed on the various stock markets because their financial performance is easy to measure and monitor. However, alongside investment in these markets, additional forms of SRI have been developed in recent years, such as impact investing, which measures the return on investment also in social terms, or green bonds—funds issued by banks to finance sustainable projects (see Fontrodona et al. (2020), p. 6; Calvo Vergez (2021)).

[40] On the necessary determination of the concept of "sustainable investment" and, in particular, on the scope of a harmonized model of financial reporting on sustainability, see Tapia Sánchez (2020). See also, Alonso A, Gonzalez CI (2021) Los productos financieros sostenibles desde el

1. On the one hand, those "investments in an economic activity that contribute to an environmental objective" (Article 2, paragraph 17)[41] and
2. On the other hand, "investments in an economic activity that contribute to a social objective" and, in particular, any investment that contributes to the fight against inequality; any investment that strengthens social cohesion, social integration, and labor relations; or any investment in human capital or in economically or socially disadvantaged communities (Article 2, paragraph 17)[42]

The concept of sustainable investment in the Regulation is therefore outlined on the basis of the concurrence of the following requirements:

1. The investment must be directed to a specific or determined economic activity and not to the company, which may carry out various economic activities.
2. There is a necessary linkage or commitment of the economic activity to an environmental and/or social objective.
3. The economic activity does not cause any significant harm to any of the environmental or social objectives set forth in the Regulation.
4. Good governance practices are monitored by the beneficiary companies.

In conclusion, an investment is sustainable for the purposes of Regulation (EU) 2019/2088 provided that while complying with the other above requirements, it does not *significantly* harm any of the environmental or social objectives set out in that Regulation. In this regard, Article 2a thereof, introduced by Regulation (EU) 2020/852 of the European Parliament and of the Council of 18 June 2020 (RIS), establishes the principle of not causing significant harm as well as mandates the European Supervisory Authorities (ESAs) to establish regulatory technical standards "specifying in detail the content and presentation of the information in relation to the 'no significant harm' principle referred to in Article 2(17) of this Regulation, consistent with the content, methodologies and presentation in respect of the sustainability indicators in relation to adverse events referred to in Article 4(6) and (7) of this Regulation."

punto de vista de los supervisores y reguladores bancarios. In: López Jiménez JM, Zamarriego A (eds) La sostenibilidad y el nuevo marco institucional y regulatorio de las finanzas sostenibles. Thomson Reuters Aranzadi, Pamplona.

[41] This environmental target will be measured "on the basis of several key efficiency indicators such as "resource efficiency" relating to energy use, renewable energy, consumption of raw materials, water and land, waste production and greenhouse gas emissions, and impact on biodiversity and the circular economy."

[42] Provided that the investments do not significantly harm any of these objectives and that the beneficiary companies follow good governance practices, in particular with regard to sound management structures, employee relations, and the remuneration of relevant personnel and tax compliance.

2.1.2.2.2 *Concretization of the Principle of Not Causing Significant Harm*

A sustainable investment may not be directed toward activities that may cause significant harm, in accordance with Article 2(17) of Regulation (EU) 2019/2088.

Article 17.1 of the RIS Regulation specifies that an economic activity shall be considered to cause significant damage to any of the environmental objectives when, taking into consideration the life cycle of the products and services provided by the economic activity in question, including the goods and assets on which it relies, the following circumstances are present:

1. Climate change mitigation: when the activity results in significant greenhouse gas emissions[43]
2. Climate change adaptation: when the activity causes an increase in the adverse effects of current and projected future climate conditions on itself or on people, nature, or assets.[44]
3. Sustainable use and protection of water and marine resources:[45] when the activity is detrimental to the good ecological status or potential of water bodies, including surface and groundwater, or to the good ecological status of marine waters
4. Circular economy: (1) when it generates significant inefficiencies in the use of materials or in the direct or indirect use of natural resources, such as nonrenewable energy sources, raw materials, or water or soil in one or more phases of the life cycle of the products, in particular in terms of durability and possibilities for the repair, upgrade, reuse, or recycling of the products; (2) if it results in a significant increase in the generation, incineration, or disposal of waste, except for the incineration of nonrecyclable hazardous waste; or, finally,

[43] Economic activity that pursues the environmental objective of mitigating climate change must make a substantial contribution to stabilizing greenhouse gas emissions by avoiding or reducing them or by enhancing their absorption. Economic activity must be consistent with the long-term temperature objective set out in the Paris Agreement. That environmental objective should be interpreted in accordance with applicable Union law, including Directive 2009/31/EC of the European Parliament and of the Council (see Recital 24 of Regulation (EU) 2020/852).

[44] An economic activity pursuing the environmental objective of adapting to climate change should make a substantial contribution to reducing or preventing current or expected future adverse climate impacts or the risks of such adverse impacts, whether on the activity itself, the people, nature, or assets. That environmental objective should be interpreted in accordance with applicable Union law and the Sendai Framework for Disaster Risk Reduction 2015–2030 (see Recital 25 of Regulation (EU) 2020/852).

[45] The environmental objective of sustainable use and protection of water and marine resources is to be interpreted in accordance with the applicable Union legislation, in particular, Regulation (EU) No. 1380/2013 of the European Parliament and of the Council (9); Directives 2000/60/EC (10), 2006/7/EC (11), 2006/118/EC (12), 2008/56/EC (13), and 2008/105/EC (14) of the European Parliament and of the Council; Council Directives 91/271/EEC (15), 91/676/EEC (16), and 98/83/EC (17); and Commission Decision (EU) 2017/848 (18), as well as with the Commission Communications of 18 July 2007, "Addressing the challenge of water scarcity and droughts in the European Union"; of 14 November 2012, "A plan to safeguard Europe's water resources"; and of 11 March 2019, "EU strategic approach to pharmaceuticals in the environment" (Recital 26 of Regulation (EU) 2020/852).

(3) if the long-term disposal of waste is likely to cause significant and long-term damage to the environment[46]
5. Pollution prevention and control: when the activity results in a significant increase in the emissions of pollutants to air, water, or soil, compared to the situation before the start of the activity[47]
6. Protection and restoration of biodiversity and ecosystems: (1) if it is significantly detrimental to good ecosystem condition and resilience or (2) if it is detrimental to the conservation status of habitats and species, and in particular those of Union interest.[48]

2.1.3 IBIPs as Supervised Financial Products

The disclosure legal framework provided for in Regulation (EU) 2019/2088 extends to the so-called *financial products* listed in Article 2(12) thereof.

In particular, its application covers the marketing and/or distribution of a wide range of products, including all so-called insurance-based investment products (IBIPs). IBIPs are considered for the purposes of EU Regulation 2019/2088, both insurance-based investment products, as defined in Article 4(2) of Regulation (EU) No. 1286/2014 of the European Parliament and of the Council, and insurance products, which are available to a professional investor and which offer a maturity

---

[46] An economic activity can contribute significantly and in various ways to the environmental objective of transition to a circular economy (see Recital 28 of Regulation (EU) 2020/852).

[47] The environmental objectives of pollution prevention and control should be interpreted in accordance with applicable Union legislation, in particular Directives 2000/60/EC, 2004/35/EC (35), 2004/107/EC (36), 2006/118/EC, 2008/50/EC (37), 2008/105/EC, 2010/75/EU, (EU) 2016/802 (38), and (EU) 2016/2284 (39) of the European Parliament and of the Council (Recital 29 of Regulation (EU) 2020/852).

[48] The environmental objectives of the protection and restoration of biodiversity and ecosystems are to be interpreted in accordance with applicable Union legislation, in particular, Regulations (EU) No. 995/2010 (40), (EU) No. 511/2014 (41), and (EU) No. 1143/2014 (42) of the European Parliament and of the Council; Directive 2009/147/EC of the European Parliament and of the Council (43); Council Regulation (EC) No. 338/97 (44); and Council Directives 91/676/EEC and 92/43/EEC (45), as well as with the Commission Communications of 21 May 2003, "Forest Law Enforcement, Governance and Trade"; of 3 May 2011, "EU Biodiversity Strategy to 2020: our life insurance and natural capital"; of 6 May 2013, "Green Infrastructure: Enhancing Europe's natural capital"; of 26 February 2016, "EU Action Plan against wildlife trafficking"; and of 23 July 2019, "Stepping up EU action to protect and restore the world's forests" (Recital 30 of Regulation (EU) 2020/852).

Economic activity can make a significant contribution to the environmental objective of protecting and restoring biodiversity and ecosystems in a number of ways, including protecting, conserving, or restoring biodiversity and ecosystems, and thus enhancing ecosystem services. These services fall into four categories, namely, provisioning services, such as food and water provisioning; regulating services, such as climate and disease control; enabling services, such as nutrient cycling and oxygen production; and cultural services, such as those providing spiritual and recreational benefits (Recital 31 of Regulation (EU) 2020/852).

value or a surrender value exposed in whole or in part, directly or indirectly, to market fluctuations.

The scope of the Disclosure Directive is concretely determined by the delimitation that the IDD makes on the type of product, defined as one "offering a maturity or redemption value that is wholly or partially, and directly or indirectly, exposed to market fluctuations" (Article 2, paragraph 17), so that the following are excluded from this consideration: (a) nonlife insurance products as listed in Annex I to Directive 2009/138/EC (nonlife insurance classes); (b) life insurance contracts where the benefits provided for in the contract are payable only in the event of death or situations of invalidity caused by accident, illness, or disability; (c) pension products that, under national law, are recognized as having the primary purpose of providing the investor with an income in retirement and that entitle the investor to certain benefits; (d) officially recognized occupational pension schemes falling within the scope of Directive 2003/41/EC or Directive 2009/138/EC; and, finally, (e) personal pension products for which national law requires a financial contribution from the employer and where neither the employer nor the employee has any choice of pension product or its provider.

2.1.4 Entry into Force

In general, Article 20.2 entered into force on March 10, 2021, although, by way of exception, its application was brought forward to December 29, 2020, for (1) the mandate of the ESA to prepare draft regulatory technical standards on the information referred to in paragraphs 1–5 of Article 4 (Article 4, paragraphs 6); (2) Article 8, paragraph 3; (3) Article 9, paragraph 5; (4) Article 10, paragraph 2; (5) Article 11, paragraph 4; and (6) Article 13, paragraph 2. For its part, the application of (1) the mandate to the ESA to develop draft technical standards for the regulation of information in relation to the principle of not causing significant harm as provided in Article 2a; (2) the corresponding mandate to the ESA to develop draft technical standards for the regulation of the content and presentation of the information referred to above and provided for in Article 8(4); (3) the mandate to the ESA to develop draft technical standards for the regulation of the content and presentation of information as set forth in Article 4a and provided for in Article 9(4); (4) the mandate to the ESA to develop draft technical standards for the regulation of the content and presentation of information under Article 8(5) and provided for in Article 9(5); (5) Article 10(2); (6) Article 11(4); and (7) Article 13(2)–(4a) and provided for in Article 9(6); and, finally, (8) the corresponding mandate to the ESA to develop draft technical standards and the presentation of information on financial products under Articles 5 and 6 of Regulation (EU) 2020/852, in accordance with points (c) and (d) of Article 11.1 and set out in Article 11(5). Finally, the fulfillment of the mandate of Article 4(7) of the ESAs to develop draft regulatory technical standards in accordance with Articles 10–14 of Regulations (EU) No. 1093/2010, (EU) No. 1094/2010 and (EU) No. 1095/2010 was delayed -no later than December 30, 2021, on the content, methodologies and presentation of the information referred to in paragraphs 1–5 of this Article, regarding sustainability indicators in relation to adverse impacts in the field of social and labor issues, respect for human rights, anti-corruption and bribery.

Finally, and in accordance with Article 20.3, the application of the disclosure obligations of financial market participants offering financial products of Article 6 of Regulation (EU) 2020/852 provided for in Articles 8(2a) and 9(4a) was postponed to the following dates: (1) no later than January 1, 2022, for the environmental targets referred to in Article 9(a) and (b) of Regulation (EU) 2020/852 and (2) no later than January 1, 2023, for the environmental targets referred to in Article 9(c)–(f) of Regulation (EU) 2020/852. Article 11(1)–(3) shall apply from January 1, 2022.

2.2 *The Specific Transparency Legal Framework for Environmentally Sustainable Investments and the Modification Brought About by EU Regulation 2020/852*

2.2.1 Objectives

As an initiative under the *European Green Deal*,[49] EU Regulation 2020/852 is the culmination of the EU's general intention in European regulation to create a European green financial system that encourages confidence and thus the promotion of sustainable investments, especially in green products, thereby avoiding "green washing."[50] Its objective is twofold: on the one hand, to lay the foundations for a unified Community system of activities to determine whether an economic activity is sustainable from an environmental point of view, also for the purposes of any public measures, standards, or labels,[51] and, on the other, to strengthen transparency in the operation of the financial system by increasing the nonfinancial disclosure obligations regulated in both Regulation (EU) 2019/2088 of the European Parliament and

[49] The European Green Pact was presented by the European Commission in 2019 as an instrument to steer European growth toward "a climate-neutral circular and resource-use economy" and in the "Action Plan: Financing Sustainable Growth."

[50] *Greenwashing* refers to all practices whereby an unfair competitive advantage is gained by marketing a financial product as environmentally friendly when, in fact, it does not meet basic environmental requirements.

[51] The Taxonomy Regulation developed, for now, only some environmental aspects. On December 31, 2021, the Commission published a report describing the provisions necessary to extend the taxonomy to economic activities that do not have a significant impact on environmental sustainability and those that significantly harm it, as well as to social objectives. In this way, economic activities could be classified into three categories: green activities, nongreen activities, and an intermediate category of activities that neither contribute to nor harm the environment. In addition, the crisis caused by the COVID pandemic has increased the perception of the importance of social issues in the field of sustainability, so these issues will be reflected in the future development of the taxonomy.

of the Council of 27 November 2019 on sustainability disclosures in the financial services sector (known as the "Disclosure Regulation") and Directive 2013/34/EU of the European Parliament and of the Council of 26 June 2013 on the annual financial statements, consolidated financial statements and related reports of certain types of undertakings.

The Regulation complements and amends certain provisions of Regulation (EU) 2019/2088 laying down harmonized rules on the transparency that both financial market participants and financial advisors must apply with respect to the integration of sustainability risks in their investment decision-making or advisory processes. In particular, it comes to amend some precepts of Regulation 2019/2088 to strengthen, in accordance with its provisions, the precontractual information disclosure obligations and periodic reports.

The Taxonomy Regulation favors the redirection of financial resources toward sustainable activities, contributing to the EU's climate objectives. But it also broadens the information received by European investors by intensifying the disclosure obligations of companies subject to Directive 2014/95/EU of the European Parliament and of the Council of 22 October 2014 amending Directive 2013/34/EU as regards disclosure of non-financial information and diversity information by certain large companies (Non-financial Reporting Directive or NFRD).[52,53] Finally, it also increases the transparency obligations of companies required to report nonfinancial information under the NFRD. These are large public interest companies with more than 500 employees. Public interest entities are those with securities admitted to trading, credit institutions, insurance companies, and others identified by Member States as being in the public interest.

2.2.2 Target Scope of Application: The Concept of Environmentally Sustainable Investments for a Unified Classification System of Regulation (EU) 2020/852

The definition of "sustainable investments" in Regulation (EU) 2019/2088 covers, in addition to economic activities with social objectives, investments in those economic activities that contribute to an environmental objective or "environmentally sustainable economic activities" within the meaning of Regulation (EU) 2020/852 of the European Parliament and of the Council of 18 June 2020, known as the "Taxonomy Regulation." From its regulation, two directional paths can be glimpsed from the

[52] The main reason why the Regulation extends the environmental disclosure obligations is precisely the relevance and impact of environmental data in determining the sustainability of investments.

[53] The Taxonomy Regulation foresees the obligation of offerors of certain financial products traded on EU markets that are offered as sustainable to provide information on their sustainability in accordance with the taxonomy. Furthermore, it is added that all other (conventional) products have to include a *disclaimer* clarifying that the underlying investments do not take into account the EU criteria on sustainable economic activities.

concept of environmentally sustainable investments: on the one hand, the one that points toward what has come to be called "financially sustainable ecology" or, in other words, the need for the financial system "to adapt progressively to support the sustainable functioning of the economy."[54] On the other hand, the notion of "sustainable finance" is also conceptually redirected from ecology to the financial system, insofar as the character of being "environmentally sustainable" requires that the flows of savings toward productive investment be maintained in the long term and not be harmful to the environment.[55]

Regulation (EU) 2020/852 of the European Parliament and of the Council of June 18, 2020, known as the "Taxonomy Regulation," aims at adopting a unified classification system for "environmentally sustainable activities," one of the measures set by the Action Plan for Financing Sustainable Growth. This system of unified criteria at the Community level makes it possible to determine the sustainability of economic activity from an environmental point of view for the purpose of determining the degree of environmental sustainability of investments in relation to public measures, standards, and labels.

2.2.2.1 Requirements: Special Reference to Environmental Objectives

"Environmentally sustainable investments" are defined by the Regulation as investments that finance one or more economic activities that can, in turn, be considered environmentally sustainable. To this end, an economic activity[56] is considered to be "environmentally sustainable" when it meets the following requirements:

1. *Substantially* contribute to one or more environmental objectives: the Regulation indicates the six objectives to be pursued by the financed economic activity. The objectives must be one or more of those set out in Article 9.[57]
2. Not to cause any significant detriment to objectives other than the above (Article 9), in accordance with Article 17.[58]

---

[54] See Recital (10) of the Taxonomy Regulations or RIS.

[55] On the bidirectional nature of the concept, see Tapia Hermida (2021), p. 9.

[56] The concept on which the system is founded is based on the investment in economic activities, so that in order to determine whether or not it falls within the scope of application of the Community regulations, it will be necessary to consider not the company, which can carry out various economic activities, but the specific economic activity.

[57] Namely, (1) mitigation of climate change, (2) adaptation to climate change, (3) sustainable use and protection of water and marine resources, (4) transition to a circular economy, (5) prevention and control of pollution, and (6) protection and restoration of biodiversity and ecosystems. These objectives are closely related, directly or indirectly, to the Sustainable Development Goals of the 2030 Agenda and to the climate neutrality and biodiversity protection objectives of the Green Pact.

[58] The Regulation attempts to give cohesion and efficiency to the sustainability objectives it submits to a common purpose, thus preventing an economic activity from being harmful to the environment despite its substantial contribution to a specific objective, which, together with the criterion of minimum social guarantees, allows it to fulfill its integrating function for sustainability. Thus,

3. Be carried out in compliance with the minimum social guarantees set out in Article 18: in other words, the activity must be aligned with the OECD Guidelines for Multinational Enterprises and the United Nations Guiding Principles on Business and Human Rights, including the principles and rights set out in the eight core conventions referred to in the International Labour Organization's Declaration on Fundamental Principles and Rights at Work and the International Bill of Human Rights. These minimum guarantees are without prejudice to the application of EU regulations where these are stricter in the areas of environment, health and safety, and social sustainability.
4. Comply with the technical selection criteria, which determine in detail the substantial contribution to an objective and with no significant detriment to the other environmental objectives of an economic activity (Article 10(3), Article 11(3), Article 12(2), Article 13(2), Article 14(2), or Article 15(2)).

2.2.2.2 Technical Criteria

Given the difficulty in the qualification of the activity, Regulation (EU) 2020/852 warns of the need to establish a series of technical selection criteria based, as far as possible, on the sustainability indicators of Regulation (EU) 2019/2088 (see Recital 20), which make it possible to determine whether an economic activity contributes substantially to one or more objectives and does not cause significant harm to the rest, so that an economic activity cannot be considered environmentally sustainable if the damage it causes to the environment is greater than the benefits it brings (see Recital 40).[59,60] They also make it possible to determine when an economic activity can substantially contribute to one or more environmental objectives by reducing the negative impact of other economic activities.[61]

In the implementation of the mandate of Regulation *(EU) 2020/852*,[62] the Commission published on April 21 the technical screening criteria for defining

---

Article 17 of the Regulation establishes the criteria for considering that an economic activity causes significant damage.

[59] The technical criteria allow the taxonomy to be a dynamic tool capable of adapting metrics and thresholds to the scientific evidence of each moment (see Murillo García (2020).

[60] For a first analysis of the programmatic approach of the cost/benefit analysis method applied by Regulation (EU) 2020/852, see Tapia Hermida (2020a).

[61] The relevance of the technical criteria is explained by their role in the applicability of the concept and, therefore, of the Regulation. Indeed, the Regulation itself recognizes their role, considering that to ensure the reliability, consistency, and comparability of sustainability-related disclosures in the financial service sector, the disclosure of information related to the 2020 Regulation should use existing sustainability indicators as far as possible, as proposed by the European Parliament in its resolution of 29 May 2018 on sustainable finance (OJ C 76, 9.3.2020, p. 23).

[62] To this end, the Regulation entrusts the Commission with determining, by means of delegated acts, the technical criteria for selecting sustainable economic activities for each objective and each relevant environmental sector, in accordance with Article 19 of the Regulation, which must also be updated periodically (Articles 10.3, 11.3, 12.2, 13.2, 14.2, and 15.2).

activities that make a substantial contribution to climate change mitigation and adaptation, i.e. the first two of the six environmental objectives of the EU taxonomy.[63] The EU Taxonomy Regulation requires investors and companies to use these criteria for disclosure, which also makes it possible to provide reliable guidance for investment decisions. For the other environmental objectives, the Regulation itself foresaw that delegated acts should be established by December 31, 2021, at the latest, with a view to their entry into force as of January 1, 2023 (Articles 12–15).

The Commission finally adopted on December 9, 2021, the *Commission Delegated Regulation (EU) 2021/2139 of June 4, 2021, supplementing Regulation (EU) 2020/852 of the European Parliament and of the Council*[64] *and establishing the technical selection criteria for determining the conditions under which an economic activity is deemed to make a substantial contribution to climate change mitigation or adaptation, and for determining whether that economic activity does not cause significant harm to any of the other environmental objectives. The aforementioned Delegated Regulation establishes two types of technical selection criteria to determine the conditions under which an economic activity is considered to contribute substantially to the achievement of (i) climate change mitigation (Annex I) and (ii) climate change adaptation (Annex II). The same criteria will be applicable to determine whether such activity causes significant harm to the other environmental objectives (Article 9 RIS). Subsequently, Delegated Regulations (EU) 2022/1214 and 2022/1288, implementing the Disclosure Regulation, amend and adjust, respectively, as regards economic activities in certain energy sectors, the content, and the presentation of information relating to the promotion of environmental or social characteristics and sustainable investment objectives in precontractual documents, on websites and in periodic reports.*

2.2.2.3 Facilitating Activities

The Regulation also contemplates and regulates the possibility of activities that directly enable other economic activities to make a substantial contribution to the environmental objectives. These are so-called "facilitating activities," which are defined in Article 16 as activities that contribute substantially to one or more of the environmental objectives established in Article 9 when they directly allow other activities to make a substantial contribution to one or more of those objectives, provided that such economic activity:

[63] Article 9 of the EU Taxonomy Regulation specifies the following six environmental objectives: (a) climate change mitigation, (b) adaptation to climate change, (c) sustainable use and protection of water and marine resources, (d) transition to a circular economy, (e) pollution prevention and control, and (f) protection and restoration of biodiversity and ecosystems.

[64] Delegated Regulation (EU) 2021/2139 entered into force 20 days after its publication in the OJEU and is applicable as of January 1, 2022 (Article 3).

(a) Does not lead to the retention of assets that undermine long-term environmental objectives, taking into account the economic life of such assets; and
(b) Should have a substantially positive environmental effect, taking into account the life cycle.

This concept includes certain activities or technologies that play an essential role in improving the environmental performance of others.

In contrast to Regulation (EU) 2019/2088, it is not sufficient that the economic activity does not significantly impair another objective, but a high level of sustainability efficiency in the economic activity is required; hence, the contribution to the marked objective of the economic activity must necessarily be substantial.

2.2.3 Insurance Companies as Obligated Parties to Disclose the Sustainability of the ISPS

2.2.3.1 General Legal Framework

The harmonized transparency legal framework is generally required, according to Article 1 of EU Regulation 2019/2088, from all "financial market participants" as well as from "financial advisors" in relation to the integration of sustainability risks and the analysis of adverse sustainability impacts in their processes and sustainability disclosures for financial products. In particular, the insurance activity consisting in the offering of insurance-based financial products presents some particularities and specialties, which shall be subject to application in this matter.

2.2.3.1.1 Insurers Offering IBIPs as Participants in the Financial Markets

The category of "market participants" for the purposes of the transparency legal framework related to sustainable investments is delimited by both EU Regulation 2019/2088 and EU Regulation 2020/852.

Thus, according to Article 2.1 of EU Regulation 2019/2088 are included under the category of "market participants" a heterogeneous cast of market operators offering financial products[65] and covering the following: "(a) any insurance undertaking offering insurance-based investment products (IBIPs); (b) any investment services firm providing portfolio management services; (c) any occupational pension fund (IORP); (d) any pension product originator: (e) any alternative investment fund manager (AIFM); (f) any provider of pan-European individual pension products; (g) any manager of qualifying venture capital funds registered in accordance with

[65] For the purposes of EU Regulation 2019/2088, any of the following are considered to be financial products in accordance with Article 2, point 12, of the Regulation: (a) any portfolio managed in accordance with point (6) of this article, (b) any alternative investment fund (AIF), (c) any IBIPs, (d) any pension product, (e) any pension scheme, (f) any UCITS, or (g) any pan-European individual pension product.

Article 14 of Regulation (EU) No. 345/2013; (h) any manager of qualifying social entrepreneurship funds registered in accordance with Article 15 of Regulation (EU) No. 346/2013; (i) any management company of undertakings for collective investment in transferable securities (UCITS management company); or (j) any credit institution providing portfolio management services" (EU Regulation 2019/2088).

For its part, Article 2.2 of EU Regulation 2020/852, while referring to the list of participants enumerated by Article 2.1 of the aforementioned EU Regulation 2019/2088 under such category, nevertheless extends its scope of application also to pension product manufacturers "to which a Member State has decided to apply this Regulation in accordance with Art. 16 of this Regulation." In order to consider them as market participants for the purposes of the aforementioned EU Regulation 2020/852, it refers to creators of pension products operating national social security schemes regulated by Regulations (EC) No 883/2004 and (EC) No 987/2009 (Article 16 EU Regulation 2019/2088).[66]

2.2.3.1.2 Insurers and Insurance Intermediaries Advising on IBIPs and Their Consideration as Financial Advisors

The general transparency legal framework extends to "financial advisors," a category that, according to EU Regulation 2019/2088, covers any of the following: (1) any insurance intermediary providing insurance advice in respect of IBIPs, (2) any insurance undertaking providing insurance advice in respect of IBIPs, (3) any credit institution providing investment advice, (4) any investment service firm providing investment advice, (5) any alternative investment fund manager providing investment advice in accordance with Article 6(4)(b)(i) of Directive 2011/61/EU, and, finally, (6) any UCITS management company providing investment advice in accordance with Article 6(3)(b)(i) of Directive 2009/65/EC.

In short, it must be concluded that under the condition of financial market participants, there is a varied and heterogeneous list of financial product creators, which includes, of course, insurance companies offering insurance-based investment products (IBIPs) and also entities that concurrently perform activities corresponding to financial market participants and financial advisors, when acting in their capacity as financial product creators, and also provide portfolio management services.

On the other hand, the concept of financial advisor covers any intermediary when providing investment or insurance advice, including the insurance intermediary (i.e., any insurance intermediary) and any insurance company providing insurance advice with respect to such investment products. Its delimitation is decisive, insofar as the Disclosure Regulation imposes on them the duty to disclose information on how

[66] In such cases, the creators of pension products referred to in Article 2(1)(d) of EU Regulation 2019/2088 shall include these creators of pension products operating national social security schemes as well as the pension products referred to in Article 2(8) of EU Regulation 2019/2088. In such a case, the definition of pension product in Article 2, point (8), of this Regulation shall be understood to include the aforementioned pension products.

they take into account sustainability risks in the selection process of the financial product they present to end investors, regardless of their sustainability preferences.

To introduce further dissonance, the regulation itself subsequently exempts the aforementioned insurance intermediaries from its provisions, although "Member States may decide to apply this Regulation to insurance intermediaries providing insurance advice in respect of IBIPs [...]" (Article 17 of the Disclosure Regulation).[67]

2.2.3.2 Exemptions: Special Reference to Small IBIP Insurance Intermediaries (with Less Than Three Employees)

The harmonized transparency rules on sustainable investment transparency under EU Regulation 2019/2088 will not be required for "insurance intermediaries providing insurance advice in respect of IBIPs nor for investment firms providing investment advice and which are undertakings, regardless of their legal form, including natural persons and self-employed persons, provided that they have fewer than three employees" (Article 17.1).

However, Member States may decide to apply this Regulation to insurance intermediaries providing insurance advice with regard IBIPs or to investment firms providing "investment advice," as defined in Article 17(1) (Article 17(2)), by notifying both the Commission and the ESAs (Article 17(3)).

2.2.4 Entry into Force

Its general entry into force was July 12, 2020, 20 days after its publication in the Official Journal of the European Union (OJEU).

However, the deadline for the entry into force of the precepts imposing on public authorities the duty to use criteria to determine whether an activity is environmentally sustainable in public measures, standards, and labels (Article 4) was postponed to January 1, 2022.[68] For the precepts reinforcing the nonfinancial reporting obligations (Articles 5–8), their entry into force was postponed to January 1, 2023.[69] In short, the information obligations imposed by EU Regulation 2020/853 have applied, in general, from July 12, 2021, although the transparency obligations of Articles 4, 5, 6, 7, and 8(1)–(3), with regard to the environmental objectives of Article 9 (a) and (b), were applicable from January 1, 2022, while with regard to the

---

[67] See Sect. 2.2.3.2.

[68] According to Article 27.2(a), "(a) Articles 4, 5, 6, and 7, and Article 8(1), (2) and (3) shall apply: (a) with respect to the environmental objectives listed in Article 9(a) and (b), as of January 1, 2022."

[69] According to Article 27.2 (b), "(e)xcept for the environmental objectives listed in Article 9 (c) to (f), as of January 1, 2023."

environmental objectives of Article 9 (c) and (f), they were applicable from January 1, 2023.

The obligations apply, for each environmental objective, 12 months after the establishment by the Commission of the corresponding technical selection criteria. The European Commission adopted, through Commission Delegated Regulation (EU) 2021/2139 of June 4, 2021, the final text of the regulatory technical standards (RTS) in order to comply with the mandate concerning the mitigation and adaptation objectives, adopted on December 31, 2020, and applied as of January 1, 2022, pursuant to—and further developing—Articles 10(4) and 11(5) of the Taxonomy Regulation.[70] For their part, the delegated acts relating to economic activities that substantially contribute to the other four environmental objectives were adopted on December 31, 2021, so that they could be applied as of January 1, 2023, in accordance with paragraph 5 of Articles 12–15.

2.2.5 Technical Development Standards and Their Application to Insurance Companies

The European Commission adopted the final version of the regulatory technical standards (RTS), which implement the Disclosure Regulation. Specifically, Commission Delegated Regulation (EU) 2022/1288 of 6 April,[71] supplementing Regulation (EU) 2019/2088, applicable from January 1, 2023, contains the regulatory technical standards specifying the details in terms of the content and presentation to be met by the information relating to the "no significant harm" principle and specifying the content, methods, and presentation of information relating to sustainability indicators and adverse sustainability impacts, as well as the content and presentation of information relating to the promotion of environmental or social features and sustainable investment objectives in precontractual documents, on websites and in periodic reports.

For its part, and in compliance with Article 8 of the Taxonomy Regulation, which requires companies subject to Article 19a or 29a of the NFRD to disclose the manner and extent to which their activities are associated with environmentally sustainable economic activities, the Commission Delegated Regulation (EU) 2021/2178 of July

---

[70] In the implementation of its mandate, the Commission adopted on December 9, 2021, *Commission Delegated Regulation (EU) 2021/2139 of June 4, 2021, supplementing Regulation (EU) 2020/852 of the European Parliament and of the Council and establishing the technical selection criteria for determining the conditions under which an economic activity is deemed to contribute substantially to climate change mitigation or adaptation, and for determining whether that economic activity does not cause significant harm to any of the other environmental objectives.*

[71] This Regulation is based on the draft regulatory technical standards submitted to the Commission by the European Banking Authority, the European Insurance and Occupational Pensions Authority, and the European Securities and Markets Authority.

6, 2021,[72] was published on December 10, 2021. The standard provides a list of KPIs (*key performance indicators*) for financial and nonfinancial companies, as well as the methodology for calculating them, and also includes reporting templates.

Article 6 sets forth the content and methodology to be followed by insurance companies, as well as in its art. 7, in their condition as financial companies, to include in the statement of nonfinancial information the degree of sustainability of their activities. More specifically, it thus determines, by reference to Annexes IX–XI, the content, methodology, and presentation of information to be disclosed by insurance companies in publishing nonfinancial information on environmentally sustainable activities. For financial companies, including insurance and reinsurance companies, it specifies the obligation to include the qualitative key performance indicators on which financial companies must disclose information and the methodology for their calculations.[73]

3 Transparency Obligations and Precontractual Information on Financial Sustainability

The rules and transparency legal framework of Regulation (EU) 2019/2088 on sustainable finance, as amended by EU Regulation 2020/852, oblige insurers as financial market participants to be transparent and to inform the financial market and their end investors, in particular, to what extent their investment decisions, naturally based on the three fundamental criteria (profitability, risk, and liquidity), have taken sustainability objectives—environmental and social—into consideration.

Specifically, the Regulation establishes a series of obligations that affect both the internal organization of the vast majority of financial institutions, including

[72] Commission Delegated Regulation (EU) 2021/2178 of 6 July 2021 supplementing Regulation (EU) 2020/852 of the European Parliament and of the Council by specifying the content and presentation of the information to be disclosed by companies subject to Articles 19a or 29a of the Directive. In particular, the implementing regulation ensures the uniform application of the disclosure requirements set out in the aforementioned Article 8 of the Taxonomy Regulation.

[73] Specifically, this qualitative information that must accompany the KPIs is specified in Annex XI of Commission Delegated Regulation (EU) 2021/2178, namely: "– contextual information to support the quantitative indicators, including the scope of assets and activities covered by the KPIs, information on data sources and limitations; – explanations of the nature and objectives of the economic activities that conform to the taxonomy and of the evolution of the economic activities that conform to the taxonomy over time, starting in the second year of application, and distinguishing between business-related elements and methodological and data-related elements; – description of compliance with Regulation (EU) 2020/852 in the financial company's strategy, product design processes and relationship with clients and counterparties; – for credit institutions that are not required to disclose quantitative information on trading exposures, qualitative information on the extent to which the trading portfolios comply with Regulation (EU) 2020/852, including the overall composition, observed trends, objectives and policy; – additional or complementary information on the strategies of the financial company and the weight of the financing of economic activities that conform to the taxonomy in its total activity."

insurance companies that offer IBIPs, and the information that they must publish on their website and include in the precontractual information of their products in relation to (1) the integration of "risks and incidents," understood as the impact that such institutions may generate in their environment in terms of sustainability; (2) financial products that promote environmental or social characteristics; and (3) financial products aimed at sustainable investments.

This set of obligations derived from these transparency rules on financial sustainability has been ordered on the basis of the following criteria:[74]

(a) Based on a subjective, internal, and organizational criterion, the legal framework requires market participants and financial advisors to develop a policy of integrating sustainability risks into their decision-making process, for which purpose it establishes duties of transparency in relation to policies regarding sustainability risks (Article 3) and the integration of sustainability risks (Article 6), with particular emphasis on the duties of transparency in relation to adverse sustainability impacts at the entity level (Article 4) as well as on remuneration policies in relation to the integration of sustainability risks (Article 5).
(b) In accordance with an objective criterion, the Regulation establishes a set of duties of transparency in the adverse sustainability impacts of financial products (Article 7).
(c) There is also a formal or documentary criterion, which brings together certain duties of transparency on the part of the website in relation to certain information at the level of the entity (Articles 3, 4, and 5) and in relation to its financial products and sustainable investments (Article 10). There is likewise a precontractual duty of transparency in the promotion of environmental or social characteristics (Article 8), on sustainable investments in precontractual information (Article 9), in the promotion of environmental or social characteristics and sustainable investments on websites (Article 10), and, finally, in the promotion of environmental or social characteristics and sustainable investments in periodic reports (Article 11).

Ultimately, Regulation (EU) 2019/2088 on sustainable finance provides that insurers offering IBIPs as financial market participants must ensure that their marketing communications do not contradict the information disclosed under the Regulation (Article 13.1).

3.1 Depending on the Means or Instrument of Dissemination

The disclosure legal framework for sustainability-related information in the financial service sector provided for in the Disclosure Regulation and EU Regulation 2020/

[74] See Tapia Hermida (2020b), p. 6.

852 establishes a set of disclosure obligations affecting the content of the website, the content of its precontractual information, and periodic reports.

The transparency obligations regarding financial sustainability will affect the information contained in the website or the precontractual information, or, finally, the periodic reports, each of them having a different content.

Therefore, the means or instrument of articulation or dissemination of the legal framework is analyzed below.

3.1.1 Disclosure on the Website

The dissemination on the website of specific content is articulated as one of the most prominent generic obligations of the transparency legal framework to the extent that insurers, as soon as they market and/or give advice, or insurance intermediaries advising on IBIPs shall endeavor, in accordance with Articles 3, 4, 5, and 10 of the Disclosure Regulation, to ensure clarity and transparency in the information published on their websites at the entity level and product level.

The main requirement for financial market participants and financial advisors is to host and maintain concise information on their websites, which must be updated by these entities. In addition, the legal framework foresees the obligation of the entities to ensure that what is published in their advertising communications does not contradict the information disclosed on their website in order to guarantee the reliability of information (Article 13).

In conclusion, the transparency legal framework on sustainable investments articulates a duty of disclosure through the website or web page of the entities subject to it and, thus, the obligation to have a corporate website or web page as an indispensable condition for compliance with the minimum content of the duty of disclosure of information via the web, which is recognized as a generic obligation. However, the consequences of noncompliance with this generic, instrumental, and prior obligation are not contemplated and typified in the following cases: (1) when the obliged entity does not have a corporate website or (2) when there is evidence of the absence or deficiency of the information provided for in the Regulation to be disclosed on the website.

3.1.1.1 About the Entity

At the entity level, an insurer offering IBIPs must publish the following information on its website, in accordance with the Disclosure Regulation:

1. Its policy of integrating sustainability risks into the decision-making process (Article 3)
2. A statement about its due diligence policies with respect to the principal adverse impact (PAI) on sustainability factors, which shall include a statement in this regard in the terms that have been developed by the Commission Delegated

Regulation (EU) 2022/1288 of 6 April 2022, supplementing Regulation (EU) 2019/2088 (Article 4 Disclosure Regulation)[75] and
3. Information on the consistency of remuneration policies with the integration of sustainability risks (Article 5)

3.1.1.2 On Financial Products

Regarding the IBIP financial products they promote, the insurers' website shall include the following information:

1. That IBIPs promoting *environmental or social characteristics* have a *sustainable investment* objective (whether or not a benchmark has been designated) or have a *carbon emission reduction* objective (Article 10),[76] which includes the following: (a) a description of the environmental or social characteristics of the sustainable investment objective (Article 10.1) and (b) information regarding the methods used for its measurement and monitoring (Article 10.1).
2. That other IBIPs that promote and/or *target sustainable investments* and a *benchmark* have been designated (Article 9)—the citation shall be accompanied by a description of the characteristics of the sustainable investment objective, as well as the method for measuring the impact of the selected sustainable investments (Articles 10.1 and 9.1),[77] in particular, (*a*) information on how the designated index meets that objective and (*b*) an explanation of why and how the designated index differs from a general market index.

The disclosure of the IBIP on the website should provide additional data on the investment strategy used by the insurer for the financial product in question, including the policy for assessing the good governance of the beneficiary companies, as well as the methods used to measure whether it meets environmental or social characteristics or achieves sustainable investment objectives (Chapter IV of

[75] Article 4 of the Commission Delegated Regulation (EU) 2022/1288, implementing Article 4 of the Disclosure Regulation, provides that the entities to which the Disclosure Regulation applies shall "publish on their website, in a specific section entitled: 'Statement regarding the main adverse impacts of investment decisions on sustainability factors', the information referred to in Article 4(1) (a), (2), (3) and (4) of Regulation (EU) 2019/2088, and in Articles 4 to 10 of this Regulation. Such information shall cover the period from 1 January to 31 December of the preceding year and shall be published in the section 'Sustainability disclosures' referred to in Article 23 of this Regulation."

[76] More specifically, it must be accompanied by (*a*) a description of the environmental or social characteristics of the sustainable investment objective; (*b*) information on the methods used to assess, measure, and monitor the environmental or social characteristics or the impact of the sustainable investments selected for the financial product; (*c*) precontractual information on the environmental or social characteristics and sustainable investments; and, finally, (*d*) promotional information on the environmental or social characteristics and sustainable investments in the periodic reports.

[77] See Sects. 3.1.2, 3.2.2.1, and 3.2.2.2.

Delegated Regulation (EU) 2022/1288 on "Publication of product-related information on the website").

3.1.2 Disclosure of Precontractual Information

3.1.2.1 About the Entity

The disclosure legal framework for sustainability-related information in the financial service sector provided for in the Disclosure Regulation establishes a set of disclosure obligations that affect not only the content of the website but also the content of its precontractual information and periodic reports.

Indeed, the generic duty to include in the precontractual information specific content at the entity level on how it integrates sustainability risks in investment decisions and the results of the assessment of their impact on the profitability of financial products derived from Regulation 2019/2088 (Sustainable Finance Disclosure Regulation or SFDR) and its content is specified in Article 6.[78] Its instrumental nature is based precisely on the purpose it is called upon to fulfill, which is none other than to reduce information asymmetries in principal-agent relationships existing between financial market participants and financial advisors, on the one hand, and potential end investors, on the other, with regard to the integration of sustainability risks, the analysis of adverse sustainability impacts, the promotion of environmental or social features, as well as sustainable investment, hence imposing on them the obligation to disclose precontractual and ongoing information to end investors when acting as agents for such end investors.

However, as regards insurance undertakings, in particular, the disclosure of this precontractual information shall take the form of the information referred to in Article 185(2) of Directive 2009/138/EEC (Solvency II)[79] or, where applicable, in accordance with Article 29(1) of Directive (EU) 2016/97.

As regards their specific content, their scope is discussed together in the corresponding section.[80]

---

[78] See Sect. 3.2.1.

[79] The information required by the aforementioned Article 185, paragraph 2, of the Solvency II Directive for life insurance undertakings comprises (a) the name or business name and its legal form; (b) the Member State in which the head office is established and, where appropriate, the branch with which the contract is to be concluded; (c) the registered office and, where appropriate, the address of the branch with which the contract is to be concluded; and, finally, (d) a specific reference to the report on the solvency and financial condition in accordance with Article 51, enabling the policyholder to have easy access to this information.

[80] See Sect. 3.2.1.1.

3.1.2.2 On Financial Products

Also, like the previous one, it is an obligation of generic content and instrumental nature, whose specific substantive content in relation to financial products is established by Regulation 2019/2088 (Disclosure Regulation or SFDR) and specified in Articles 7, 8, and 9.2–9.3, and its scope is analyzed jointly by product in the corresponding section.[81]

To ensure the comparability and comprehensibility of environmental or social features, insurers marketing IBIPs that promote such features shall confirm the information on such promotion in the annexes to the documents or information referred to in Article 6, paragraph 3, and Article 11, paragraph 2, of the Disclosure Regulation. They must also clarify, by means of a declaration, that such products do not have a sustainable investment objective. For the same purpose and to ensure a level playing field with financial products targeting sustainable investments, precontractual, periodic, and website information on products promoting environmental or social features must also mention the proportion of sustainable investments (Chapter III of the Delegated Regulation (EU) 2022/1288).

3.1.3 Regular Disclosure of Sustainable Products

The disclosure legal framework for sustainability-related information in the financial service sector under the Disclosure Regulation includes a set of disclosure obligations that affect the content of periodic reports.

The Disclosure Regulation (SFDR) typifies as a generic obligation the inclusion in the periodic reports of information related to the promotion of environmental or social characteristics and sustainable investments. The obligation to submit periodic reports with a specific minimum content is thus configured as an obligation of an instrumental nature.

Article 11 contains the specific information to be included in the periodic reports according to the type of financial product:

(a) Thus, for financial products, including IBIPs that promote, among others, environmental or social features, or a combination thereof, provided that the companies in which the investment is made observe good governance practices (Article 8.1), the periodic reports must contain a description of the degree to which the environmental or social features have been complied with. In this regard, Annex IV of the Delegated Regulation (EU) 2022/1288 sets out the template for the periodic reporting template for these financial products.
(b) In relation to both IBIPs aiming at sustainable investments (Articles 9.1 and 9.2), and those aiming at reducing carbon emissions (Article 9.3), the periodic reports shall include express reference to: (1) the overall sustainability impact of the

[81] See Sect. 3.2.2.

financial product using relevant sustainability indicators; or (2) where a benchmark index has been designated, a comparison of the overall sustainability impact of the financial product based on the designated index and a general market index using sustainability indicators. The Delegated Regulation (EU) 2022/1288 establishes in this regard in its Annex V the model template for periodic reporting of these financial products.

(c) Both for IBIPs investing in an economic activity contributing to an environmental objective, and subject to Article 5 of Regulation (EU) 2020/852 and for those promoting environmental features, subject to Article 6 of Regulation (EU) 2020/852, the information to be collected refers to the information required in particular in such Articles, namely: (1) information on the environmental objective (s) set out in Article 9 of this Regulation to which the investment underlying the financial product contributes, and (2) a description of how and to what extent the investments underlying the financial product are allocated to economic activities that qualify as environmentally sustainable pursuant to Article 3 of this Regulation.

(d) Finally, for those IBIPs not subject to Article 8(1) or Article 9(1), (2) or (3) of Regulation (EU) 2019/2088, the information to be included in the periodic report in accordance with the provisions of the sectoral legislation referred to in Article 6(3) and Article 11(2) of that Regulation shall be accompanied by the following statement: "The investments underlying this financial product do not take into account the EU criteria for environmentally sustainable economic activities". (Article 7 Regulation (EU) 2020/8952).

The content of this obligation has been further developed by Delegated Regulation (EU) 2022/1288[82] requiring financial market participants to disclose a minimum set of quantitative and qualitative, standardized, and comparable indicators demonstrating how each financial product complies with the environmental or social characteristics it promotes or the sustainable investment objective it seeks to achieve.[83] Thus, with regard to the publication related to the product in periodic reports, the aforementioned Delegated Regulation dedicates Section 1 of its Chapter V (Articles 50–57) to establishing the indicators related to the promotion of environmental or social characteristics, while it reserves Section 2 of the same

---

[82] Delegated Regulation (EU) 2022/1288 complements the Disclosure Regulation by implementing its mandate to the European supervisory authorities to develop draft regulatory technical standards to specify in detail their content and presentation (Articles 11.4 and 11.5), which it is, in principle, is required as of January 1, 2022, although the ESAs have requested the Commission to adopt a different implementation date to clarify that the first periodic report should be published in 2023 for the 2022 financial year.

[83] Such indicators should be relevant to the design and investment strategy of the financial product as described in its precontractual information. In particular, to ensure consistency between precontractual information disclosures and periodic information disclosures, financial market participants should communicate in their periodic disclosures the specific sustainability indicators referred to in the precontractual information and that are used to measure how environmental or social features are met or how the sustainable investment objective is achieved.

Chapter V to products with a sustainable investment objective (Articles 58–63) and, finally, develops in its Section 4 the publication of periodic information on financial products with investment options for the investor or several of those investment options that qualify the financial product as one that promotes environmental or social characteristics (Articles 65–67).

3.1.4 Review of Disclosed Information

Regulation (EU) 2019/2088 closes the transparency legal framework on financial sustainability by incorporating in Article 12 the obligation of financial market participants to ensure that they keep published information up to date in accordance with the transparency obligations concerning policies on sustainability risks (Article 3) as well as remuneration policies in relation to the integration of sustainability risks (Article 5) and, finally, in accordance with the obligation to publish the promotion of environmental or social features and sustainable investments on their website (Article 10). The modification or revision of this published information must include a clear explanation on the same website (paragraph 1).

This obligation also extends, in accordance with Article 12(2), to financial advisors in relation to any information published in accordance with policies relating to sustainability risks (Article 3) and remuneration policies in relation to the integration of sustainability risks (Article 5).

3.1.5 Transparency of Insurers in Nonfinancial Statements

Regulation (EU) 2020/852 extends, through its Article 8, the list of nonfinancial disclosure obligations regulated in Directive 2013/34/EU of the European Parliament and of the Council on the annual financial statements, consolidated financial statements and other related reports of certain types of undertakings (transposed into law by Law 11/2018 of December 28).

3.1.5.1 Subjective Scope of the Obligation

On the one hand, and by reference to Article 19a of Directive 2013/34/EU of the European Parliament and of the Council of 26 June, this covers large, medium, and small companies, including insurance companies, which are public interest entities.[84]

[84] Such entities are required by Article 19a of Directive 2013/34/EU to include in the management report a *nonfinancial statement* containing information to the extent necessary to understand the development, performance, and position of the company and also the impact of its activity, relating at least to environmental and social issues, as well as concerning personnel, respect for human rights, and the fight against corruption and bribery.

On the other hand, and by reference to Article 29a of Directive 2013/34/EU of the European Parliament and of the Council of 26 June, EU Regulation 2020/852 also extends to those public interest insurance companies that are parent companies of a large group, provided that, at their balance sheet closing dates, they have an average number of employees exceeding 500 during the financial year (Article 2, paragraph 1, letter c).[85]

3.1.5.2 Content and Presentation of the Information

In general, Article 8 of the Taxonomy Regulation subjects these companies to the duty to disclose, in connection with the nonfinancial information on them, a description of how and to what extent the activities carried out by such companies are related to economic activities that can be classified as environmentally sustainable in accordance with the Taxonomy Regulation.[86]

Regarding the content and presentation of this information, and in compliance with the mandate of Article 23 of the Regulation to complete paragraphs 1 and 2 of Article 8 of the Regulation, the Commission published on December 10, 2021, the Commission Delegated Regulation (EU) 2021/2178 of July 6, 2021.[87] It specifies the rules for the content and presentation of the information to be disclosed under these paragraphs, including the methodology to be used for compliance with their provisions. Specifically, it establishes common rules applicable to both financial (Article 7) and nonfinancial institutions (Article 2). Thus, in particular, for financial institutions, such as insurance companies, the key performance indicators (KPIs) and the methodology for their calculation are specific and different according to the type of financial institution. The disclosure of the KPIs shall be accompanied by qualitative information (Articles 3–6).

However, the rules common to financial and nonfinancial entities, as well as, specifically, to financial entities that apply to insurance companies offering IBIPs or IBIPs, including unit-linked insurance, are of particular note. Among the former, the

[85] In this case, such entities must include in the consolidated management report a consolidated nonfinancial statement containing information to the extent necessary to understand the development, performance, and position of the group as well as the impact of its activity, relating at least to environmental and social issues, as well as to personnel matters, respect for human rights, and the fight against corruption and bribery. More specifically, it must provide information similar to that contained in Article 19 bis, in relation to the group.

[86] Nonfinancial companies shall disclose, in particular, (1) the proportion of the company's turnover derived from financial products associated with economic activities that can be qualified as environmentally sustainable according to the Taxonomy Regulation, as well as (2) the proportion of its total fixed assets and the proportion of its operating expenses related to assets or processes associated with economic activities that are considered environmentally sustainable.

[87] Commission Delegated Regulation (EU) 2021/2178 of 6 July 2021 supplementing Regulation (EU) 2020/852 of the European Parliament and of the Council by specifying the content and presentation of the information to be disclosed by companies subject to Articles 19a or 29a of the Directive.

following stand out: (a) the obligation for any entity, financial or not, to publish the corresponding KPIs as from the 2003 financial year; (b) the obligation for the KPIs to initially cover the climate adaptation and mitigation objectives, with the following objectives to be published at least 12 months after the date of application of the corresponding RTS; and (c) the obligation to use the same currency in the financial statements. Regarding the latter, the Regulation includes a series of exclusion parameters in the calculation of KPIs.[88]

3.2 *Depending on Its Content*

3.2.1 Regarding Internal Organization

Even if not expressly provided for in the Disclosure Regulation (SFDR), in order to comply with internal transparency obligations, the financial market participants concerned must approve a policy for the integration and assessment of sustainability risks in their investment decision-making process or investment advisory service prior to their transparency, disclosure, and information obligations in this area. The rationale is that the information provided on the prior analysis and assessment of sustainability factors during the investment advice and decision-making process increases the resilience of the real economy and the stability of the financial system and can ultimately influence the risk/return ratio of financial products.

In addition, and although the Regulation does not expressly provide for it either, it seems that the transparency legal framework on financial sustainability imposes on these entities the need to review all their internal manuals, policies, and procedures in order to adapt them to the contents of the Regulation and to avoid any inconsistency arising from its entry into force.

3.2.1.1 Publication of Policies Related to Sustainability Risks and Their Integration in Investment Decision-Making

The Disclosure Regulation (SFDR) requires insurers offering or marketing insurance-based investment products (IBIPs), regardless of IBIPs and the target market, to publish in writing their policies on the integration of sustainability risks into their investment decision-making process and to ensure the transparency of such integration (Article 3).

In this sense, the governance of these entities should not only have a clear investment policy on the incorporation of sustainable finance risks, but it should also be communicated and published in writing. In turn, policies related to advice on

[88] The parameters excluded from this calculation are (1) sovereign debt, (2) derivative financial instruments, and (3) companies not subject to the *NFRD*.

sustainability issues, as well as the adverse impacts of investment choices, should also be incorporated into the policy.

In particular, Article 6 of SFDR has an impact on the content that the legal framework also imposes as part of the precontractual information regarding transparency in the integration of sustainability risks, which is specified in the duty to communicate to potential investors the way in which sustainability risks are integrated in their investment decision-making process, in the case of financial market participants, or in their investment or insurance advice, in the case of financial advisors, the sustainability risks in the profitability of the financial products they offer as well as an assessment of the potential impact of such risks on the profitability of the financial products (paragraphs 1(a) and 2(b), respectively). This obligation extends even in cases where sustainability risks are not significant as financial market participants must include, along with the above descriptions, a "clear and concise explanation of the reasons for this."[89]

Specifically, the legal framework differentiates between financial market participants and advisors in relation to the minimum precontractual information obligation.

The insurers concerned, as financial market participants, shall include in the disclosed precontractual information the following: (1) a description of how sustainability risks are integrated into investment decisions and (2) the results of the assessment of the potential impact of sustainability risks on the profitability of the financial products they offer. However, where financial market participants consider sustainability risks to be insignificant, the descriptions referred to in the first paragraph shall include a clear and concise explanation of the reasons for this (Article 6.1).

The precontractual information required from insurers and insurance intermediaries advising on IBIPs shall be limited to the following: (1) a description of how sustainability risks are integrated into investment decisions and (2) the results of the assessment of the potential impact of sustainability risks on the profitability of financial products. On the other hand, where sustainability risks are considered to be insignificant, the descriptions must consist of a clear and concise explanation of the reasons for this (Article 6.2).

3.2.1.2 Publication of Remuneration Policies in Relation to Sustainability Risks

Specifically, Article 5 of the Disclosure Regulation (SFDR) obliges financial market participants and financial advisors to include in their remuneration policies, which they must already have in place in advance, information on the consistency of these policies with the integration of sustainability risks (paragraph 1), with a mandate to

[89] See Sect. 3.1.2.1.

create and maintain in accordance with the relevant sectoral guidelines and legislation (paragraph 2).

Consequently, this information should be included in the remuneration policies required of insurers offering insurance-based investment products.

3.2.1.3 Publication of the Main Adverse Events (PAIs) at the Entity Level

This is one of the most important obligations at the entity level insofar as every market participant or noninsurance intermediary financial advisor must add its specific information on the web or make public, in the investment process, its investment policy on sustainability factors, following a proportionality criterion or, in other words, taking into consideration its size and nature and the scale of its activities.

Its articulation obliges the entity to integrate in its adopted processes, including in particular its due diligence processes, those related to the analysis of the main adverse effects (PAIs), material or possibly material, of investment decisions on sustainability factors, understanding for such purposes by PAIs, the effects of advice and investment decisions that have negative effects on sustainability factors or the negative impact that investment or advice decisions may have on sustainability factors (environmental or social).

Thus, they must carry out a prior analysis of the due diligence policies in relation to such adverse events, taking into account their size and nature and the scale of their activities, as well as the types of financial products they offer (letter a), Article 4.1, Regulation 2019). Such analysis is therefore established as a prior step to the duty to declare the policy in relation to the main adverse events at two levels: at the subjective level (Article 4) and at the objective level (Article 7).[90]

On the subjective level, the rule differentiates between financial market participants and financial advisors, who are not required to include PAI disclosures.[91]

Insurance entities offering IBIPs—included within these categories both (1) those that exceed at the balance sheet date an average number of 500 employees during the financial year (Article 4.3) and (2) those that are parent companies of a large group according to Article 3(7) of Directive 2013/34/EU and exceed at the group's balance

---

[90] On the analysis of the main adverse events for each product, see *infra*, subheading 3.2.2.3. On the Declaration of PAIs with Respect to Each Product.

[91] Financial advisors are not required to include a statement about their due diligence policies in relation to material adverse events (PIAs) but must issue and publish on their websites information about the following: (1) whether they take into account adverse material incidences on sustainability factors when providing investment or insurance advice, taking into account their size and nature, as well as the scale of their activities and the types of financial products on which they provide advice, or (2) the reasons why they do not take into account the main adverse impacts of investment decisions on sustainability factors when providing investment or insurance advice and, where applicable, information on whether and when they plan to take such adverse impacts into account (Article 4.5).

sheet date, on a consolidated basis, an average number of 500 employees during the financial year (Article 4.4)[92]—shall issue and publish on their websites a statement about their due diligence policies in relation to the principal adverse impacts (PAIs) of investment decisions on sustainability factors or, in case such impacts are not taken into account, a clear justification why these are not taken into consideration and if and when they intend to consider them—except for insurers with more than 500 employees that are always obliged to publish such a statement (Article 4.1).[93]

This policy statement on major adverse events shall contain, at a minimum, the following: (a) information on its policies for identifying and prioritizing adverse material sustainability impacts and key sustainability indicators; (b) a description of the adverse material impacts and any actions taken or planned in relation to them; (c) brief summaries of engagement policies, if any; and (d) a reference to responsible business codes of conduct and internationally recognized standards for due diligence and reporting (Article 4.2 Disclosure Regulations). In this regard, Chapter II of the Commission Delegated Regulation (EU) 2022/1288 of 6 April 2022 supplementing the Disclosure Regulation (SFDR) aims to specify the content, methodology, and presentation of information on sustainability indicators and adverse sustainability impacts. To this end, it establishes standardized templates for the presentation of this information, which in any case must contain summary explanations of the key terms used in them.

The publication of the information on the website of the insurers concerned is set every June 30 as a cut-off date and in relation to the previous fiscal year. Thus, the identification of major adverse events must be carried out on at least four specific dates during that given reference period, and the average result must be disclosed annually (Article 4 Delegated Regulation (EU) 2022/1288). In order to ensure that end investors can compare how insurers have taken into account major adverse events over time, insurers must provide a year-by-year historical comparison of their reports for at least the previous five reporting periods, where available (Article 10 Delegated Regulation (EU) 2022/1288).

3.2.2 About the Product Features*

The pillar of the transparency legal framework under the SFDR is based, not exclusively but mainly, on the set of transparency obligations in relation to product features. In general terms, both financial market participants and financial advisors marketing and/or advising on any financial product in relation to potential adverse sustainability impacts or products promoting environmental, social, and good

[92] Specifically, Articles 4.3 and 4.4 imposed such obligation on these entities with effect from June 30, 2021.

[93] Insurers, which must comply with this transparency obligation by December 30, 2022, must include the following: (a) a clear and reasoned explanation of how the insurance-based investment product takes into account the main adverse events and (b) a statement that the information relating to these events is included in the reports submitted on an annual basis.

corporate governance features (Article 8) or products with specific sustainability objectives (Article 9.1 and 9.2), including emission reduction (Article 9.3), must add minimum content on the website and in the precontractual information provided to their investor clients. However, in the case of the insurance sector, the Regulation only imposes this obligation on insurance companies offering and/or advising IBIPs, and insurance intermediaries are not excluded in principle (Article 17).

3.2.2.1 On "Sustainable" Products (with Environmental or Social Characteristics)

The transparency legal framework includes, as part of the minimum content to be integrated into the precontractual information regarding financial products, the duty of the subject entities to provide their investors with information on their financial products when they promote environmental or social features, provided that the invested companies observe good governance practices (Article 8 of the Disclosure Regulation (SFDR).

The precontractual information of the IBIPs with promoted environmental or social characteristics shall contain a specific explanation on whether or not they comply and their scope, based on the following specific mentions and indications, namely: (a) how such characteristics are complied with and (b) whether—and in what way—the benchmark is consistent with them, in case one has been designated, as well as where a method of calculation of such benchmark can be found. However, and in relation to IBPIs, provided for in Article 6 of Regulation (EU) 2020/852, i.e. specifically for those promoting environmental characteristics, they shall include therein, in addition to that provided for in Article 6(1) and (3) of Regulation (EU) 2019/2088 or Disclosure Regulation (SFDR), the statement provided for in Article 6 of Regulation (EU) 2020/852.[94]

In any case, the provisions of Article 8 of the Disclosure Regulation (SFDR) must be complemented by the provisions of the regulatory technical standards (Article 8.3 and 8.4).[95] In relation to them, a standardized model is outlined in which with

---

[94] Specifically, Article 6 of Regulation (EU) 2020/852 requires the following statement to be incorporated in relation to products promoting environmental features: "The 'no significant harm' principle applies only to investments underlying the financial product that meet the EU criteria for environmentally sustainable economic activities. The investments underlying the rest of the financial product do not take into account the EU criteria for environmentally sustainable economic activities."

[95] In the execution of this mandate, on February 8, 2021, the ESAs published a final report on the draft regulatory technical standards, which are key for entities to implement their regulations. Among its important modifications, one of its main novelties is the precontractual information contained in relation to "sustainable" products, i.e. those that promote environmental or social characteristics. The project details the content, methodology, and form of presentation of the information on (1) the main adverse sustainability events (PIAS) to be reported by entities and (2) "sustainable" products or products that promote environmental or social characteristics and products with a sustainable investment objective. In relation to these, it outlined a standardized

different sections, three aspects are clearly indicated: (1) if the product intends to make sustainable investments, (2) if it promotes environmental or social characteristics but does not pursue a sustainable objective, and (3) if an index has been designated for the achievement of the environmental or social characteristics. In particular, Annex II of Commission Regulation (EU) 2022/1288 of 6 April sets out a model for structured precontractual information.[96]

But it must also include such information in more detail on its website for each product with environmental or social characteristics (Article 10.1 Disclosure Regulation or (SFDR)). Specifically, they must incorporate the following on the website: (a) a description of the environmental or social characteristics of the sustainable investment objective; (b) information on the methods used to assess, measure, and monitor the environmental or social characteristics, including their sources of information, the selection criteria relating to the underlying assets, and the relevant sustainability indicators used to measure the environmental or social characteristics or the overall impact of the IBIPs or IBIP in terms of sustainability; (c) the information referred to in Articles 8 and 9; and, finally, (d) the information referred to in Article 11. Such information shall be clear, succinct, and understandable to investors. It shall be published in an accurate, true, clear, nonmisleading, simple, and concise manner and in a prominent and easily accessible place on the website (*last paragraph* of the aforementioned Article 10.1).

3.2.2.2 On Products with a Specific Sustainability Goal

In the field of transparency required in the precontractual information of financial products, Article 9 of Regulation (EU) 2019/2088 includes, as a specific obligation, the obligation to provide certain information when a product is aimed at sustainable investments, although it differentiates between the following products:

---

model in which different sections clearly indicate three aspects: (1) whether the product aims to make sustainable investments, (2) whether it promotes environmental or social characteristics but does not pursue a sustainable objective, and (3) whether an index has been designated for the achievement of environmental or social characteristics.

[96]The standard form of precontractual information in relation to Article 8 of the Disclosure Regulation and Article 6 of the RIS is composed of the following sections: (a) "What environmental or social features does this financial product promote?" (b) "Does this financial product take into account the main adverse impacts on sustainability factors?" (c) "What investment strategy does this financial product follow?" (d) "What is the intended asset allocation for this financial product?" (e) "To what extent, at a minimum, do sustainable investments with an environmental objective conform to the EU taxonomy?" (f) "What is the minimum proportion of sustainable investments with an environmental objective that do not conform to EU taxonomy?" (g) "What is the minimum proportion of sustainable investments?" (h) "What investments are included in '#2 Other' and what is their purpose?" (i) "Has a specific index been designated as a benchmark to determine whether this financial product is in line with the environmental or social features it promotes?" (j) "Where can I find more product-specific information online?".

1. Financial products, including IBIPs, with specific sustainability targets and assigned benchmarks, which information shall be accompanied by (a) information on how the designated benchmark is aligned with such target and (b) an explanation of why and how such designated benchmark differs from a general market benchmark (Article 9.1).
2. Financial products, including IBIPs, with specific sustainability objectives that lack such index, whose information must include an explanation of how this objective is achieved (Article 9.2).
3. Financial products, including IBIPs, which have, in particular, the objective of reducing carbon emissions, the disclosure of which must be accompanied by a detailed explanation of how the low-carbon objective is ensured with a view to meeting the long-term global warming objectives of the Paris Agreement (Article 9.3). In this regard, however, where an EU climate transition benchmark or an EU benchmark aligned to the Paris Agreement in accordance with Regulation (EU) 2016/1011 of the European Parliament and of the Council is not available, the information referred to in Article 6 of Regulation (EU) 2019/2088 or Disclosure Regulation (SFDR) shall include a detailed explanation of how the ongoing effort to achieve the low-carbon target with a view to meeting the long-term global warming objectives of the Paris Agreement is carried out (Article 9.3, paragraph 2).

Where such precontractual information is to be provided by financial market participants, such as insurers offering IBIPs, it must also include two additional disclosures:

(a) Firstly, the method used to calculate the benchmarks assigned in relation to IBIPs both with sustainable targets and with benchmarks and in relation to financial products aiming at reducing carbon emissions with an EU climate transition benchmark or an EU benchmark aligned with the Paris Agreement (Article 9.4).
(b) Secondly, and whenever IBIPs with sustainability objectives invest in an economic activity that contributes to an environmental objective, they shall refer to the information relating to Article 5 of Regulation (EU) 2020/852, namely, (1) information on the environmental objective(s) set out in Article 9 of this Regulation to which the investment underlying the financial product contributes and (2) a description of how and to what extent the investments underlying the financial product are allocated to economic activities that qualify as environmentally sustainable under Article 3 of this Regulation.

Finally, the provisions of Article 9 of the aforementioned SFDR must be complemented by the provisions of the regulatory technical standards (Article 9.5), so that information must be included (a) on how the aforementioned sustainability objectives are met and (b) on whether and how the benchmark is consistent with them, if one has been designated, as well as where a method for calculating the benchmark can be found.

With reference to the content of the standard template for financial products targeting sustainable investments, Annex III of Commission Regulation (EU) 2022/1288 of 6 April establishes a structured precontractual disclosure template,[97] which should clearly indicate that they pursue a sustainable objective and whether a benchmark has been designated to measure the achievement of the objective.[98]

Finally, and as with products with sustainable features, also for each investment product with sustainable objectives, insurers must include such information in more detail on their website for each IBIP with environmental or social features (Article 10.1 of the Disclosure Regulation). Specifically, they must incorporate on the website the following: (a) a description of the environmental or social characteristics of the sustainable investment objective; (b) information on the methods used to assess, measure, and monitor the impact of the sustainable investments selected for the financial product, including their sources of information, the selection criteria relating to the underlying assets, and the relevant sustainability indicators used to measure the environmental or social characteristics or the overall impact of the financial product in terms of sustainability; (c) the information referred to in Articles 8 and 9; and, finally, (d) the information referred to in Article 11. Such information shall also be clear, succinct, and understandable to investors. It shall be published in an accurate, true, clear, nonmisleading, simple, and concise manner and in a prominent and easily accessible place on the website (last paragraph of Article 10.1).

3.2.2.3 On the Declaration of PAIs with Respect to Each Product

Secondly, the obligation to disclose adverse events through their inclusion in the precontractual information extends, in an objective manner, to each of the financial products. When a participant carries out such an analysis, it must also provide

[97] Previously, and in the execution of such mandate, the AES published on February 8, 2021, a final report on the new version of the regulatory technical standards (RTS) of the disclosure regulation structuring such precontractual information, composed of different sections.

[98] The standard form of precontractual information in connection with Article 9, paragraphs 1–4a, of the Disclosure Regulation and Article 5, paragraph 1, of the RIS consists of the following sections: (a) "What is the sustainable investment objective of this financial product?" (b) "Does this financial product take into account the main adverse impacts on sustainability factors?" (c) "What investment strategy does this financial product follow?" (d) "What is the asset allocation and the minimum proportion of sustainable investments?" (e) "To what extent, at a minimum, are sustainable investments with an environmental objective compliant with EU taxonomy?" (f) "What is the minimum proportion of sustainable investments with an environmental objective that do not conform to EU taxonomy?" (g) "What is the minimum proportion of sustainable investments with a social objective?" (h) "What investments are included in 'No. 2 Unsustainable' and what is their purpose? Are there any minimum environmental or social safeguards?" (i) "Has a specific benchmark been designated to meet the sustainable investment objective" in the case of a financial product referred to in Article 9(1) of Regulation (EU) 2019/2088? (j) "Where can you find more product-specific information online?"

appropriate information on each financial product, which, according to Article 7 of the SFDR, must reflect a minimum content. Thus, on the one hand, it must contain a clear and reasoned explanation of the extent to which the financial product takes into account the main adverse effects on the sustainability factors. On the other hand, it must also contain an express statement that the information on the principal adverse impacts on sustainability factors is included in the information to be disclosed in accordance with Article 11(2) (Article 7.1).

To ensure the comparability of the PAI statement on sustainability, Annex I of the Delegated Regulation (EU) 2022/1288 also establishes standardized templates for the presentation of this information, which in any case must contain summary explanations of the key terms used in them.

In the event that an insurer offering IBIPs does not take into account the adverse impacts of investment decisions on sustainability factors, it must nevertheless complete its precontractual transparency by expressly providing for each financial product a clear justification as to why it does not take into account the adverse impacts of investment decisions on sustainability factors and a reasoned explanation as to why it does not do so, including, where appropriate, information on whether and when it plans to take into account such adverse impacts (Article 7.2).

4 Conclusions

The study provides some interesting implications for the precontractual activity of insurers when they market unit-linked life insurance. Its significance lies in the fact that the management and marketing of portfolios related to unit-linked life insurance, and insurance-based investment products in general, have subjected the insurance industry to a new complex and detailed legal framework of information transparency obligations, beyond those relating to the assessment and reporting of financial risks in their investment policies. Its ultimate purpose is none other than to shape the mandatory sustainability information on how the financial market participants and/or financial advisors integrate ESG or sustainability criteria into the governance procedures of the insurers themselves and on the quality and profitability of the products, as well as to inform policyholders, as end investors, of the social and environmental impacts of such products, decisions, and investment policies within the framework of their marketing and distribution policies.

It must be concluded that under the condition of financial market participants, there is a varied and heterogeneous list of financial product creators, which includes, of course, insurance companies offering insurance-based investment products (IBIPs) and also those entities that concurrently perform activities corresponding to financial market participants and financial advisors, when acting in their capacity as financial product creators, as well as providing portfolio management services, that is, the insurance intermediary (i.e., any insurance intermediary) and any insurance company providing insurance advice with respect to such investment products.

In their capacity as financial market participants and/or financial advisors, both insurers and distributors of insurance-based investment products are required to provide an analysis of all "sustainability risks" with negative effects on the financial performance of the investment and/or to give advice, where appropriate, in this regard, meaning with respect to any environmental, social, or governance event or condition that, if occurring, could have an actual or potential material adverse effect on the value of the investment.

In terms of the content and scope of information related to ESG/ESG criteria, the basis of legal framework required of the insurance industry marketing insurance-based investment product is established by Regulation (EU) 2019/2088 of 27 November 2019 and amended and implemented by Regulation (EU) 2020/852 of 18 June 2020 on establishing a framework to facilitate sustainable investment, that strengthen, in accordance with its provisions, the pre-contractual information disclosure obligations and periodic reports and favors the redirection of financial resources toward sustainable activities, contributing to the EU's climate objectives, but does not in any way exhaust the entire framework.

This basis legal framework is complemented and developed by other legal instruments, such as draft technical standards for the regulation of the content and presentation of the information. The purpose of all of them is to contribute to setting out more specific and standardized disclosure requirements with regard to such investments, specifying the details in terms of content and presentation to be met by the information relating to the "no significant harm" principle and specifying the content, methods, and presentation of information relating to sustainability indicators and adverse sustainability impacts, as well as the content and presentation of information relating to the promotion of environmental or social features and sustainable investment objectives in precontractual documents, on websites and in periodic reports. Thus, KPIs (key performance indicators) are a kind of indicators to calculate the environmental impact as well as the environmental sustainability of activities linked to investment decisions.

The transparency legal framework for the disclosure of sustainability information is based on a series of obligations that affect both the internal organization of the vast majority of insurance companies that offer IBIPs and the information that they must publish on their website and include in the precontractual information of their products in relation to (1) the integration of "risks and incidents," understood as the impact that such institutions may generate in their environment in terms of sustainability, (2) financial products that promote environmental or social characteristics, and (3) financial products aimed at sustainable investments.

Specifically, it imposes on insurer companies a set of obligations that can been categorized as follows. In relation to the first group, the one based on a subjective, internal, and organizational criterion, Regulation (EU) 2019/2088 requires insurance companies and financial advisors to develop a policy of integrating sustainability risks into their decision-making process, for which purpose it establishes duties of transparency in relation to policies regarding sustainability risks (Article 3) and the integration of sustainability risks (Article 6). Of particular importance, however, is the fulfillment of the duties of transparency with regard to the adverse impacts on sustainability at the entity level (Article 4), as well as of remuneration policies in relation to the integration of sustainability risks (Article 5).

Secondly, in accordance with *objective criteria*, the Regulation establishes a set of duties of transparency in the adverse sustainability impacts of financial products (Article 7).

Finally, there is also *formal documentation criteria*, which bring together certain duties of transparency on the website in relation to certain information at the level of the entity (Articles 3, 4, and 5) and in relation to its financial products and sustainable investments (Article 10), as well as transparency in the promotion of environmental or social characteristics included in precontractual information (Article 8), in sustainable investments in precontractual information (Article 9), in the promotion of environmental or social characteristics and sustainable investments on websites (Article 10), and, finally, in the promotion of environmental or social characteristics and sustainable investments in periodic reports (Article 11).

Furthermore, for certain insurance companies, those considered to be of public interest, it is required of them to include in the consolidated annual report a consolidated nonfinancial statement containing information, to the extent necessary for an understanding of the development, performance, and position of the group, and the impact of its activities, relating at least to environmental and social issues, as well as to personnel matters, respect for human rights, and the fight against corruption and bribery.

As a final conclusion, the new Regulation on sustainability-related disclosures in the financial service sector applicable to the marketing of insurance-based investment products reinforces precontractual information on the sustainability risks of investments. It seems to achieve the objectives of the synthesis and standardization of procedures and information content. However, the specificity, complexity, diversity, and the methodology of their calculation, while providing a priori quantitatively accurate information for the investor, is of little use if it is not possible to filter out what really reflects a pattern and presents an improvement in terms of asset selection. On the other hand, it does not eliminate the risk of greenwashing, and it cannot be ruled out that some insurance companies, which know how their various indicators are being calculated, try to report to the market what is in their best interest.

References

Alonso A, Gonzalez CI (2021) Los productos financieros sostenibles desde el punto de vista de los supervisores y reguladores bancarios. In: López Jiménez JM, Zamarriego A (eds) La sostenibilidad y el nuevo marco institucional y regulatorio de las finanzas sostenibles. Thomson Reuters Aranzadi, Pamplona

Calvo Vergez J (2021) La delimitación del concepto de inversión financiera sostenible. El papel de los llamados "bonos verdes". Revista Aranzadi de Derecho Medioambiental 50:119–144, digital edition

Campiglio E, Dafermos Y, Monnin P et al (2018) Finance and climate change: what role for central banks and financial regulators? Nat Clim Change 8:462–468. https://doi.org/10.1038/s41558-018-0175-0

Di Marco R, Dong T, Malatincová R, Reuter M, Strömsten T (2022) Symbol or substance? Scrutinizing the 'risk transparency premise' in marketized sustainable finance: the case of TCFD reporting. Bus Strateg Environ 32(6):3027–3052. https://doi.org/10.1002/bse.3285
Eccles RG, Klimenko S (2019) The investor revolution. Harv Bus Rev 97:106–116
Enciso Alonso-Muñumer M (2020) Transparencia y sostenibilidad: nuevos retos de la información no financiera. Revista de Derecho del Mercado de Valores 27:242–281
Esty DC, Karpillow Q (2019) Harnessing investor interest in sustainability: the next frontier in environmental information regulation. Yale J Regul 36:625–692. https://ssrn.com/abstract=3809880
Fontrodona J, Muller P, Marín García S (2020) La inversión sostenible y responsable. Introducción a la guía para inversores particulares. Cuadernos de la Cátedra CaixaBank de Responsabilidad Social Corporativa 43:1–31
Garcia Gimenez U, Gonzalez-Palenzuela A (2021) Nueva normativa de divulgación de información relativa a la sostenibilidad en el sector de los servicios financieros. In: López Jiménez JM, Zamarriego A (eds) La sostenibilidad y el nuevo marco institucional y regulatorio de las finanzas sostenibles. Thomson Reuters Aranzadi, Pamplona, p 950
Landi G, Sciarelli M (2019) Towards a more ethical market the impact of ESG rating on corporate financial performance. Soc Responsib J 15(1):11–27. https://doi.org/10.1108/SRJ-11-2017-0254
Leipziger D (2010) The Corporate Responsibility Code Book, revised second edition
Maldonado Molina FJ (2000) Los seguros de vida unit-linked. Derecho de los Negocios 121:1
Martinez Lopez MJ (2019) Directrices de la AEVM sobre factores de riesgo conforme al reglamento de folletos: aplicación al examen y aprobación de los factores de riesgo a la luz del Reglamento delegado 2019/980. Revista de Derecho del Mercado de Valores 24, digital edition
Martínez MT, Sánchez Calero Guilarte J (eds) (2019) Nuevas tendencias de Derecho Europeo y del Derecho español en las sociedades cotizadas, vol 7. Servicio de Publicaciones Facultad de Derecho. Colección "Actas y Homenajes"
Mayorga Toledano MªC (2015) La protección del inversor minorista en el Reglamento UE 1286/2014, sobre los documentos de datos fundamentales". Revista de Derecho del Mercado de Valores, 16:7, digital edition
Muñoz Pérez AF (2019) Los mercados de capitales y el impulso de las finanzas sostenibles. Revista de Derecho del Mercado de Valores 25, digital edition
Murillo García UE (2020) Reglamento de Taxonomía de la UE de Actividades Sostenibles. Boletín Económico 3126. https://doi.org/10.32796/bice.2020.3126.7077
Palá Laguna R (2019) Directrices acerca de cómo supervisar los factores de riesgo del folleto informativo, Análisis GA_P, 16 de mayo de 2019. https://www.ga-p.com/wp-content/uploads/2019/05/Directrices-de-la-ESMA-acerca-de-c%C3%B3mo-supervisar-los-factores-de-riesgo.pdf. Accessed 21 Apr 2024
Tapia Hermida AJ (2019) Fomento de la implicación a largo plazo de los accionistas en las sociedades cotizada. In: Martínez MT, Sánchez Calero Guilarte J (eds) Nuevas tendencias de Derecho Europeo y del Derecho español en las sociedades cotizadas, vol. 7. Servicio de Publicaciones Facultad de Derecho. Colección "Actas y Homenajes", pp 131–139
Tapia Hermida AJ (2020a) Sostenibilidad financiera en el mundo posterior al COVID19. Revista de Derecho Bancario y Bursátil 159:31–74
Tapia Hermida AJ (2020b) Sostenibilidad financiera en la Unión Europea: El Reglamento (UE) 2019/2088 sobre las finanzas sostenibles. La Ley Unión Europea 77:1–16
Tapia Hermida AJ (2021) Sostenibilidad financiera. Reus, Madrid
Tapia Sánchez MªR (2020) La Taxonomía UE: una regla de oro de las finanzas sostenibles. Revista de Derecho del Mercado de Valores 27:193–241

Isabel Rodríguez Martínez is an Assistant Professor of Commercial Law at UNED University (Madrid) and is accredited as a University Professor. She held the role of Professor of Commercial Law at the University CEU Cardenal Herrera until 2023, shortly after her PhD in Law at the University of Valencia, where she held the role of research fellow at the Department of Commercial Law "Manuel Broseta Pont." She was also a researcher at the Polytechnic University of Valencia.

In recent years, she has been active in the field of corporate governance and sustainability. She is a frequent speaker in academic events, has participated in research projects, and has published academic papers and books on this subject. As a result of her specialization, her research effort has been extended to the field of sustainability and financial products. Her recent publications include works such as the "OECD Guidelines for Multinational Enterprises and the OECD Due Diligence Guidance for Responsible Business Conduct," in BATALLER GRAU, J, BOQUERA MATARREDONA, J., Dirs., Responsabilidad social y sostenibilidad. El marco de actuación de la empresa," ed. Tirant lo Blanch, 2023, pp. 231–268, and "Nuevo régimen de transparencia y divulgación de la información relativa a la sostenibilidad en el sector de los servicios financieros," in MARTÍNEZ-ECHEVARRÍA GARCÍA DE DUEÑAS, A. (Dir.) Gobierno Corporativo, Sostenibilidad y Reputación, ed. Thomson Reuters Aranzadi, Cizur Menor, 2022, pp. 315–360.

Sustainability of Agricultural Insurance Systems: Challenges from a European Approach

Alicia Mateos-Ronco

1 Introduction

Agriculture is one of the economic activities most exposed to risk because of its intrinsic connection with the natural environment. Climate event variability and the evolution and liberalisation of international markets have heightened uncertainty in farming. Producers have to cope with new risks and growing social concerns about environmental and food safety issues. In addition, most farmers have to make decisions about planting crops or replacing their livestock holdings without actually knowing what price their production might fetch at the time of harvesting or slaughtering. The result is highly variable farm incomes and considerable exposure to significant losses or low earnings in some years.

Farming in Europe consists of complex systems in which social and ecological components are strongly linked. The diversity of actors and pathways to make these systems more resilient requires flexible, coordinated and comprehensive policies that encompass their complexity (Soriano et al. 2023). The economic and social viability of farms and farming households is crucial to safeguarding the resilience and sustainability of agricultural and agri-food systems. However, the growing risk exposure of European farming is impacting the well-being of producers and the economic and social sustainability of farms, driving the demand for innovation in risk management instruments and spurring public intervention through the development of support policies. Hence, one of the main aspects of public policy backing for European agriculture is to secure a decent standard of living for farmers. Ensuring stable, decent income levels is a policy target that also aims to guarantee the well-

A. Mateos-Ronco (✉)
Universitat Politècnica de València, Faculty of Business Administration and Management, Centre for Research in Business Management (CEGEA), València, Spain
e-mail: almaron@esp.upv.es

J. Bataller-Grau et al. (eds.), *Sustainability and the Insurance Market*, AIDA Europe Research Series on Insurance Law and Regulation 10,
https://doi.org/10.1007/978-3-031-72186-1_9

being of farm families, and therefore, farm income is a relevant policy proxy for this viability (Finger and El Benni 2021).

Risks are growing in agricultural systems. Anticipating the likelihood of the occurrence, frequency and severity of events in agriculture is increasingly difficult, compounded by rising liberalisation (and price volatility), greater quality and price requirements from the agri-food industry and large-scale retailers (reducing producers' room for manoeuvre) and climate change. Market risks and price volatility coupled with the uncertainty generated by the political and environmental context are pivotal for European farms (Meraner and Finger 2019). In the European Union (EU), the latest common agricultural policy (CAP) reforms underscore the political interest in managing producer risks and unlocking new support measures. However, the emergence of new insurance mechanisms in Europe is still limited, compared to other countries, such as the United States and Canada, which have rolled out new insurance tools in recent years (Agricultural Risk Coverage, Price Loss Coverage) (Pieralli et al. 2021), although there are still significant differences in risk management policies between these countries and the EU (European Parliament 2014).

In line with the increasing complexity of agricultural risks, agricultural policies and measures are becoming more intricate, more targeted to specific policy objectives and tailored to specific farms. The EU has gradually redirected its support mechanisms from market management to decoupled payments and income support over the years. The 2013 CAP reform included the income stabilisation tool (IST), which allowed 70% compensation for any income loss over 30% of a historical average benchmark (Pieralli et al. 2021; Severini et al. 2019). In June 2018, the European Commission presented its proposals for the post-2020 CAP, in which the first goal was to ensure a fair level of income for agricultural producers.[1] The EU's risk management toolbox was expanded, enabling member states to step up support levels for agricultural and livestock insurance to 70% of premiums and to pump payments into mutual funds on an annual basis. This seems to indicate a public-private partnership approach to agricultural insurance in the EU, which is comparable to the US crop insurance programme (Meuwissen et al. 2018). It also factors in risk variation across member states, which makes for a diverse European agricultural insurance landscape.

Research has often underscored the need to approach income risk management analysis from a contextualised and regional standpoint. In economic terms, agricultural income can be defined from a farm-household-level perspective, where total household income shapes the family's spending choices. Keeping the diversity of farm households in mind is pivotal in this approach when mapping out new policies (Finger and El Benni 2021).

This environment moulds agricultural producers' attitudes towards farm management and using tools designed to reduce and, where applicable, offload some of the

[1] "Member States will have to support risk management tools under rural development to help farmers manage production and income-related risks which are outside their control" (European Commission 2018b).

risks. Producers' risk management attitudes and preferences change as the political, economic and social context in which they operate evolves (Bozzola and Finger 2021). Effective (and diverse) risk exposure, risk attitude and risk perception and the complex interrelationships between them need to be considered together to better understand producers' response to risk and their likely uptake of risk management tools (Iyer et al. 2020).

The situation outlined above poses fresh challenges for research into the sustainability of agricultural insurance systems, some of which are addressed in this paper. Firstly, the emergence of new risks (price volatility, market risks) calls for progress in devising new products (insurance lines, coverages) to safeguard the viability and continuity of farms. How these new risk management tools can be integrated into insurance business models and practice needs to be identified, given that EU policies are pushing for public-private agreements on insurance as a fairer way of allocating public funds to agriculture. Accordingly, this paper performs an analysis of the current situation in some EU countries. Secondly, conducting this assessment on a national basis entails analysing the feasibility of tools which secure the income level of agricultural producers. It also takes into account (1) the fit of these new products in the relevant legislative framework (EU policies, World Trade Organization and others), (2) the economic and social background and the configuration and features of the markets that producers operate in and (3) the insurance preferences of producers by reviewing the sparse evidence on how they rate insurance attributes, i.e. which aspects of insurance are crucial to farmers' willingness to pay. This approach, which advocates a role for stakeholders (especially producers) in drawing up insurance, could lead to greater uptake by target groups and, consequently, increase the likelihood of these insurance products being successful (Gosh et al. 2021). This national approach is conducted from the Spanish perspective, enabling the generalisation of initiatives for use in other European countries with similar characteristics in the field of agricultural insurance.

This chapter is organised as follows. The next section puts the scope of the study into context by describing EU agricultural policies and their goal of stabilising and protecting farm income against the risks inherent to farming. Section 3 then explores the disparate geographical distribution of risk in EU farming systems, the variability in farm incomes across the EU and the consequent uneven roll-out of risk management tools. Section 4 reviews the development of agricultural insurance in the EU with particular reference to new insurance models, such as revenue and income insurance, and their relationship with producers' risk preferences and perceptions. Finally, Sect. 5 addresses the Spanish agricultural insurance system, one of the most highly developed in Europe, while Sect. 6 sets out the main conclusions and future strands for research in risk management and agricultural insurance sustainability.

2 EU Agricultural Policies and Agricultural Risk Protection

Uncertainty and risk in agriculture stem from a multitude of factors, such as hazards related to weather, pests and diseases, as well as changes in both market conditions and the policy context in which farmers operate and trade (Iyer et al. 2020). Climate change is driving the intensity and frequency of adverse climate events, triggering production losses, damaging farmland and assets and threatening livelihoods in many areas around the world. Increased exposure to risk and the impact of climate change will further exacerbate agriculture's challenges. Meanwhile, issues such as the recent Covid-19 pandemic have demonstrated how events outside the agricultural industry can also disrupt its operations, leading to unexpected fallout in labour and input markets.

Risks can be categorised by their source and consequences. The five main types of risks in agriculture are divided into production risks, which are caused, for example, by drought, floods, pests and diseases; market risks (input and output prices, price spikes); enterprise risks, i.e. risks related to the functioning of public bodies which are triggered by unexpected changes in government policies; personal risks, for example due to the death or serious illness of producers or farm workers; and financial risks (insolvency, funding difficulties). All these risks ultimately have a bearing on producers' income, with the extent depending on the frequency, randomness and distribution of the risk in question and the correlation between the events and the scale of the losses incurred.

Notwithstanding the inherent exposure of farming, the impact of disasters in the end hinges on the ability of producers to anticipate, cope with, withstand and recover from their adverse effects. It is thus essential to embrace proactive risk management to prevent potentially hazardous events from turning into disasters. Resilience and disaster risk reduction therefore must become part and parcel of modern agri-food systems (FAO 2021). Against this background, risk management should enable the agricultural industry to address the threefold challenge of supplying safe and nutritious food to a growing population, providing sustainable livelihoods along the agri-food chain and managing the planet's natural resources sustainably. Meeting this threefold challenge requires a systematic approach. In its *Farm-to-Fork* strategy, the European Commission has put together a legislative framework for sustainable food systems that will be adopted at the end of 2023 after broad consultation and impact assessment, seeking to accelerate and facilitate the transition to sustainable food systems. To this end, this framework aims to promote policy coherence at EU and national levels and integrate sustainability into all food-related policies.[2]

The OECD's recent proposals on risk management in agriculture (OECD/FAO 2021) present a resilience-based approach to managing the impacts of natural-

[2]More information about this initiative can be found at https://ec.europa.eu/info/law/better-regulation/have-your-say/initiatives/13174-Sustainable-EU-food-system-new-initiative_en.

hazard-induced disasters.[3] The shift from risk-coping to a resilient approach emphasises the importance of ex ante planning to prevent and mitigate the adverse effects of disasters before they occur, enabling producers to be better prepared to recover from adversity and helping the sector to adapt and change to reduce its vulnerability to future disasters. Indeed, some OECD countries are already steering cooperation between governments, producers and other stakeholders towards innovative policy measures, governance arrangements and on-farm strategies to step up their resilience to natural-hazard-induced disasters. In some countries, scientific-knowledge-based information and decision-support tools on climate that provide options and strategies for adapting to those risks are made available to producers. Nature-based physical solutions are also being rolled out to prevent and mitigate natural hazard risks and their impacts, using on-farm practices that harness the potential of agricultural land to lessen specific natural hazard risks and improve soil health. Partnerships and relationship building between stakeholders in the agricultural industry are being fostered to enhance strategies that avert the effects of natural disasters, while contingency plans and simulation exercises are being prioritised to help ensure that stakeholders are better equipped to respond to disasters and also to learn from them.

European agricultural policies, such as the CAP, have underscored the crucial role of risk management tools (El Benni et al. 2016; Meuwissen et al. 2018). The production of an agricultural holding is bound up with several potential outcomes, which have varying likelihoods. Many factors cannot be controlled by the farmer even though they have a direct impact on their holding's earnings, and this confirms the importance of using risk management tools to run businesses and safeguard sustainable farming.

Farm households draw on a variety of risk management strategies based on the types and levels of risk they face, the range of solutions available and the government's willingness to support them (OECD 2020c). In most cases, producers also have to cope with and manage many risks at the same time. This can exert a compounding effect and can lead to cascading results, where one kind of risk feeds into the occurrence of another. Hence, risks cannot be analysed separately as one risk may affect others. This interrelationship calls for a systemic approach, which is crucial in seeking solutions to mitigate the vulnerability and sensitivity of agricultural systems to different types of risk and their interrelated effect (Lupton et al. 2020). Some policy initiatives therefore advocate addressing risk management more holistically by looking at issues and strategies that target multiple sources of risk (Komarek et al. 2020).

Risk management strategies combine market-based approaches and government intervention, including a wide range of tools and instruments, such as (1) financial management by, for example, handling borrowing and cash flow correctly;

---

[3] *Agricultural resilience* is defined as the ability to prepare and plan for, absorb, respond to, recover from and more successfully adapt to and transform in response to natural hazards and other risks (OECD 2020a).

(2) diversification of income sources by bundling production options with different risk profiles and tapping into other non-agricultural activities; (3) production techniques that combine the choice of inputs and outputs; (4) marketing techniques, including expanding sales, concentrating production and marketing at source through cooperatives, risk transfer in the food chain via vertical integration and using futures contracts; (5) insurance systems, in which government support can be arranged through subsidies or by managing the system; and (6) social, fiscal and agricultural safety nets.

Over the last two decades, there has been a significant increase in public support for risk management tools in agriculture, particularly in disaster assistance, agricultural insurance, income stabilisation schemes and producer tax-saving accounts. These tools make farms more resilient by enabling producers to cope with the financial impact of adverse events. Nevertheless, they also discourage producers from being more proactive in investing in risk reduction measures (Glauber et al. 2021). Public support for risk management is warranted when the output of risk-averse farmers is below the level which maximises earnings because risk-neutralising contingency markets are not available or do not work properly (OECD 2020c). Virtually, all OECD countries and some large emerging economies support agricultural risk management, although the extent and focus of this support varies considerably. For example, agricultural insurance subsidies for OECD countries have increased nearly fivefold since 2005 to over USD 10 billion in 2019 (OECD 2020b). Total support for the agricultural sector stood at USD 817 billion per year in 2019–2021 in 54 OECD countries, up by 13% from USD 720 billion in 2018–2020. The European Union and the United States, both major agricultural producers, together account for two-thirds of this total. However, this increase is also partly down to temporary factors, such as support for producers and consumers during the Covid-19 pandemic (OECD 2022).

In most cases, agricultural support policies, including risk management, need to be aligned with the international rules in the World Trade Organization's (WTO's) Agreement on Agriculture (AoA). Government subsidies granted at the national level have to meet specific conditions in order to be compatible with WTO rules and thus be included in what is known as the green box. Any failure to comply with these conditions has to be reported to the WTO and will go into the amber box, which has a total expenditure ceiling for each country.

Nonetheless, although public intervention is justified to remedy market failures, it has been challenged because it hampers the development of market solutions by transferring support to producers, which often leads to rent-seeking. This intervention therefore needs to be assessed in terms of its cost-effectiveness and its impact on producers' decisions and markets (OECD 2020c). The analysis of public support for risk management tools should make a distinction between the different levels of risk faced by farmers since standard fluctuations in production, price and climate events do not necessarily require public response. These risks can be appropriately managed by farmers as part of their normal business strategy (OECD 2009), for example, by investing in irrigation technologies that mitigate the adverse impact of drought or by diversifying crop choice to prevent high variability of earnings in the event of large price fluctuations in any one crop. Conversely, infrequent and catastrophic events (drought, flooding, outbreak of a highly contagious disease) may require a public policy response because coping with the loss is beyond the capacity of individual market producers.

Consequently, public agricultural policies need to provide safety nets to deal with natural disasters and other major market shocks on the supply or demand side. However, private risk management tools should be at the core of insurance schemes. Building the private market for risk management is essential, with or without public support, and public policy safety nets should not crowd out the private market (Cordier 2014). Walters and Preston (2018) showed the value of insurance for producers and the importance of using a combination of public and private risk management tools. In light of recent trends in agricultural and economic policy, other researchers have highlighted the pressure to increase the volume of market methods and individual cost sharing associated with reducing income risks in agriculture (Janowicz-Lomott et al. 2015).

2.1 Farm Income Stabilisation

Growing price volatility in agricultural markets, meaning persistently low prices and constant price fluctuations, has led to a global crisis with major ramifications for stakeholders operating at various economic levels: farmers (production), intermediaries (marketing) and customers (consumption) at the micro, meso and macro levels, respectively (Mustafa et al. 2023). Price volatility is the main source of uncertainty, and identifying and measuring it calls for comprehensive real-time information on internal and external factors, usually referred to as price dynamics. This phenomenon has been further compounded by the current high inflation rates, which are driving price increases to record peaks in most regions around the world.

The economic literature suggests that price volatility runs in waves, which overlap during crises, leading to irreversible price increases. Studying past food shocks is therefore of particular importance in understanding food crises and assessing agricultural markets. This concern led to the launch in 2016 of the Global Network Against Food Crises (GNAFC), founded by the EU, the Food and Agriculture Organization (FAO) and the World Food Programme (WFP) of the United Nations. It is "an alliance of humanitarian and development actors united by the commitment to tackle the root causes of food crises and promote sustainable solutions through shared analysis and knowledge, strengthened coordination in evidence-based responses and collective efforts across the Humanitarian, Development and Peace (HDP) nexus".[4]

[4]More information about the Global Network Against Food Crises (GNAFC) can be found at https://www.fightfoodcrises.net/about/en/.

Farm income volatility comes from the instability of natural and market conditions resulting from the special features of agricultural production and markets shaped by climate events, faster growth in supply than in demand, lower prices, poor mobility in terms of production factors (land, capital and labour) and low opportunity costs of labour. According to the European Commission (2018a), up to 20% of farmers reported falls in income of more than 30% compared to the previous year, with farms in Italy, Poland, Spain and Greece especially affected, followed by Cyprus, Slovenia, Malta and Latvia. Furthermore, the emergence of new types of risks tied to production, price and income has led to diverse producer risk profiles across EU regions.

One of the main drivers of government subsidies and support for agriculture has been the stabilisation of farm incomes. Successive reforms of the CAP since 1992 have been designed to provide agricultural producers with income support, which has varied from the initial direct payments coupled with production factors (land area, livestock) to the subsequently more usual uncoupled and non-product specific ones.

The EU's CAP allocates a large part of its budget to supporting and stabilising the farm incomes of its producers through direct payments, market support and border protection. Although this support is lower than it was three decades ago, it is still high. Mitchel and Baker (2019) estimated EU agricultural support in 2018 at 20% in terms of the OECD's "producer support estimate" (PSE) indicator, which calculates this figure as a share of total farm income. These levels, which vary significantly between member states, are above the OECD average and also above the average for other countries, such as China, the United States, Russia, Canada, Brazil and Australia. The European Commission estimates put the share of direct support in the shape of agricultural factor income[5] for the EU at 23.4% in 2020, varying widely among member states from 7% in Malta to 49% in Estonia, with Spain below the EU average at 18%. This variable agricultural support is a consequence of the member states' diverse agricultural structures, and although the CAP can help improve this variability, it is best addressed through national policies (European Commission 2018a).

However, current CAP tools are not counter-cyclical. Support in the shape of Pillar I direct payments and Pillar II rural development policies for less well-off areas, agri-environmental measures, and farm restructuring and investment is geared not towards mitigating farm income instability but rather towards supporting particular quantities of agricultural resources, such as land, livestock and other farm inputs. These amounts are set per measure and do not change over time to offset variations in farm market income. As a result, there is an obvious inability of this

[5]The agricultural factor income measures the income derived from agricultural activities that can be used for the remuneration of own and rented production factors: labour, land and capital. European Commission, Directorate-General for Agriculture and Rural Development. Available at https://agridata.ec.europa.eu/extensions/DashboardIndicators/FarmIncome.html.

CAP subsidy policy to react to the high volatility and fluctuations in farm market income in some cases (Bojnec and Ferto 2019; Severini et al. 2016).

3 Regional Differences in Risk Management: A European Analysis

The robust interrelationships between policy measures, external factors and farm-household-level decision-making influence the extent to which agricultural policy objectives and farm-household well-being are achieved. The resilience of farming systems needs to be addressed from a regional standpoint as producers, producer organisations, service providers and various supply chain actors are embedded in local environments (Meuwissen et al. 2019). A system approach in this context enables a broader, more complex and holistic understanding of risks in agriculture and how they are managed by sundry actors (farmers, agribusiness and international organisations) (Lupton et al. 2020). In short, risk preferences are context-dependent and differ across various fields of farm-level decision-making (Meraner and Finger 2019).

Risk perception is highly subjective and bound up with cultural and structural factors. Cafiero et al. (2005) provided a description anchored in three key aspects: the frequency of occurrence of the adverse event, the average value of the loss and the independence of the probability of occurrence. Farmers' willingness to use risk management tools is related to perceived business risk, the subjective likelihood of loss and the expected value of that loss, which may differ from the objective business risk. Individual risk aversion, producer indebtedness, average income levels and the odds of having very low farm income may also affect the willingness to reduce farm income distribution (Cordier 2014).

Research has sought to furnish a geographical overview of the level and distribution of risk in EU agriculture (Bielza et al. 2008) by providing a map of the risk of regional average yield reduction below a certain level for the main crops (wheat, barley, field beans, grain maize, rapeseed, sunflowers, potatoes, sugar beets). The picture is extremely uneven with a fair degree of stability in most central EU regions and a high risk of yield reduction in the peripheral ones (Mediterranean, Romania and some Scandinavian areas). The risk of drought is obviously higher in the southern regions, though is not uniform, and a large area of significant drought risk has been identified around the Baltic Sea and, to a lesser extent, in some regions along the Danube. Too much rain at harvest time is problematic in the east of the EU. The risk of frost, which affects all types of crops, increases towards the northeast, with specific local risks. The risk of biomass reduction in grassland seems to be scattered, with some concentration in parts of southern Spain, the Alps, Romania and Bulgaria, north-west Scotland[6] and the southern Rhine Valley.

Moreover, different types of agriculture have diverse sources of income volatility because agriculture-specific risks affect the various types of farming differently. The income volatility of cereal agriculture is mainly related to yields and production prices, while in livestock, poultry and pig production, it is largely driven by output-input price ratio volatility. As a result, income risk levels differ significantly between types of agriculture. Accordingly, producers need to tailor their risk management strategies to their specific type of farming, the size of their holdings and their financial structure (Cordier 2014).

3.1 Farm Income Variability Across the EU

The CAP for the period 2023–2027 is built around ten key targets focused on social, environmental and economic goals, one of which is precisely "to ensure a fair income for farmers". This means supporting decent farm income and the resilience of the agricultural sector across the EU in order to enhance long-term food security and agricultural diversity, as well as to ensure the economic sustainability of agricultural production (European Commission 2023). According to the European Commission (2018a), EU farm income, as measured by entrepreneurial income per family-work unit, is still significantly below the average economic income, as measured by the average wage, although this gap has narrowed over time. However, the situation varies from one member state to another. The ten regions with the highest income per worker in agriculture are Belgium, the Netherlands, the northern part of France, Italy and Germany, the east of the UK[6] and southern Sweden. Factors such as greater labour productivity and specialisation in intensive and high-value production, together with larger farm size, account for these differences. By production type, pig and poultry farms and wine and horticulture holdings have the highest farm income per worker, while grazing livestock and mixed crops have the lowest.

There are many factors to take into account when assessing the level of income in the sector and its differences between EU member states. Firstly, structural farm changes have an impact on farm income insofar as most of them involve investments whose expected returns are mid to long term, thus conditioning current income levels. Another factor is the gradual, continuing outflow of labour from agriculture, which increases the amount of income per person, albeit not symmetrically across sectors due to income volatility. A farm's economic viability determines its resilience in the event of a short-term fall in farm revenue as a result of low production levels, low prices or high costs. The highest resilience indicators, as measured by the

[6]References to the UK as a member of the EU have been kept in this paper in cases where the information refers to studies conducted prior to Brexit.

holding's asset-to-debt ratio, are in countries such as Denmark, France, Slovakia and Estonia, while Italy and Ireland have lower levels.

Farm income support is, on average, 12% of farm turnover in the EU and represents around one third of farm income across the EU (European Commission 2018a), although it may be higher in some sectors (grazing livestock), and especially in crisis-hit areas. The correlation between the concentration of agricultural income support and the concentration of land, as most direct payments are granted per eligible hectare of land, means the level of support varies widely between and within member states. Income support and land are more concentrated in eastern European countries, contrasting with fewer payments and less land concentration in western and southern European countries, with a few exceptions. Accordingly, the Communication on the Future of Food and Farming[7] and the proposal for a new Multi-annual Financial Framework 2021–2027[8] advocate a more balanced distribution of these supports, and the Impact Assessment[9] accompanying the Commission's proposal for the CAP after 2020 looks at ways to achieve this through mechanisms to reduce direct payments to large farms and redistribute income support to small and medium-sized ones.

Agricultural policy design needs to consider three distinct aspects of farm income (Finger and El Benni 2021): the income issue, given that average income levels have frequently been used as an indicator to proxy the well-being of farms and the farming sector; the variability issue, since the variability of income over time reflects the income risk faced by farmers; and the inequality issue, which refers to income distribution across the farm population and includes income inequality within the farm population compared to non-agricultural sectors.

3.2 Agricultural Risk Management Tools

Risk management programmes in OECD countries cover a variety of risks associated with natural disasters, from drought or flood to multiple-peril yield insurance. Most countries provide some protection against natural disasters through disaster assistance programmes and/or crop insurance programmes. Protection against short-term price and income declines is common in countries such as the United States. The main tools for publicly supported agricultural risk management are summarised in the following policy packages (Glauber et al. 2021): ex-post disaster assistance,

---

[7] European Commission (2017). Available at https://eur-lex.europa.eu/legal-content/EN/TXT/PDF/?uri=CELEX:52017DC0713&from=EN.

[8] European Commission. Available at https://ec.europa.eu/commission/publications/factsheets-long-term-budget-proposals_en.

[9] European Commission (2018). Impact assessment for "CAP towards 2020". Available at: https://eur-lex.europa.eu/legal-content/EN/TXT/PDF/?uri=CELEX:52018SC0301&from=EN.

agricultural insurance programmes, income stabilisation schemes and tax and savings measures.

Disaster Assistance Programmes compensate producers after a loss. While in some countries (e.g. the United States) these programmes are statutory and the producer knows in advance whether and how much compensation they would be eligible for in the event of a loss, in most cases, the programmes are post hoc, i.e. the government makes a decision to intervene after the loss occurs. This approach is also used to address the impact of economic crises on the sector, such as in cases of export closures due to animal disease outbreaks. The United States and Canada have used these kinds of programmes, and virtually, all European member states have provided ad hoc payments in cases of agricultural disasters in recent years (European Commission 2017b).

Agricultural Insurance , as will be seen below, guarantees producers a level of yield or income in exchange for the payment of premiums, which reflect the instrument's underlying risk. The idea behind insurance is to pool risks, i.e. to combine the risks faced by a large number of individuals who pay premiums into a common fund, which is used to cover losses sustained by any individual in the pool. In this sort of tool, indemnities are set according to the experience of a producer's actual yields or to regional performance indexes, climate results and other correlated variables but not to an individual's performance. While there are examples of fully private agricultural insurance schemes, most of them are government subsidised or supported because the risks to be covered are not insurable as a market-determined premium would be too high.

Income Stabilisation Programmes usually target stabilising producers' incomes in relation to the average of recent years, which may encompass the producer's entire farm or individual crops covered by agricultural insurance programmes. These income stabilisation schemes usually set an income floor and not a ceiling. Such schemes are in place, albeit with differences, in the United States and Canada, along with some OECD countries and a number of European member states, e.g. Italy, Spain and Hungary. Severini et al. (2019) provided an ex ante assessment of the effects of the income stabilisation tool (IST), which was being discussed at the moment they were writing, on income variability and levels as well as on income inequality in the Italian farming population. Their study compared the current income situation with that resulting from a hypothetical implementation of IST under different policy scenarios, taking into account reduced levels of CAP direct payments. The results showed that IST stabilised farm income, raised its level and reduced inequality among Italian producers and was more effective in reducing income inequality when farmers paid contributions to mutual funds that were proportional to their income as opposed to flat-rate payments. More recently, and once this tool had been rolled out for the apple sector, Rippo and Cerroni (2023) showed that greater specialisation in crop production coupled with greater exposure to risk and previous experience with mutual funds were conducive to producers' participation in IST. El Benni et al. (2016) investigated the influence of Swiss farms and farmers' characteristics on IST potential indemnification, finding more likely and higher indemnities for part-time and low-income farmers, which could brand the IST as a transfer instrument hampering structural change.

Tax and Saving Measures help producers smoothen their incomes by encouraging savings in tax-deferred savings accounts or government-matched accounts, whereby the government matches producers' savings deposits up to a pre-set amount and allows producers to withdraw these sums, often without penalty, in years when revenue falls below a pre-determined level. Some countries, such as Austria, Canada, France, Germany (an exception used only for small farms) and the United States, allow producers to use cash accounting rather than accrual methods, i.e. to recognise income and expenses at the time the cash flow (receivables and payables) occurs, which makes reporting income and expenses for tax purposes more flexible. Other countries also offer producers income-averaging measures which smoothen out variable taxable income and reduce their tax burden. This is the case in Australia, Canada, France, Germany, Ireland, Norway, the United Kingdom and the United States (OECD 2020d).

The role of public support for agricultural risk management instruments needs to be carefully assessed as it may result in cost biases in risk management strategies. Producers tend to opt for tools that are subsidised, more for their income support aspect than their risk management features (Antón 2015). This makes producers less efficient in using risk management tools as it encourages adverse selection, moral hazard[10] and riskier production decisions. A critical question in assessing public risk management policies is whether the policy addresses a market failure or whether, precisely because it is a subsidised policy, it leads to crowding out of the private market (futures and options markets, cash forward contracts, production and market contracts, and private agricultural insurance) or reduces the incentives for producers to adopt on-farm strategies that would otherwise be in place in the absence of such subsidies (Glauber et al. 2021), as noted above. Risk-averse producers will make farm management decisions that cut losses and risk exposure yet at the same time generate opportunity costs in terms of foregone income. This also describes the potential critical effects of subsidising risk management tools (El Benni et al. 2016) since coverage against income variability may encourage riskier production decisions.

One of the mechanisms through which agricultural support policies can interfere with production decisions is their impact on farmer's risk aversion (Hennessy 1998). For example, decoupled CAP payments[11] may alter producers' risk aversion if risk tolerance increases with wealth, which can affect production in two ways: (1) the

[10]Moral hazard occurs when producers change their behaviour because of the presence of the risk management programme such that the probability of a loss is increased. Adverse selection occurs when the producers know more about the underlying risk than the provider of the risk management programme, which can affect their choice to participate in the programme (Glauber et al. 2021).

[11]Decoupled payments are fixed-income transfers that do not depend on the producer's production decisions, production levels or market conditions.

choice of output mix and (2) input decisions, where the level of use of an input affects the output variability (Koundouri et al. 2009). Several empirical studies analysing the impact of decoupled agricultural programmes on production and land allocation decisions have confirmed the role of these risk effects.

Furthermore, experience in the use of risk management tools has exposed inefficiencies in their design, which need to be addressed and remedied if they are to make the agricultural sector more sustainable. Ex-post disaster policies and agricultural insurance subsidies sometimes overlap in protecting and compensating for catastrophic risk, and while subsidies for insurance schemes have been used as a means to deploy ad hoc assistance, experience shows that it is often politically difficult to remove this ad hoc assistance even when agricultural insurance systems are firmly established. As for income stabilisation programmes, there is as yet little experience and analysis as to their impact. Finally, tax and savings measures may be effective in helping producers mitigate income variability with fewer market distortions and externalities, but they are unlikely to be sufficient in isolation to manage the most catastrophic events. Further discussion and quantitative assessment of policy options to protect producers from the increasing risk of extreme income losses brought about by catastrophic climate events is therefore essential (Boysen et al. 2022).

4 Agricultural Insurance in the EU

Most agricultural insurance schemes in the EU are conventional, such as single-peril insurance, combined insurance and yield insurance, and are generally privately run. Their development in each country basically depends on two variables: producers' needs (risk level) and financial support for the insurance system in each member state. This development is therefore strongly contingent on the availability of other risk management tools and the public sector's role, especially in terms of ad hoc aid measures (Bielza et al. 2008).

Single- and multiple-peril crop insurance schemes are in place in several parts of Europe. Almost all member states have private single-peril insurance. Single-peril hail insurance is the most highly evolved insurance product and exists in all EU countries. In fact, it is the main insurance product available in some countries (Belgium, Germany, the Netherlands and Ireland). This may be due to the low level of public support for agricultural insurance schemes and the fact that these are the countries with the lowest climate risks. In some Nordic and Baltic countries, there is less demand for crop insurance. In other countries, both single-peril and combined insurance are available (Bulgaria, Czech Republic, Hungary, Poland, Portugal, Slovakia, Slovenia and Sweden), coinciding with areas with the greatest risks (frost, drought, rainfall at harvest time). However, cover against drought, one of the toughest systemic risks to insure against, is not usually included in combined insurance, although it is built into the all-climate peril cover furnished by yield insurance, which underwrites the main production risks. In Greece and Cyprus, for example, the public sector provides a compulsory insurance system.

Since there is a strong correlation between risk and the insurance coverage of the peril, the countries with the highest levels of risk are the ones with the highest levels of insurance coverage (Spain, Italy and Austria). Moreover, the countries with the greatest public sector involvement in the agricultural insurance system are the ones with coverage of highly systemic risks, such as drought. Consequently, the Spanish agricultural insurance system is the most highly developed in Europe; Italy, France, Luxembourg and Austria also have a well-developed insurance system covering most risks. There are subsidies, at least in part, for single-peril or yield insurance in Austria, Belgium, Croatia, France, Italy, Lithuania, Hungary, Malta, the Netherlands, Portugal and Spain. Germany is the only country that offers non-subsidised multiple-peril insurance. The largest programmes have been rolled out in Italy and Spain, where premium subsidies account for over 65% of yield insurance.

Some countries have started to implement new insurance lines. Several types of indexed-based schemes have been devised in France, Spain, Germany and Switzerland. Italy was one of the first member states to introduce revenue insurance for grain, a type of insurance widely used in the United States. Exploratory work on the design and economic viability of this type of coverage has also been carried out in Spain. However, income/revenue insurance has not developed in Europe to the same extent as yield insurance, as discussed below. France has also introduced a new type of subsidised insurance for certain crops, which provides cover against rising production costs, yield losses and losses due to other factors, such as poor quality and price reductions (Santeramo and Ramsey 2017).

The successive CAP reviews back crop insurance premium subsidies by EU member states. Nonetheless, there is still discussion as to how insurance market intervention should be designed to effectively promote programme uptake. Market failure is a necessary, but not sufficient, condition for government intervention, given that other factors, such as public costs, economic sustainability and by-product distortions, also need to be considered (García-Azcárate 2014). Critics point out that subsidising agricultural insurance discourages the use of other more cost-effective risk management and resilience tools, such as investing in irrigation systems and crop diversification. It may also encourage farmers to cultivate land or raise livestock in marginal areas, thereby further contributing to and exacerbating environmental degradation. Like other agricultural subsidies, it can also lead to distortions in production decisions, resulting in distortions in world trade and global prices, with the consequent knock-on effects for the Common Market Organisation (CMO) (Glauber et al. 2021). Additionally, public subsidies may lead to an increase in premiums and cross-subsidise private insurance companies.

Conversely, a properly designed agricultural insurance system may be less distortionary than other agricultural support measures, such as ex-post disaster payments (Chang and Zilberman 2014). Furthermore, it might also be more straightforward to tie insurance uptake to other requirements, such as compliance with environmental standards and best farming practices. Likewise, catastrophe insurance coverage could be made compulsory for producers who sign up for other counter-cyclical loss programmes, which would boost demand for insurance and reduce adverse selection problems that emerge when this demand comes from farms with high levels of risk (Santeramo and Ramsey 2017).

The feasibility of implementing an EU-wide crop insurance programme, as is the case in the USA, which has the world's largest subsidised agricultural insurance programme, is hampered by the diversity of member states' farming systems. Moreover, the CAP's redistributive aspect and the distortions a common EU insurance scheme would introduce hinder the prospects of achieving political support for a unified European agricultural insurance system (García-Azcárate 2014). This is compounded by difficulties in delivering unified service in system management and distortions resulting from asymmetric information, which can lead to adverse selection and moral hazard problems. Consequently, the CAP has preferred to foster the implementation of agricultural insurance programmes developed individually by member states and for certain crops.

4.1 Revenue and Income Insurance in the EU

Crop revenue insurance is a unique product because the cover underwrites crop risk and highly systematic price risk. This insurance indemnifies the shortfall in the producer's gross income resulting from low yield, low prices and a combination of both. If indemnification is triggered by a price drop, income insurance policies might have to indemnify almost all policyholders at the same time. Thus, the standard insurance approach is that systematic (or systemic) risks are not insurable per se (Tiwari et al. 2021).

Revenue and income insurance has not yet developed in the EU in the same way as other risk protection, although it is a target for agricultural insurance policies with a view to delivering income stability for agricultural producers. However, the budgetary consequences of these risk management schemes are uncertain due to their dependence on market prices (Pieralli et al. 2021). These authors assessed the potential budgetary impact of importing certain risk management models used in the United States that protect against revenue losses (Agriculture Risk Coverage) and market price declines (Price Loss Coverage) into the EU CAP. Their findings showed that the payouts made under these two risk management models are sensitive to the reference prices which trigger coverage and to the programme's participation fees.

The uptake of these agricultural insurance models is still somewhat limited in the EU due to the high premiums (especially in the case of multiple-peril insurance, where available), the high loss threshold triggering insurance coverage (30%) and the lack of on-farm data and information, which leads to information asymmetry (European Commission 2017a). Subsequently, the Omnibus Regulation amending the four CAP regulations[12] reduced the loss threshold for triggering coverage to 20% and increased aid intensity rates from 65% to 70%.

The choice of reference prices is critical in the design of these instruments as they have a major impact on payouts and represent one of the most difficult political decisions for these programmes. In terms of the different revenue insurance programmes, futures prices at harvest are the most common variable to determine the average price for insurance purposes as this generates no transaction costs (Mahul 2003; Coble et al. 2000). However, there is no consensus as to the best approach for rating price risk. It is widely recognised that market-based price risk measures are to be preferred, but this mechanism does not exist for all the crops covered by revenue insurance. Mateos-Ronco and Server (2020) drew up a composition index or model for the average seasonal price or representative market field price to be used for citrus fruit revenue insurance purposes in Spain. The price risk reliably represents the market field prices in the country's different production areas and is based on real market information. However, the model has to be designed so that calculations are replicable using this information and cannot be controlled by any of the market participants. The idea is that an increase in the number of variables that make up the price risk lessens the chances of results being tampered with. Goodwin et al. (2000) reviewed alternative approaches to rating price risk, such as the use of historical series of futures prices, the use of proportional errors under the assumption of normality and the use of existing options markets to derive market-based price risk measures. The recognition of these problems has led to the development of a variety of approaches providing modelling techniques that provide an accurate price. The distribution of market prices may also be sensitive to market conditions.

4.2 Farmers' Risk Preferences

Managing the risks associated with income variability is a fundamental issue for farmers as, apart from bankruptcy, which is the ultimate consequence of catastrophic events, the variability of income and the risk of income loss lead to sub-optimal production decisions every year and also to sub-optimal investment decisions. The result is weaker farm competitiveness through short-term loss of productivity and long-term loss of innovation (Cordier 2014). Understanding the factors that drive farmers' insurance demands is fundamental to evaluating the system's sustainability and to choosing measures that encourage farmers to take out insurance.

Farmers' risk preferences can be broken down into risk attitude and risk perception. Risk attitude reflects an agent's general willingness to consistently assume risk, whereas risk perception can be defined as an assessment of the uncertainty of the risk

[12] Available at https://www.consilium.europa.eu/es/policies/cap-simplification/omnibus-regulation-agriculture/.

content inherent to a particular situation (Pennings et al. 2002). Risk attitudes, risk perception and their interaction are fundamental determinants of risk management and the use of specific risk management tools (Pennings and García 2004; Pennings and Wansink 2004; Just and Just 2016).

The extensive literature on this subject has empirically shown the effect (positive and negative) of a number of independent variables relating to farm households' risk perceptions and risk preferences (Feyisa et al. 2023). Some of them are related to farm characteristics (physical capital, farm size, ownership and types of assets, capital ownership), the human capital of the farm household (age and education of household head, family size) and household location. The economic literature has also pointed out that experience of extreme events (drought, floods, earthquakes, civil war, negative financial shocks) impacts risk attitude over time. However, these aspects cannot be observed and are consequently extremely difficult to measure. This is evidenced by the large body of literature analysing the risk preferences of European farmers with highly diverse results, depending on the methods used and the space, time and types of farms (Iyer et al. 2020). This literature, in general, seems to reveal that European farmers are risk averse, although this claim is not in fact backed up by any statistical analysis of the underlying estimates. A comparative analysis of absolute risk aversion estimates is complicated by the fact that these estimates depend on the prices, quantities or incomes used in their calculation. Farmers' risk preferences change considerably when measured using different methods and over time (Finger et al. 2023). In other words, applying the same elicitation method to the same producer at different points in time yields different risk preference estimates.

Changes in producers' risk attitudes are associated with major changes in agricultural policies and, to some extent, with weather shocks. Pennings et al. (2002) found greater time instability in farmers' aversion to profit variance, while aversion to extreme events, as expressed through the asymmetry of earnings, proved to be more stable over time. Likewise, Moschini and Hennessy (2001) argued that changes in policy interventions can lead to a context of uncertainty, which generates considerable risk for agricultural investment, and under these conditions, risk aversion tends to rise. However, EU policies geared towards stabilising producer incomes, when implemented long enough and not constantly reformed, tend to trigger more risk-neutral or even risk-friendly behaviour, although more knowledge of these relationships in the specific context of decision-making in the agricultural sector is needed.

Identifying risk determinants and their impacts coupled with a full understanding of the response to farm-level risks is of paramount importance in designing support for producers' risk management strategies and developing better risk management tools and policies (Finger et al. 2018).

Most studies assessing farmers' willingness to pay (WTP) for an insurance policy have been based on the expected utility theory (EUT) as the foremost paradigm for explaining decision-making under uncertainty. Farmers' WTP has been calculated by comparing the monetary amounts involved in insured and uninsured scenarios based on whether they take out a policy or not. In terms of the certainty equivalent, the difference between these scenarios is always positive for risk-averse farmers, and their maximum WTP for taking out insurance is considered (Pérez-Blanco et al. 2016). However, other studies have shown that decisions about taking out insurance are often not consistent with maximising expected utility (Babcock 2015; Carter et al. 2015; Du et al. 2016) and that the likelihood of taking out insurance decreases as premiums increase, even though the higher values of these costs increase farmers' expected utility. Gómez-Limón and Granado-Díaz (2023) found relationships between WTP for index-based hydrological drought insurance in Spain and policy design (in relation to sums insured, level of excesses and contract term), the socio-economic characteristics of farmers (full-time farmers, crops, risk aversion) and the insurance premium subsidy. Bannor et al. (2023) similarly argued that in addition to the defining features of the insurance (price and premium period, risk covered, type of participation and sum insured), some socio-economic variables of the farm and the farmer, such as the age, experience and educational level of the farmer and the size of the household and farm, may play a key role in the willingness to pay for an insurance product.

In any case, the literature supports the view that actions geared towards increasing the intensity of aid as much as possible, making the provision of other aid contingent on taking out an insurance policy and fostering knowledge and information about this type of risk management instrument, would help improve its uptake and implementation by producers.

5 The Spanish Agricultural Insurance System

Agricultural insurance is probably one of the most efficient and best-known tools for managing agricultural risks. Spain has a higher incidence of climate-associated risks than other European countries with less extreme conditions. Therefore, in Spain, this type of insurance policy has experienced rapid growth and has been accepted as an efficient way of sharing the risks involved in agricultural production. The exceptional nature of climate risks and their additional nature to the other factors of uncertainty affect all economic activities and therefore support mechanisms from society as a whole for the strategic agricultural industry are warranted.

The Spanish agricultural insurance system, which is heavily dependent on subsidies, also has certain peculiarities that make it stand out from insurance used in other countries. Its present configuration, which can be described as wide-ranging and complex, has its roots in the 1978 Law of Combined Agricultural Insurance and its subsequent amendments. The system's complexity is due to the participation of both public bodies and private companies, each of which has a special contribution to make. The insurance sector applies insurance techniques to agriculture, while the public sector plans and leads subsidy management.

The system is based on the relationship between representatives of the private sector, policyholders and insurance companies, in the shape of an insurance contract. Agricultural producers are represented in the system by professional organisations and agricultural cooperatives, while insurers are represented by their professional association, Agroseguro, the Spanish Association of Combined Agricultural Insurance Companies, S.A. Various central and regional government administrations also participate in the contractual relationship, with the Spanish Ministry of Agriculture taking a planning and financial role (subsidising insurance costs) and the Ministry of the Economy (Directorate General of Insurance and Pension Funds) supervising and regulating the insurance scheme. The Insurance Compensation Consortium also plays an important role. This public body, subject to private business legislation, is the system's obligatory reinsurer, with responsibility for controlling the proper functioning of the loss adjustment system. Finally, the Ministry of Agriculture, through its subsidiary, the State Agricultural Insurance Entity (ENESA), coordinates the different organisations involved (Mateos-Ronco and Server 2011).

This system is required to cover damages to crop production, animal rearing, fish farming and forestry projects in Spain[13] caused by all kinds of natural phenomena. The model is based on the solidarity of the system as a whole in offsetting losses; on one hand, there is a coinsurance pool of private insurance companies, controlled by Agroseguro, in which premiums from a certain region or industry may be used to pay damages in another region or industry. In addition, policyholders are required to insure all the fields they use to grow the same crop, and so they cannot choose to insure only the fields exposed to the highest risks.

Besides its strong dependence on subsidies, the Spanish farmers' insurance system is also characterised by its actuarial strength (Garrido and Bardají 2009), which has evolved steadily since 1978; by its independence from crop selection and production levels, as shown by the lack of evidence to prove that insurance has a stimulating effect on these aspects; and, finally, by the absence of phenomena such as adverse selection and moral hazard. Subsidies from the Ministry of Agriculture vary between 8% and 45% of the cost of premiums for producers, depending on the type of product and policy conditions. Some regional governments also provide additional, albeit smaller, subsidies (Burgaz 2000).

Insurance policies are now frequent in many Spanish farming sectors. The latest available statistics (Agroseguro 2021) show a total of more than 409,000 insurance policies in force, €15.59 billion in sums insured and 6.25 million hectares of insured land. The percentage of production insured by the system varies greatly by sector, but in some cases (persimmon, non-citrus fruit trees, extensive arable crops, bananas, table grapes), it is close to or greater than 80%.

There are several reasons for the expansion and robustness of the agricultural insurance system in Spain: its extended coverage, which now includes all climate risks in agriculture; the participation of private insurance companies, with the government's role being restricted to coordination, promotion and publicity; the

[13]The legal requirement establishes that insurance must be taken out gradually according to produce, areas and risks, until roll-out is complete. The requisites that a risk should comply with to be included in an insurance policy are a technical feasibility study to establish the risk insurance conditions and the existence of sufficient funds to meet the requirements of subsidies on the cost of insurance policies.

importance of producers' organisations participation on the operational and decision-making bodies of ENESA (Ministry of Agriculture), which makes it possible to match the insurance products that are available directly with the sector's actual needs; agricultural insurance as the only tool for coverage against natural disasters, which means that there is no need to turn to ad hoc support in the event of a loss and people are encouraged to take out insurance; coordinated participation and initiatives by the government and other organisations; continuous technical improvement of the system, which has gradually brought the insurance system in line with the agricultural and geographical circumstances of Spanish farming and its inherent risks; public support for the system, which the government sees as a key aspect of an effective income policy; and the government's role as a re-insurer through the Insurance Compensation Consortium, which has enabled private insurance companies to engage in the coverage of new risks (Burgaz 2000).

The implementation of income and revenue insurance in Spain is one of the current guidelines for the Spanish agricultural insurance system. However, there are regulatory and technical constraints that restrict the development of these tools. The regulatory constraints stem from the national legal framework since Spanish legislation (1978 *Law of Combined Agricultural Insurance*) only provides for agricultural insurance to cover risks arising from natural agents and adverse climate events and does not include income and revenue coverage. However, recent EU legislation has extended the support for risk management tools[14] by allowing member states to grant support for risk management tools based on their needs, such as financial contributions to insurance premiums and financial contributions to mutual funds. This support may be awarded to promote risk management tools that help farmers manage production and income risks associated with their agricultural operations over which they have no control. In these cases, member states establish the eligibility conditions for these tools in terms of the types and coverage of eligible instruments, the methodology for the calculation of losses and the triggering factors for compensation, and the rules for the constitution and management of mutual funds and other risk management tools.

In practice, the configuration of income and revenue insurance should be in line with the World Trade Organization's Marrakesh Agreement on Agriculture as well as the criteria identified by the European Commission in its Regulation (EU) 2021/2115. Compliance with both requirements means the government can participate financially in income insurance and income safety net programmes. The following conditions have to be met to be eligible for these payments:

[14] Regulation (EU) 2021/2115 of the European Parliament and of the Council of 2 December 2021 establishing rules on support for strategic plans to be drawn up by Member States under the common agricultural policy (CAP Strategic Plans) and financed by the European Agricultural Guarantee Fund (EAGF) and by the European Agricultural Fund for Rural Development (EAFRD) and repealing Regulations (EU) No. 1305/2013 and (EU) No. 1307/2013 (OJEU 06-12-2021). *Art. 76, Risk management tools.*

1. Support is granted only for covering losses that exceed a threshold of at least 20% of the average annual income of the farmer in the preceding 3-year period or a 3-year average based on the preceding 5-year period, excluding the highest and lowest income figures.
2. The support is limited to one or more percentages not exceeding 70% of the eligible costs.

Member states ensure that any overcompensation resulting from combining interventions using these tools with other public or private risk management schemes is avoided.

The technical constraints to implementing these insurance models involve several aspects, such as the varying exposure of agricultural production to market risks and the coverage of CAP direct aid, which already protects against this type of risk in some sectors. Consequently, this type of insurance is more attractive in sectors that are less reliant on direct CAP support. Moreover, it is essential to have reliable data on farm gate prices, production costs and yields. Studies conducted to explore the feasibility of this coverage in the Spanish agricultural insurance system point to some critical issues (ENESA 2018). Using indexed data, i.e. linked to a regional yield, climate results or other correlated variables, would entail less moral hazard, although it might be more contentious as it would not be tied to each individual's specific situation. Furthermore, the introduction of insurance could result in changes in the price variability system, which might be altered due to an increase in supply or interference from the sector itself or even distortions in the selling price.

As of the time of writing this paper, some pilot schemes have been run in this line of insurance (Bielza et al. 2002; Aguado and Garrido 2008). In the 2003–2004 season, an experimental potato income insurance programme was launched (ENESA 2018), which provided an additional price guarantee. This covered both the adverse consequences of climate risks and poor market price performance. However, it was discontinued due to poor uptake by farmers and legal restrictions. In 2009–2011, *Agroseguro* commissioned some exploratory studies to move forward with the technical design of income and/or revenue insurance in some agricultural sectors (Mateos-Ronco and Server 2020). In 2017, a working group was set up in the Ministry of Agriculture (ENESA) to examine the feasibility of implementing income and/or revenue insurance. A pilot experiment in the shape of income insurance (which requires fewer variables than revenue insurance in actuarial calculations) was conducted in the cereal sector. Two alternative formulas were studied: as coverage in addition to crop yield insurance or as independent income insurance. In the first case, the producer would have to take out crop yield insurance to cover catastrophic damage as well as additional coverage against catastrophic price shocks. If only production damage were sustained on the farm, the insured producer would be compensated under the terms of the relevant crop yield insurance contract. However, although there is no prospect of this study's proposals actually being implemented, technical work has continued with a view to assessing its possible technical specifications (average prices, premiums, etc.).

Future strands in risk management include actions to be taken by producers and also by the agricultural insurance industry. In the former case, this involves adapting crops and varieties, seeking out new cultivation areas, changes in cultivation practices (sowing dates, pruning, etc.) and, in general, stepping up preventive measures according to the risks. The future direction of agricultural insurance includes continuing to enhance the coverage of the insurance lines available and tailoring them to the adverse effects of climate change on the sector. The main climate events of recent years in Spain (drought in 2017, hail in 2018, cold drop in 2019) seem to be clearly correlated with climate change, leading to more damaging and widespread events. Further steps should be taken in the search for a technical balance to meet the indemnities that arise. Better coverage is required, premiums need to be aligned with a solid actuarial basis to cope with the increase in risks, reinsurance has to be tailored to the new situation and a sufficient stabilisation reserve should be built up to tackle greater volatility (Agroseguro 2019).

The Ministry of Agriculture's strategy for future action on agricultural insurance is anchored in a proactive perspective (Ministerio de Agricultura, Alimentación y Medio Ambiente 2016). The action strands are based on (1) improving the coordination and transparency of information between system actors by providing access to common registers and enhancing the use of computer systems for information transfer, (2) using resources more efficiently to extend risk cover by coordinating risk management support policies and streamlining the procedure for granting subsidies, (3) building a risk management culture in the industry by fostering a proactive mindset on the part of producers and putting in place measures to convey and publicise the idea of agricultural insurance as effectively protecting against agricultural risks and (4) further research and analysis of new coverage (income insurance, revenue insurance), producer demand for coverage and risks and, in general, adaptation to the sector's actual needs.

6 Conclusions and Some Future Lines of Research

Farm viability is crucial to ensuring the sustainability of farming and food systems. However, growing risk exposure is increasingly affecting producers' well-being and, consequently, the economic and social sustainability of their agricultural business. Hence, public policies in support of European agriculture point to the significance of risk management as a means to ensure stable, decent farm income levels that secure a good standard of living for people who rely on agriculture as their livelihood.

The current approach to agricultural risk management emphasises the leading role of stakeholders in designing policies and tools to support risk management and the need for them to adopt a proactive stance in managing these risks. The comprehensive and participatory approach to risk management as an extension of the current holistic view is based on these premises.

Experience shows the need for a close partnership with stakeholders in developing risk management policy toolkits to define ex ante the various levels of responsibility for risk management and the scope of existing policy tools. Risk management must go beyond simply targeting producers and public institutions and should involve the input of all stakeholders that can interfere with the mechanisms underlying risk management. Along these lines, Bertolozzi-Caredio et al. (2021) point out that progress in risk management should not be restricted to strategies against shocks (droughts, price drops) but should instead focus on the ability to anticipate long-term challenges such as climate change and changes in consumer preferences. Accordingly, they suggest that this approach be founded on three avenues: developing learning and knowledge networks, fostering new forms of partnerships and mapping out integrated policy and financial instruments.

Meanwhile, the current thrust of policies to support producers in natural hazard risk management is to encourage them to be more proactive in preventing the adverse impacts of natural disasters and to adapt and transform their businesses in response to future climate and natural hazard risks. Risk management from a resilience approach (OECD/FAO 2021) entails addressing the challenge of how to provide assistance to producers in the event of a disaster without discouraging a more resilient recovery anchored in their use of active strategies to reduce their vulnerability.

Producer support policies, such as direct payments, risk management tool subsidies and technical assistance, need to be appropriately designed so that they do not merely reduce the cost of risk but rather serve as add-ons and, most importantly, incentives for producers to adopt robust on-farm strategies to prepare for, mitigate and prevent natural hazard risks in the long term. In this context, governments must support agricultural stakeholders in building their resilience to natural-hazard-induced disasters by providing training and extension services as well as targeted and science-based information about risk, assessing agricultural damage and losses in the wake of a disaster and investing in appropriate public infrastructure for the reduction of disaster risks. A holistic approach to risk management will help achieve complementarity between the tools by preventing overcompensation and lessening adverse selection and moral hazard behaviour. Public support for risk management should target compensation for market failures, with aid being restricted to administrative costs and catastrophic risk losses (Glauber et al. 2021).

Risk management in agriculture inevitably has to adapt to the new conditions of its setting. Farms are increasingly complex economic units with diversified revenue streams (agri-tourism, energy production), varied use of technology, greater significance of off-farm work, multiple and dispersed ownership and even greater geographical dispersion of farms. However, alongside these complex economic entities, there are also small farms that are extremely important in many European countries, and this explains why farm structures have developed in highly heterogeneous systems. This is compounded by the increasing exposure of European farmers to production risks and market and policy risks due to policy environments. European agriculture is evermore exposed to climate change and significant policy changes, and support for risk management in agriculture is increasingly prominent in the CAP. Hence, greater understanding is needed about the relationships and ramifications of producers' risk preferences and their instability over time coupled with the impact of agricultural support measures on these preferences. These measures are becoming increasingly more complex in line with the intricate scenario of risks for agricultural activity in the EU, and this means that assessing them calls for a change of outlook.

In Spain, guidelines for the future in agricultural risk management also underscore producers' proactive role in their strategies for preventing and adapting to the adverse effects of uncertainty, volatility and climate events as part of their farm management. To this end, there is a robust agricultural insurance system in place, which is one of the most developed in the EU, built on the principle that insurance is the public support tool for risk management and consequently a condition for prioritising access to other public policy aid. The transparency and accessibility of the system and the availability of information for sound decision-making are crucial to win producers' trust. Engagement in the system of various tiers of government (Ministry of Agriculture, Ministry of Economy, regions) and private organisations requires appropriate coordination and information transfer coupled with flexible, simple document management (procedures, forms, subsidy payments) to deliver certainty and ease of understanding for policyholders. This diverse participation by public and private bodies requires a common course of action on agricultural insurance which is also coordinated with other public policies (taxation).

Farmers need increasingly sophisticated insurance models with higher levels of protection and affordable costs, and they are also keen to engage in the insurance design and implementation stages. Further study and research into the risks faced by producers which capture farmers' perceived importance of the different types of risks are needed. This multiple-peril approach entails significant challenges, such as the intense data requirements needed to understand how risks are interconnected and how their knock-on effects are generated.

The system's future development is designed to foster the introduction of insurance in some sectors with lower uptake rates; explore the potential roll-out of income insurance in certain crops and regions by assessing its economic, legal and fiscal suitability; examine the feasibility of revenue insurance in those cases where income insurance has already been introduced (which would require the availability of real data on farm revenue to perform the actuarial calculations); proactively champion Spain's position with the EU and the CAP on agricultural insurance bearing in mind its special climate variabilities, like other Mediterranean countries, and its vulnerability to climate change; and propose the extension of its robust agricultural insurance system to other member states. It is also essential to put in place mechanisms to enhance the system in terms of policyholder loyalty, implementation and retention, which means reviewing the demand for cover and risks, devising new coverage tailored to producers' actual needs, delivering more bespoke insurance (with particular reference to insured yields), developing new indexed and technology-based insurance and leveraging IT in taking out and tracking insurance (Ministerio de Agricultura, Alimentación y Medio Ambiente 2016).

References

Agroseguro (2019) Cambio climático: efectos en el seguro agrario y retos de futuro. Jornada El seguro agrario ante el desafío del cambio climático, Madrid, November 2019. https://www.mapa.gob.es/es/enesa/publicaciones/efectosdelcambioclimaticoobservadosenelseguroagrarioyretosdefuturo_tcm30-521509.pdf

Agroseguro (2021) 2021 en cifras. https://agroseguro.es/conocenos/cifras-mas-destacadas/

Aguado S, Garrido A (2008) Modelización de primas para un seguro de ingresos en el fresón de Huelva. Rev Esp Estud Agrosoc P 215:127–154

Antón J (2015) Risk management in agriculture: what role for policy in the new common agricultural policy? In: McMahon J, Cardwell M (eds) Research handbook on EU agriculture law. Edward Elgar, Northampton

Babcock BA (2015) Using cumulative prospect theory to explain anomalous crop insurance coverage choice. Am J Agric Econ 97:1371–1384. https://doi.org/10.1093/ajae/aav032

Bannor RK, Oppong-Kyeremeh H, Amfo B, Kuwornu JKM, Kwabena Chaa Kyire S, Amponsah J (2023) Agricultural insurance and risk management among poultry farmers in Ghana: an application of discrete choice experiment. J Agric Food Res 11:100492

Bertolozzi-Caredio D, Bardají I, Garrido A, Berry R, Bijttebier J, Gavrilescud C, Harizanovae C, Jendrzejewski B, Meuwissen MMP, Ollendorf F, Pinsard C, Rommel J, Severini S, Soriano B (2021) Stakeholder perspectives to improve risk management in European farming systems. J Rural Stud 84:147–161

Bielza M, Garrido A, Sumpsi JM (2002) Income insurance as a tool for the stabilization of farm income: an application in the Spanish olive oil sector. Agric Resour Econ 2(1):21–43

Bielza M, Conte C, Dittman C, Gallego J, Stroblmair J (2008) Agricultural insurance schemes. European Commission, JRC Ispra, Institute for the Protection and Security of Citizens, Ispra, Italy. https://agriculture.ec.europa.eu/system/files/2020-02/ext-study-insurance-full-report-rev_2008_en_0.pdf

Bojnec S, Ferto I (2019) Do CAP subsidies stabilise farm income in Hungary and Slovenia? Agr Econ–Czech 65(3):103–111

Boysen O, Boysen-Urban K, Matthews A (2022) Stabilizing European Union farm incomes in the era of climate change. Appl Econ Perspect:1–25. https://doi.org/10.1002/aepp.13298

Bozzola M, Finger R (2021) Stability of risk attitude, agricultural policies and production shocks: evidence from Italy. Eur Rev Agric Econ 48(3):477–501

Burgaz FJ (2000) Insurance system and risk management in Spain. In: OECD (ed) Income risk management in agriculture. OECD Publishing, Paris. https://doi.org/10.1787/9789264189584-en

Cafiero C, Capitanio F, Cioffi A, Coppola A (2005) Risks and crisis management in agriculture. Study for the European Parliament's Committee on Agriculture and Rural Development, October, 76 p, IP/B/AGRI/ST/2005-30

Carter M, Elabed G, Serfilippi E (2015) Behavioral economic insights on index insurance design. Agric Financ Rev 75:8–18. https://doi.org/10.1108/AFR-03-2015-0013

Chang HH, Zilberman D (2014) On the political economy of allocation of agricultural disaster relief payments: application to Taiwan. Eur Rev Agric Econ 41(4):657–680. https://doi.org/10.1093/erae/jbt037

Coble KH, Heifner RG, Zuniga M (2000) Implications of crop yield and revenue insurance for producer hedging. J Agric Resour Econ 25:432–453

Cordier J (2014) Comparative analysis of risk management tools supported by the 2014 Farm Bill and the CAP 2014-2020. European Parliament, Directorate-General for Internal Policies, Agriculture and Rural Development, IP/B/AGRI/IC/2014-044

Du X, Feng H, Hennessy DA (2016) Rationality of choices in subsidized crop insurance markets. Am J Agric Econ 99:732–756. https://doi.org/10.1093/ajae/aaw035

El Benni N, Finger R, Meuwissen M (2016) Potential effects of the Income Stabilization Tool (IST) in Swiss agricultural. Eur Rev Agric Econ 43:475–502

ENESA (Entidad Estatal de Seguros Agrarios) (2018) Estudio de la puesta en marcha de los seguros de ingresos o de rentas en España. Observatorio de Calidad del Seguro Agrario. Ministerio de Agricultura y Pesca, Alimentación y Medio Ambiente, Madrid. https://www.mapa.gob.es/es/enesa/publicaciones/180524observatoriodelseguroagrario-segurodeingresos_tcm30-450343.pdf

European Commission (2017a) Modernising & simplifying the CAP. Economic challenges facing EU agriculture. Directorate General for Agriculture and Rural Development, Brussels. https://agriculture.ec.europa.eu/system/files/2018-05/soc_background_final_en_0.pdf

European Commission (2017b) Study on risk management in EU agriculture: final report. Directorate General for Agriculture and Rural Development, Brussels. https://doi.org/10.2762/387583

European Commission (2018a) Ensuring viable farm income. CAP specific objectives.... explained. Brief No 1. Agriculture and rural development. https://agriculture.ec.europa.eu/system/files/2021-01/cap_specific_objectives_-_brief_1_-_ensuring_viable_farm_income_0.pdf

European Commission (2018b) EU budget: The Common Agricultural Policy beyond 2020. http://europa.eu/rapid/press-release_MEMO-18-3974_en.htm

European Commission (2023) Key policy objectives for the new CAP. Agriculture and rural development. https://agriculture.ec.europa.eu/common-agricultural-policy/cap-overview/cap-2023-27/key-policy-objectives-new-cap_en#documents

European Parliament (2014) Comparative analysis of risk management tools supported by the 2014 Farm Bill and the CAP 2014–2020. Directorate-General for Internal Policies. Policy Department B: Structural and Cohesion Policies. https://op.europa.eu/en/publication-detail/-/publication/a72eb8cc-faf0-11e5-b713-01aa75ed71a1

FAO (2021) The impact of disasters and crises on agriculture and food security. FAO, Rome. https://doi.org/10.4060/cb3673en

Feyisa AD, Maertens M, De Mey Y (2023) Relating risk preferences and risk perceptions over different agricultural risk domains: insights form Ethiopia. World Dev 162:106137. https://doi.org/10.1016/j.worlddev.2022.106137

Finger R, El Benni N (2021) Farm income in European agriculture: new perspectives on measurements and implications for policy evaluation. Eur Rev Agric Econ 48(2):253–265. https://doi.org/10.1093/erae/jbab011

Finger R, Dalhaus T, Allendorf J, Hirsch S (2018) Determinants of downside risk exposure of dairy farms. Eur Rev Agric Econ 45(4):641–674

Finger R, Wüper D, McCallum C (2023) The (in)stability of farmer risk preferences. J Agric Econ 74(1):155–167. https://doi.org/10.1111/1477-9552.12496

García-Azcárate T (2014) Why a European agricultural insurance scheme is not a good solution. EuroChoices 13(3):41–45

Garrido A, Bardají I (2009) Strategies for the management of risks and crises in Spanish agriculture. Rev Esp Estud Agrosoc P 221(1):175–205

Glauber J, Baldwin K, Antón J, Ziebinska U (2021) Design principles for agricultural risk management policies. OECD food, agriculture and fisheries papers, no. 157. OECD Publishing, Paris. https://doi.org/10.1787/1048819f-en

Gómez-Limón JA, Granado-Díaz R (2023) Assessing the demand for hydrological drought insurance in irrigated agriculture. Agric Water Manage 276:108054. https://doi.org/10.1016/j.agwat.2022.108054

Goodwin BK, Roberts MC, Coble KH (2000) Measurement of price risk in revenue insurance: implications of distributional assumptions. J Agric Resour Econ 25:195–214

Gosh RK, Gupta S, Singh V, Ward PS (2021) Demand for crop insurance in developing countries: new evidence from India. J Agric Econ 72(1):293–320

Hennessy DA (1998) The production effects of coupled and decoupled agricultural income support policies. Am J Agric Econ 80:46–57

Iyer P, Bozzola M, Hirsch S, Meraner M, Finger R (2020) Measuring farmer risk preferences in Europe: a systematic review. J Agric Econ 71(1):3–26
Janowicz-Lomott M, Lyskawa K, Rozumek P (2015) Farm income insurance as an alternative for traditional crop insurance. Proc Econ Financ 33:439–449
Just DR, Just RE (2016) Empirical identification of behavioral choice models under risk. Am J Agric Econ 98(4):1181–1194
Komarek AM, De Pinto A, Smith VH (2020) A review of types of risk in agriculture: what we know and what we need to know. Agric Syst 178:102738. https://doi.org/10.1016/j.agsy.2019.102738
Koundouri P, Laukkanen M, Myyrä S, Nauges C (2009) The effects of EU agricultural policy changes on farmer's risk attitudes. Eur Rev Agric Econ 36(1):53–77. https://doi.org/10.1093/erae/jbp003
Lupton S, Meuwissen M, Ingrand S (2020) Editorial introduction to the special issue risk management in agriculture. Agric Syst 178
Mahul O (2003) Hedging price risk in the presence of crop yield and revenue insurance. Eur Rev Agric Econ 30:217–239
Mateos-Ronco A, Server RJ (2011) Drawing-up the official adjustment rules for damage assessment in agricultural insurance: results of a Delphi survey for fruit crops in Spain. Technol Forecast Soc 78:1542–1556
Mateos-Ronco A, Server RJ (2020) Risk management tools for sustainable agriculture: a model for calculating the average price for the season in revenue insurance for citrus fruit. Agronomy 10:198. https://doi.org/10.3390/agronomy10020198
Meraner M, Finger R (2019) Risk perceptions, preferences and management strategies: evidence from a case study using German livestock farmers. J Risk Res 22(1):110–135
Meuwissen M, de Mey Y, van Asseldonk M (2018) Prospects for agricultural insurance in Europe. Agric Financ Rev 78(2):174–182
Meuwissen M, Feindt P, Spiegel A, Termeer C, Mathijs E, de Mey Y, Finger R, Balmann A, Wauters E, Urquhart J, Vigani M, Zawalińska K, Herrera H, Nicholas-Davies P, Hansson H, Paas W, Slijper T, Coopmans I, Vroege W, Ciechomska A, Accatino F, Kopainsky B, Poortvliet PM, Candel J, Maye D, Severini S, Senni S, Soriano B, Lagerkvist CJ, Peneva M, Gavrilescu C, Reidsma P (2019) A framework to assess the resilience of farmer systems. Agric Syst 176(1026):56
Ministerio de Agricultura, Alimentación y Medio Ambiente (2016) Executive summary Sistema de seguros agrarios 2025. Subdirección General de Análisis, Prospectiva y Coordinación, Madrid. https://www.mapa.gob.es/es/enesa/publicaciones/resumenejecutivoprospectiva_tcm30-581258.pdf
Mitchel I, Baker A (2019) New estimates for EU agricultural support: an "Un-common" agricultural policy. Center for Global Development. https://www.cgdev.org/publication/new-estimates-eu-agricultural-support-un-common-agricultural-policy
Moschini G, Hennessy DA (2001) Uncertainty, risk aversion, and risk management for agricultural producers. Handbook of agricultural economics 1(A), pp 87–153
Mustafa Z, Vitali G, Huffaker R, Canavari M (2023) A systematic review on price volatility in agriculture. J Econ Surv:1–27. https://doi.org/10.1111/joes.12549
OECD (2009) Managing risk in agriculture: a holistic approach. OECD Publishing, Paris. https://doi.org/10.1787/9789264075313-en
OECD (2020a) Strengthening agricultural resilience in the face of multiple risk. OECD Publishing, Paris. https://doi.org/10.1787/2250453e-en
OECD (2020b) Producer and consumer support estimates database. OECD. https://www.oecd.org/unitedstates/producerandconsumersupportestimatesdatabase.htm
OECD (2020c) Income risk management in agriculture. https://read.oecd-ilibrary.org/agriculture-and-food/income-risk-management-in-agriculture_9789264189584-en#page6
OECD (2020d) Taxation in agriculture. OECD Publishing, Paris. https://doi.org/10.1787/073bdf99-en

OECD (2022) Agricultural policy monitoring and evaluation 2022. Reforming agricultural policies for climate change mitigation. OECD Publishing, Paris. https://doi.org/10.1787/7f4542bf-en
OECD/FAO (2021) Building agricultural resilience to natural hazard-induced disasters: insights from country case studies. OECD Publishing, Paris. https://doi.org/10.1787/49eefdd7-en
Pennings JME, García P (2004) Strategic risk management behavior: what can utility functions tell us?. Agricultural and Applied Economics Association (AAEA) 2004 Annual meeting, August 1–4, Denver, CO. https://doi.org/10.22004/ag.econ.20388
Pennings JME, Wansink B (2004) Channel contract behavior: the role of risk attitudes, risk perceptions, and channel members' market structures. J Bus 77(4):697–724
Pennings JME, Wansink B, Meulenberg M (2002) A note on modeling consumer reactions to a crisis: the case of the mad cow disease. Int J Res Mark 19(2):91–10
Pérez-Blanco CD, Delacámara G, Gómez CM (2016) Revealing the willingness to pay for income insurance in agriculture. J Risk Res 19:873–893. https://doi.org/10.1080/13669877.2015.1042505
Pieralli S, Pérez Domínguez I, Elleby C, Chatzopoulos T (2021) Budgetary impacts of adding agricultural risk management programmes to the CAP. J Agric Econ 72(2):370–387
Rippo R, Cerroni S (2023) Farmer's participation in the Income Stabilisation Tool: evidence from the apple sector in Italy. J Agric Econ 74(1):273–294. https://doi.org/10.1111/1477-9552.12508
Santeramo FG, Ramsey AF (2017) Crop insurance in the EU: lessons and caution form the US. EuroChoices 16(3):34–39. https://doi.org/10.1111/1746-692X.12154
Severini S, Tantari A, Di Tommaso G (2016) Do CAP direct payments stabilise farm income? Empirical evidences from a constant sample of Italian farms. Agric Econ 4:1–17
Severini S, Di Tommaso G, Finger R (2019) Effects of the Income Stabilization Tool on farm income level, variability and concentration in Italian agriculture. Agric Econ 7:23
Soriano B, Garrido A, Bertolozzi-Caredio D, Accatino F, Antonioli F, Krupin V, Meuwissen MPM, Ollendorf F, Rommel J, Spiegel A, Tudor M, Urquhart J, Vigani M, Bardají I (2023) Actors and their roles for improving resilience of farming systems in Europe. J Rural Stud 98:134–146
Tiwari S, Coble KH, Barnett BJ, Harri A (2021) Hedging the price risk inherent in revenue protection insurance. J Agric Appl Econ 53(4):510–530
Walters C, Preston R (2018) Net income risk, crop insurance and hedging. Agric Financ Rev 78(1):135–151. https://doi.org/10.1108/AFR-05-2017-0036

Alicia Mateos-Ronco agricultural engineer and Doctorate in Agronomy. Tenured lecturer in the Department of Economics and Social Sciences at the Faculty of Business Administration and Management of the Polytechnic University of Valencia (Spain) and member of the Centre for Research in Business Management (CEGEA) and other international scientific associations. She has directed or taken part in diverse research projects on the subject of agricultural insurance with international (Italian Institute of Services for the Food Market (ISMEA)) and Spanish organisations (Spanish Ministry of the Environment and Rural and Marine Affairs; Agroseguro). She has carried out research in the fields of agricultural insurance, business management, social economy and foresight. She is the author of many scientific publications, including articles, books, book chapters and international congress papers.

Pension and Sustainability: The Case of Employee Capital Plans in Poland

Janina Petelczyc

1 Introduction

In this chapter, the undeniable reality of anthropogenic climate change is acknowledged, as confirmed by the Intergovernmental Panel on Climate Change (IPCC) (2021). The negative consequences for future generations will escalate if the goals set forth in the climate agreement are not met. The insurance industry is not immune to the effects of climate change, and various methods of addressing this risk have been observed (as seen in studies by Mills in Mills 2009, Stechemesser et al. in Stechemesser et al. 2015, and Raymond et al. in Raymond et al. 2020). The chapter suggests that the *climate-related pension risk* faced by future retirees must also be considered. This risk is a combination of investment risk and climate risk, which will ultimately affect the quality of life of future pensioners. Even high pension benefits cannot ensure a decent life if the world is plagued by weather disasters, resource scarcity, and wars, resulting from climate change. Hence, while designing future pensions for generations that will retire in the next 20–50 years, it is crucial to consider not just the investment risk but also the impact of climate change on life quality.

The pension industry is susceptible to both climate and investment risks, but it also has the potential to contribute to these problems. Currently, financial markets—of which private insurance and pension institutions are part—contribute to climate change as a major source of financing for, e.g., coal, gas, or oil (Bingler et al. 2020; Reclaim Finance 2021). However, pension funds have the capacity to address these challenges if they adjust their investment policies to sustainability needs. It has been demonstrated that a 'green transition' requires not only public capital but also capital

J. Petelczyc (✉)
Warsaw School of Economics, Department of Social Insurance, Warsaw, Poland
e-mail: jpetel@sgh.waw.pl

J. Bataller-Grau et al. (eds.), *Sustainability and the Insurance Market*, AIDA Europe Research Series on Insurance Law and Regulation 10,
https://doi.org/10.1007/978-3-031-72186-1_10

from private entities, including insurance sector and pension fund investments (Della Croce et al. 2011; Chebanov 2019; Owen 2021). As a result, addressing the *climate-related pension risk* is not feasible without the participation of financial markets, including the insurance and pension sector.

In this chapter, we examine the *climate-related pension risk* in the Polish occupational pension system from two angles. Firstly, we investigate the perspectives of the participants. In a representative survey conducted among Poles, including participants of Employee Capital Plans, we asked questions such as: Do they consider anthropogenic climate change as a significant challenge? Are they interested in investing sustainably? And, if so, what conditions would they consider for this type of investment? The second, complementary perspective is a legal and non-financial analysis based on the stakeholder theory. We examine whether the market for additional employee pension plans in Poland is regulated in a way that supports sustainable investments. If individual investors wish for their pension contributions to be invested sustainably, would their views be taken into account? In this chapter, we outline the concept of sustainable investments against the backdrop of environmental (E), social (S), and governance (G) criteria. These criteria address contemporary issues such as environmental and climate concerns, as well as workers' rights and other human rights. The EU's ESG taxonomy serves as a classification system that provides a list of sustainable economic activities and allows for the evaluation of an investment's sustainability (Camilleri 2018). We have chosen Poland because it is one of a few Central and Eastern European (CEE) countries that have recently introduced new, quasi-obligatory Employee Capital Plans (in Polish: Pracownicze Plany Kapitałowe (PPK)). According to the Financial Supervision Authority, at the end of 2022, there were 2,894,375 individuals in those plans (KNF 2023). There are also three other, less popular, but still important capital pension plans: Individual Retirement Account, Individual Retirement Security Account, and Employee Pension Plans. This suggests a potentially larger pool of individuals who may demand more sustainable investments of their contributions from the pension funds. It is worth adding that ethically managed funds in the CEE region have a small market share and have not yet entered the occupational capital pension fund market. However, their number is increasing, and Poland has the most well-developed segment of these types of funds in the region, although it is still small compared to Western Europe (Adamska et al. 2016).

2 Theoretical Framework and Hypothesis Development

In this chapter, we base on the stakeholder theory, focusing on individuals who are pension members as its core and situating it within the institutional and legal framework of the Polish supplementary occupational pension fund system. The concept of stakeholder theory was first introduced by Richard Edward Freeman in the early 1980s. It is a central concept of modern business ethics, positing that organizations have a duty to consider the interests of all their stakeholders, not just shareholders. It means that, e.g., managers of insurance or pension investment funds must consider the consequences of the institution's activity with a bigger picture in mind, and their goals should be broader than ensuring a high return on investment.

According to the above-mentioned theory, institutional investors should also minimize the negative social and environmental cost of generating profits imposed on stakeholders. A stakeholder is a broad notion describing every member of a group or an individual that can affect a company (Freeman 1984). It is up to the company, including pension or other insurance fund, to determine which groups of stakeholders—if not all—should be considered in the formation of its investment and other policies (Donaldson and Preston 1995).

A theory of stakeholder identification was developed by Ronald K. Mitchell, Bradley R. Agle, and Donna J. Wood. They tried to understand how stakeholders are identified and how their relative importance is determined. The authors argue that the identification and salience of stakeholders is a complex and dynamic process that is influenced by a variety of factors, including the organization's goals and strategies, the actions of other stakeholders, and the legal and regulatory environment in which the organization operates (Mitchell et al. 1997). This last aspect is particularly important in our chapter, in which we analyse not only the attitude of individual participants of Employee Capital Plans towards climate change and sustainable investments but also the possibilities of their influence on the investment policy of the funds. Individual investors are widely recognized as important stakeholders in the fund industry. Studies show that individual investors play a significant role in the financial markets and that their investment decisions can impact market trends and performance (Kaniel et al. 2012; Agrawal and Hockerts 2021).

Moreover, what is important, from the point of view of this chapter, is that individuals invest more in firms with clear and concise financial disclosures (Lawrence 2013). There are a bunch of papers showing that institutional investors may be interested in sustainable investments (e.g. van Duuren et al. 2016, Morgan Stanley 2019; Murad 2017), and stakeholders may demand more information related to sustainability, including information on ESG investments (Aras and Crowther 2009). But a study conducted in the UK in 1990–2005 shows that managers' awareness has a minor impact on their investment policies because of a lack of demand (Pfeifer and Sullivan 2008). Further studies conducted in 2015 and 2017 confirm that portfolio managers, by and large, fail to consider ESG issues in their investment analysis because of the absence of demand from clients and investors (CFA Institute 2017).

It is, however, an unresolved issue whether participants of occupational pension plans in CEE countries were interested in sustainable investments. There is a study on Polish individual investors showing that even though they consider climate change as an important issue and are in favour of ESG investments, their propensity to sustainable investments decreases if the returns are lower than from traditional investments (Petelczyc 2022). But this study does not take into account the specificity of future pensioners, who always invest with a long-term perspective and are exposed to *climate-related pension risk.* This risk, from the perspective of future pensioners, is related not only to financial security and lower returns on investments and potential insolvency of pension funds but also to conditions of life deteriorated by climate change, including increased costs of food, housing, and healthcare, which can affect the conditions of living for pensioners. We assume that individuals who are participants of capital pension schemes may perceive these challenges more acutely than institutional investors. The significance of this issue is evident as the shift in the retirement system in Poland, decreasing the role of the first public pillar, leads to the expansion of additional capital pension plans. As a result, individuals are now responsible for managing their own retirement savings and investing their money in a manner that will provide for them in their later years. Therefore, our first hypothesis is that ***Polish retail investors who are participants of Employee Capital Plans (PPK) and consider climate change as an important issue are interested in ESG investment***.

The second important aspect of this analysis is to answer the question of whether participants of Employee Capital Plans in Poland are considered stakeholders by pension managers. Are Employee Capital Plans governed democratically in the sense that individual participants have an impact on the investment policy of the fund? The studies on the stakeholders of pension plans conducted so far in countries of Western Europe and in the United States indicate the dominant role of financial experts in management and pension investment policy (McCarthy 2014; Natali 2018; Nölke 2020; Golka and van der Zwan 2022). Financial experts have also been found to occupy a dominant position in CEE financial systems (Orenstein 2009; Naczyk 2018). However, the interests of banks and asset managers could be in conflict with those of individual investors, especially in the context of short- and long-term perspectives. Participants of pension funds could typically prioritize long-term stability and security in their investment strategies, including climate risk, which means that they can be more interested in sustainable investments. Pension fund managers may, in turn, prioritize short-term gains over long-term sustainability due to different investment goals, perspectives, and risk profiles. It is therefore crucial which stakeholders and to what extent are taken into account when creating investment policy.

According to a study by Evan McGaughey, increased democratization of the governance of pension funds could boost the sustainability of their investments (McGaughey 2021). As we have shown, more individuals are becoming shareholders in more than one company on the stock markets due to pension deregulation and the decreasing role of the 'first' public pension pillar (Sandberg 2008; McCarthy 2014). However, even those capital owners who care about the environment, human rights, or business ethics lack the ability to influence how their retirement funds are allocated, as financial institutions manage these investments on their behalf (McGaughey 2021). So far, social dialogue in Poland is rather at a very low level (Czarzasty 2019; Gajderowicz et al. 2021) which leads to the second hypothesis, according to which the ***current willingness of participants of Employee Capital Plans in Poland to engage in sustainable investments is irrelevant because participants are not considered stakeholders***.

3 Methodology

To test the first hypothesis, we analyse data from two phases of the Omnibus survey, which were carried on in Poland in January and February 2021. The study was conducted by a specialized polling institute (SW Research) that used the computer-assisted web interviewing (CAWI) method. The survey, which took the form of an Internet panel, included weights based on gender, age, income groups, and educational quotas. From the whole sample, we separated those respondents who are members of Employee Capital Plans (PPK). The sample consists of 2416 Poles, 1299 women, and 1117 men, including 1142 retail investors (people who invest in the capital market, including capital pension policyholders). From the database, we extracted those people who are participants of Employee Capital Plans. As a result, we have a sample of 346 Poles with 173 women and 173 men. Respondents were asked about their attitude towards human-caused climate change, ESG investments, the importance of pro-environment and pro-social values, and their readiness to forgo higher profits in an attempt to attain environmental goals. To test our first hypothesis about the opinion on human-caused climate change, we asked a question with six possible answers. Below are the provided options:

1. 'Climate change is currently one of the greatest threats to modern civilization.'
2. 'Climate change is a threat but is one of many dangerous phenomena.'
3. 'Climate change is not a particularly significant threat.'
4. 'Climate change is not a dangerous phenomenon at all.'
5. 'There is no such thing as human-caused climate change.'
6. 'It's hard to say/I don't know/I have no opinion.'

We simplified the answers into three categories, ranked from most important to least important:

1. 'Climate change is an important problem.'
2. 'Climate change is not an important problem.'
3. 'I don't know/It's hard to say.'

The dependent variable is based on the question about the attitude towards pro-environmental investment (E from ESG) of the participants of PPKs: *If you were to choose a fund, how much impact environmental considerations would have on your choice?* The answers were:

1. 'Not at all important'
2. 'Slightly important'
3. 'I don't know/hard to say'
4. 'Fairly important', and
5. 'Very important'

Answers 1, 2, and 3 indicate that environmental considerations are either not important for or not taken consciously into consideration by a given respondent, whereas answers 4 and 5 indicate the opposite. For the bigger picture, we also ran a binomial regression using a sample of all 1142 retail investors. The dependent variable was based on the question of propensity to sacrifice part of the profit for ESG investments, which we recorded as:

0. 'willingness to make a financial sacrifice for ESG' and
1. 'the lack of willingness to make a financial sacrifice for ESG'

The independent tested variables include membership in Employee Capital Plans, as well as age, gender, monthly net income, educational level, the population of the locality of residence, and attitude towards human-caused climate change. Those variables were included in the first model designed to test hypothesis 1.

Testing of the second hypothesis required a multidisciplinary approach. We conducted an analysis of the legal acts on Employee Capital Plans, namely:

1. The Act of October 4, 2018 on Employee Capital Plans (Dz. U. z 2023 r. poz. 46)
2. Explanatory Memorandum to the Act of October 4, 2018 on Employee Capital Plans

The analysis starts by reviewing the relevant laws and regulations governing Employee Capital Plans with special attention put on the role of employers and employees in their management. We analysed how often and in what context participants appear in the Act. This analysis of legal provisions allowed us to evaluate whether employees who are participants in Employee Capital Plans can be considered stakeholders and what (if any) impact they have on fund investments. As part of our analysis, we also examined the legal provisions regarding investment policies of Employee Capital Plans to identify opportunities and conditions for incorporating sustainable investing practices into these plans. We also analysed the first reports of companies in which Employee Capital Plans are investing to see whether ESG criteria are met in their investment policy.

4 Individual Perspective Results

The first of the research hypotheses relates to the attitude to climate change and the willingness of people who are participants of Employee Capital Plans to invest in ESG. First, we analyse their attitude towards climate change. Therefore, the respondents were asked: *What is your personal opinion on human-induced climate change?* As one can see (Fig. 1), the majority of the respondents (74%) consider human-caused climate change as an important problem.

To test the initial hypothesis, it is, however, essential to confirm whether there is a statistical correlation between the participants of Employee Capital Plans who acknowledge the significance of climate change and their expressed endorsement of ESG investments. The analysis supports the hypothesis that there is a statistically significant dependence between a person's attitude towards climate change and their willingness to choose funds with pro-environmental investments. The more important the climate change is for a respondent, the more important environmental issues

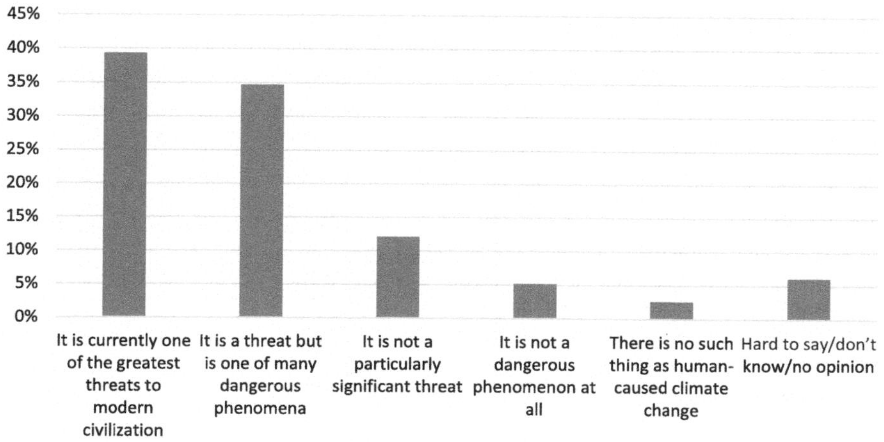

Fig. 1 Opinion on human-induced climate change (Source: The author)

Table 1 Cross table, attitude towards human-caused climate change with pro-environment investment importance (Source: The author)

			Pro-environment investment importance			
			Not important	No opinion	Important	Total
Attitude towards human-caused climate change	Climate change is an important problem	Count	11	50	195	256
	Climate change is not an important problem	Count	10	16	43	69
	No opinion	Count	1	12	8	21
Total		Count	22	78	246	346
Pearson Chi-square		Value 26.062 [a]	Df 4	Asymptotic significance (two sided) <0.001		
Nominal by nominal		V Cramer	0.194	<0.001		

are for their investment decisions, with $\chi 2 = 26.062$, $p < 0.001$. However, this association is weak, at the level of 0.194 at the Cramer's V (Tables 1, 2, and 3).

Therefore, evidence supports the first hypothesis, and there are no grounds for rejecting it. Almost 3/4 of the respondents who are participants of Employee Capital Plans consider climate change to be a significant problem. At the same time, most people who see the problem of climate change want pro-environmental investments to be made when their contributions are taken into account. However, a deeper analysis shows that participants of Employee Capital Plans do not differ from other retail investors in terms of the conditions under which they want pro-environmental

Table 2 Willingness to accept a different return rate from ESG funds as compared to traditional investments among members of PPKs and all retail investors (Source: The author)

	Members of PPKs $N = 336$	All retail investors $N = 1142$
Only if the likely return on the investment would be higher than the average return on a traditional investment.	33.8%	29.3%
Only if the likely return on the investment would be at least equal to the return on a traditional investment.	34.1%	32.7%
Also when the likely returns on the investment would be lower than one from a traditional investment.	9.2%	9.7%
I am not interested in this type of investment; I prefer traditional funds.	10.7%	13.6%
I don't know/It's hard to say.	12.1%	14.6%

Table 3 Odds ratio from binomial logistic regression for the readiness to forgo profits in favour of ESG among retail investors (Source: The author)

	Odds ratio
Attitude towards human-caused climate change	0.364***
Gender	0.723
Age	1.232
Income	0.912
Education	1059
Being a participant in Employee Capital Plan	0.722
Pro-environmental investments	0.877
Constant (coefficient)	34,612**

$^{***}p \leq 0.01$; $^{**}p \leq 0.05$; $^{*}p \leq 0.1$

investments. In this research, retail investors are those having capital pension accounts (individual or occupational) or investing in treasury bonds, shares, and other equity instruments, namely people who invest their money in the capital market. Less than 10% of them are likely to invest in ESG also when the likely returns on the investment would be lower than one from a traditional investment, whether it is all retail investors or only policyholders of Employee Capital Plans (see Table 2).

Table 3 presents the results of the estimated binomial regression model. The model was used to ascertain the effects of being a participant of an Employee Capital Plan, as well as age, gender, income, education, propensity to pro-environment investments, and attitude towards climate change on the likelihood that respondents would forgo a part of their profits to engage in ESG investments. This logistic regression model was statistically significant $\chi 2 = 25.653$, $p < 0.001$. Out of seven predictor variables, only one was statistically significant. The model shows merely a decreased odds of forgoing profits among people who perceive climate change as not important. Their odds of forgoing higher profits decrease by a factor of 0.364. It means that any other variable, including being a participant of an Employee Capital Plan, has proven to be statistically insignificant.

Fig. 2 Hosmer and Lemeshow test for the model

Step	Chi-square	df	Significance
1	4,483	8	,811

The Hosmer and Lemeshow goodness-of-fit test yielded a non-significant p-value of 0.811, signifying a strong alignment between the statistical model and the observed data, thus affirming the model's suitability for the analysis (see Fig. 2).

Participants of Employee Capital Plans do not differ from the general population. The binomial regression model did not show their greater inclination to pro-environmental investments. However, in accordance with the initial assumptions, most of these people perceive climate change as a significant problem and would like their investments to be more pro-environmental (although most do not want to do it at the expense of lower own profits).

5 Employee Capital Plans Regulatory Perspective Results

Since we already know that under certain conditions, participants of Employee Capital Plans in Poland would like to invest more pro-environmentally, we need to answer the question as to whether they have any influence on the investment policy of the funds and if they are perceived as stakeholders. Employee Capital Plans are regulated in the Act of October 4, 2018 on Employee Capital Plans (Dz. U. z 2023 r. poz. 46.). This Act regulates almost all the issues connected to this pension provision. To verify our second hypothesis, we need to analyze this Act in two respects: (1) the role of the participants in the whole process and (2) the investment policy of the funds.

According to the legal definition (article 2 of the above-mentioned Act), a participant is *an individual who has reached the age of 18, on behalf of whom the employing entity has concluded an agreement on running an Employee Capital Plan with a financial institution.* For the purpose of this chapter, we consider participants as retail investors as their private contributions to pension provisions are invested in the capital market. The word 'participant' appears in the document as many as 350 times. A closer analysis shows that, in most cases, they concern formal and legal issues:

(a) Forms of declarations, resignation, and participation (articles 4, 14, 18, 19, and 23)
(b) Financing of contributions (articles 25, 27, 28, 31, 32, 33, and 35)
(c) Collecting and providing information on the accumulated funds (article 74)
(d) Formalities related to the divorce or death of participants (articles 21, 80, 81, 85, and 86)
(e) Forms and terms of payment (articles 96, 97, 98, 99, 100, 101, 102, and 105)

Under the analyzed Act, options for influencing the selection of funds by participants of Employee Capital Plans are highly limited. There are only two possible

Table 4 Investment limits based on the age of the participant of an Employee Capital Plan (Source: analizy.pl)

	Equity securities (shares, investment certificates, participation units in investment funds)	Bonds (treasury bonds, treasury bills, certificates of deposit, and other negotiable securities)
More than 20 years up to 60 years old	60–80%	20–40%
20 years before 60 years old	40–70%	30–60%
10 years before 60 years old	25–50%	50–75%
5 years before 60 years old	10–30%	70–90%
60 years old	Max. 15%	Min. 85%

options. The first concerns the choice of the financial institution with which the employer will sign the agreement. According to article 7 point 3 of the Act, 'The employing entity, in agreement with the trade union organization operating in this employing entity, selects the financial institution with which an agreement on managing the Employee Capital Plans will be concluded'. The selection of the financial institution with which an agreement on managing the Employee Capital Plan is made by the employer represents a limited form of influence of participants. It is only exercised at the beginning of the implementation of the Employee Capital Plan in the company and only by members of the unions or other representative groups of employees.

The second option concerns the individual influence of participants on the choice of the sub-fund but not on the investment policy of these sub-funds. According to the Act, the so-called defined date funds allocate higher proportions of investments into shares for younger people and into safer options, such as treasury bonds for older people, thus reducing investment risks for the latter group (see Table 4). Every participant is assigned to the defined date funds, depending on how many years he/she is missing until 60 years old.

However, in accordance with article 45, a participant may submit to the fund an application for conversion into a sub-fund other than the one designated for his/her age group. This solution responds to the different needs of participants related to their attitude to risk rather than to dissatisfaction with the investment policy. To sum up, a participant in a Polish Employee Capital Plan has practically no influence on the investment policy of the funds in which he/she invests his/her money for old age. Therefore, there are no grounds for rejecting the second hypothesis as according to this analysis, participants of Employee Capital Plans are not perceived as stakeholders in accordance with the law.

However, if, in accordance with the above-proven declarations, most of the Employee Capital Plan participants are interested in pro-environmental investments, it is worth analysing whether the legislator provided for sustainable investments in the Act. The investment policy of Employee Capital Plans is described in the Explanatory Memorandum for the Act and Chapter 6 of the Act, *Investment and pension funds, where the funds of the Employee Capital Plans are accumulated.* The Explanatory Memorandum highlights two main aspects related to the creation and investment of Employee Capital Plans. Firstly, it concerns the *enhancement of the potential for individual income growth and GDP, which in the long term contributes to strengthening the stability of the pension system and the growth of pension benefits.* The second most important aspect is the emphasis on the safety of investments, especially through the introduction of 'defined date funds', described earlier in this chapter. The term 'sustainable investment' does not appear either in the Act or in the Explanatory Memorandum. However, the legal guidelines regarding investment policy are precisely detailed in article 37 of the Act. Special attention should be paid to the proportion of assets to be invested on the Warsaw Stock Exchange (WIG-20 and mWIG-40 indices) in the equity securities part. It is:

1. A minimum of 40% of the value of assets in shares included in the WIG20 index
2. A maximum of 20% of the value of assets in shares included in the mWig40 index
3. A maximum of 10% of the value of assets in shares, rights to shares, pre-emptive rights or other equity instruments issued by public companies listed on the Warsaw Stock Exchange other than those listed in points 1 and 2.

Since such a large part of assets is invested on the Warsaw Stock Exchange, it is worth checking whether companies listed on the WIG-20, where a minimum of 40% of assets of Employee Capital Plans should be invested, are sustainable in terms of ESG. According to the ESG monitor, reports of companies listed in the WIG20 are very extensive and often raise climate-related issues, but they lack specific information. For persons with a vested interest in environmental issues, one of the major drawbacks of those reports is the absence of clear metrics on carbon footprint reduction, as well as inadequate transparency regarding supply chain information. In effect, WIG20 is the second-to-last of ten indices included in the Global ESG Monitor 2022 (Hofstetter and Diegelmann 2023). However, this marks only the beginning of non-financial reporting in the European Union. With the expansion of the scope of entities required to report and the accumulation of experience in this area, it is likely that, following the trend observed in France, reporting institutions will place increasing emphasis on reducing their carbon footprint (Mésonnier and Nguyen 2021). As of now, Employee Capital Plan funds in Poland do not consider their participants as stakeholders, and there is no requirement for them to invest in alignment with ESG criteria.

6 Conclusions and Discussion

From our research, it appears that participants of Employee Capital Plans in Poland are not different from the general population, and most of them believe that climate change is a significant issue caused by human activity. At the same time, they are interested in environmentally friendly investment options, including those within their own pension funds. While it is only true under certain conditions regarding profit, we can conclude that individuals who are members of Employee Capital Plans are interested in sustainable investments to some extent. However, a binomial regression analysis revealed that these types of investments are only of interest to fund participants when they provide at least the same level of returns as traditional investments. These findings suggest the need for further research. The study is limited by the insufficient number of explanatory variables, particularly those that could more accurately assess the extent to which retail investors, including participants of Employee Capital Plans, are willing to sacrifice some profits in favour of responsible investments. There is also a need to further analyse *climate-related pension risk.* As for now, it refers mostly to the risk that pension, insurance, and other financial institutions face due to the potential impacts of climate change on the value of their investments. Climate change poses significant risks to pension funds as it can affect the performance of their investments, particularly those in carbon-intensive sectors such as energy, utilities, and mining. It can also increase the costs of insurance, which may impact the profitability of pension funds' investments. It is worth noting that the risk associated with the investment policy of pension funds is not solely financial, and it poses a risk to the participants of Employee Capital Plans as well. This risk is related to the state of the world in the coming decades, the risk of weather catastrophes, limited access to basic resources, rising costs of living, etc. Raising awareness among individual members about the impact of pension funds' investment policies on this risk could potentially increase pressure to shift towards a more environmentally friendly investment policy. Further exploration of those aspects is required through both quantitative and qualitative research.

It turns out in the latter part of the analysis, however, that the pressure of individual participants of Employee Capital Plans alone in the current legal state may not be enough. The study revealed that the opinions of individual members of Employee Capital Plans do not hold significant relevance to pension fund managers under the current legal provisions. Firstly, the level of influence of the Employee Capital Plan participants is restricted to a minimum as they can only collectively select a financial institution to manage their funds or individually choose a sub-fund that differs only in the approach to investment risk. Secondly, the investment policy of funds under Employee Capital Plans in Poland is largely predetermined and restricts the choice of more sustainable companies. This is due to the strict definition of investment criteria, which limits the number of eligible companies. The analysis confirms this as it shows that the companies in the WIG20, where Employee Capital Plans must invest a significant portion of their assets, are far from being sustainable. It seems, therefore, that in light of the presented research results, an EU Sustainable

Finance Disclosure Regulation (SFDR) may be an insufficient solution, at least for the countries of Central and Eastern Europe, including Poland. SFDR aims to increase transparency and accountability in sustainable finance by introducing harmonized disclosure requirements for financial market participants and financial advisers. Under this Regulation, financial market participants disclose information about how environmental, social, and governance (ESG) factors are integrated into their investment decision-making process and about the impact of their investment decisions on sustainability. If a financial institution reports that it does not take ESG factors into account in its investment decisions, it may face reputational risks but not any other consequences. In a system where stakeholders such as individual participants have little influence on the selection of the fund, and in fact none on its investment policy, this solution may not be enough to really change the investments of Employee Capital Plans.

The findings presented in this chapter indicate that both Polish individual participants in the pension capital market and the institutional frameworks themselves will likely need to evolve in response to the growing recognition of long-term climate risks. It is important to ensure that savings in capital pension funds do not finance a future that will be more difficult to live in.

References

Adamska A, Dąbrowski T, Grygiel-Tomaszewska A (2016) Socially responsible investment in post-communist and developed European countries. La Revue d'études comparatives Est-Ouest (RECEO) 3:7–43

Agrawal A, Hockerts K (2021) Impact investing: review and research agenda. J Small Bus Entrep 33(2). https://doi.org/10.1080/08276331.2018.1551457

Aras G, Crowther D (2009) Corporate sustainability reporting: A study in disingenuity? J Bus Ethics 87(1):279–288

Bingler J, Pinson L, McCully P (2020) Five years lost: how finance is blowing the Paris carbon budget. Urgewald, December 2020. https://www.urgewald.org/en/medien/five-years-lost-how-finance-industry-blowing-paris-carbon-budget

Camilleri MA (2018) The corporate governance reporting in the European Union. The British Academy of Management (BAM) conference: driving productivity in uncertain and challenging times, Bristol Business School, University of the West of England

CFA Institute (2017) Environmental, social and governance survey. https://www.cfainstitute.org/-/media/documents/survey/esg-survey-report-2017

Chebanov S (2019) "Green" economy: role of sovereign funds. Mirovaia ekonomika i mezhdunarodnye otnosheniia 63(3):C5–12

Czarzasty J (2019) Collective bargaining in Poland: a near-death experience. In: Müller T, Vandaele K, Waddington J (eds) Collective bargaining in Europe: towards an endgame, vol 2. ETUI European Trade Union Institute, Brussels

Della Croce R, Kaminker C, Stewart F (2011) The role of pension funds in financing green growth initiatives. OECD working papers on finance, insurance and private pensions, no. 10, OECD Publishing

Donaldson T, Preston LE (1995) The stakeholder theory of the corporation: concepts, evidence, and implications. Acad Manag Rev 20(1):65–91

Freeman RE (1984) Strategic management: a stakeholder approach. Pitman

Gajderowicz T, Grotkowska G, Jakubowski M, Wrona S (2021) Formal or real social dialogue? Industrial relations and privatisation in education in Poland. In: Sorensen TB, Grimaldi E, Gajderowicz T (eds) Rethetoric or game changer: social dialogue and industrial relations in education midst EU governance and privatisation in Europe. ETUCE-CSEE, Brussells
Golka P, van der Zwan N (2022) Experts versus representatives? Financialised valuation and institutional change in financial governance. New Polit Econ 27(6):1017–1030
Hofstetter A, Diegelmann M (2023) Global ESG Monitor Transparency Ranking Poland 2022. www.globalESGmonitor.com
IPCC (2021) Climate change 2021: the physical science basis. In: Masson-Delmotte V, Zhai P, Pirani A, Connors SL, Péan C, Berger S, Caud N, Chen Y, Goldfarb L, Gomis MI, Huang M, Leitzell K, Lonnoy E, Matthews JBR, Maycock TK, Waterfield T, Yelekçi O, Yu R, Zhou B (eds) Contribution of working group I to the sixth assessment report of the intergovernmental panel on climate change. Cambridge University Press, Cambridge, p 4
Kaniel R, Liu S, Saar G, Titman S (2012) Individual investor trading and return patterns around earnings announcements. J Financ 67(2)
KNF (2023) Informacja dotycząca pracowniczych planów kapitałowych (PPK) - III kwartał 2022 roku. https://www.knf.gov.pl/?articleId=80633&p_id=18
Lawrence A (2013) Individual investors and financial disclosure. J Account Econ 56(1):130–147
McCarthy MA (2014) Turning labor into capital: pension funds and the corporate control of finance. Polit Soc 42(4):455–487
McGaughey E (2021) Sustainable pensions, democratic governance and EU law. Eur J Soc Secur 23(3):279–297
Mésonnier J-S, Nguyen B (2021) Showing off cleaner hands: mandatory climate-related disclosure by financial institutions and the financing of fossil energy. https://ssrn.com/abstract=3733781
Mills E (2009) A global review of insurance industry responses to climate change. Geneva Papers 34:323–359. https://doi.org/10.1057/gpp.2009.14
Mitchell RK, Agle BR, Wood DJ (1997) Toward a theory of stakeholder identification and salience: defining the principle of who and what really count. Acad Manag Rev 22(4):853–886
Morgan Stanley (2019) Sustainable signals: individual investor interest driven by impact, conviction and choice. Morgan Stanley Institute for Sustainable Investing. https://www.morganstanley.com/content/dam/msdotcom/
Murad SA (2017) Environment, social, and governance (ESG) criteria and preference of managers. Cogent Bus Manag 4(1). https://doi.org/10.1080/23311975.2017.1340820
Naczyk M (2018) When finance captures labor's capital: dominant personal pensions, resurgent occupational provision in Central and Eastern Europe. Soc Policy Adm 52(2)
Natali D (2018) Occupational pensions in Europe: Trojan horse of financialization? Soc Policy Adm 52(2)
Nölke A (2020) Financialization and the crisis of democracy. In: Mader P, Mertens D, van der Zwan N (eds) The Routledge international handbook of financialization. Routledge, London
Orenstein MA (2009) What happened in east European (political) economies?: A balance sheet for neoliberal reform. East Eur Polit Soc 23(4):479–490
Owen R (2021) Lessons from Government Venture Capital Funds to enable transition to a low carbon economy: the U.K. case. In: IEEE transactions on engineering management
Petelczyc J (2022) The readiness for ESG among retail investors in Central and Eastern Europe. The example of Poland. Glob Bus Rev 23(6). https://doi.org/10.1177/09721509221114754
Pfeifer S, Sullivan R (2008) Public policy, institutional investors and climate change: a UK case-study. Clim Change 89:245–262. https://doi.org/10.1007/s10584-007-9380-y
Raymond C, Horton RM, Zscheischler J, Martius O, AghaKouchak A, Balch J, Bowen SG, Camargo SJ, Hess J, Kornhuber K, Oppenheimer M, Ruane AC, Wahl T, White K (2020) Understanding and managing connected extreme events. Nat Clim Change 10:611–621. https://doi.org/10.1038/s41558-020-0790-4
Reclaim Finance (2021) Banking on climate chaos, fossil fuels finance report 2021. https://reclaimfinance.org/site/wp-content/uploads/2021/03/BOCC__2021_vF.pdf

Sandberg J (2008) The ethics of investing, making money or making difference? Acta Universitatis Gothoburgensis, Goeteborg

Stechemesser K, Endrikat J, Grasshoff N, Guenther E (2015) Insurance companies' responses to climate change: adaptation, dynamic capabilities and competitive advantage. Geneva Papers Risk Insur Issues Pract 40:557–584. https://doi.org/10.1057/gpp.2015.1

van Duuren E, Plantinga A, Scholtens B (2016) ESG integration and the investment management process: fundamental investing reinvented. J Bus Ethics 138:525–533. https://doi.org/10.1007/s10551-015-2610-8

Janina Petelczyc, PhD, works in the Department of Social Insurance at the Warsaw School of Economics. She focuses on research on social security systems, particularly pension systems and pension fund investments. She is a member of the Occupational Pensions Stakeholder Group at EIOPA.

The manufacturer's authorised representative in the EU is Springer Nature Customer Service Centre GmbH, Europaplatz 3, 69115 Heidelberg, Germany. If you have any concerns regarding our products, please contact ProductSafety@springernature.com

Printed and bound by CPI Group (UK) Ltd, Croydon, CR0 4YY
01/10/2026
02225950-0010